DISCARD
go with grace

by
George Alexopoulos

HAMBURG // LONDON // LOS ANGELES // TOKYO

Go with Grace Vol.1
created by George Alexopoulos

Layout and Lettering - Camellia Cox and Jennifer Carbajal
Cover Layout - James Lee

Editor - Carol Fox
Digital Imaging Manager - Chris Buford
Managing Editor - Sheldon Drzka
Production Manager - Elisabeth Brizzi
VP of Production - Ron Klamert
Editor-in-Chief - Rob Tokar
Publisher - Mike Kiley
President and C.O.O. - John Parker
C.E.O. and Chief Creative Officer - Stuart Levy

A  Manga

TOKYOPOP Inc.
5900 Wilshire Blvd. Suite 2000
Los Angeles, CA 90036

E-mail: info@TOKYOPOP.com
Come visit us online at www.TOKYOPOP.com

ISBN: 1-59816-709-X

First TOKYOPOP printing: August 2006
10 9 8 7 6 5 4 3 2 1
Printed in the USA

NO MORE.

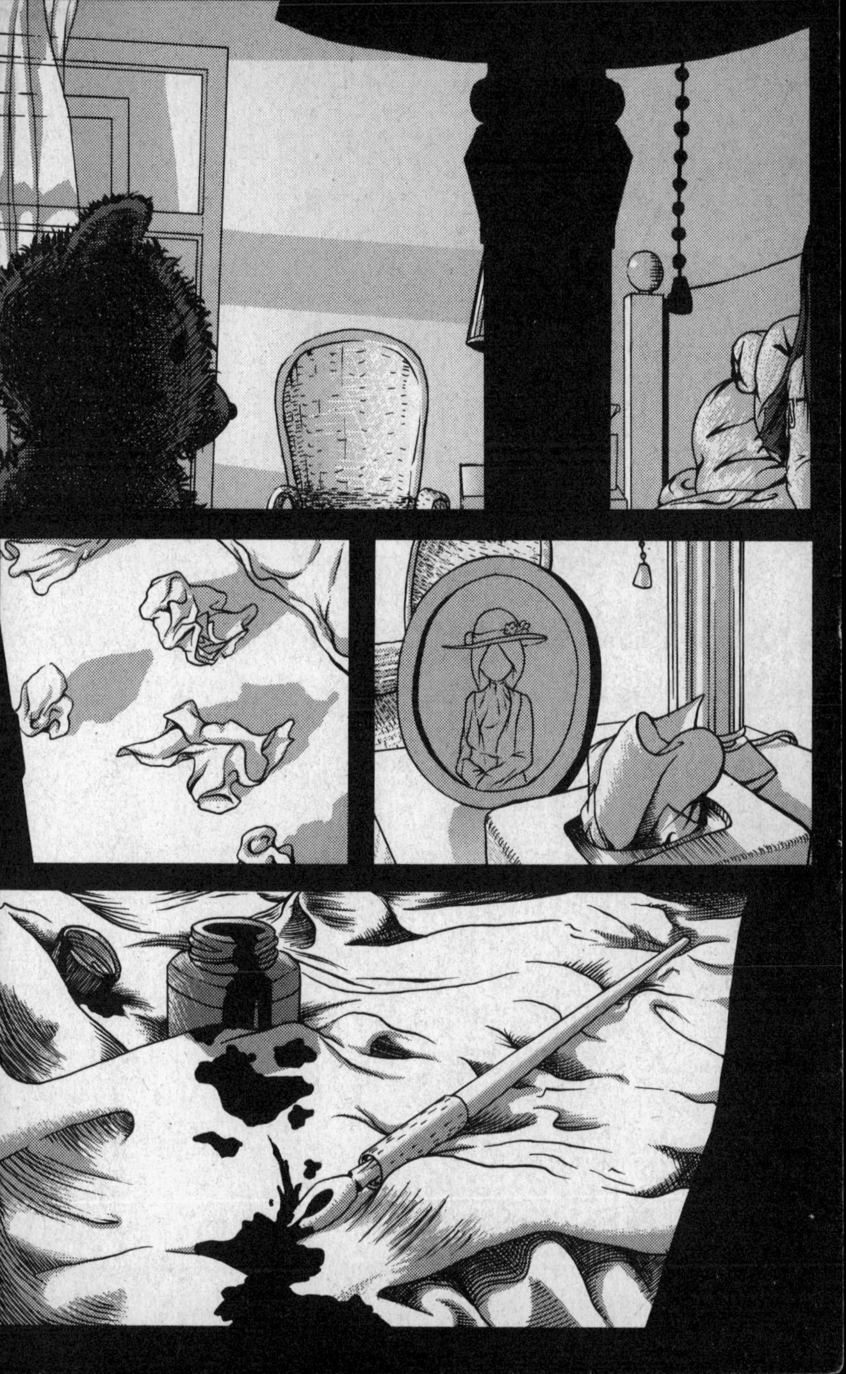

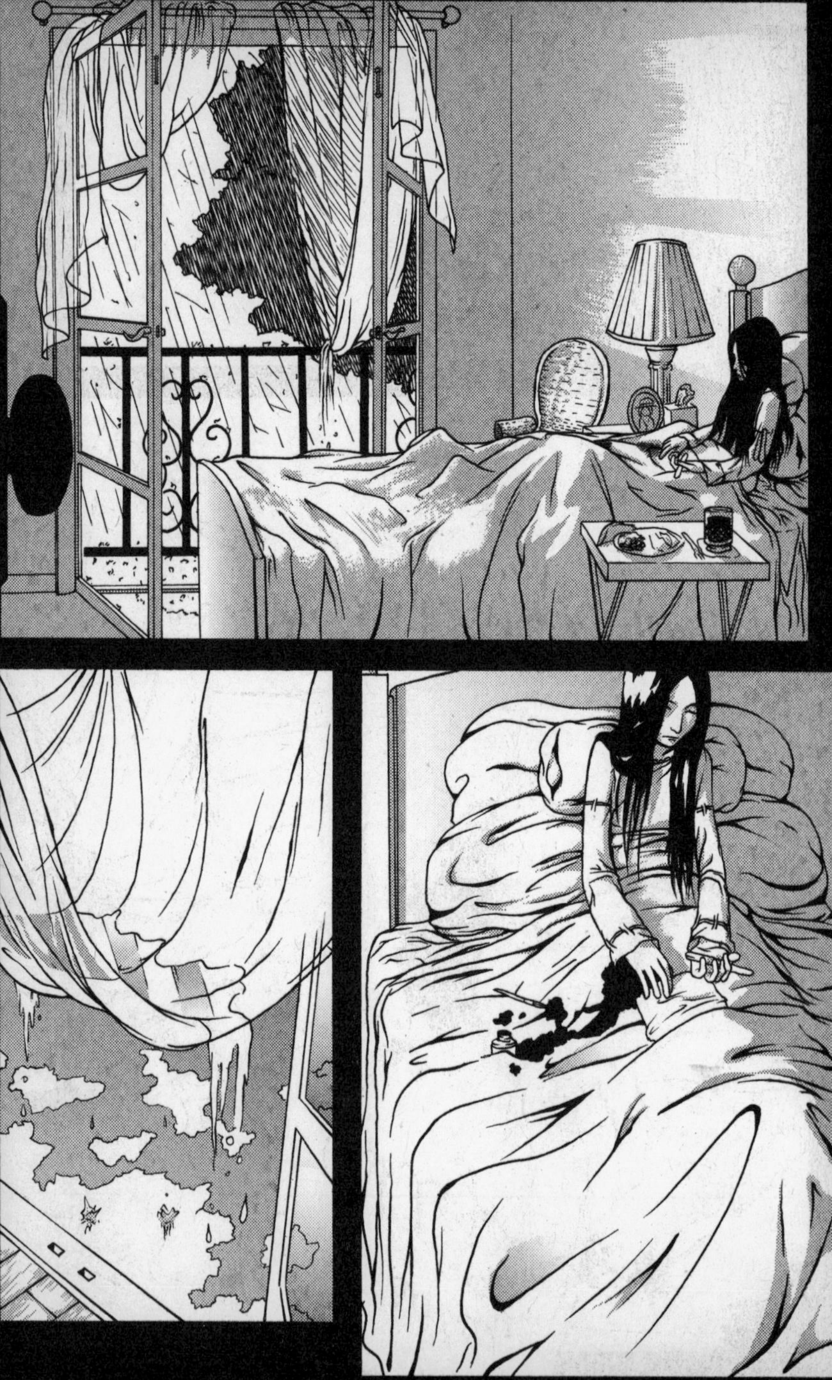

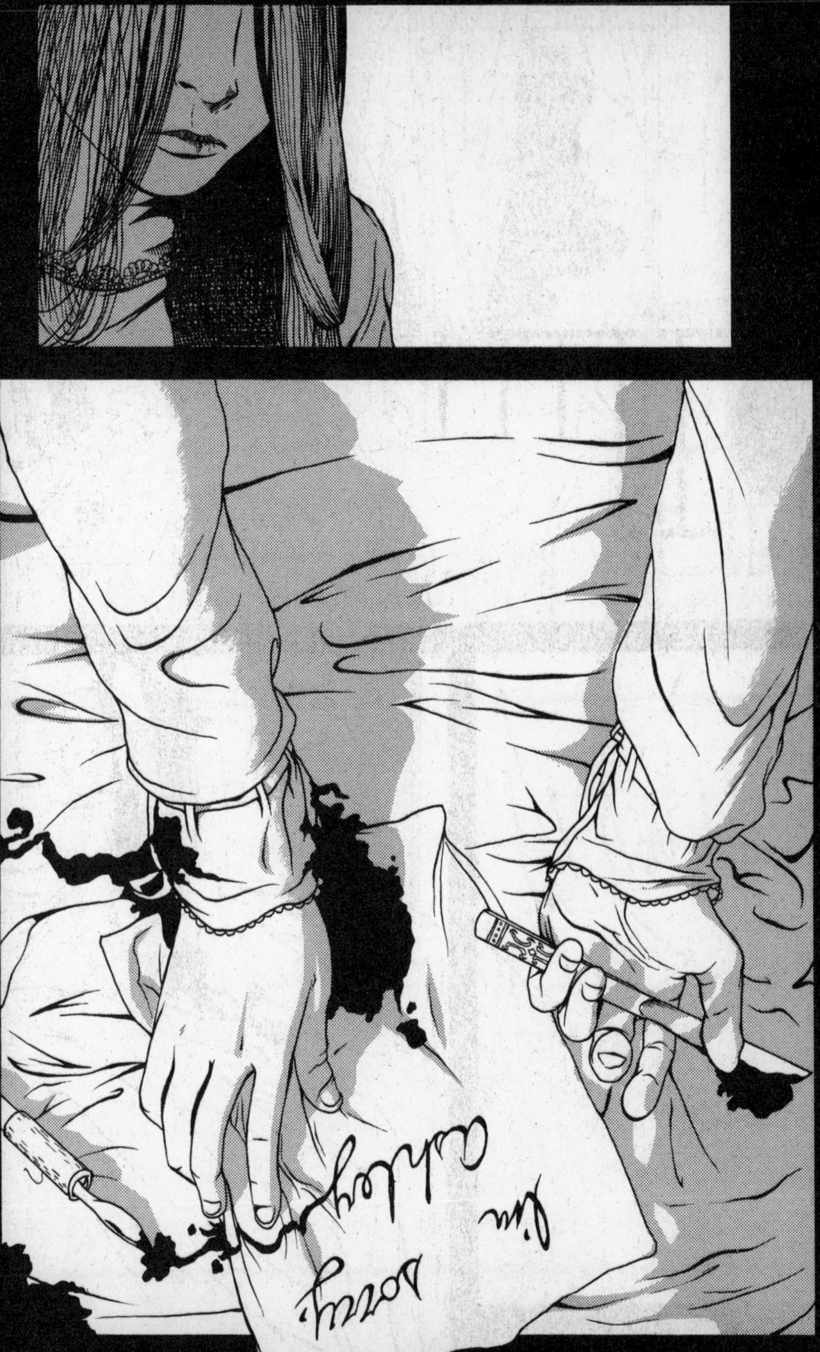
I'm always sorry.

Go With Grace

Table of Contents

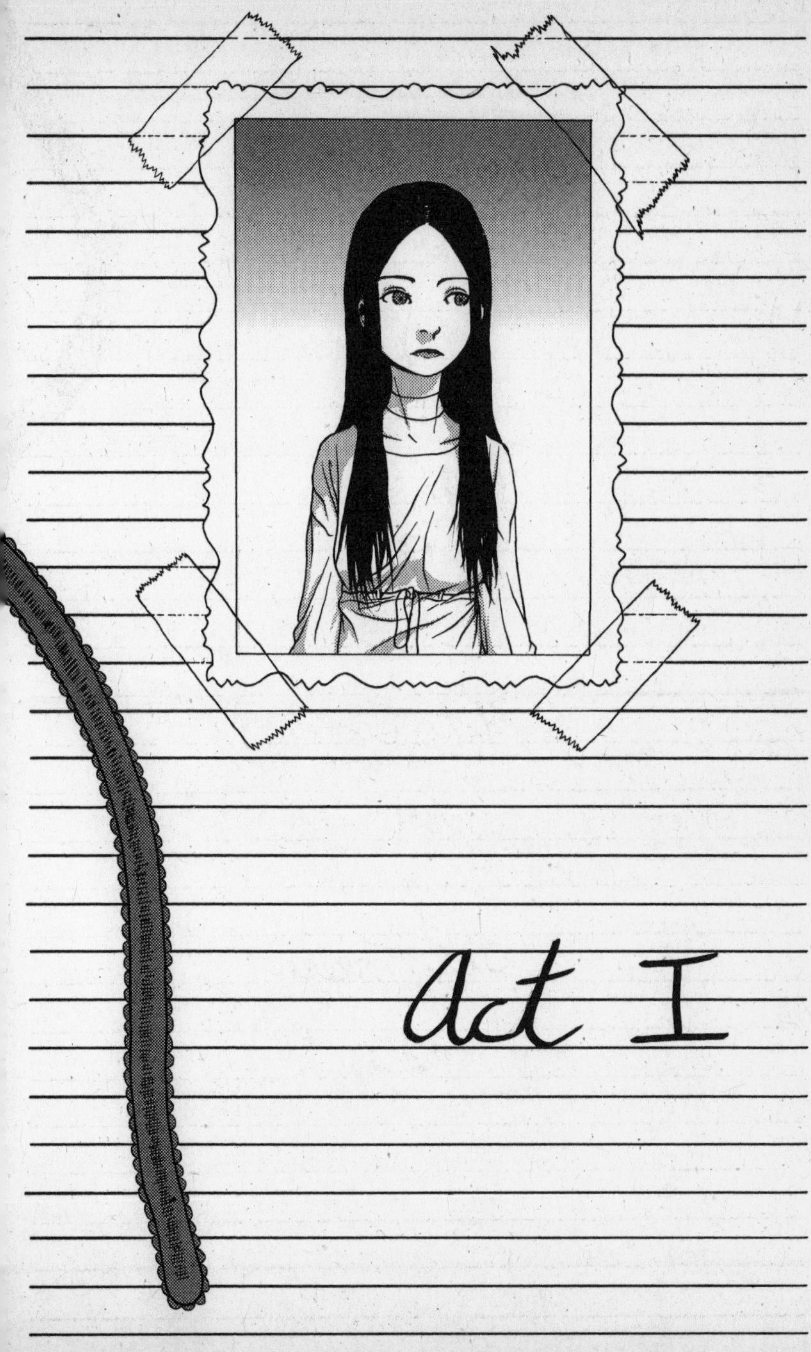
Act I

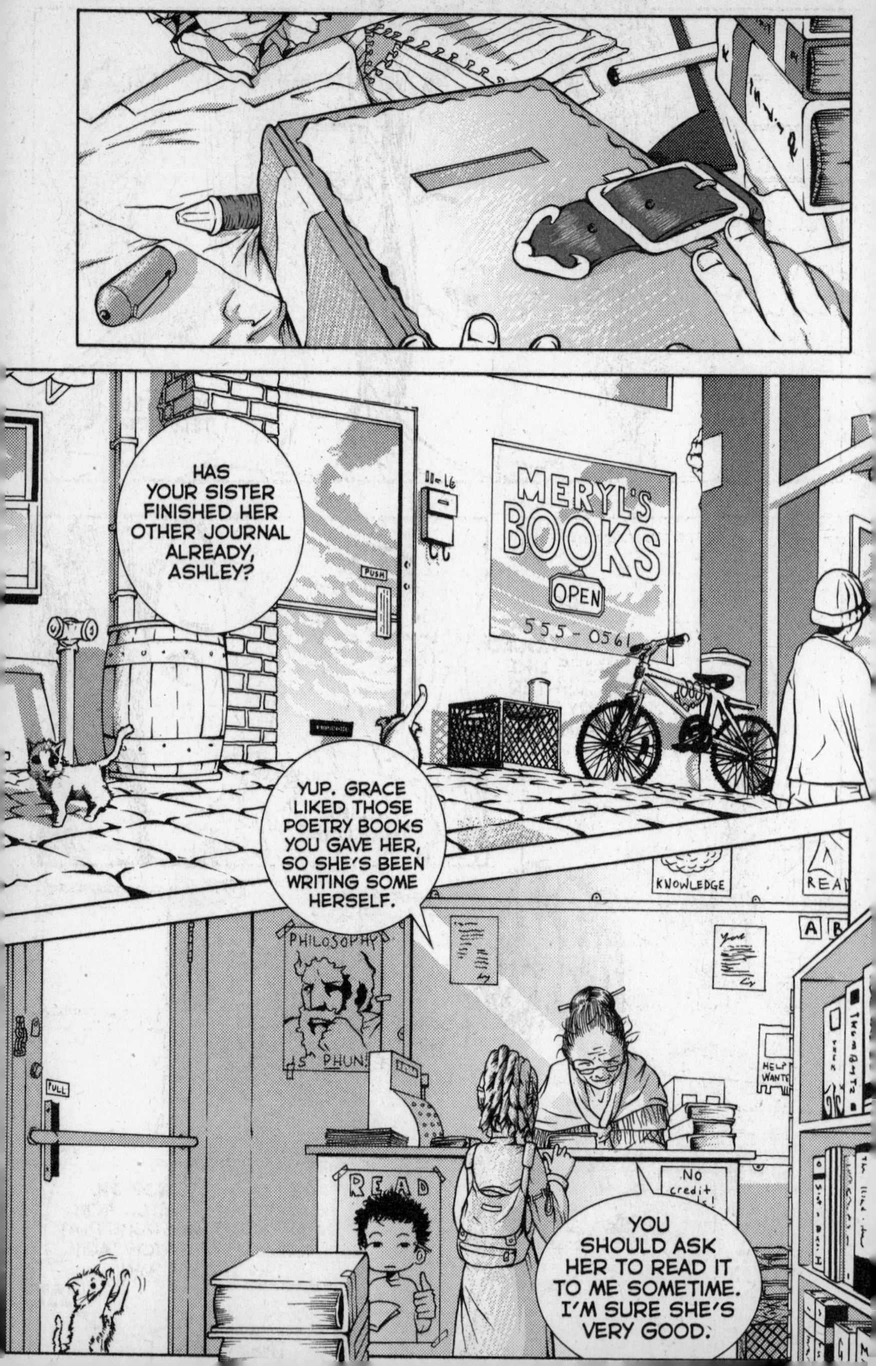
11-16
PUSH
MERYL'S BOOKS
OPEN
555-0561
HAS YOUR SISTER FINISHED HER OTHER JOURNAL ALREADY, ASHLEY?
YUP. GRACE LIKED THOSE POETRY BOOKS YOU GAVE HER, SO SHE'S BEEN WRITING SOME HERSELF.
KNOWLEDGE
PHILOSOPHY IS PHUN!
PULL
READ
No credit
YOU SHOULD ASK HER TO READ IT TO ME SOMETIME. I'M SURE SHE'S VERY GOOD.

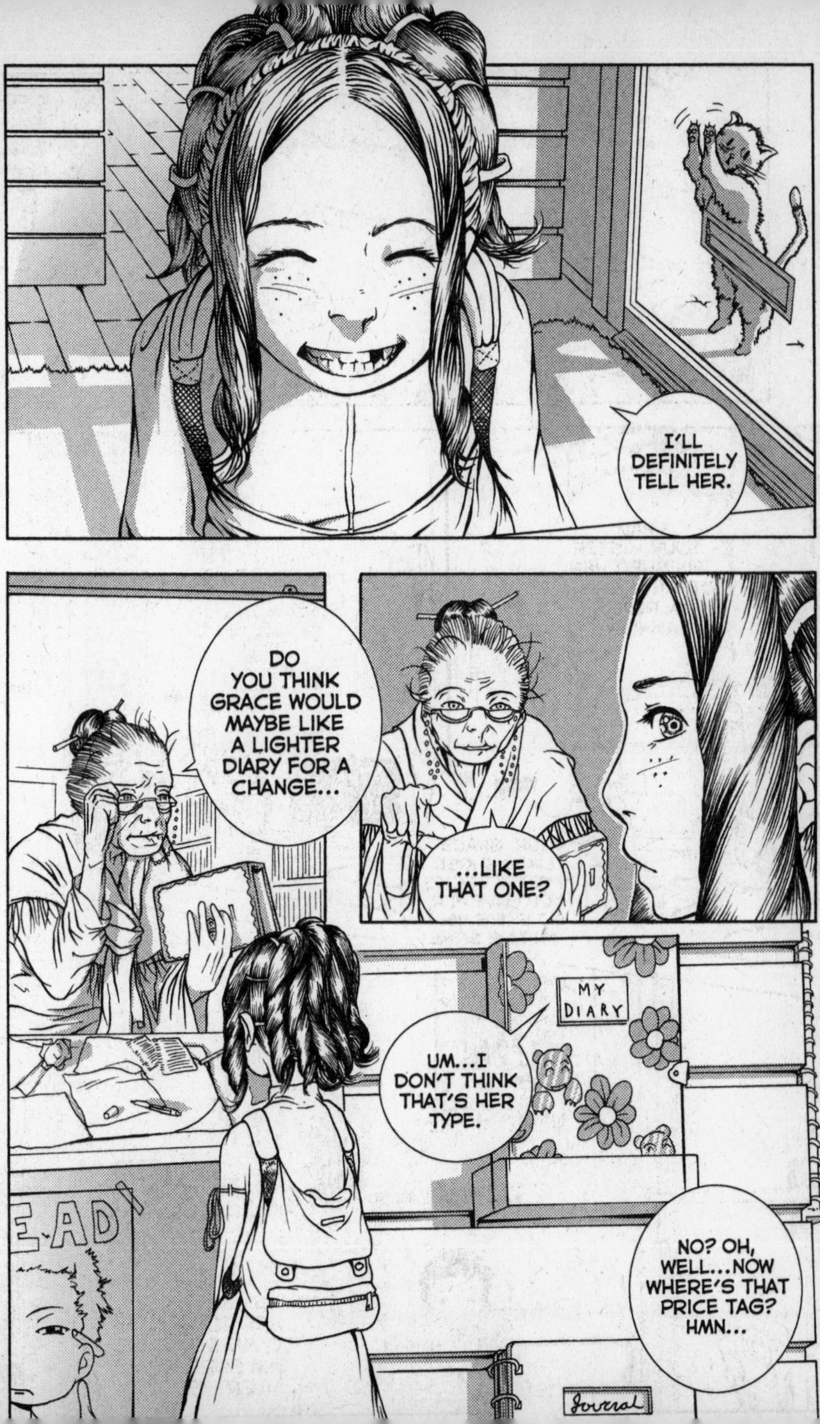
I'LL DEFINITELY TELL HER.
DO YOU THINK GRACE WOULD MAYBE LIKE A LIGHTER DIARY FOR A CHANGE...
...LIKE THAT ONE?
MY DIARY
UM...I DON'T THINK THAT'S HER TYPE.
NO? OH, WELL...NOW WHERE'S THAT PRICE TAG? HMN...
Journal

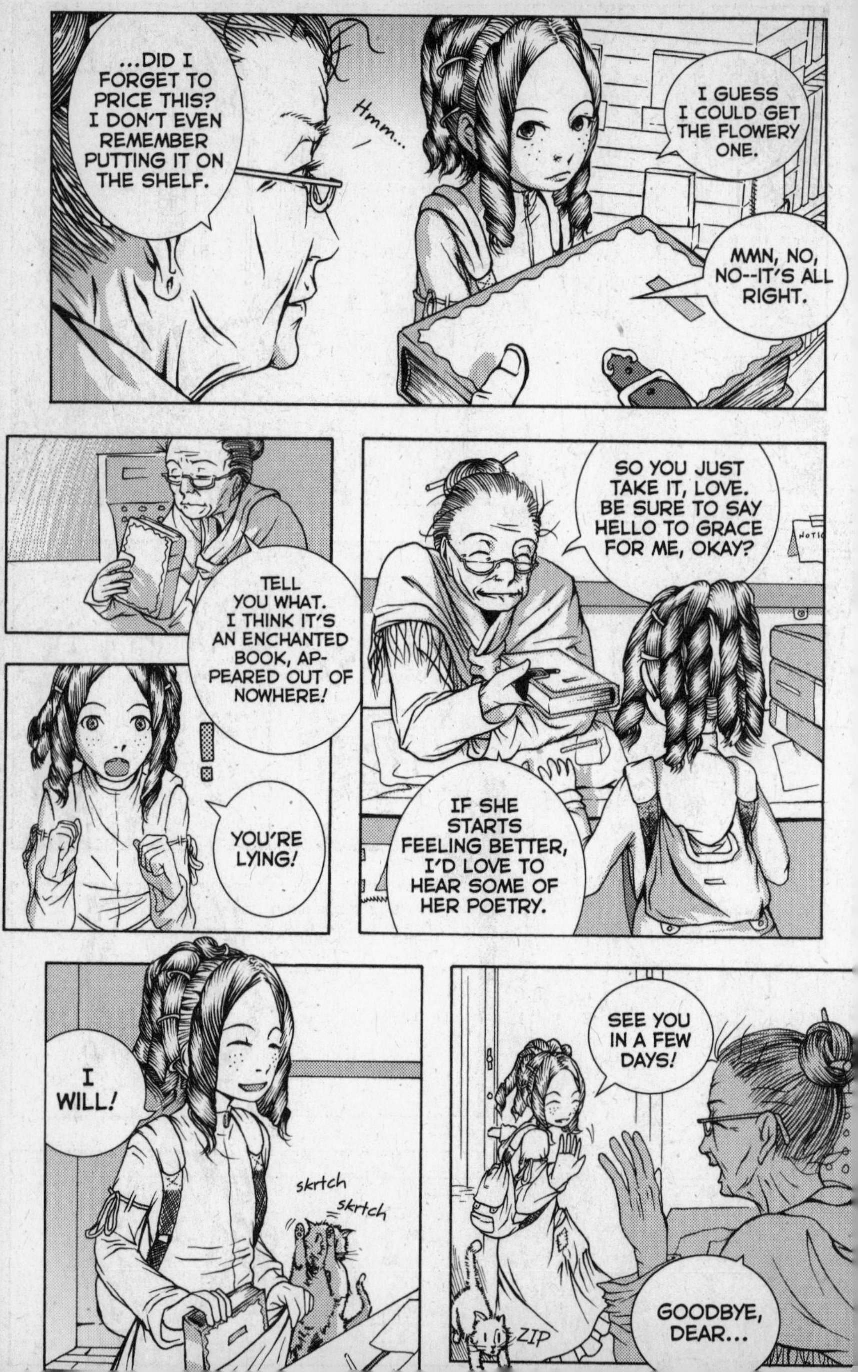
...DID I FORGET TO PRICE THIS? I DON'T EVEN REMEMBER PUTTING IT ON THE SHELF.
Hmm...
I GUESS I COULD GET THE FLOWERY ONE.
MMN, NO, NO--IT'S ALL RIGHT.
TELL YOU WHAT. I THINK IT'S AN ENCHANTED BOOK, AP-PEARED OUT OF NOWHERE!
!!
YOU'RE LYING!
SO YOU JUST TAKE IT, LOVE. BE SURE TO SAY HELLO TO GRACE FOR ME, OKAY?
IF SHE STARTS FEELING BETTER, I'D LOVE TO HEAR SOME OF HER POETRY.
I WILL!
skrtch
skrtch
SEE YOU IN A FEW DAYS!
ZIP
GOODBYE, DEAR...

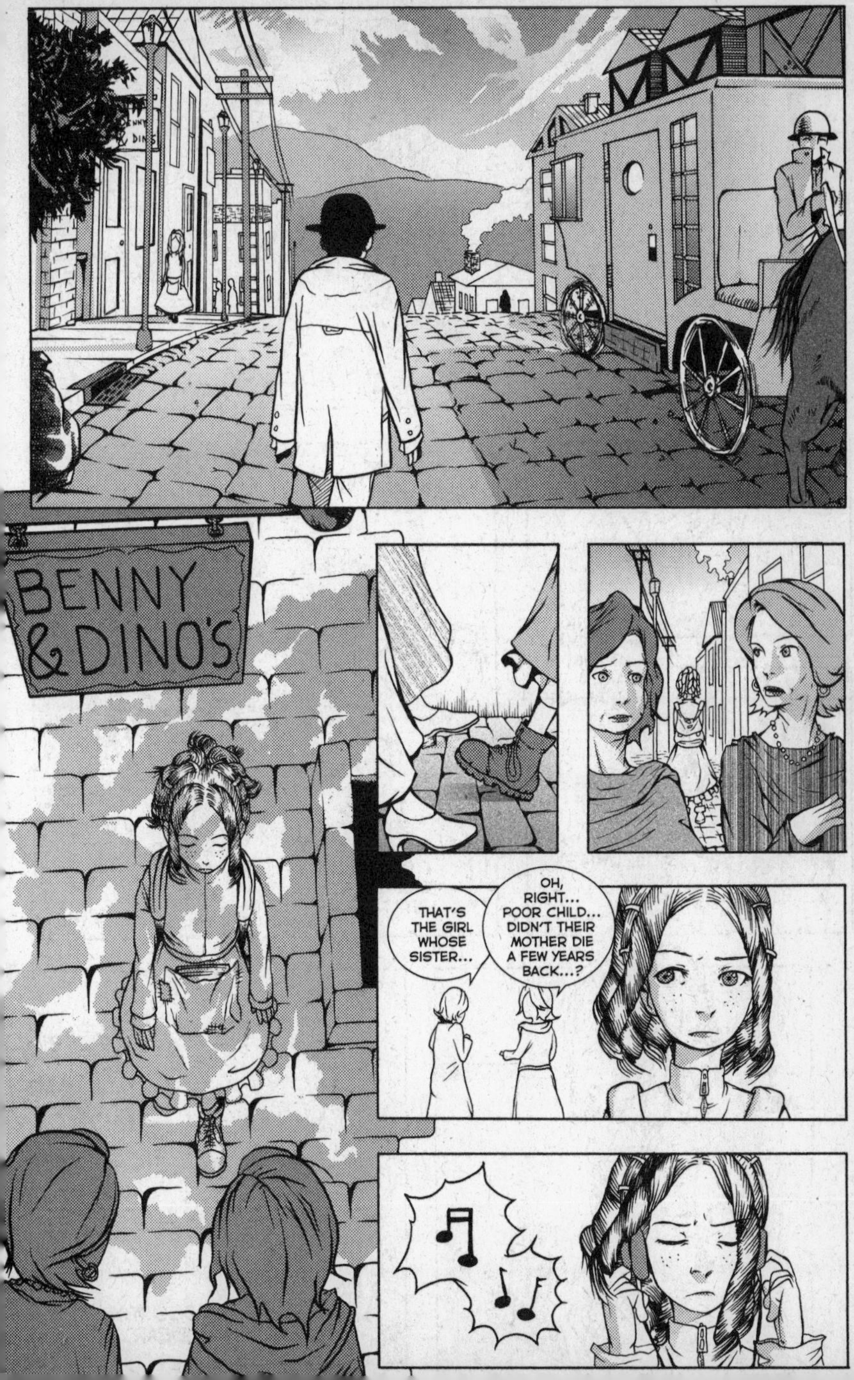
BENNY & DINOS
BENNY &DINO'S
THAT'S THE GIRL WHOSE SISTER...
OH, RIGHT... POOR CHILD... DIDN'T THEIR MOTHER DIE A FEW YEARS BACK...?

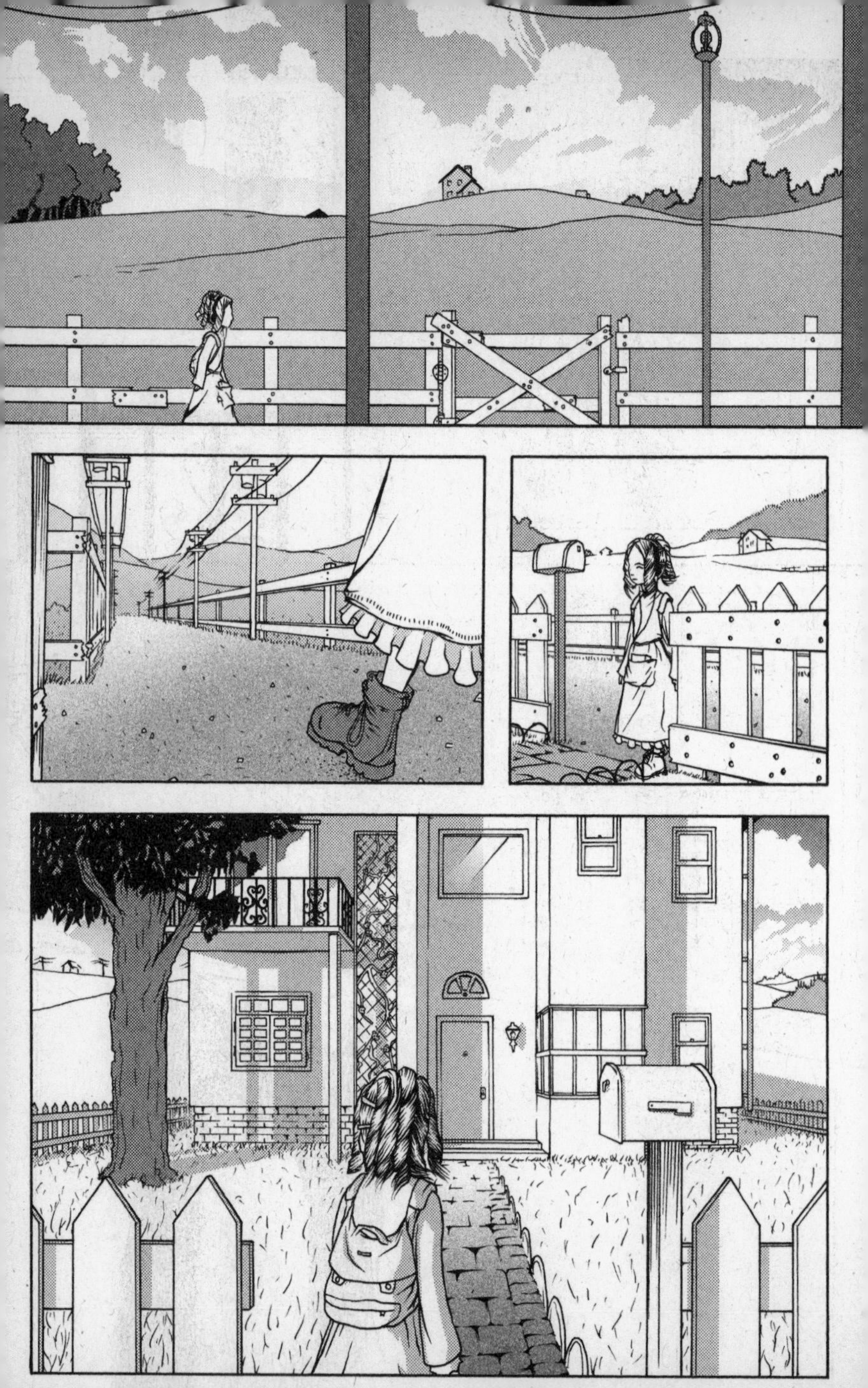

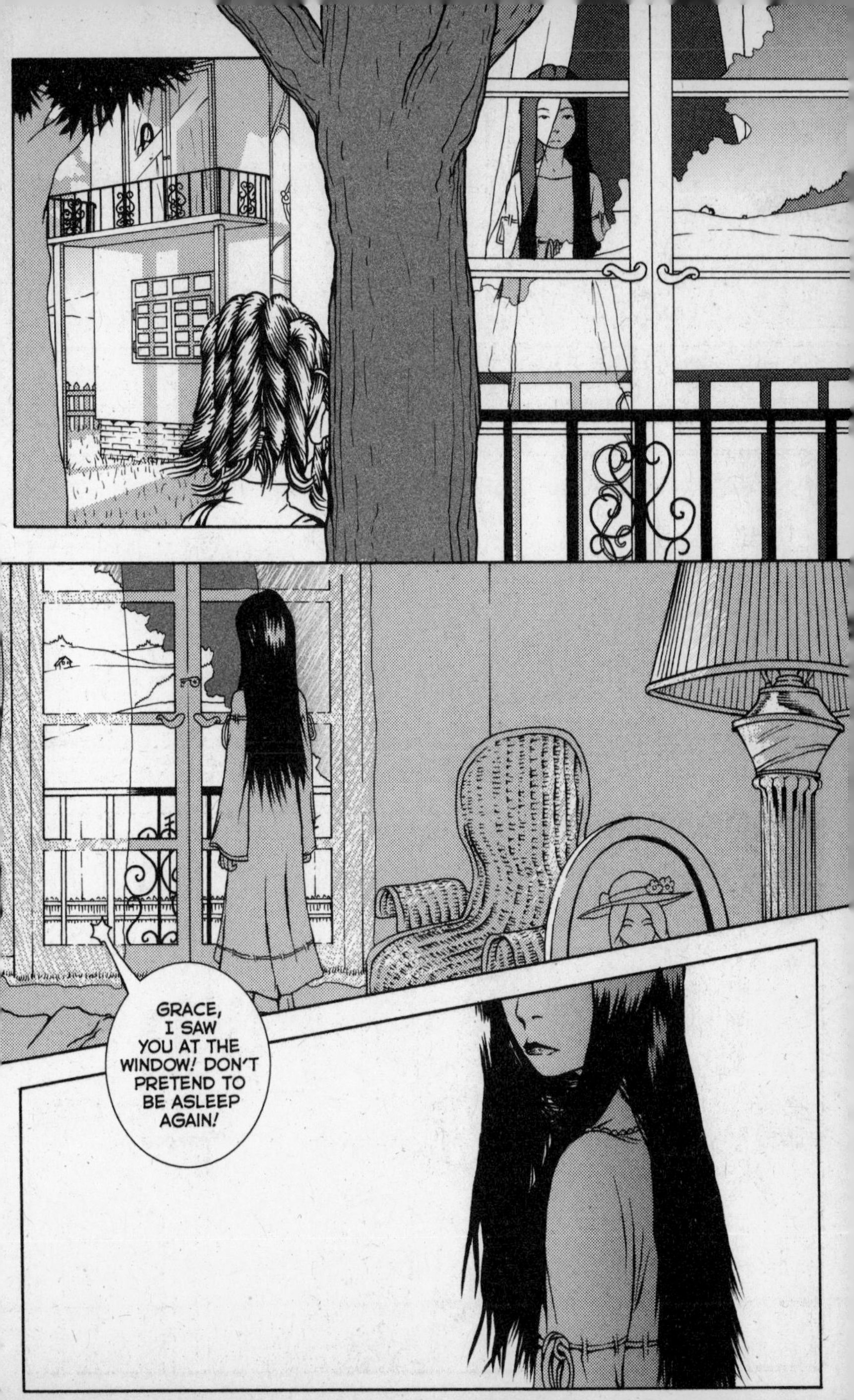
GRACE, I SAW YOU AT THE WINDOW! DON'T PRETEND TO BE ASLEEP AGAIN!

YOU WON'T BELIEVE ALL THE STUFF I GOT FOR YOU TODAY!

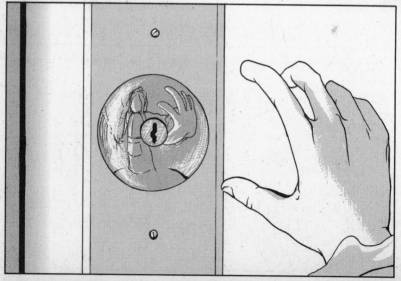

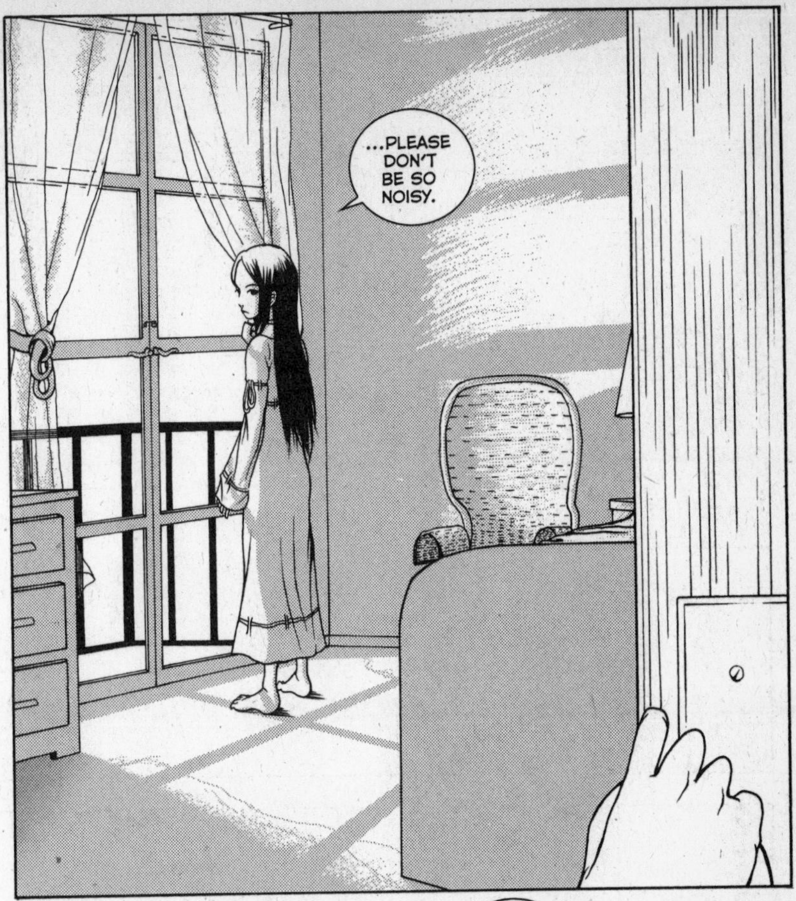
...PLEASE DON'T BE SO NOISY.
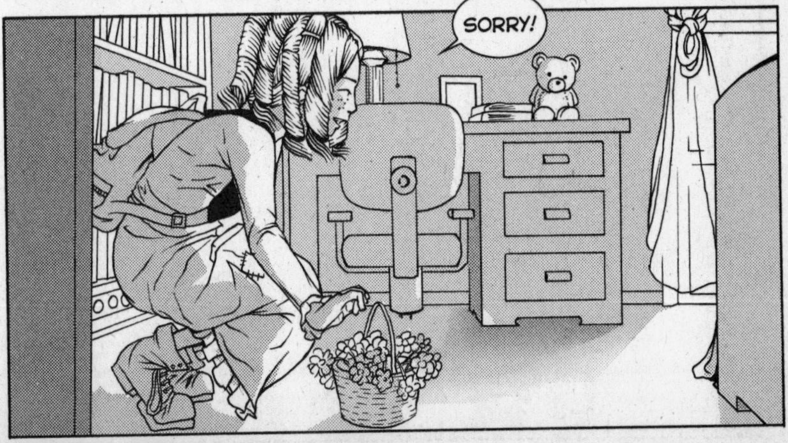
SORRY!

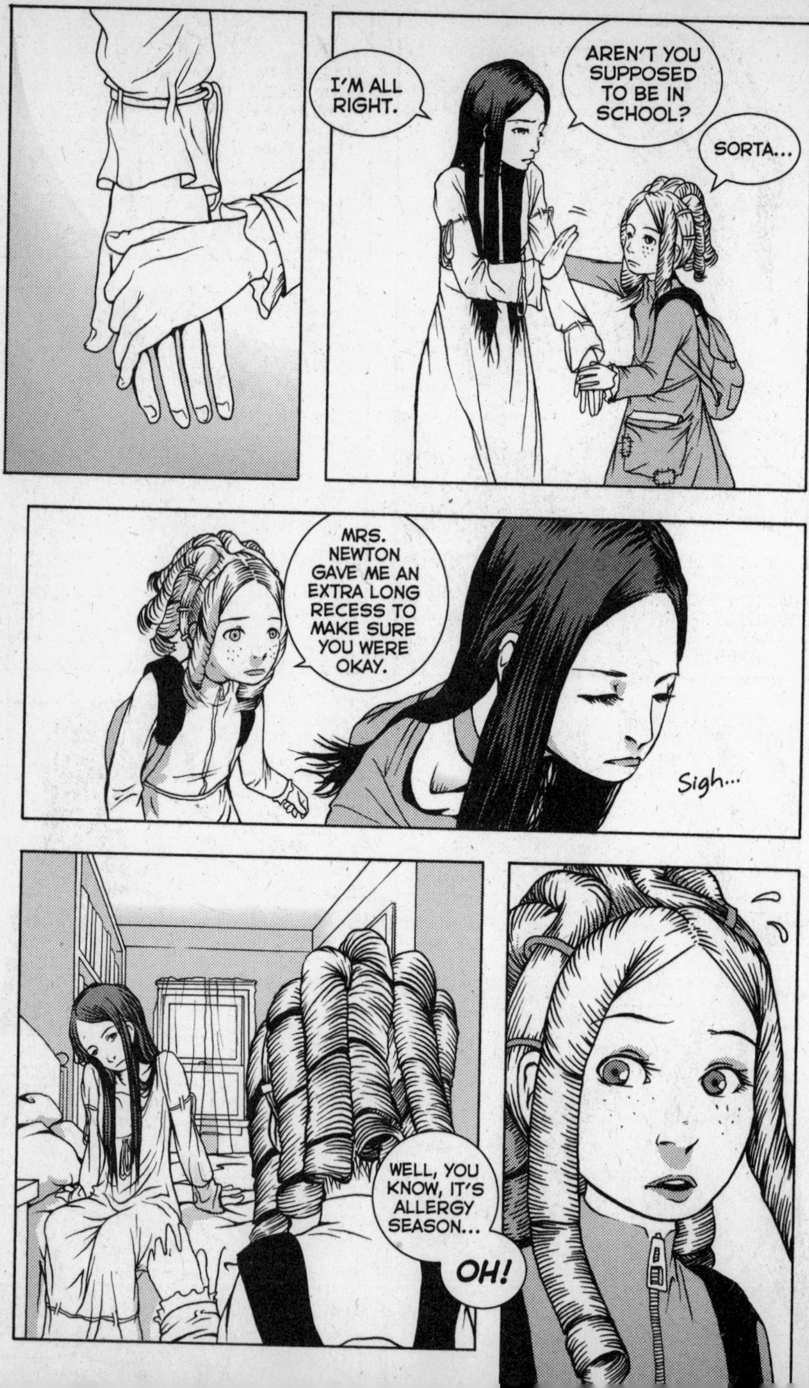
I'M ALL RIGHT.
AREN'T YOU SUPPOSED TO BE IN SCHOOL?
SORTA...
MRS. NEWTON GAVE ME AN EXTRA LONG RECESS TO MAKE SURE YOU WERE OKAY.
Sigh...
WELL, YOU KNOW, IT'S ALLERGY SEASON...
OH!

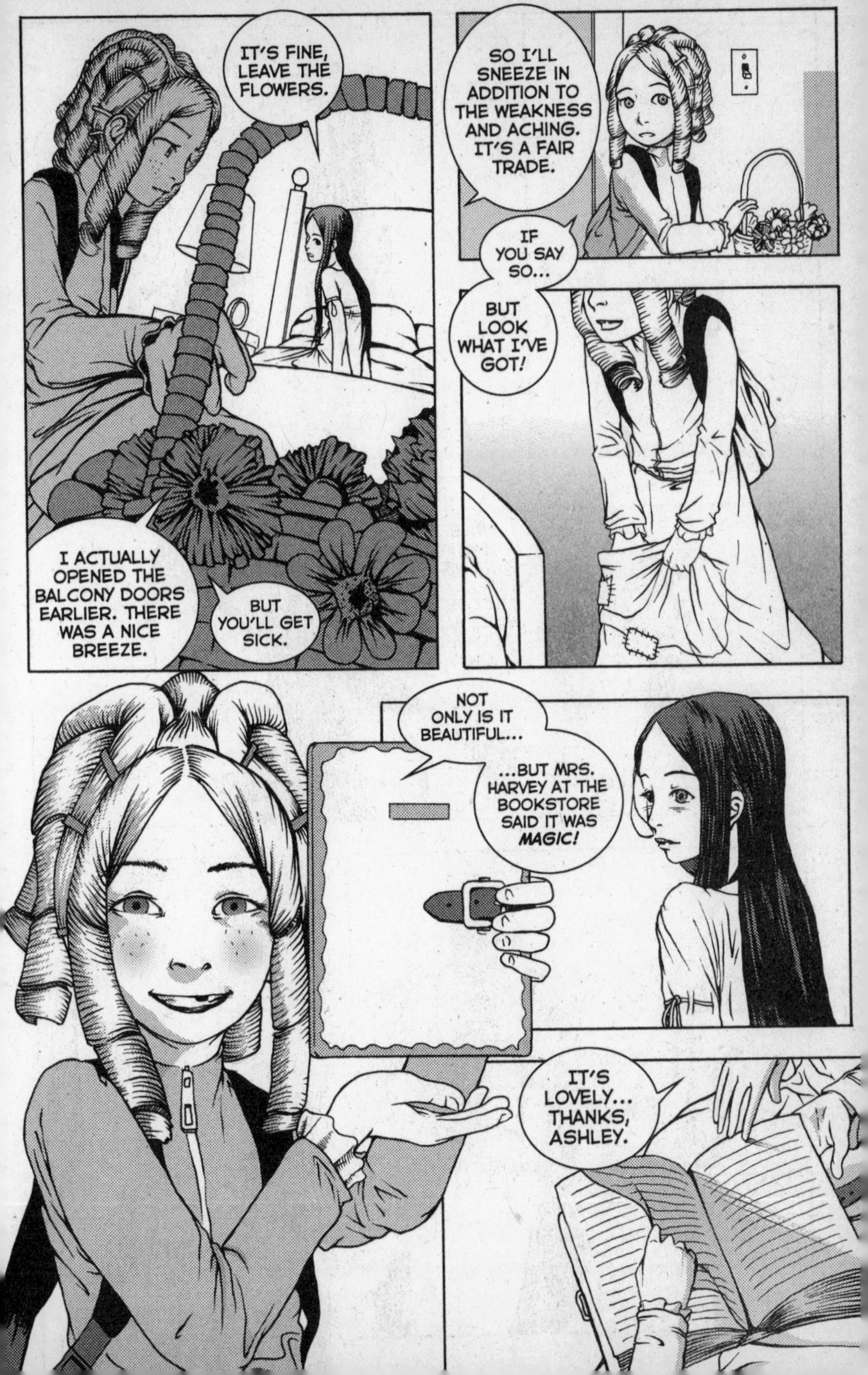
IT'S FINE, LEAVE THE FLOWERS.
I ACTUALLY OPENED THE BALCONY DOORS EARLIER. THERE WAS A NICE BREEZE.
BUT YOU'LL GET SICK.
SO I'LL SNEEZE IN ADDITION TO THE WEAKNESS AND ACHING. IT'S A FAIR TRADE.
IF YOU SAY SO...
BUT LOOK WHAT I'VE GOT!
NOT ONLY IS IT BEAUTIFUL...
...BUT MRS. HARVEY AT THE BOOKSTORE SAID IT WAS *MAGIC!*
IT'S LOVELY... THANKS, ASHLEY.

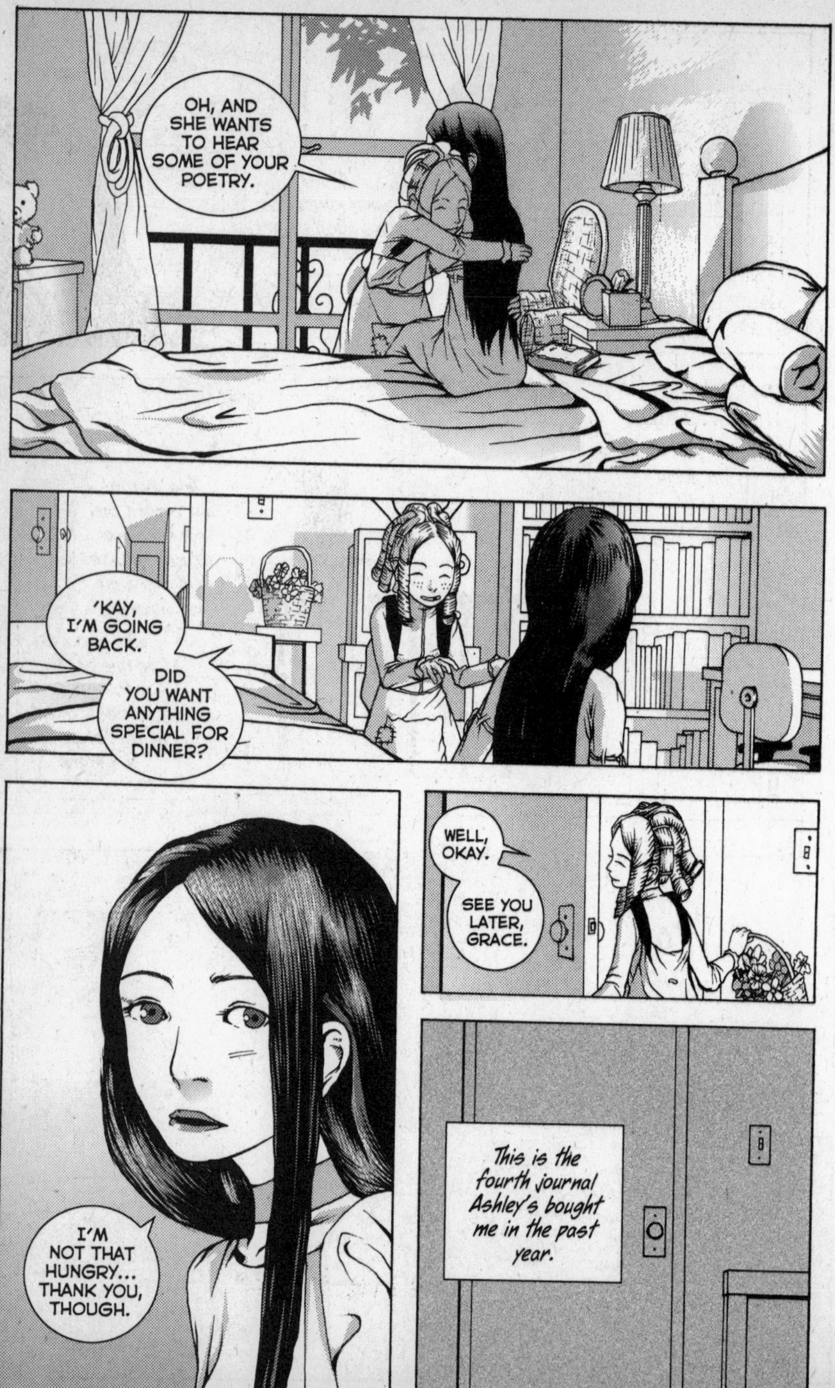
OH, AND SHE WANTS TO HEAR SOME OF YOUR POETRY.
'KAY, I'M GOING BACK.
DID YOU WANT ANYTHING SPECIAL FOR DINNER?
I'M NOT THAT HUNGRY... THANK YOU, THOUGH.
WELL, OKAY.
SEE YOU LATER, GRACE.
This is the fourth journal Ashley's bought me in the past year.

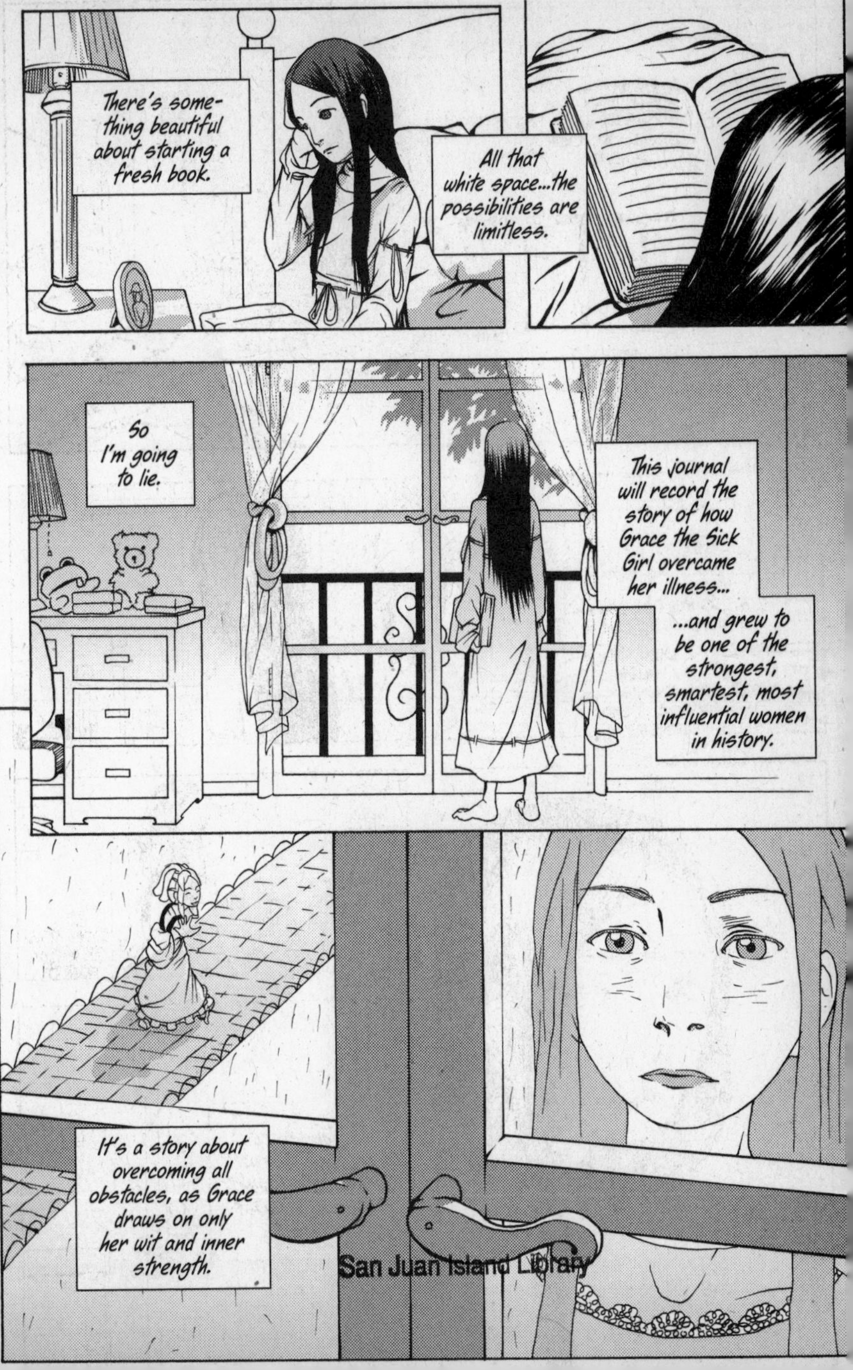
There's some-thing beautiful about starting a fresh book.
All that white space...the possibilities are limitless.
So I'm going to lie.
This journal will record the story of how Grace the Sick Girl overcame her illness...
...and grew to be one of the strongest, smartest, most influential women in history.
It's a story about overcoming all obstacles, as Grace draws on only her wit and inner strength.

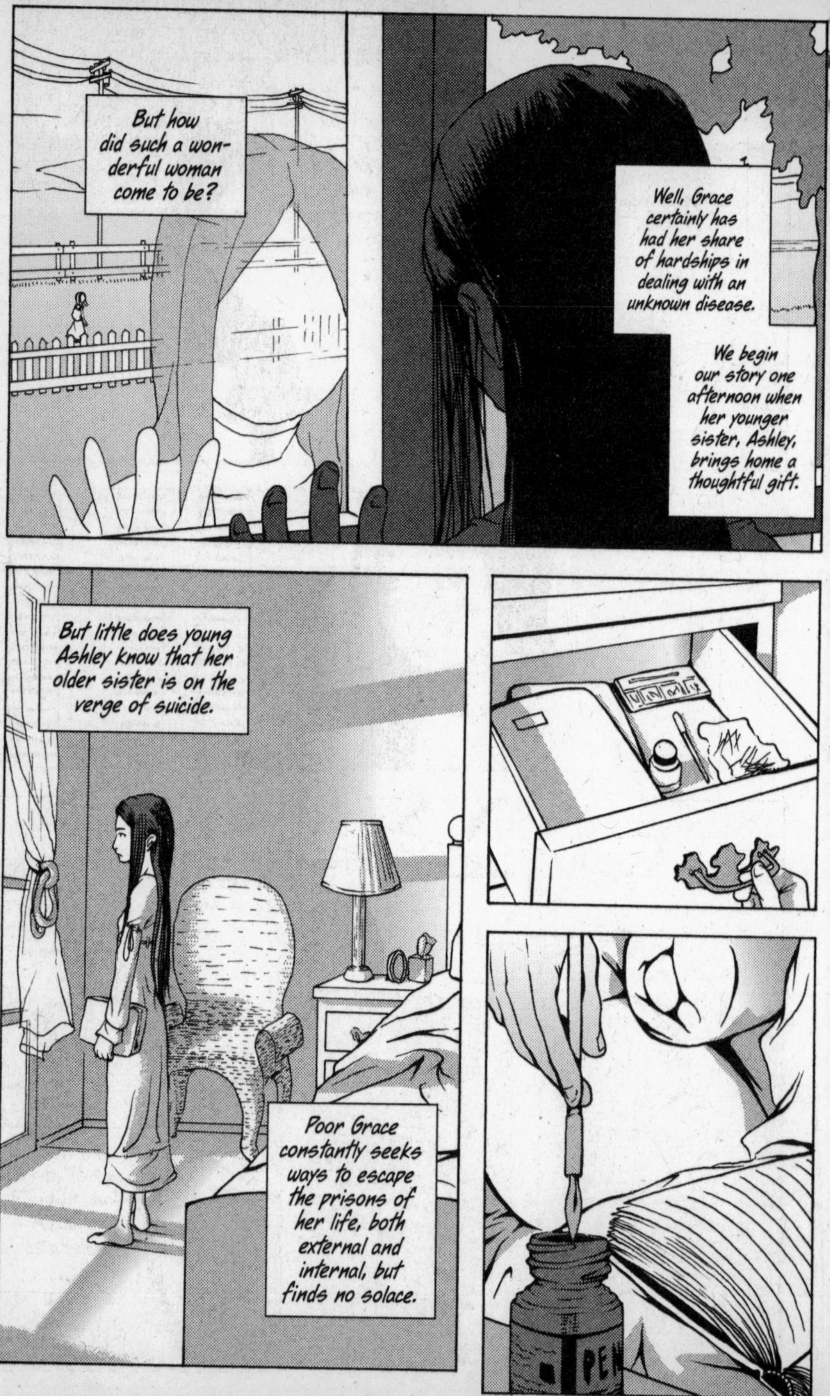
But how did such a wonderful woman come to be?
Well, Grace certainly has had her share of hardships in dealing with an unknown disease.
We begin our story one afternoon when her younger sister, Ashley, brings home a thoughtful gift.
But little does young Ashley know that her older sister is on the verge of suicide.
Poor Grace constantly seeks ways to escape the prisons of her life, both external and internal, but finds no solace.

She dreams of a release she knows only death can provide.

But Grace lives on, if only for the sake of her sister.

And so we find her alone for hours on end, with no company but her ever-growing depression.

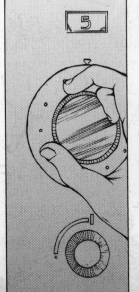

WIN FREE CA$H!

I find that I'm more mentally sound if every day is the same.

If I catch myself doing something I'll remember, I immediately stop.

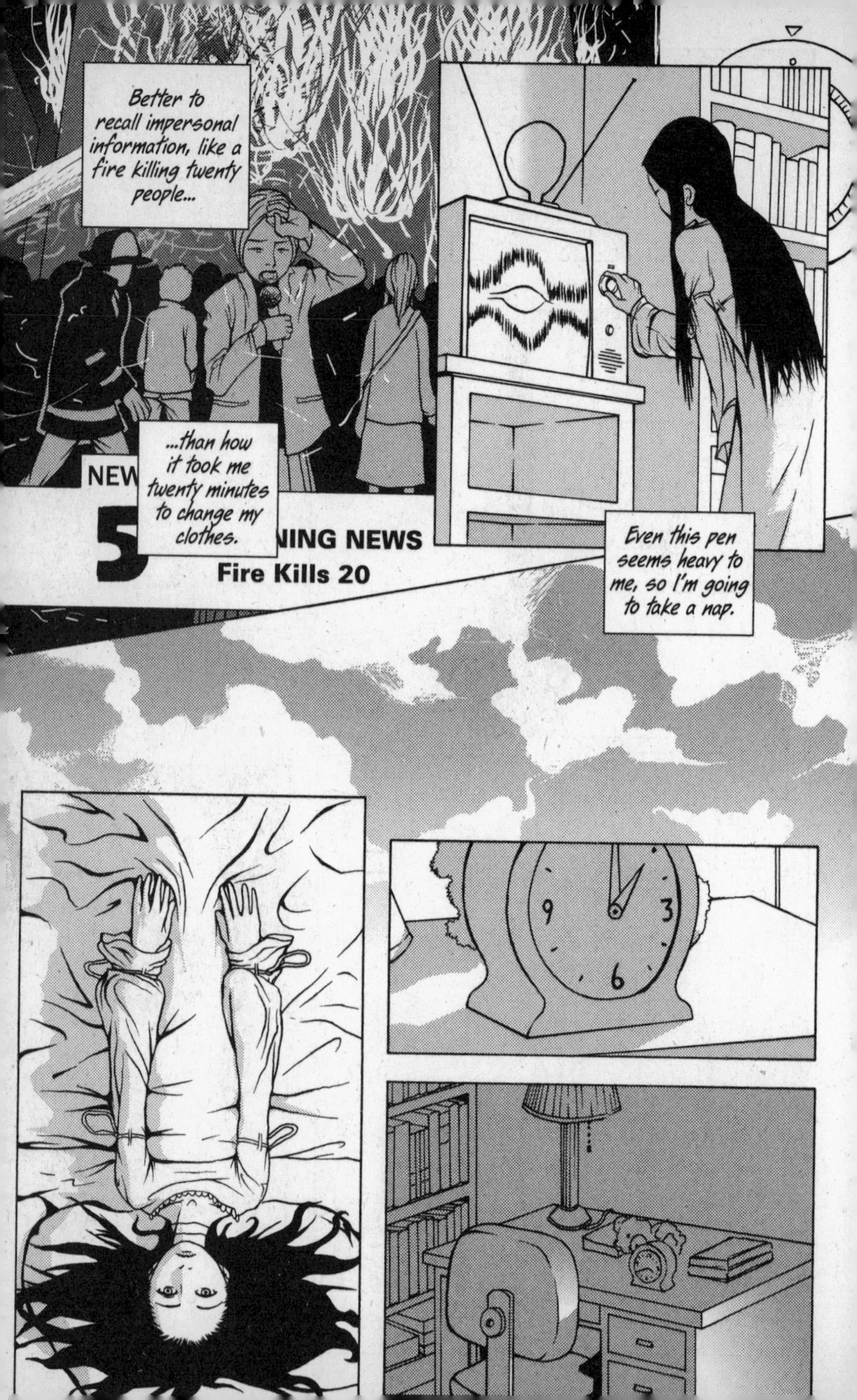
Better to recall impersonal information, like a fire killing twenty people...
...than how it took me twenty minutes to change my clothes.
NEW
5
NING NEWS
Fire Kills 20
Even this pen seems heavy to me, so I'm going to take a nap.
9
3
6

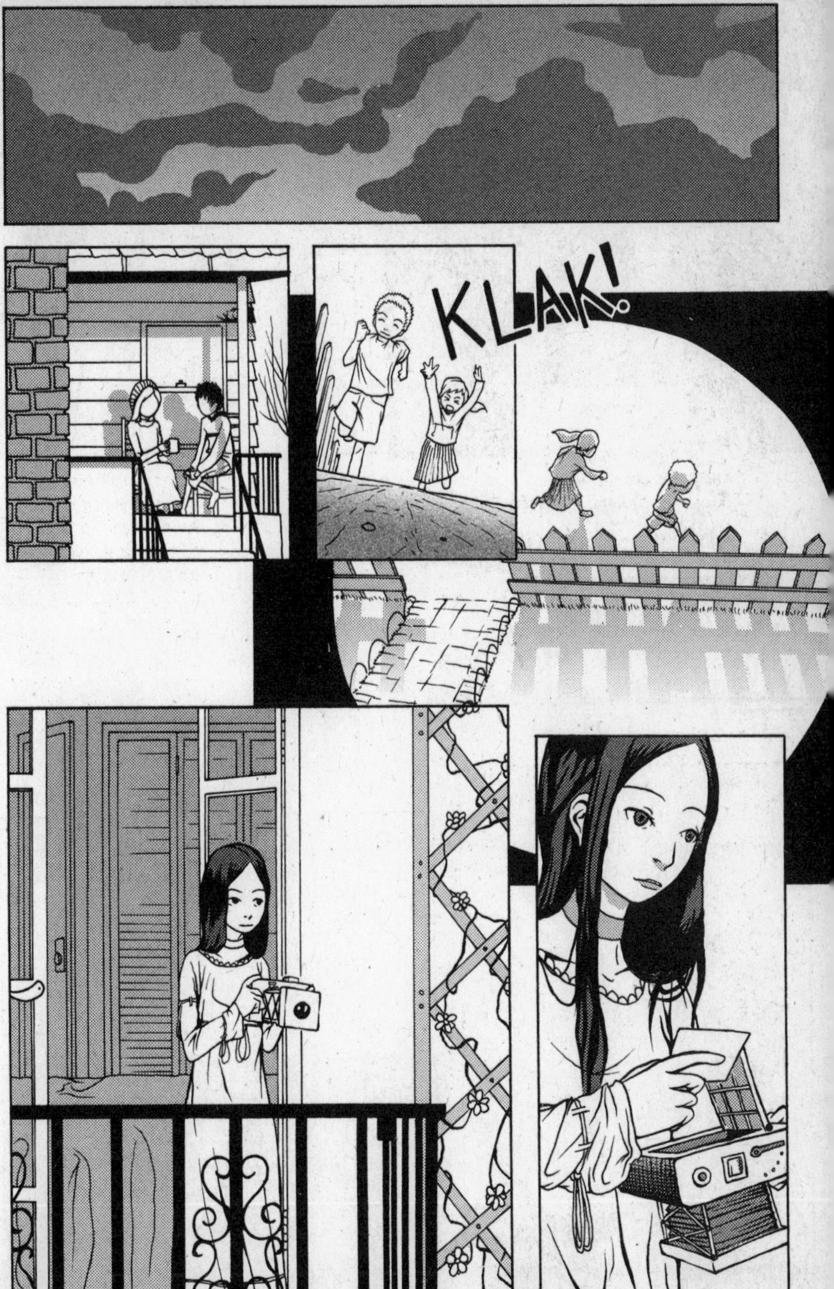
KLAK!

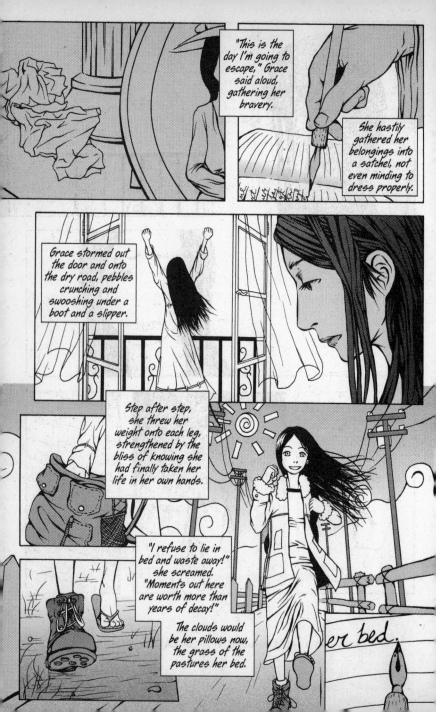

"This is the day I'm going to escape," Grace said aloud, gathering her bravery.

She hastily gathered her belongings into a satchel, not even minding to dress properly.

Grace stormed out the door and onto the dry road, pebbles crunching and swooshing under a boot and a slipper.

Step after step, she threw her weight onto each leg, strengthened by the bliss of knowing she had finally taken her life in her own hands.

"I refuse to lie in bed and waste away!" she screamed. "Moments out here are worth more than years of decay!"

The clouds would be her pillows now, the grass of the pastures her bed.

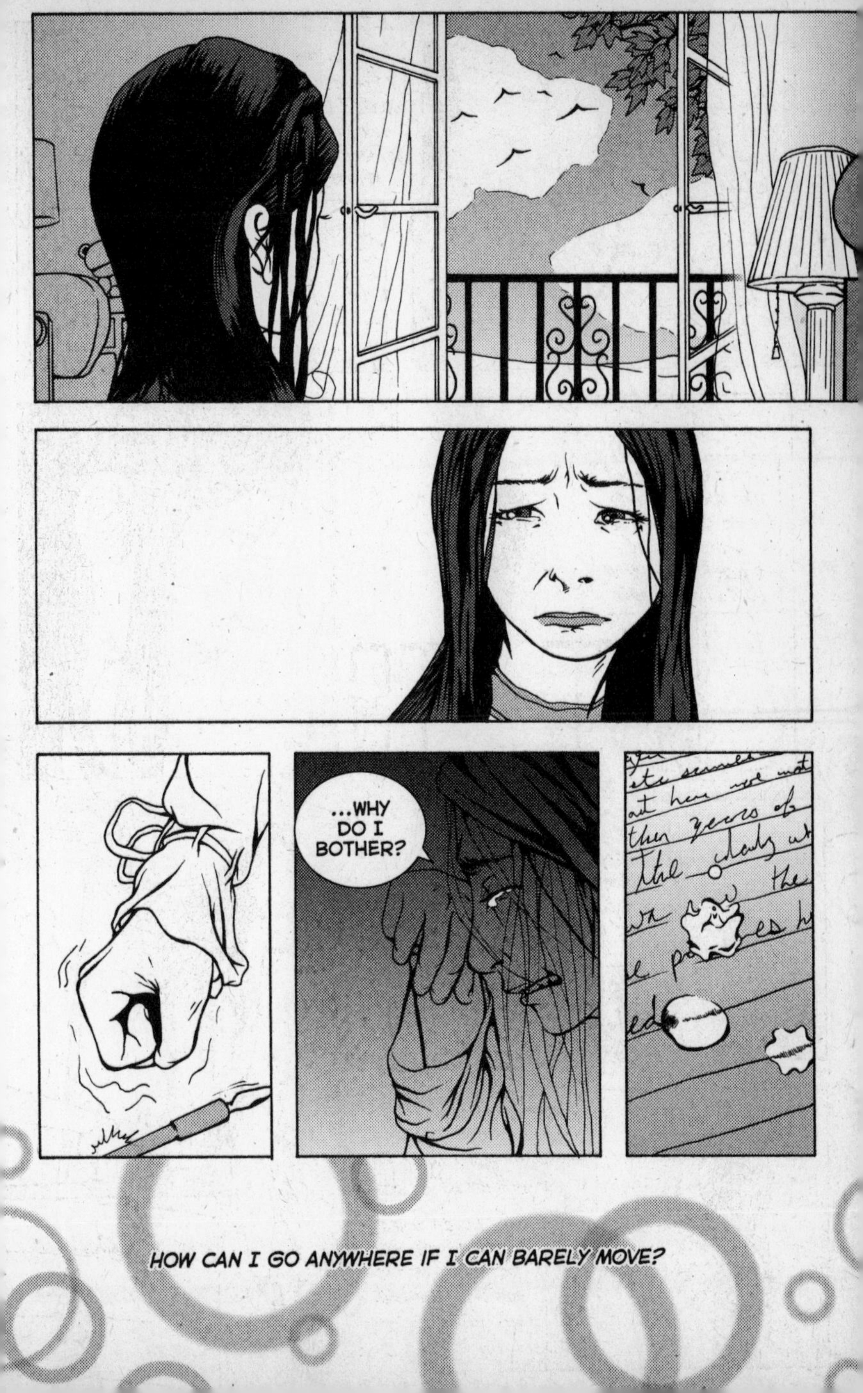
...WHY DO I BOTHER?
HOW CAN I GO ANYWHERE IF I CAN BARELY MOVE?

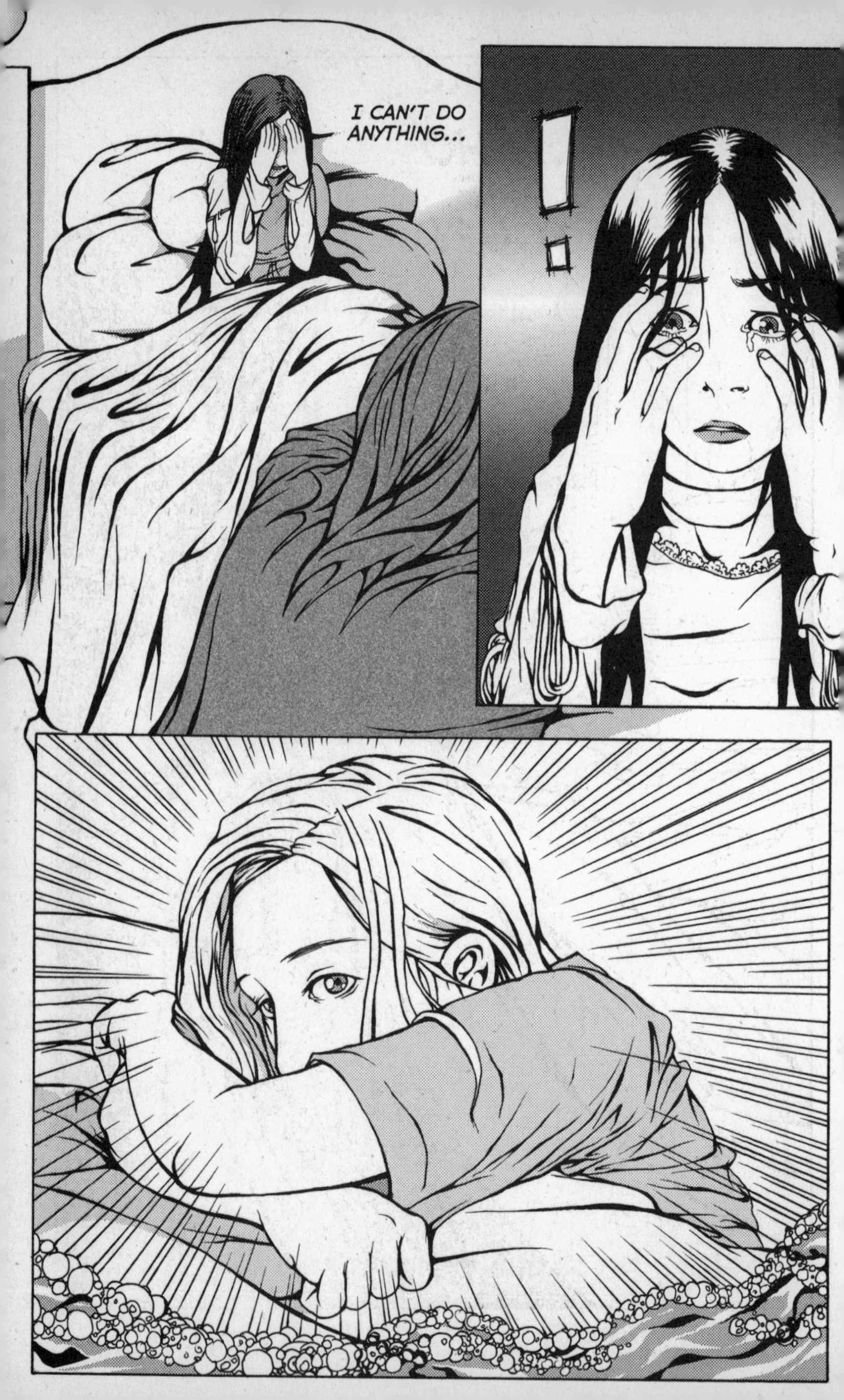
I CAN'T DO ANYTHING...
!

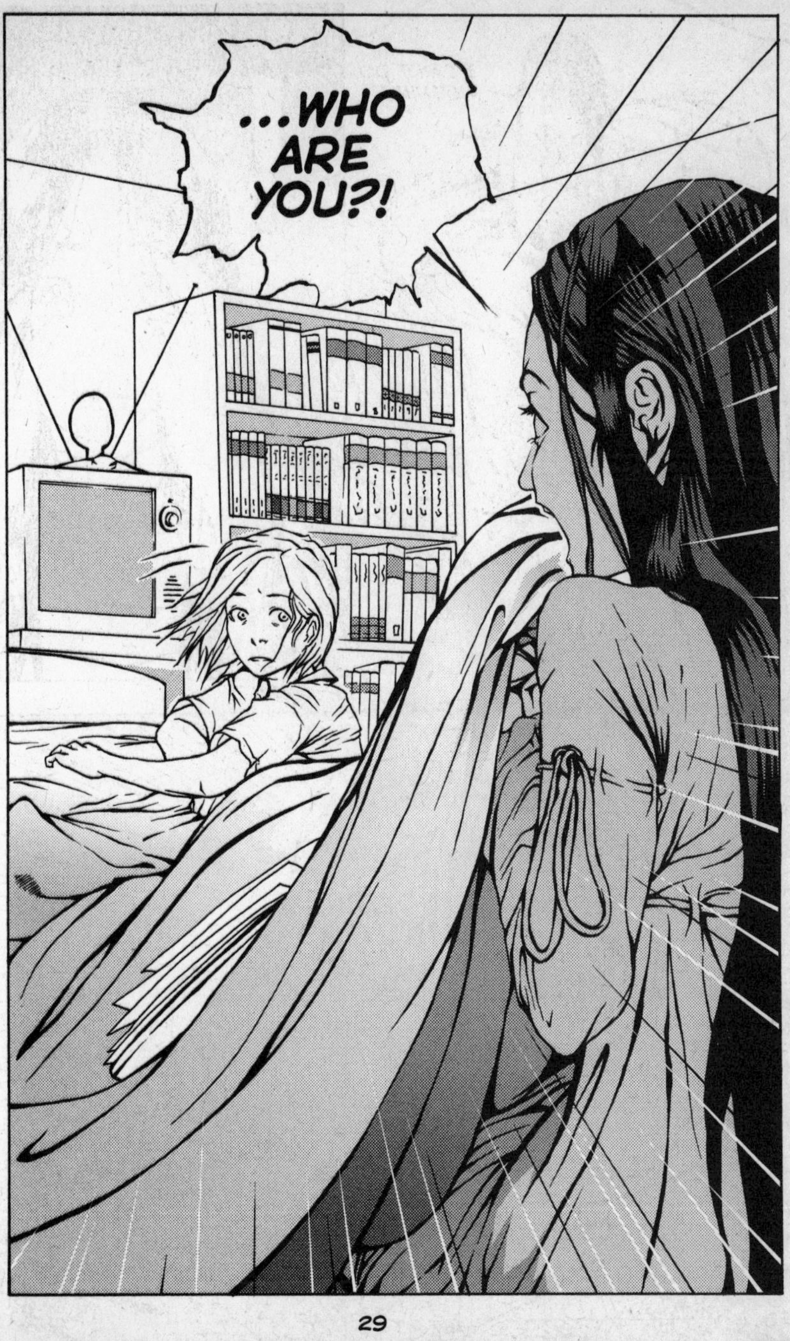
...WHO ARE YOU?!

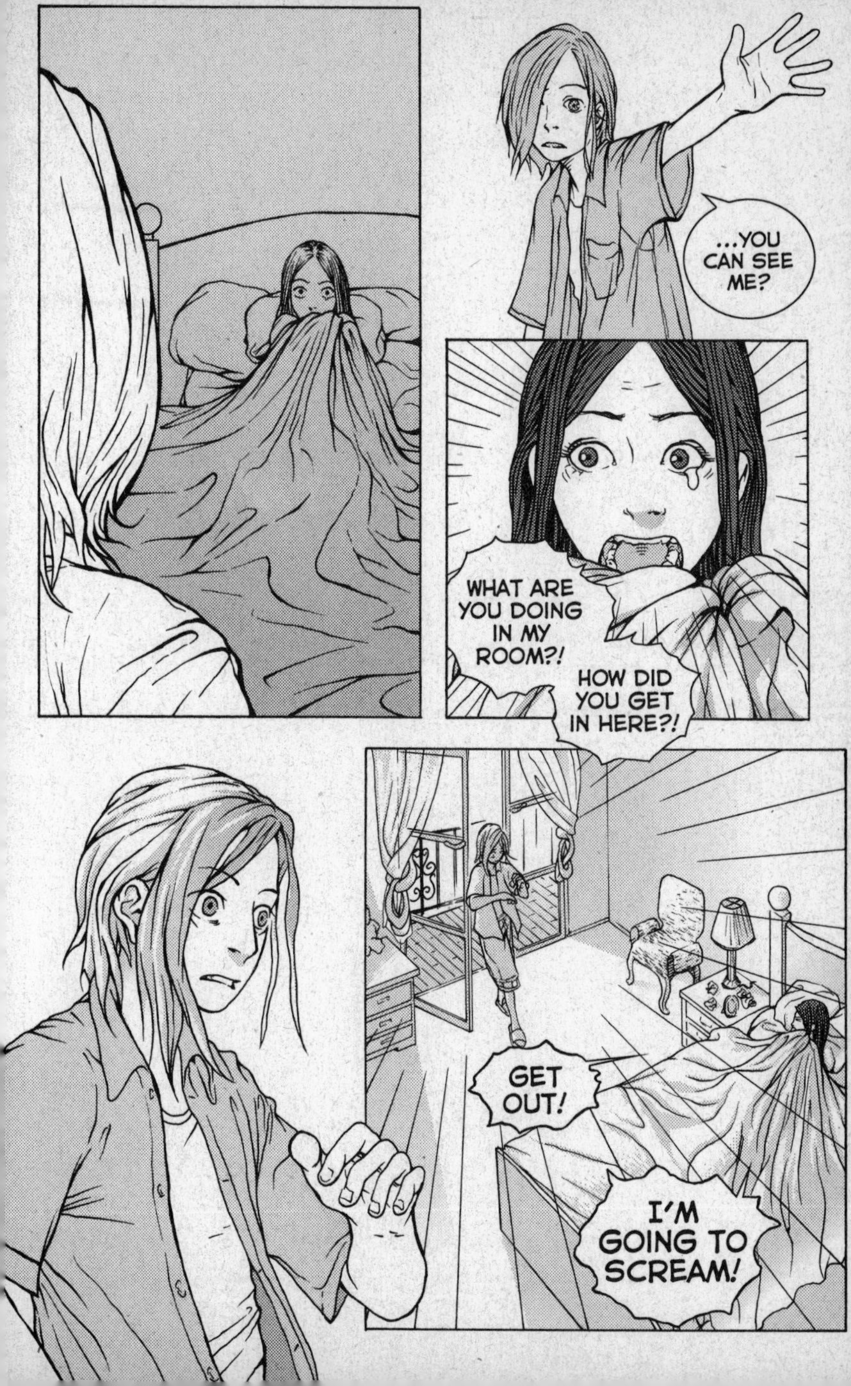
...YOU CAN SEE ME?
WHAT ARE YOU DOING IN MY ROOM?!
HOW DID YOU GET IN HERE?!
GET OUT!
I'M GOING TO SCREAM!

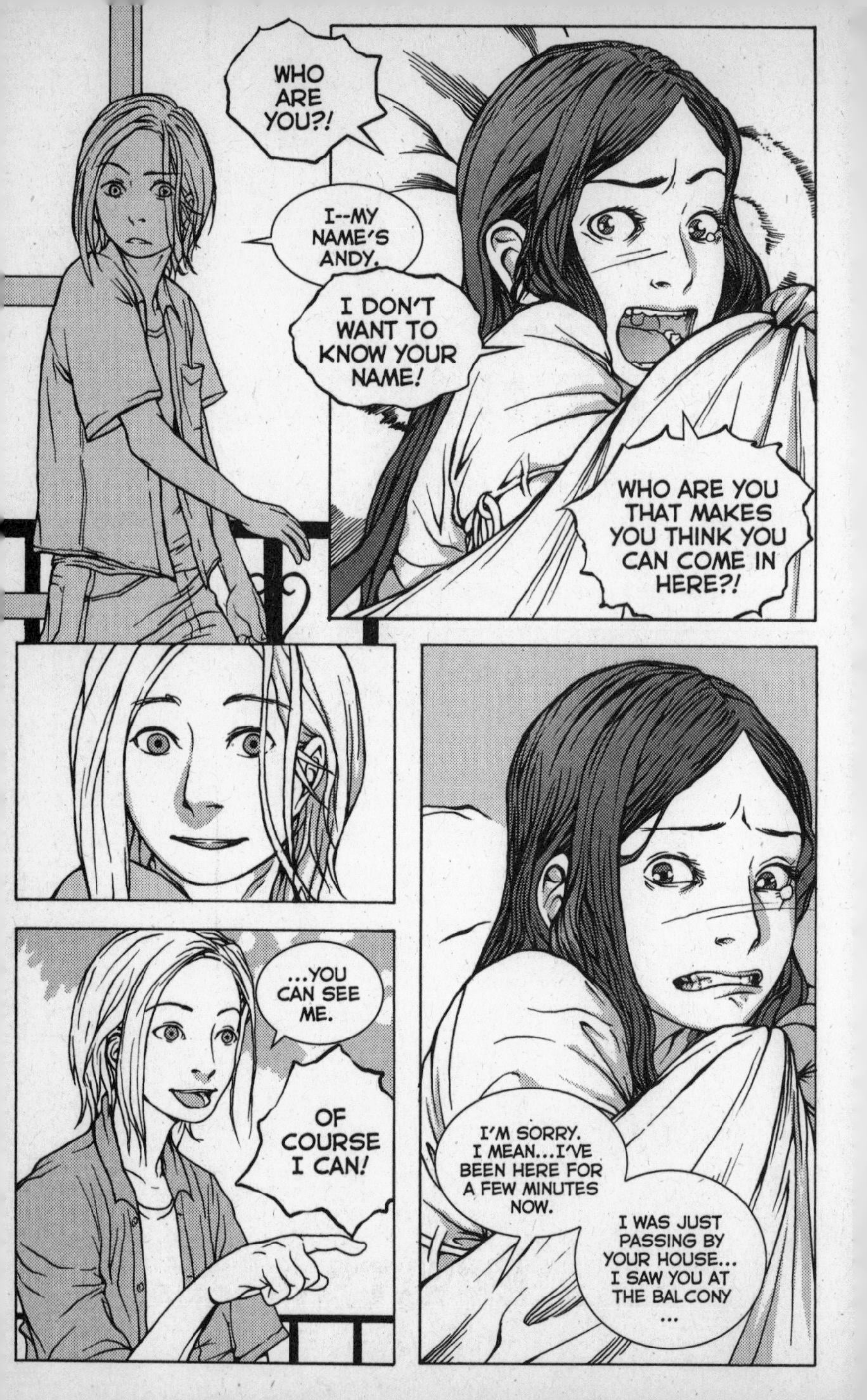
WHO ARE YOU?!
I--MY NAME'S ANDY.
I DON'T WANT TO KNOW YOUR NAME!
WHO ARE YOU THAT MAKES YOU THINK YOU CAN COME IN HERE?!
...YOU CAN SEE ME.
OF COURSE I CAN!
I'M SORRY. I MEAN...I'VE BEEN HERE FOR A FEW MINUTES NOW.
I WAS JUST PASSING BY YOUR HOUSE... I SAW YOU AT THE BALCONY ...

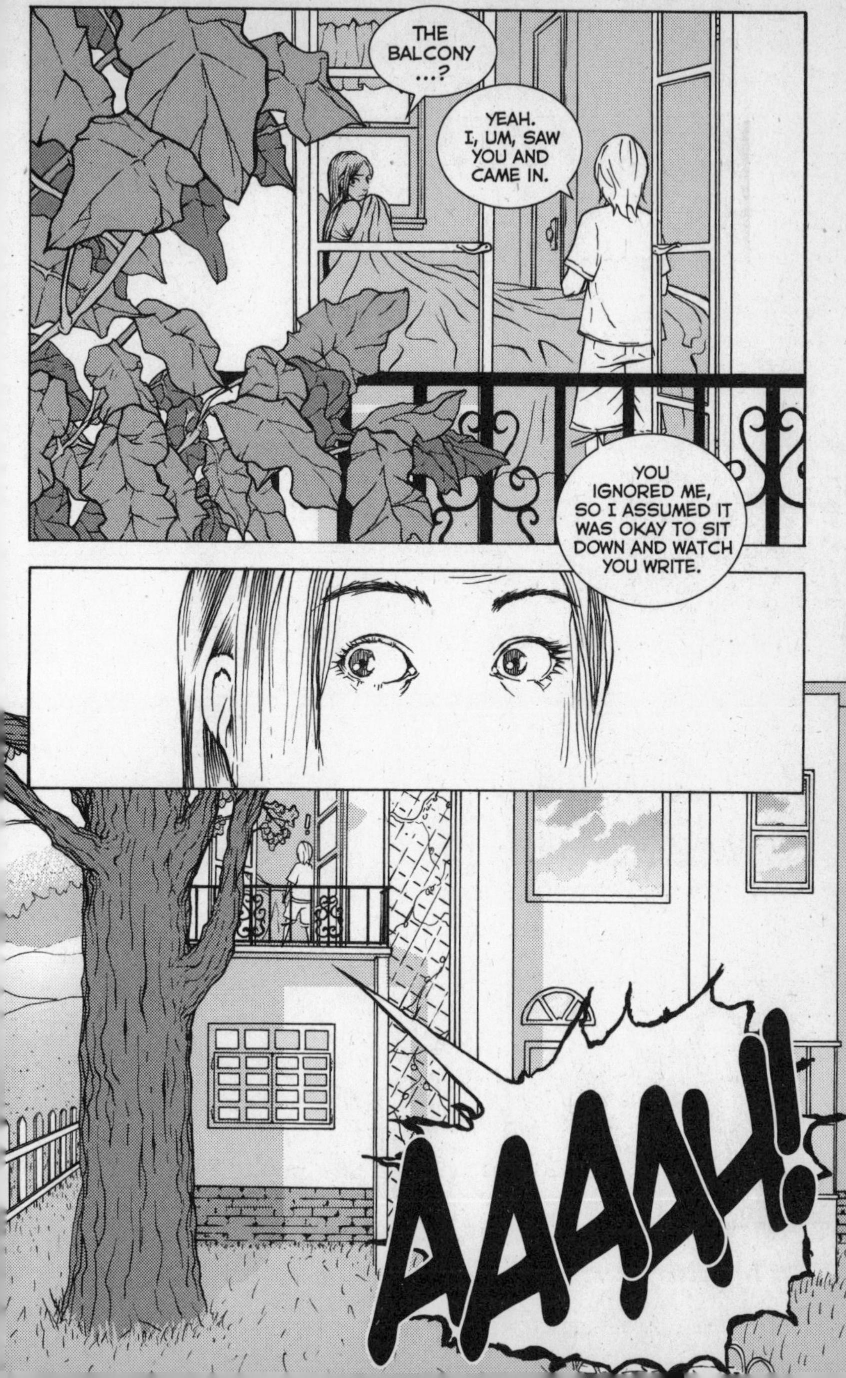

THE BALCONY ...?
YEAH. I, UM, SAW YOU AND CAME IN.
YOU IGNORED ME, SO I ASSUMED IT WAS OKAY TO SIT DOWN AND WATCH YOU WRITE.
!
AAAH!!

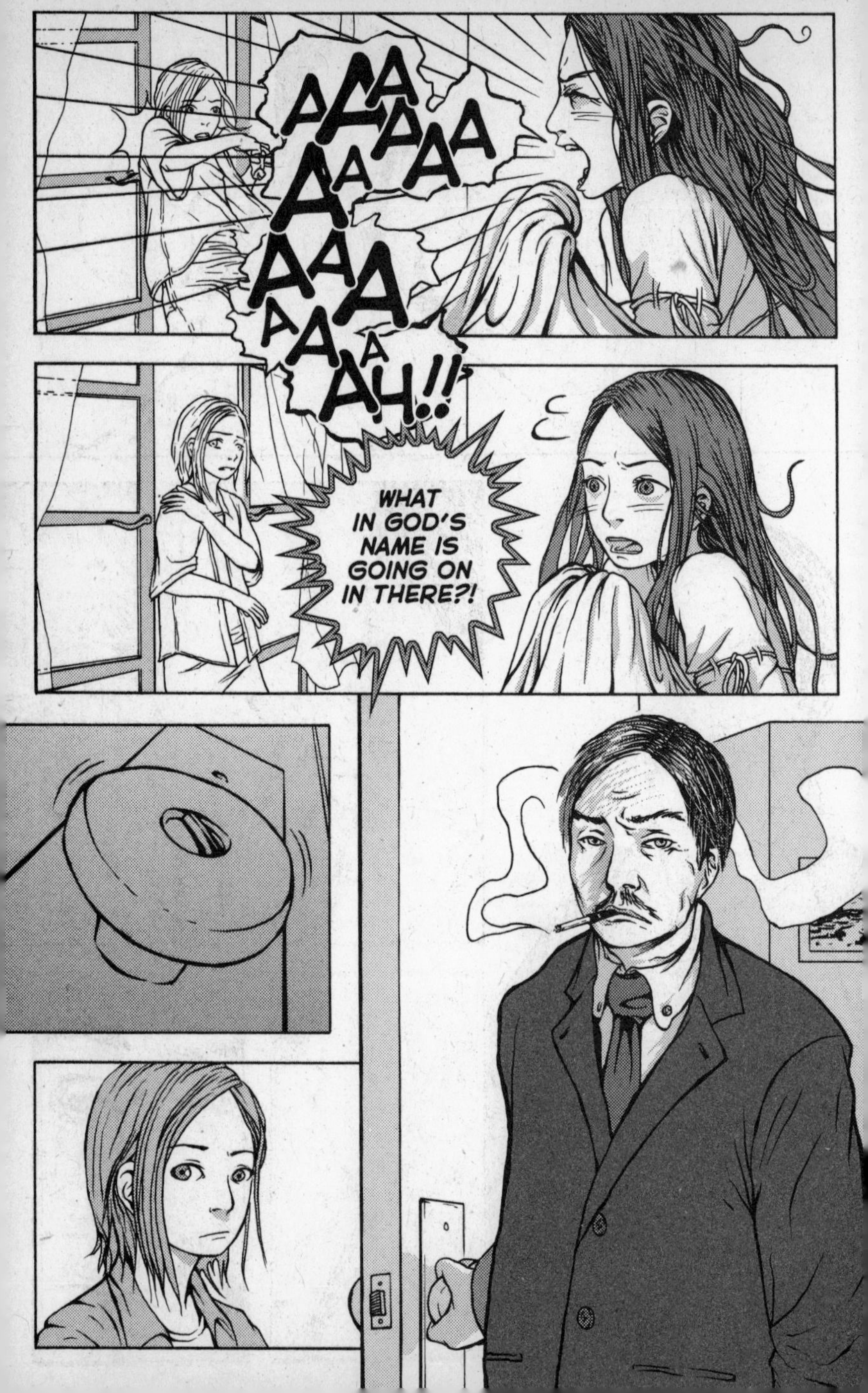
AAAAAAAAAAAAAAAAH!!
WHAT IN GOD'S NAME IS GOING ON IN THERE?!

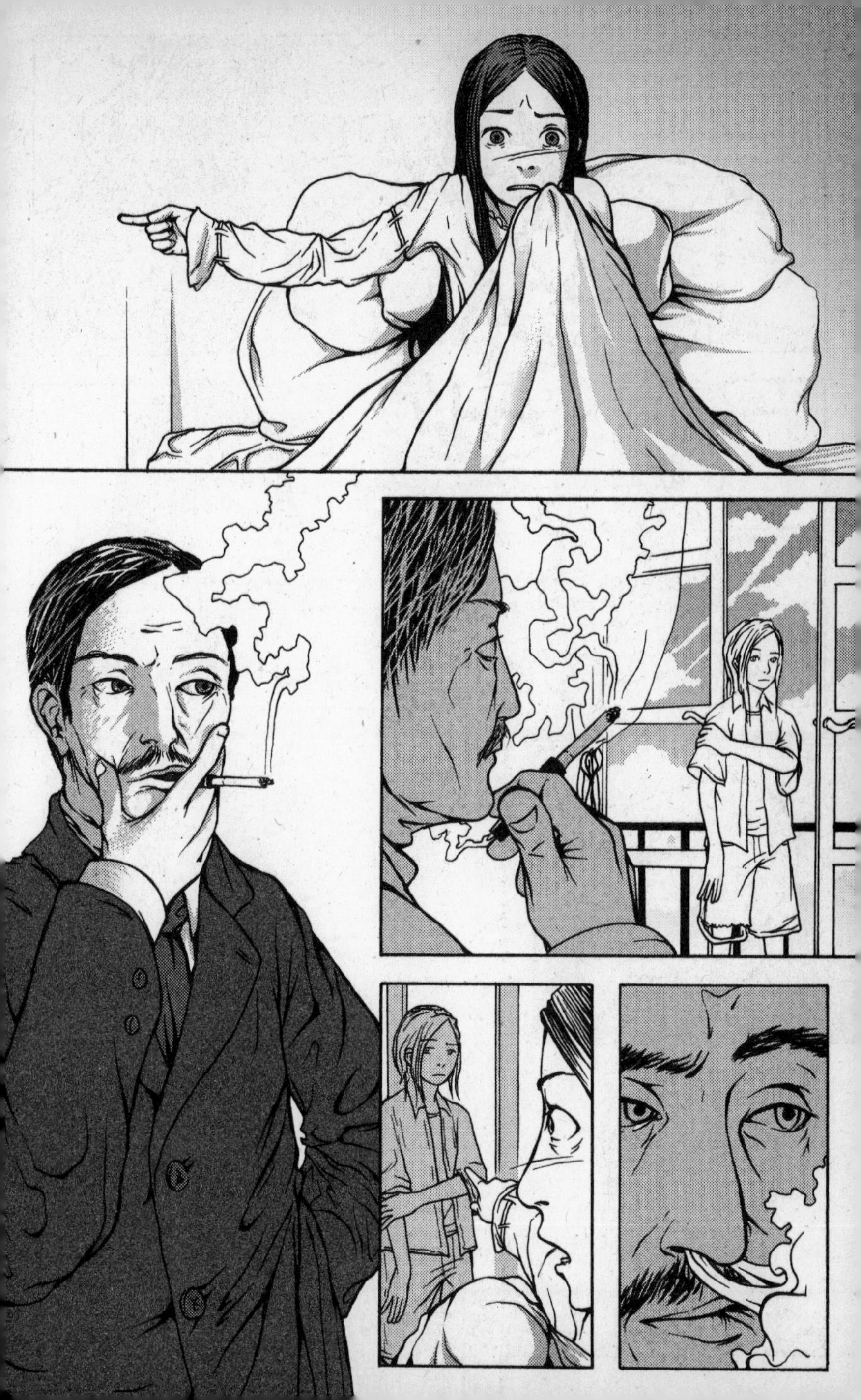

WHAT?

YOU DON'T SEE...?!

...YOUR BALCONY?

SPEAK UP, GIRL!

BOTHERING ME? SCREAMING AS IF SOMEONE WAS ABOUT TO BURN THE HOUSE DOWN?

I'M SORRY. PLEASE, JUST... DON'T BRING THE SMELL OF SMOKE IN HERE. I TOLD YOU IT MAKES ME NAUSEOUS.

YOU *TOLD* ME?

I COME UP HERE AND THIS IS THE APPRECIATION I GET? I GIVE YOU A ROOF TO LIVE UNDER AND A NICE BED TO SLEEP IN--

...IT'S NOTHING. SORRY FOR BOTHERING YOU.

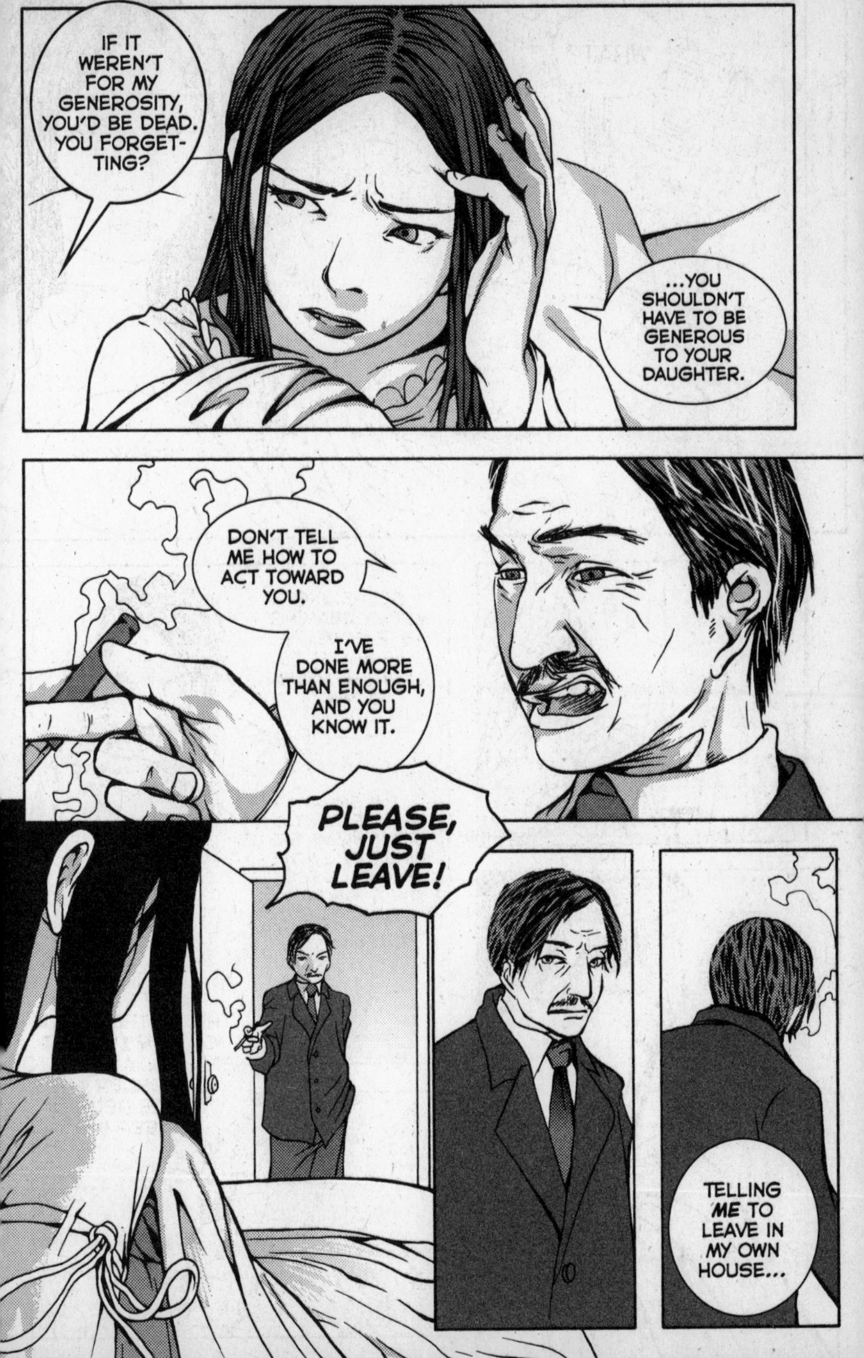
IF IT WEREN'T FOR MY GENEROSITY, YOU'D BE DEAD. YOU FORGET-TING?
...YOU SHOULDN'T HAVE TO BE GENEROUS TO YOUR DAUGHTER.
DON'T TELL ME HOW TO ACT TOWARD YOU.
I'VE DONE MORE THAN ENOUGH, AND YOU KNOW IT.
PLEASE, JUST LEAVE!
TELLING *ME* TO LEAVE IN MY OWN HOUSE...

SLAM!

WHOA, IT SMELLS IN HERE...

WHOEVER YOU ARE, JUST GET OUT!

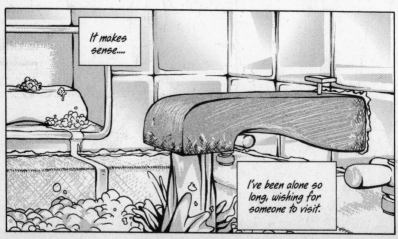

It makes sense....

I've been alone so long, wishing for someone to visit.

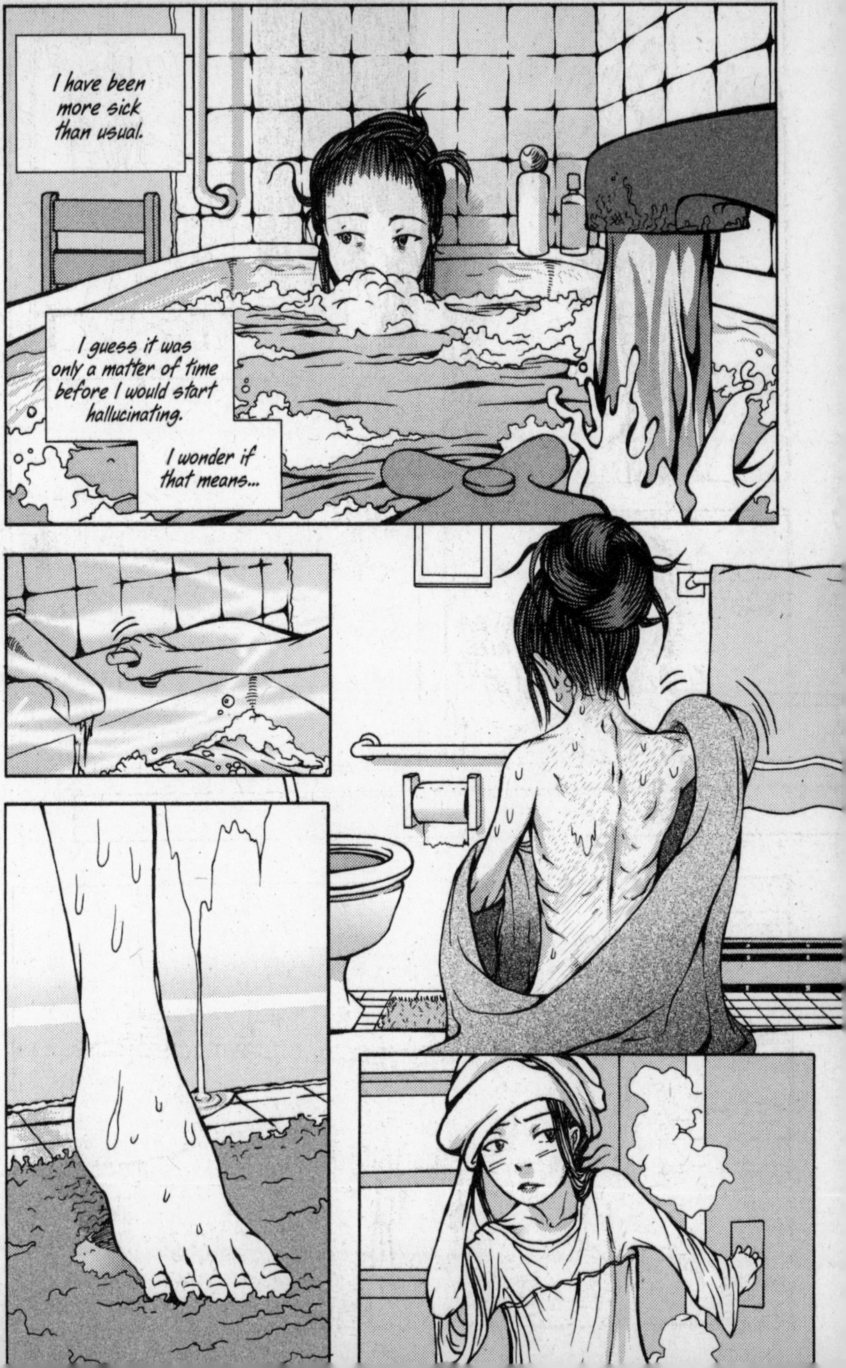
I have been more sick than usual.
I guess it was only a matter of time before I would start hallucinating.
I wonder if that means...

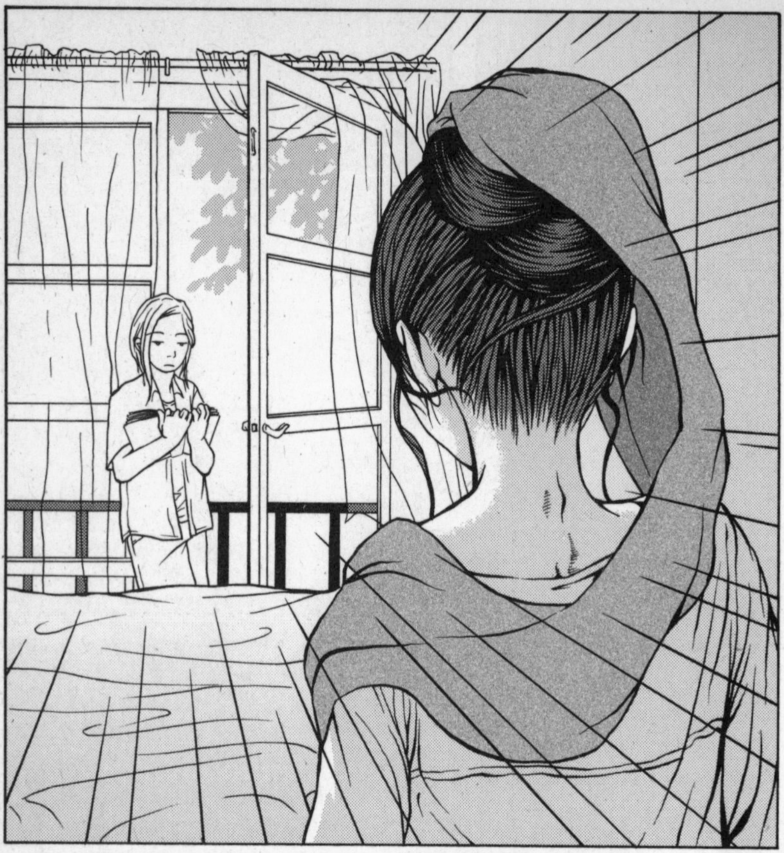

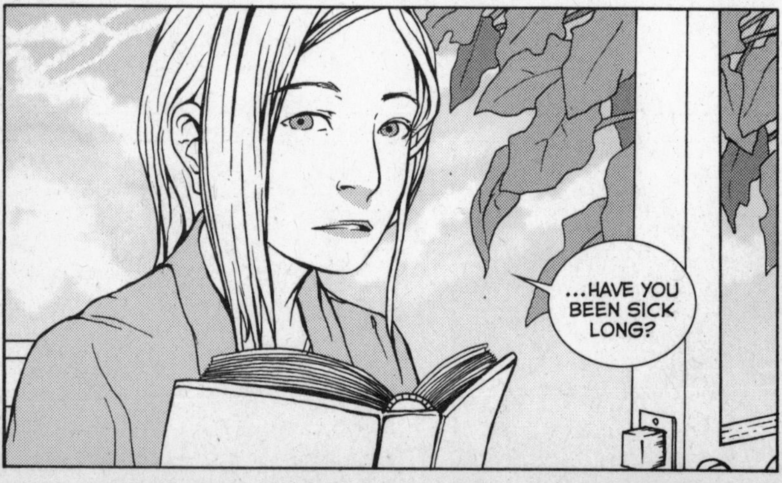
...HAVE YOU BEEN SICK LONG?

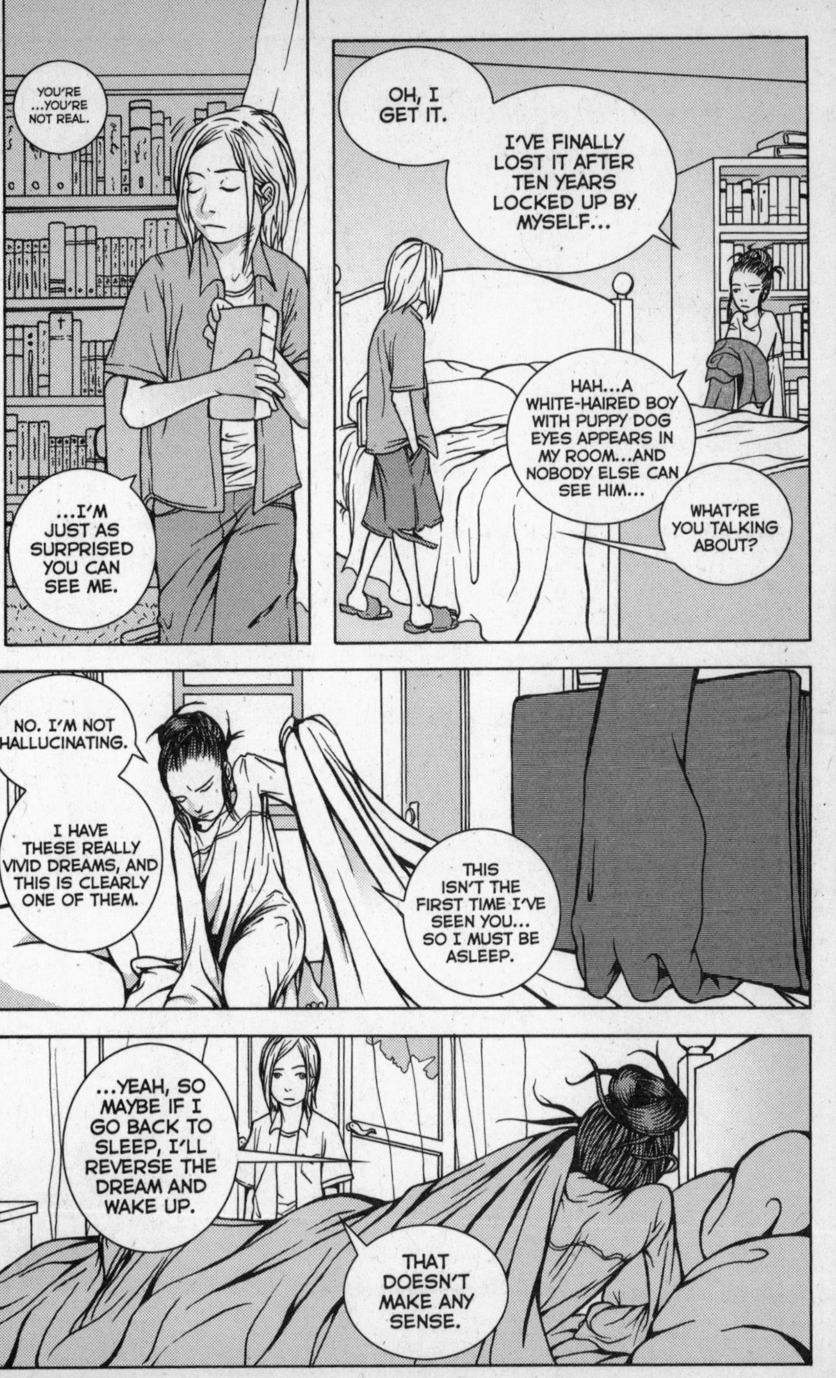
YOU'RE ...YOU'RE NOT REAL.
...I'M JUST AS SURPRISED YOU CAN SEE ME.
OH, I GET IT.
I'VE FINALLY LOST IT AFTER TEN YEARS LOCKED UP BY MYSELF...
HAH...A WHITE-HAIRED BOY WITH PUPPY DOG EYES APPEARS IN MY ROOM...AND NOBODY ELSE CAN SEE HIM...
WHAT'RE YOU TALKING ABOUT?
NO. I'M NOT HALLUCINATING.
I HAVE THESE REALLY VIVID DREAMS, AND THIS IS CLEARLY ONE OF THEM.
THIS ISN'T THE FIRST TIME I'VE SEEN YOU... SO I MUST BE ASLEEP.
...YEAH, SO MAYBE IF I GO BACK TO SLEEP, I'LL REVERSE THE DREAM AND WAKE UP.
THAT DOESN'T MAKE ANY SENSE.

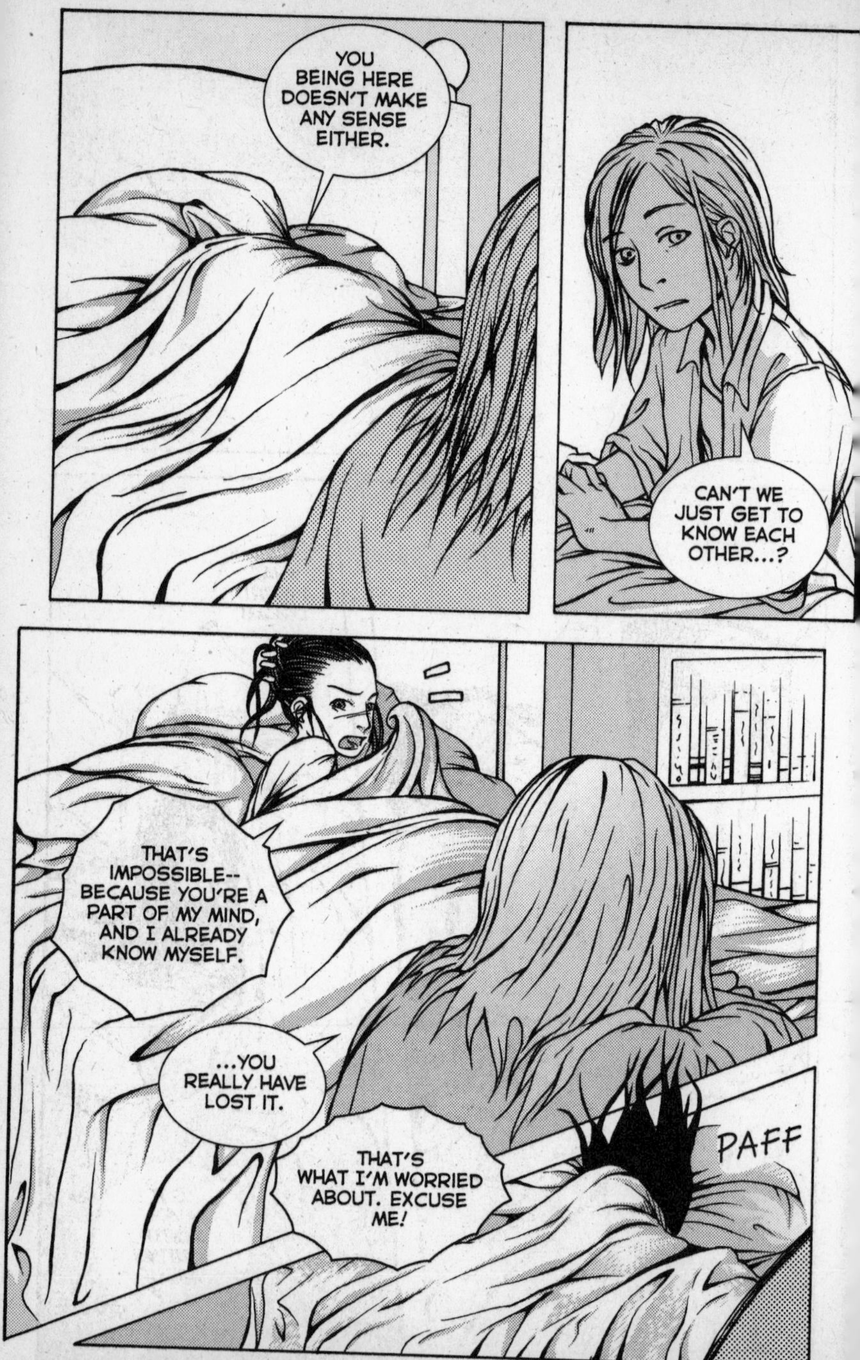
YOU BEING HERE DOESN'T MAKE ANY SENSE EITHER.
CAN'T WE JUST GET TO KNOW EACH OTHER...?
THAT'S IMPOSSIBLE-- BECAUSE YOU'RE A PART OF MY MIND, AND I ALREADY KNOW MYSELF.
...YOU REALLY HAVE LOST IT.
THAT'S WHAT I'M WORRIED ABOUT. EXCUSE ME!
PAFF

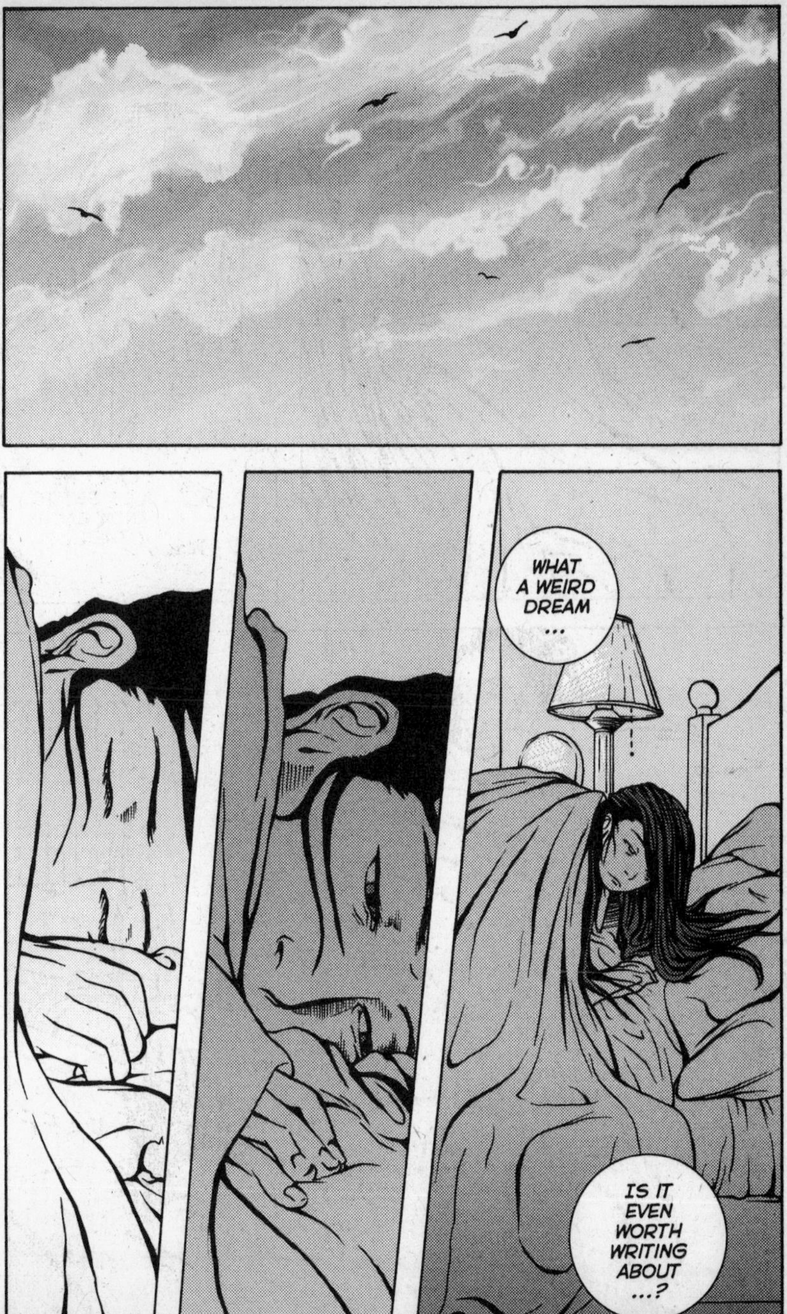
WHAT A WEIRD DREAM ...
IS IT EVEN WORTH WRITING ABOUT ...?

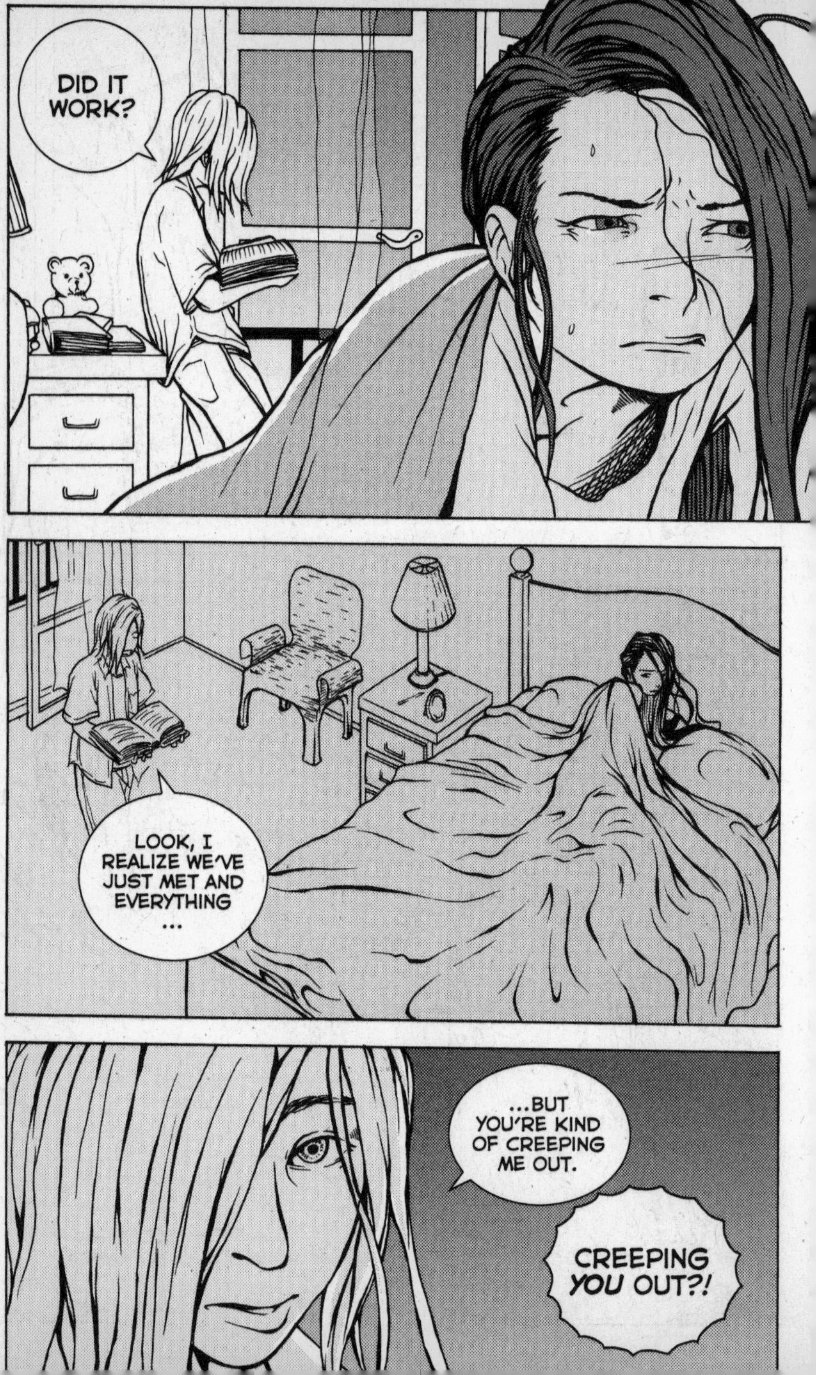
DID IT WORK?
LOOK, I REALIZE WE'VE JUST MET AND EVERYTHING ...
...BUT YOU'RE KIND OF CREEPING ME OUT.
CREEPING *YOU* OUT?!

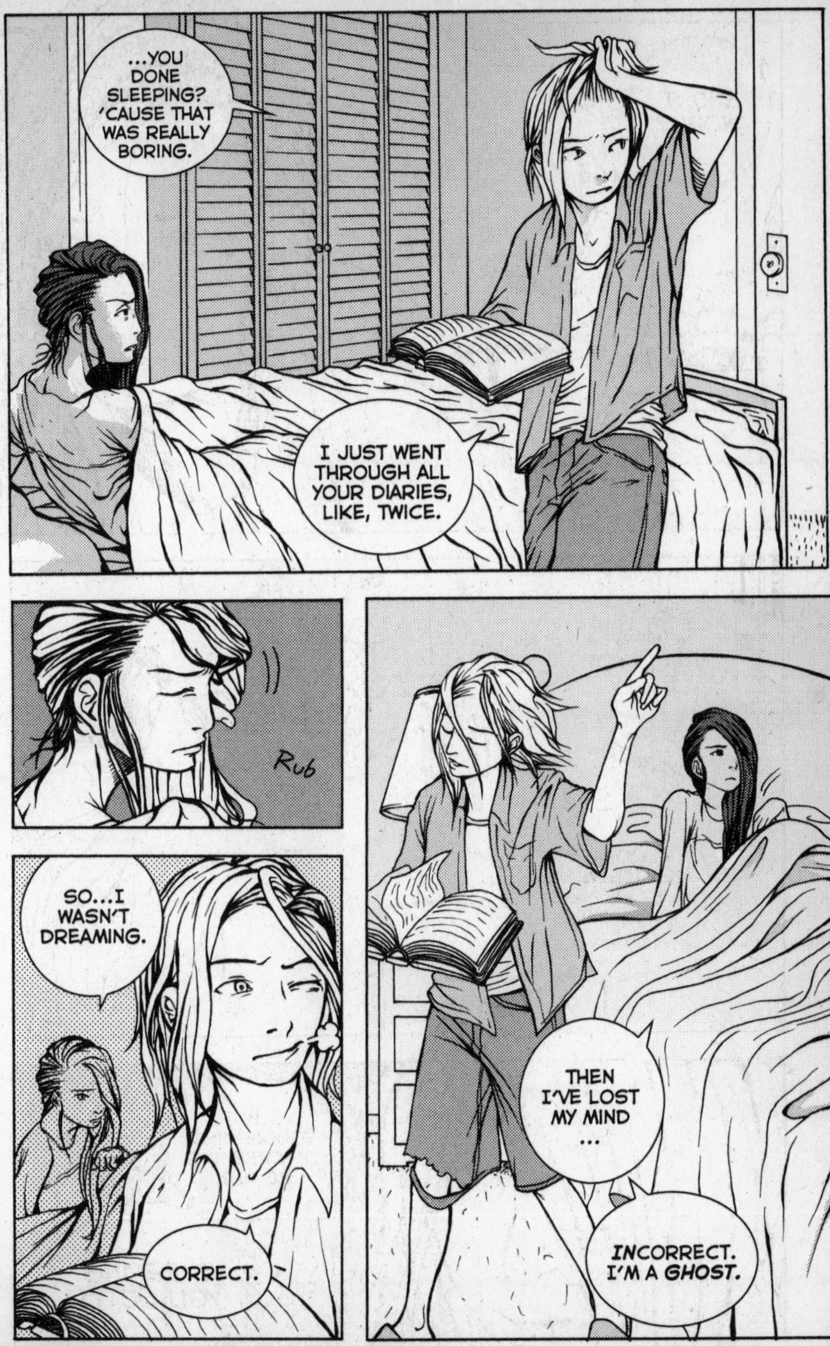
...YOU DONE SLEEPING? 'CAUSE THAT WAS REALLY BORING.
I JUST WENT THROUGH ALL YOUR DIARIES, LIKE, TWICE.
Rub
SO...I WASN'T DREAMING.
CORRECT.
THEN I'VE LOST MY MIND ...
*IN*CORRECT. I'M A ***GHOST***.

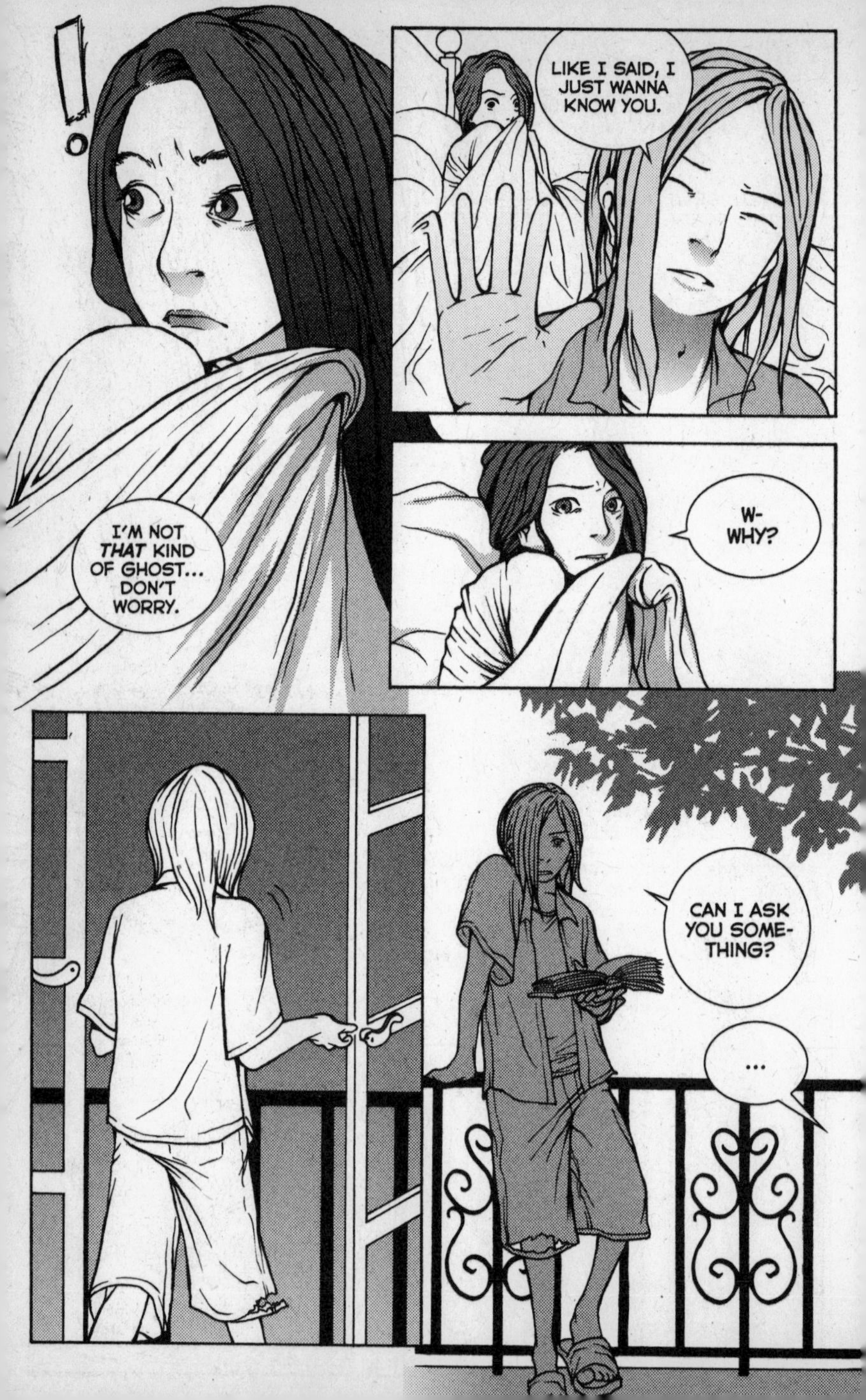
LIKE I SAID, I JUST WANNA KNOW YOU.
W- WHY?
!
I'M NOT *THAT* KIND OF GHOST... DON'T WORRY.
CAN I ASK YOU SOME- THING?
...

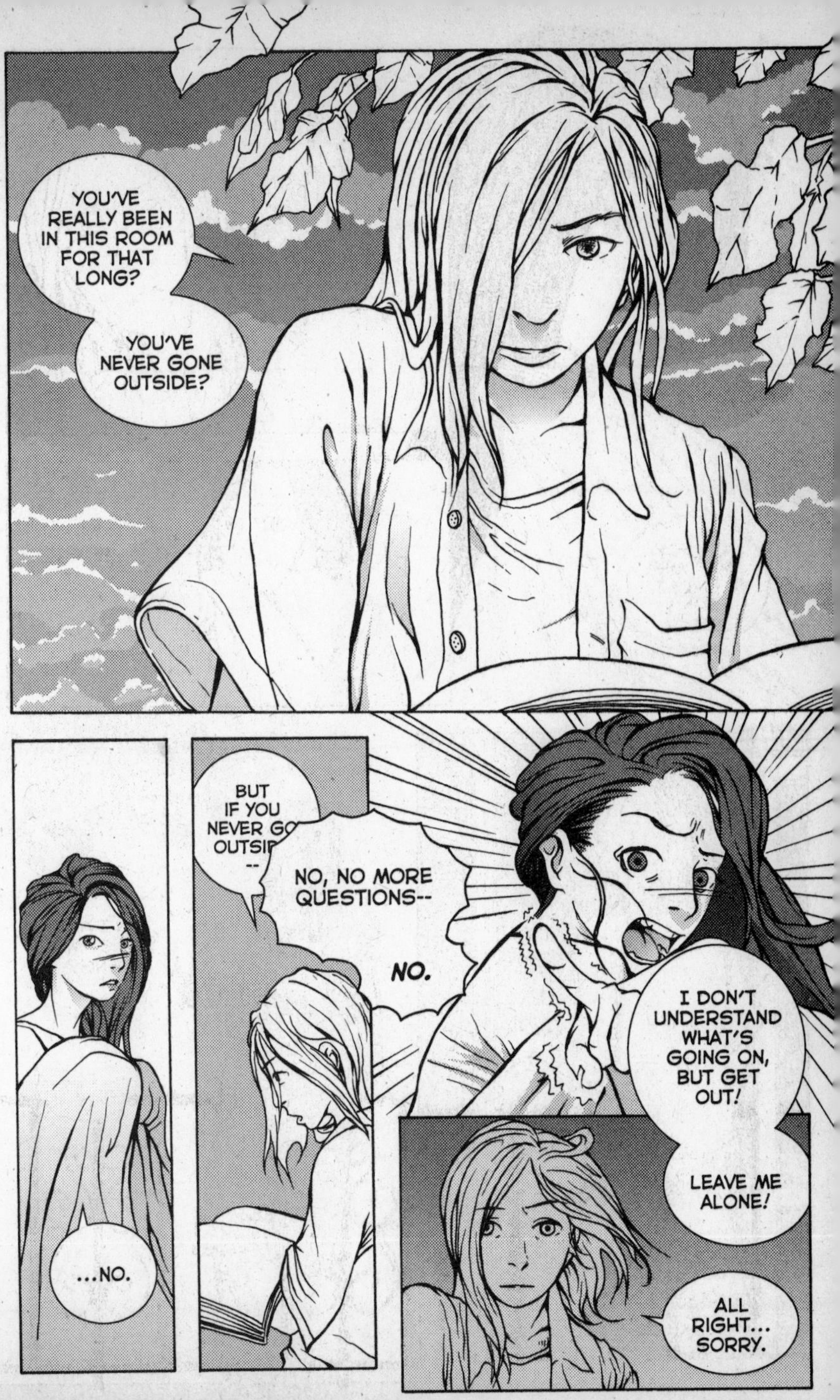
YOU'VE REALLY BEEN IN THIS ROOM FOR THAT LONG?
YOU'VE NEVER GONE OUTSIDE?
...NO.
BUT IF YOU NEVER GO OUTSI --
NO, NO MORE QUESTIONS--
NO.
I DON'T UNDERSTAND WHAT'S GOING ON, BUT GET OUT!
LEAVE ME ALONE!
ALL RIGHT... SORRY.

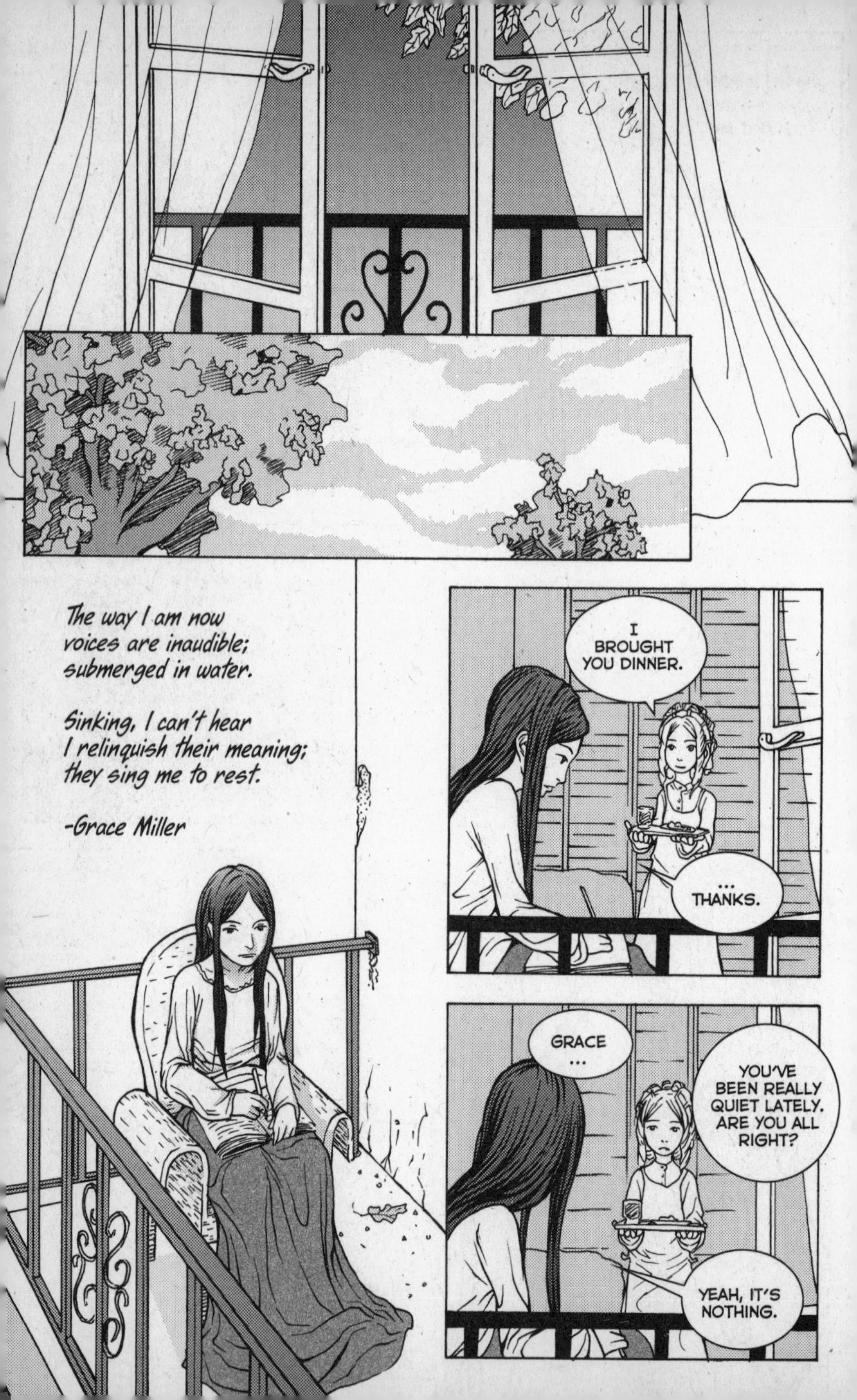
The way I am now
voices are inaudible;
submerged in water.
Sinking, I can't hear
I relinquish their meaning;
they sing me to rest.
-Grace Miller
I BROUGHT YOU DINNER.
... THANKS.
GRACE ...
YOU'VE BEEN REALLY QUIET LATELY. ARE YOU ALL RIGHT?
YEAH, IT'S NOTHING.

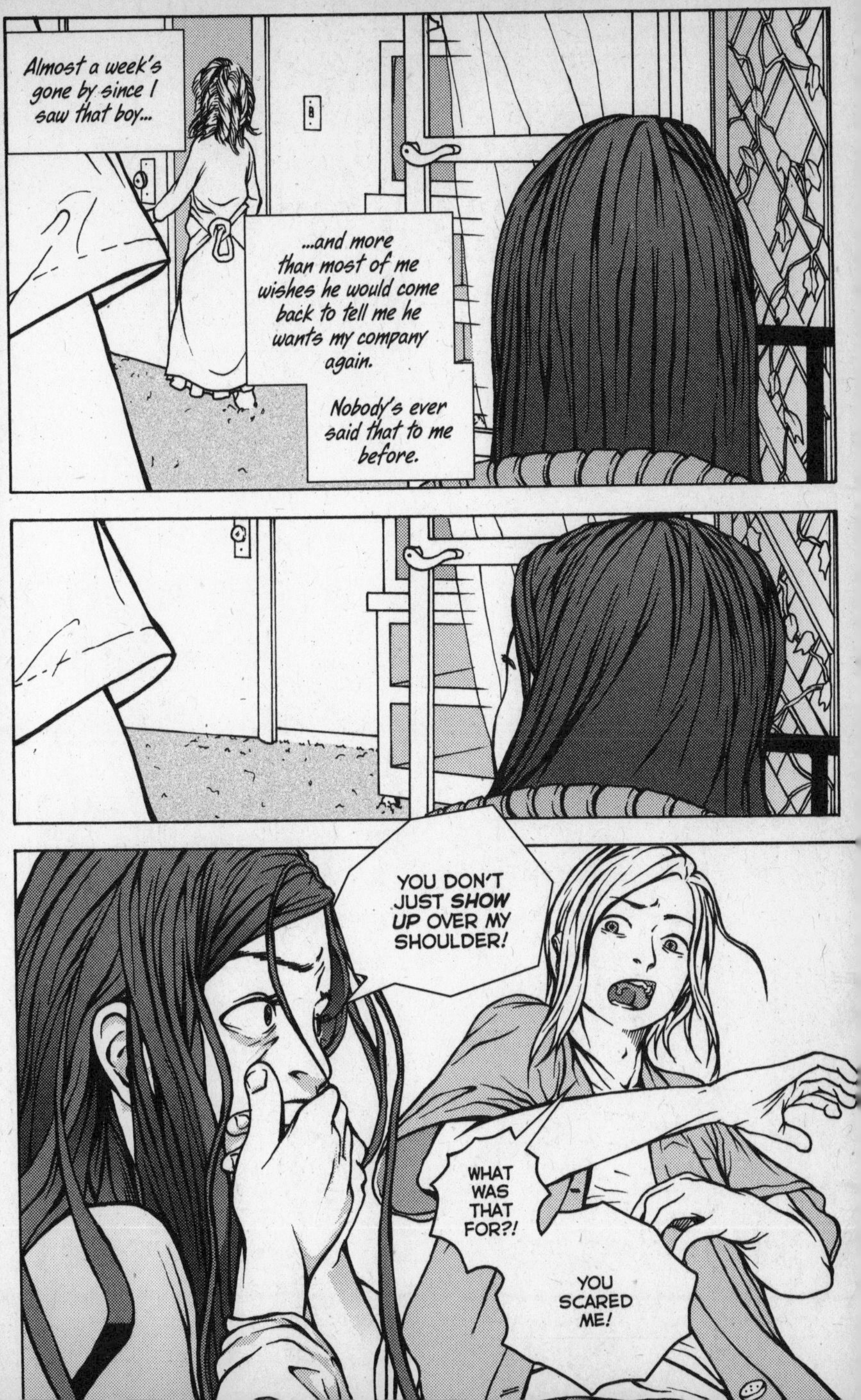

Almost a week's gone by since I saw that boy...
...and more than most of me wishes he would come back to tell me he wants my company again.
Nobody's ever said that to me before.
YOU DON'T JUST SHOW UP OVER MY SHOULDER!
WHAT WAS THAT FOR?!
YOU SCARED ME!

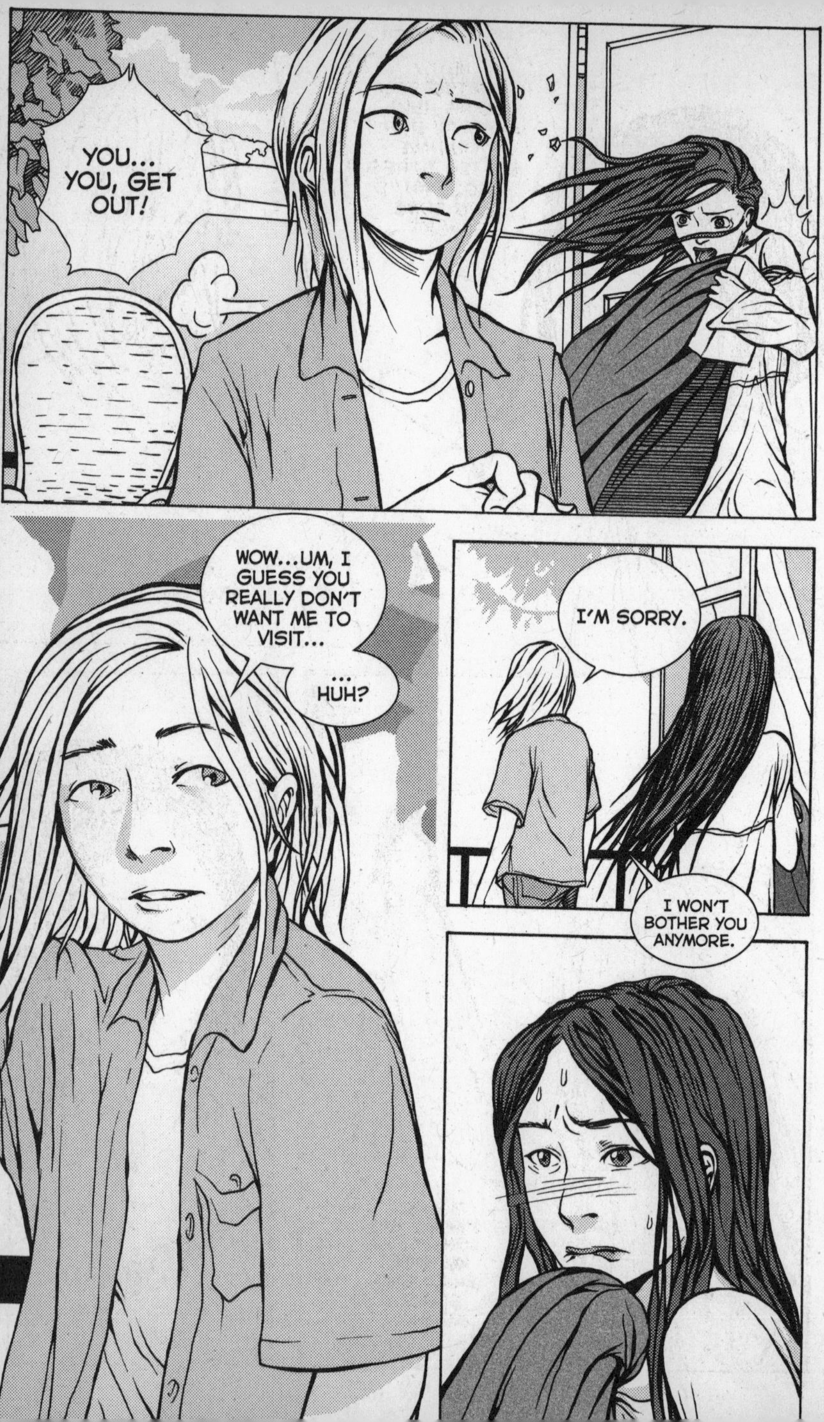
YOU... YOU, GET OUT!
WOW...UM, I GUESS YOU REALLY DON'T WANT ME TO VISIT...
... HUH?
I'M SORRY.
I WON'T BOTHER YOU ANYMORE.

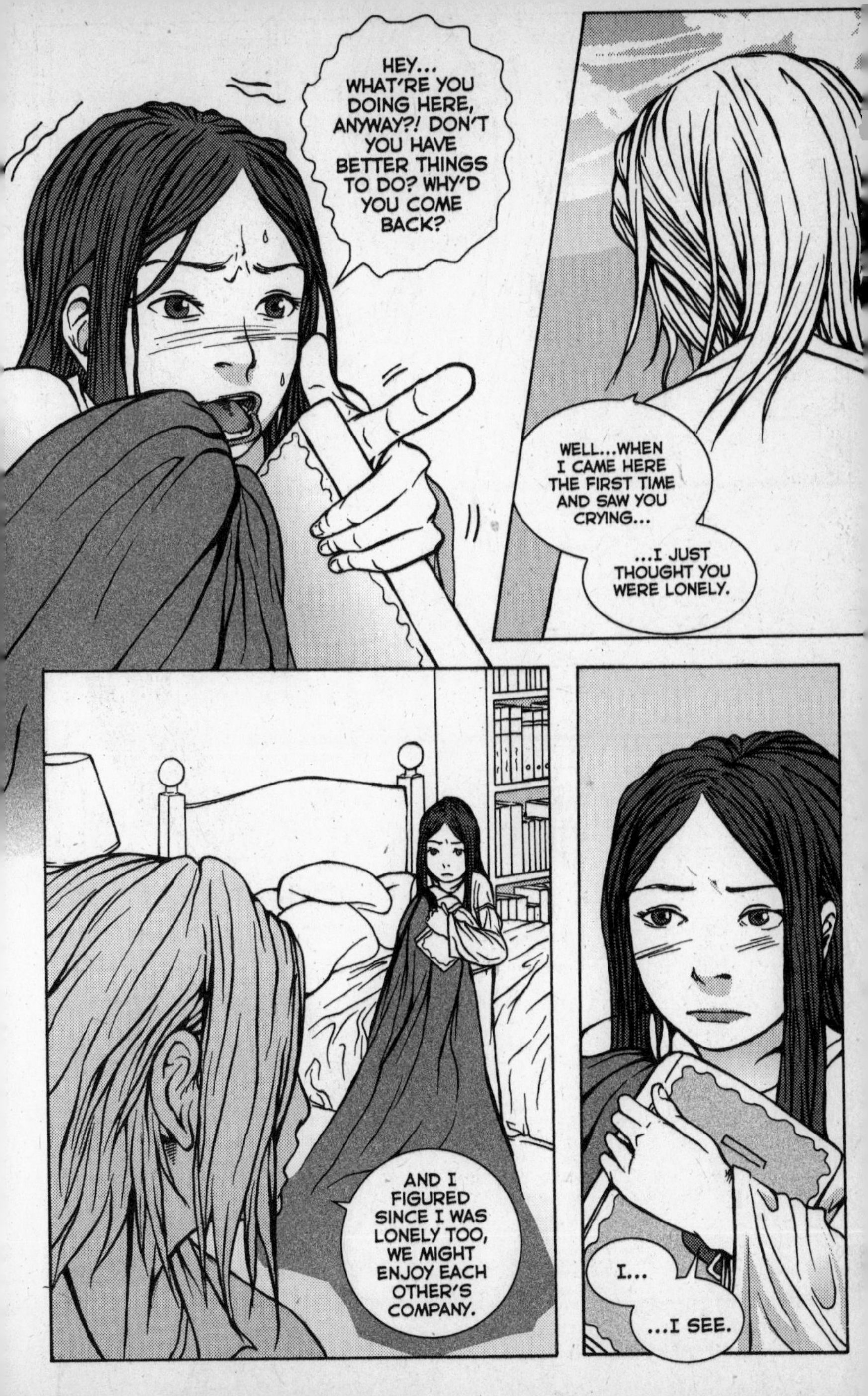
HEY... WHAT'RE YOU DOING HERE, ANYWAY?! DON'T YOU HAVE BETTER THINGS TO DO? WHY'D YOU COME BACK?
WELL...WHEN I CAME HERE THE FIRST TIME AND SAW YOU CRYING...
...I JUST THOUGHT YOU WERE LONELY.
AND I FIGURED SINCE I WAS LONELY TOO, WE MIGHT ENJOY EACH OTHER'S COMPANY.
I...
...I SEE.

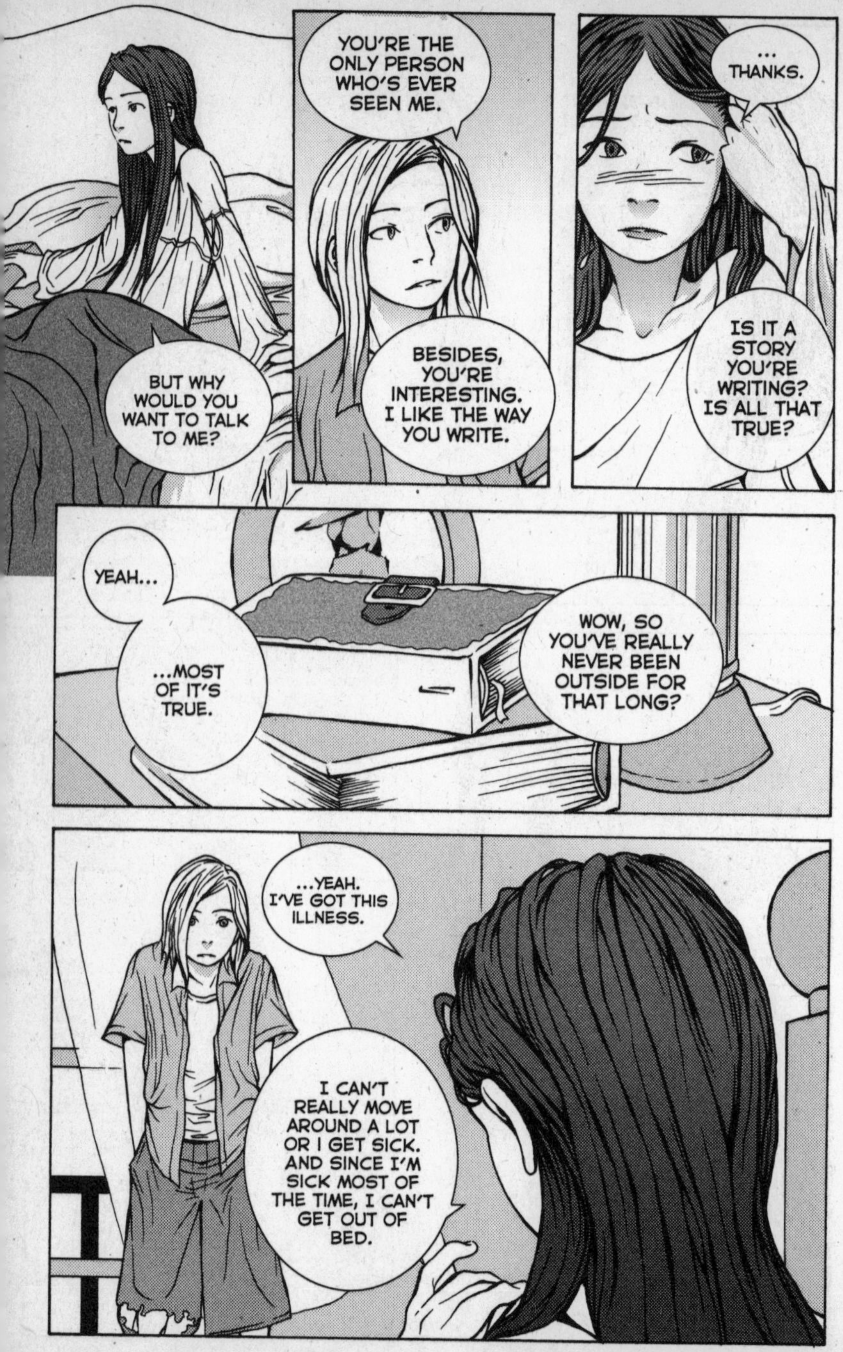
BUT WHY WOULD YOU WANT TO TALK TO ME?
YOU'RE THE ONLY PERSON WHO'S EVER SEEN ME.
BESIDES, YOU'RE INTERESTING. I LIKE THE WAY YOU WRITE.
... THANKS.
IS IT A STORY YOU'RE WRITING? IS ALL THAT TRUE?
YEAH...
...MOST OF IT'S TRUE.
WOW, SO YOU'VE REALLY NEVER BEEN OUTSIDE FOR THAT LONG?
...YEAH. I'VE GOT THIS ILLNESS.
I CAN'T REALLY MOVE AROUND A LOT OR I GET SICK. AND SINCE I'M SICK MOST OF THE TIME, I CAN'T GET OUT OF BED.

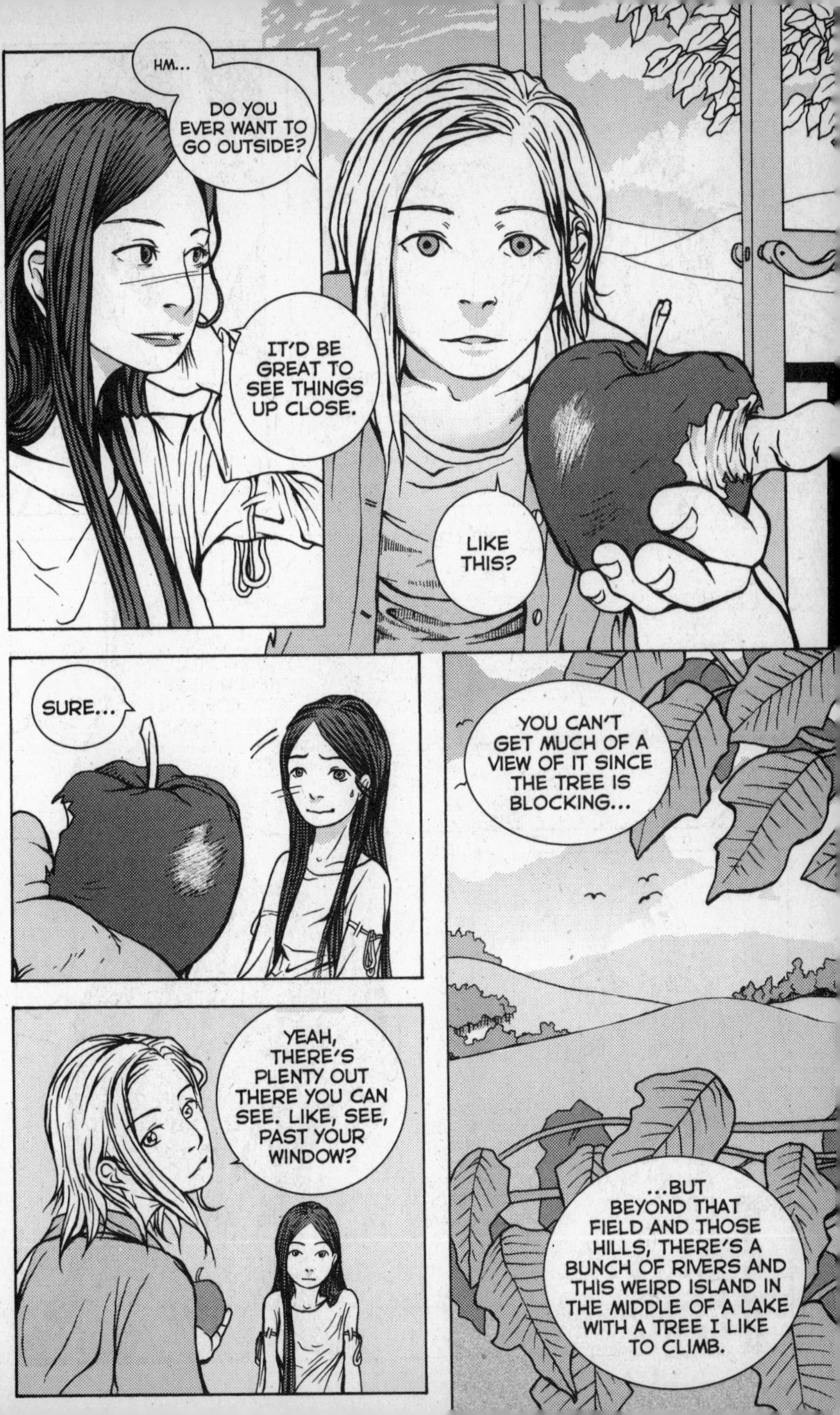
HM...
DO YOU EVER WANT TO GO OUTSIDE?
IT'D BE GREAT TO SEE THINGS UP CLOSE.
LIKE THIS?
SURE...
YOU CAN'T GET MUCH OF A VIEW OF IT SINCE THE TREE IS BLOCKING...
YEAH, THERE'S PLENTY OUT THERE YOU CAN SEE. LIKE, SEE, PAST YOUR WINDOW?
...BUT BEYOND THAT FIELD AND THOSE HILLS, THERE'S A BUNCH OF RIVERS AND THIS WEIRD ISLAND IN THE MIDDLE OF A LAKE WITH A TREE I LIKE TO CLIMB.

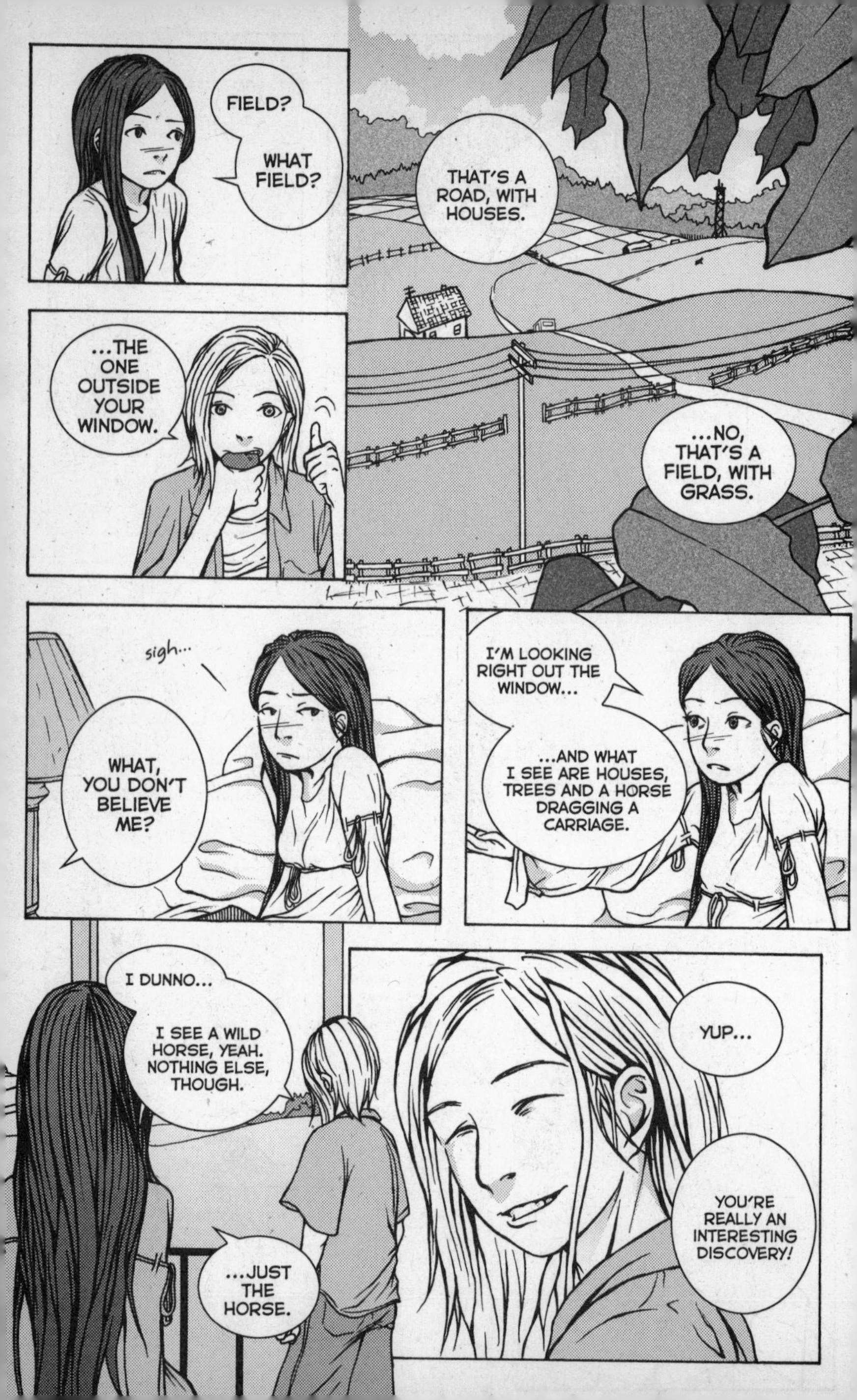
FIELD?
WHAT FIELD?
THAT'S A ROAD, WITH HOUSES.
...THE ONE OUTSIDE YOUR WINDOW.
...NO, THAT'S A FIELD, WITH GRASS.
sigh...
WHAT, YOU DON'T BELIEVE ME?
I'M LOOKING RIGHT OUT THE WINDOW...
...AND WHAT I SEE ARE HOUSES, TREES AND A HORSE DRAGGING A CARRIAGE.
I DUNNO...
I SEE A WILD HORSE, YEAH. NOTHING ELSE, THOUGH.
...JUST THE HORSE.
YUP...
YOU'RE REALLY AN INTERESTING DISCOVERY!

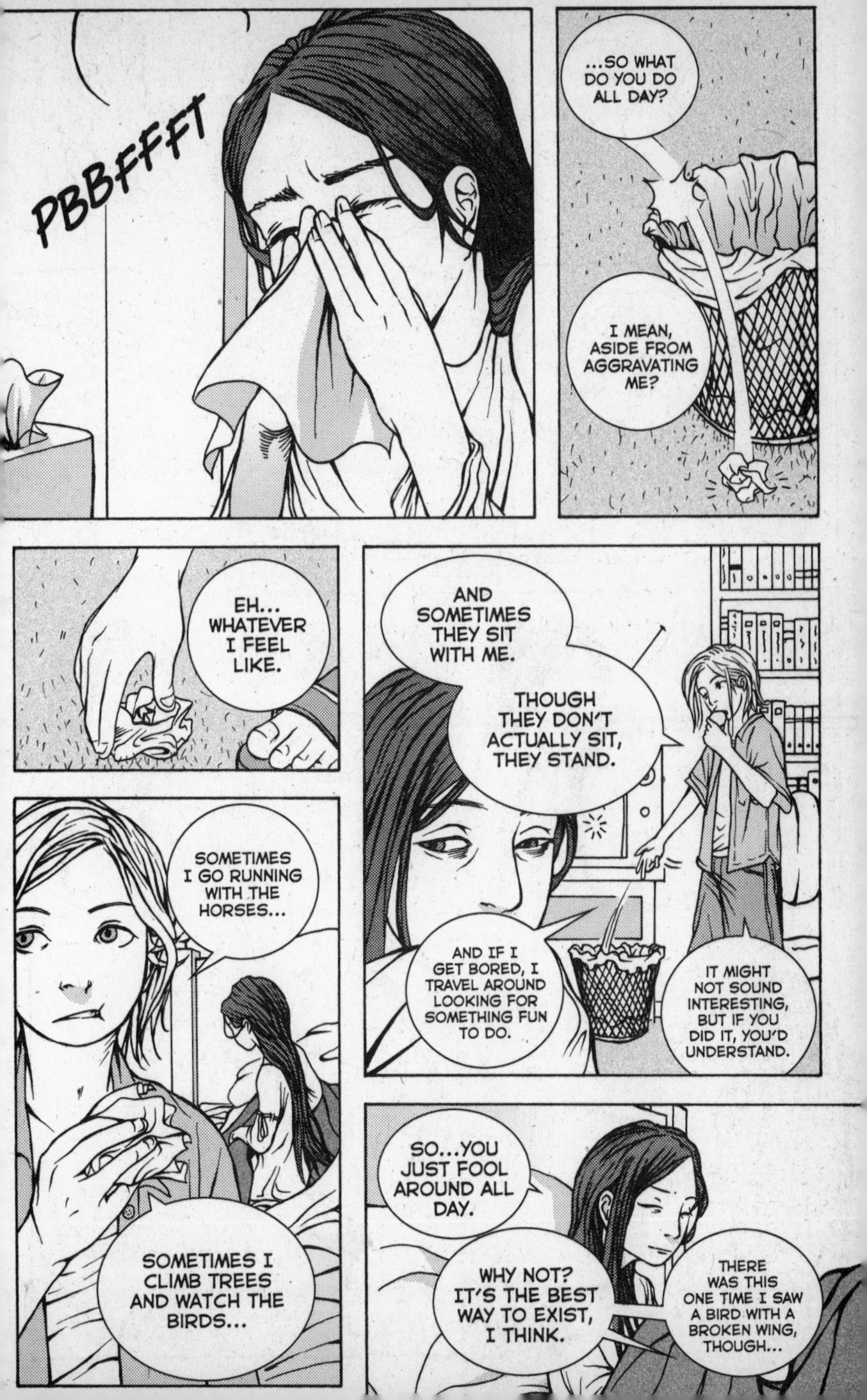
PBBFFFT
...SO WHAT DO YOU DO ALL DAY?
I MEAN, ASIDE FROM AGGRAVATING ME?
EH... WHATEVER I FEEL LIKE.
SOMETIMES I GO RUNNING WITH THE HORSES...
SOMETIMES I CLIMB TREES AND WATCH THE BIRDS...
AND SOMETIMES THEY SIT WITH ME.
THOUGH THEY DON'T ACTUALLY SIT, THEY STAND.
AND IF I GET BORED, I TRAVEL AROUND LOOKING FOR SOMETHING FUN TO DO.
IT MIGHT NOT SOUND INTERESTING, BUT IF YOU DID IT, YOU'D UNDERSTAND.
SO...YOU JUST FOOL AROUND ALL DAY.
WHY NOT? IT'S THE BEST WAY TO EXIST, I THINK.
THERE WAS THIS ONE TIME I SAW A BIRD WITH A BROKEN WING, THOUGH...

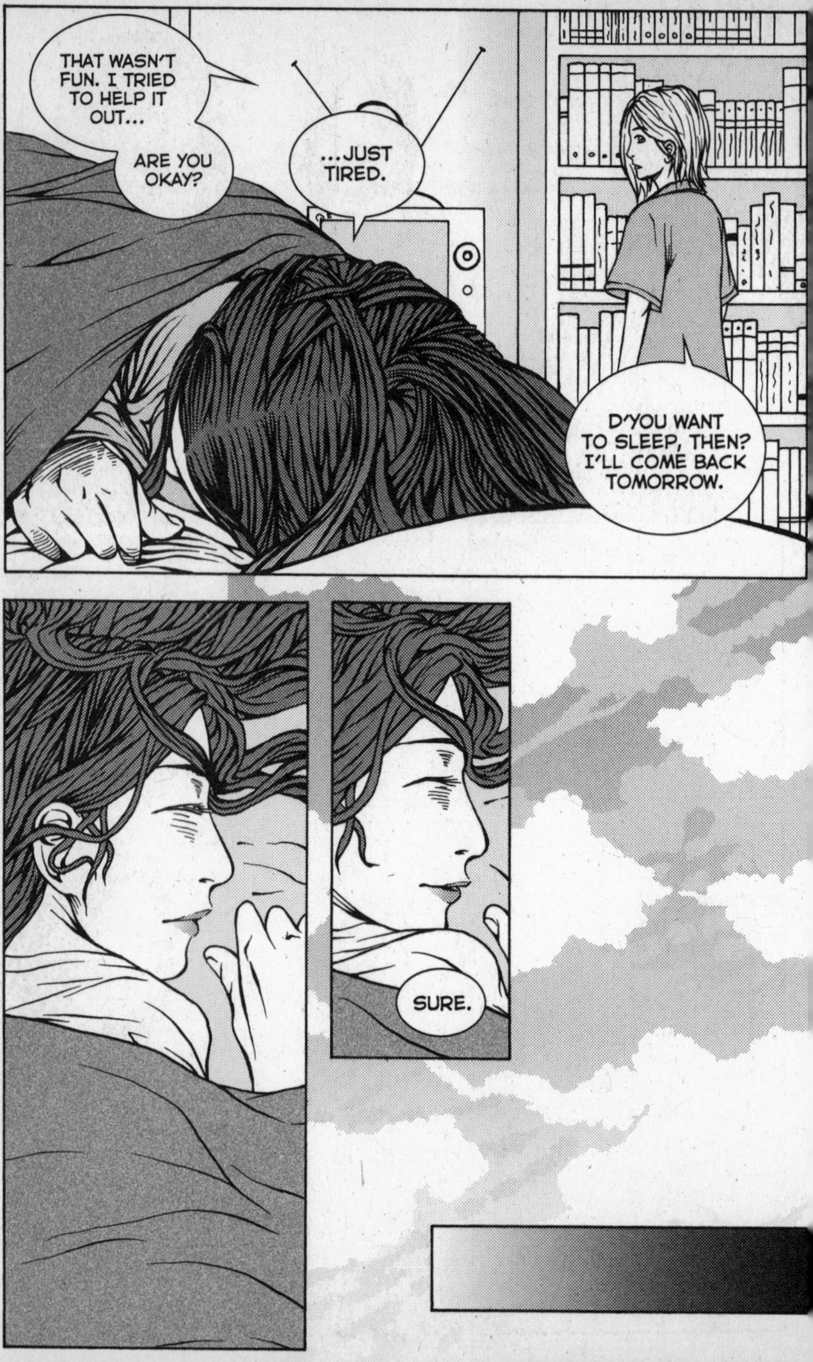
THAT WASN'T FUN. I TRIED TO HELP IT OUT...
ARE YOU OKAY?
...JUST TIRED.
D'YOU WANT TO SLEEP, THEN? I'LL COME BACK TOMORROW.
SURE.

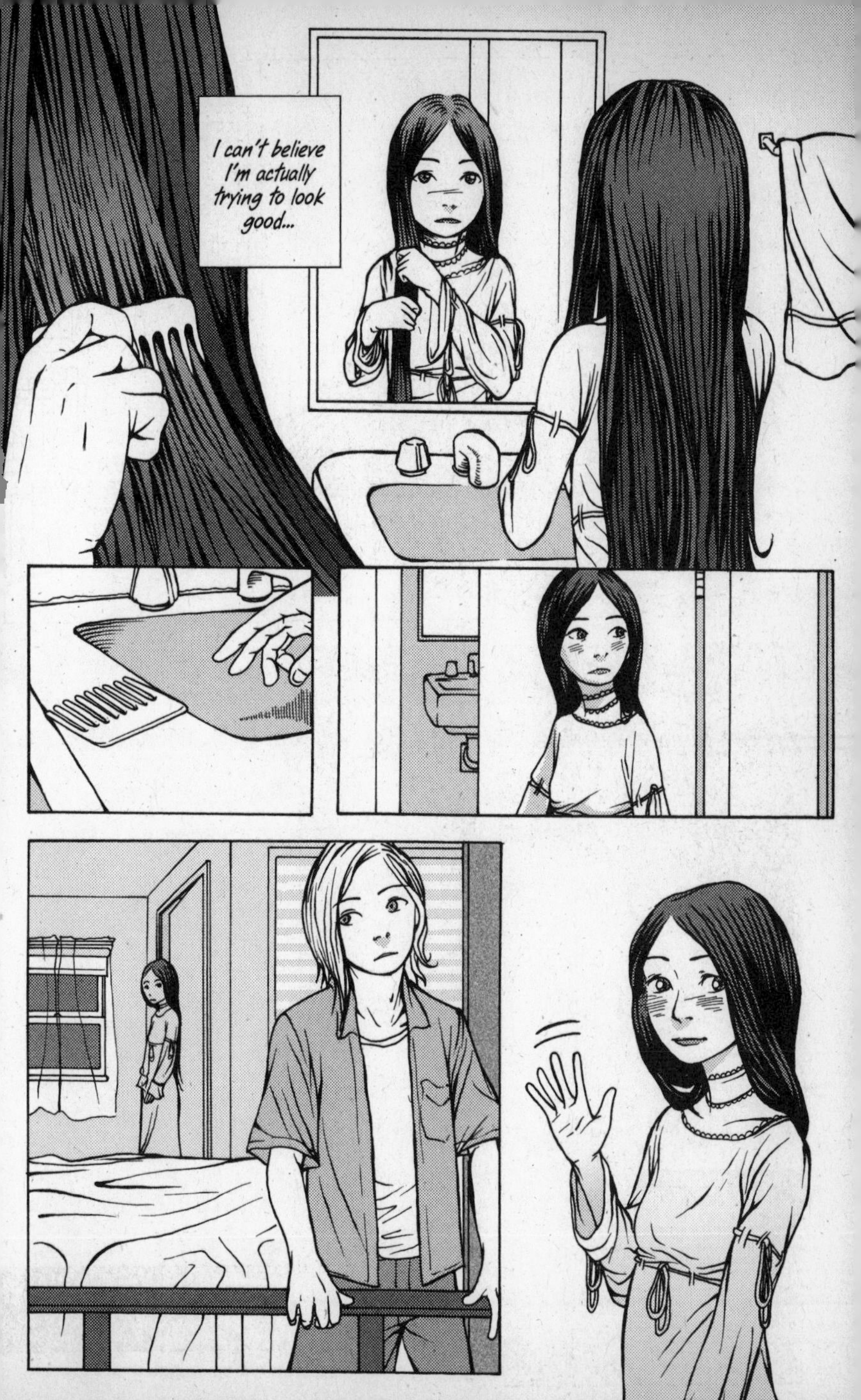
I can't believe I'm actually trying to look good...

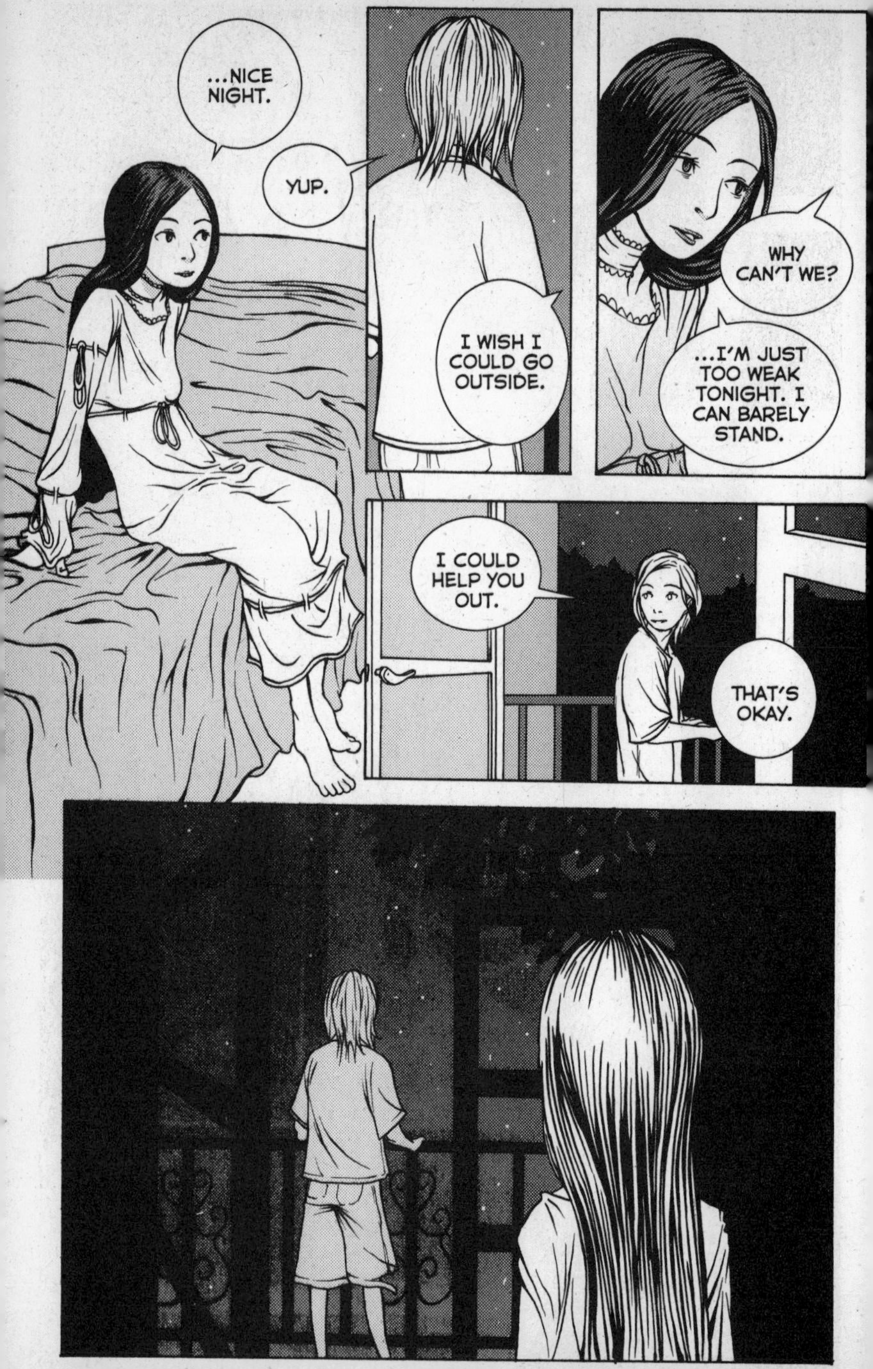
...NICE NIGHT.
YUP.
I WISH I COULD GO OUTSIDE.
WHY CAN'T WE?
...I'M JUST TOO WEAK TONIGHT. I CAN BARELY STAND.
I COULD HELP YOU OUT.
THAT'S OKAY.

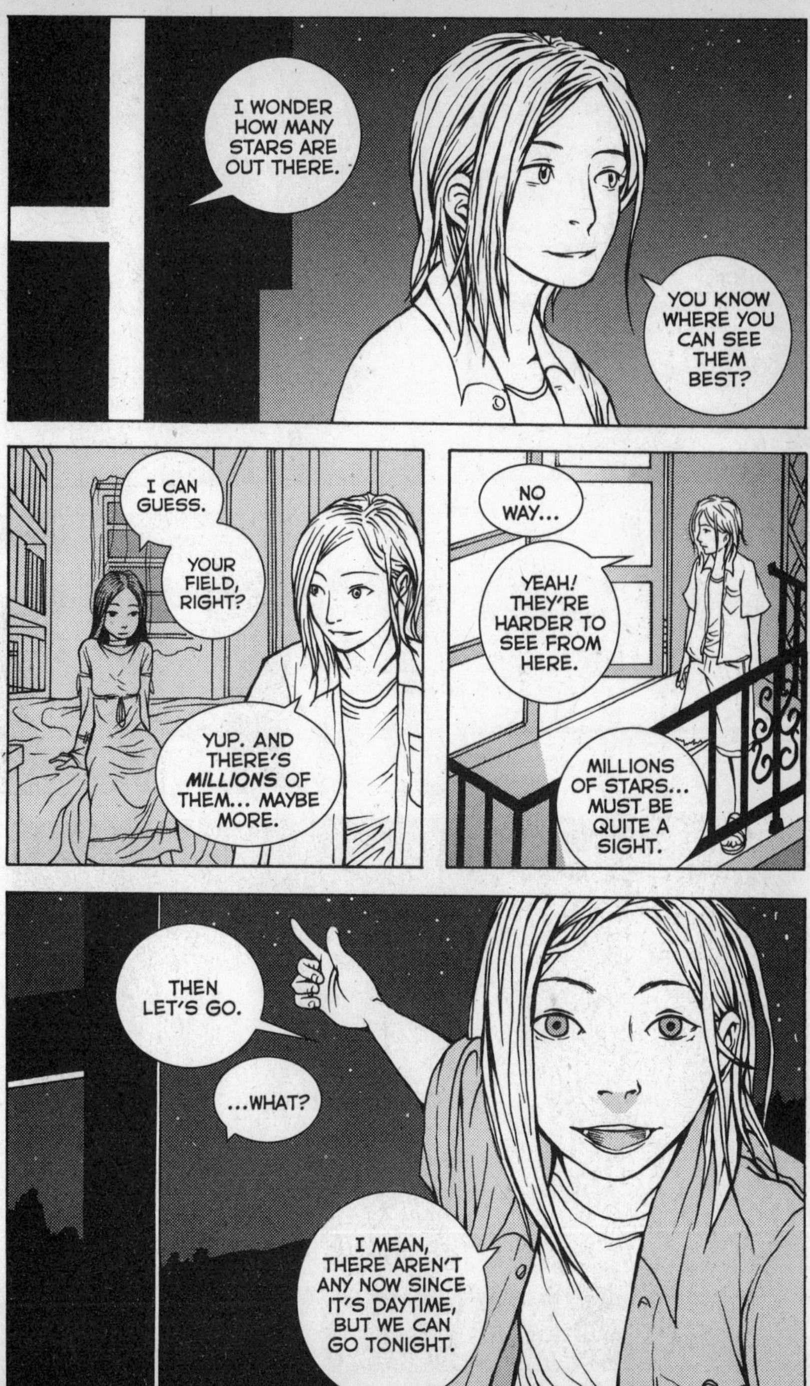
I WONDER HOW MANY STARS ARE OUT THERE.
YOU KNOW WHERE YOU CAN SEE THEM BEST?
I CAN GUESS.
YOUR FIELD, RIGHT?
YUP. AND THERE'S *MILLIONS* OF THEM... MAYBE MORE.
NO WAY...
YEAH! THEY'RE HARDER TO SEE FROM HERE.
MILLIONS OF STARS... MUST BE QUITE A SIGHT.
THEN LET'S GO.
...WHAT?
I MEAN, THERE AREN'T ANY NOW SINCE IT'S DAYTIME, BUT WE CAN GO TONIGHT.

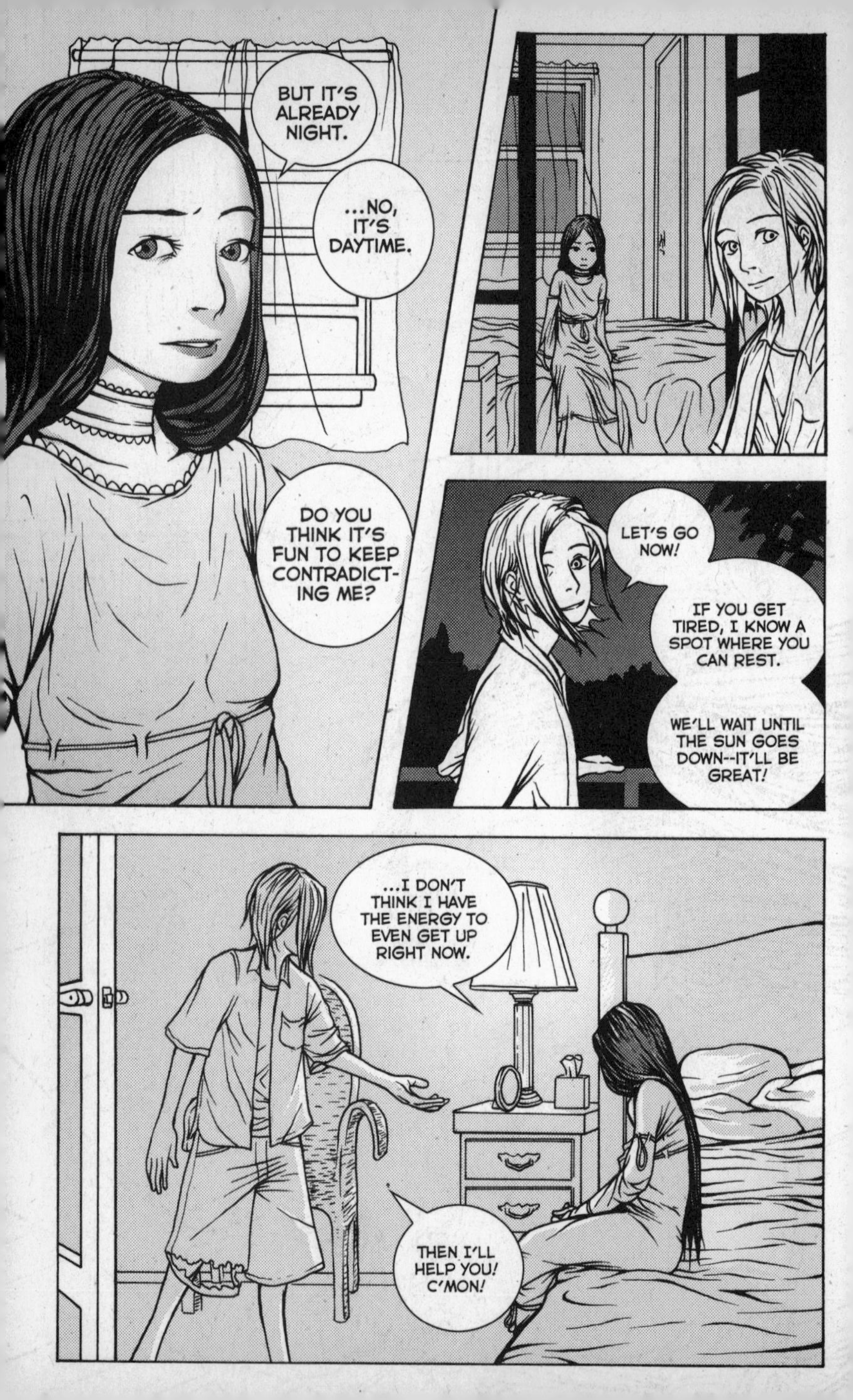
BUT IT'S ALREADY NIGHT.
...NO, IT'S DAYTIME.
DO YOU THINK IT'S FUN TO KEEP CONTRADICT-ING ME?
LET'S GO NOW!
IF YOU GET TIRED, I KNOW A SPOT WHERE YOU CAN REST.
WE'LL WAIT UNTIL THE SUN GOES DOWN--IT'LL BE GREAT!
...I DON'T THINK I HAVE THE ENERGY TO EVEN GET UP RIGHT NOW.
THEN I'LL HELP YOU! C'MON!

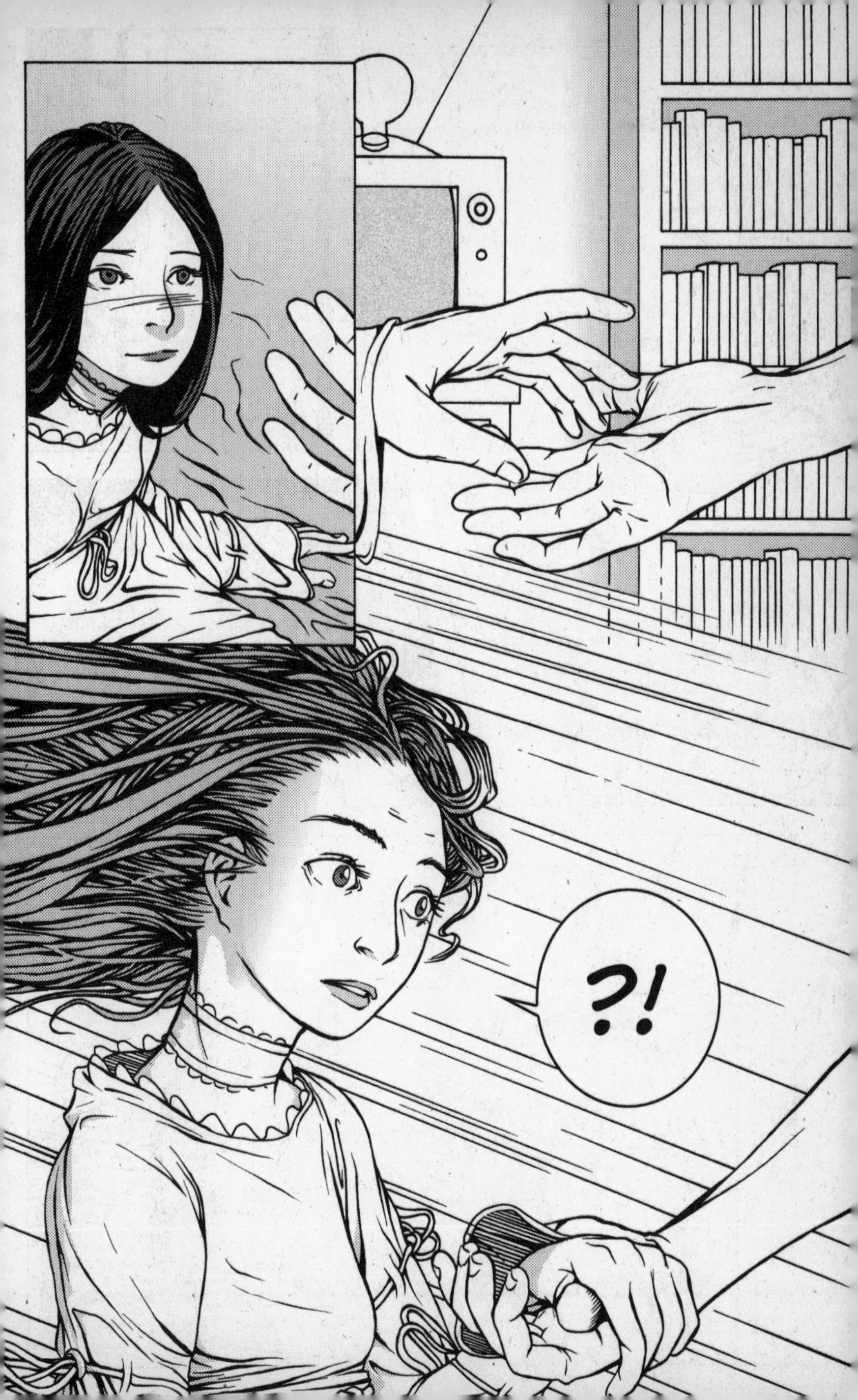
?!

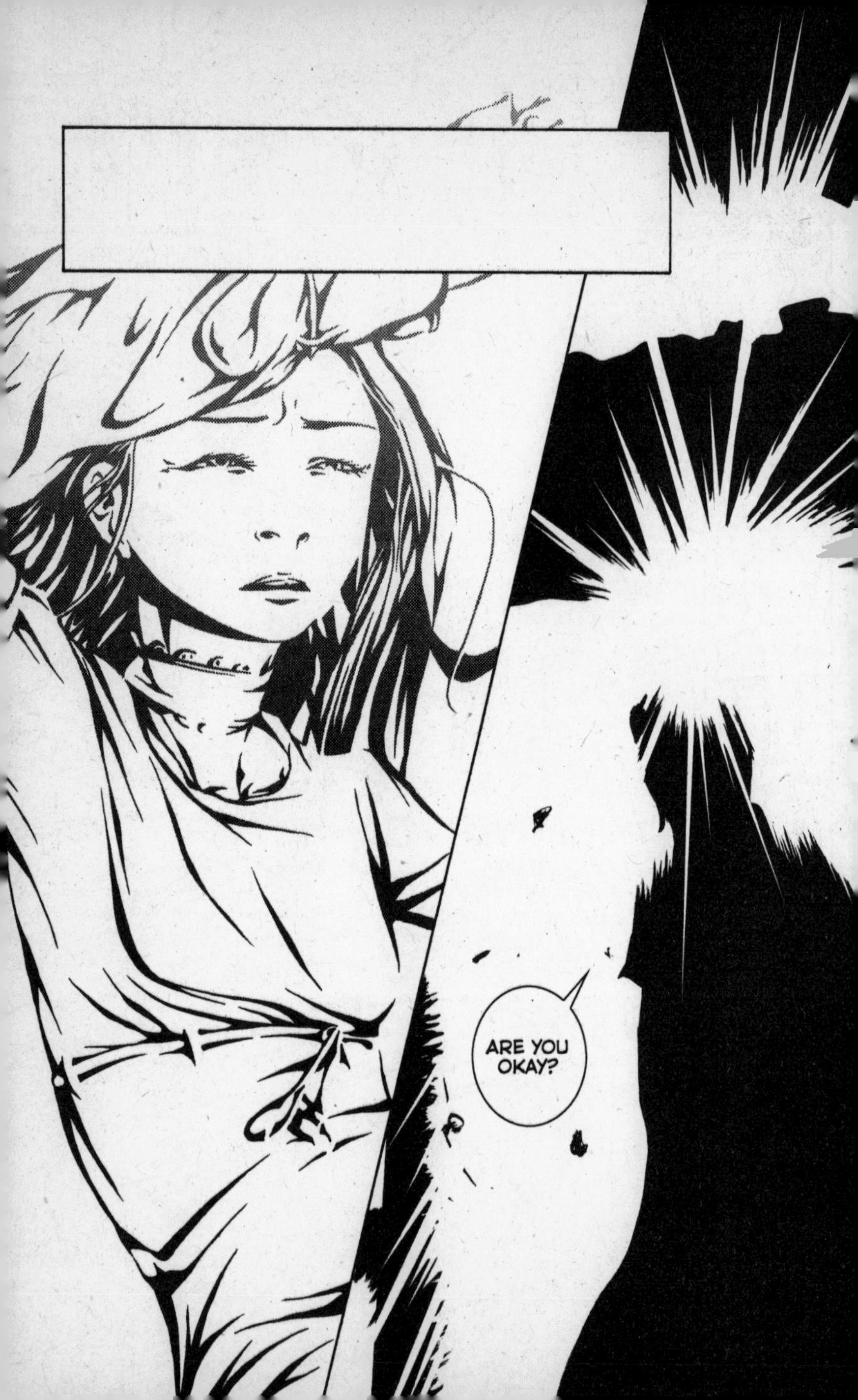
ARE YOU OKAY?

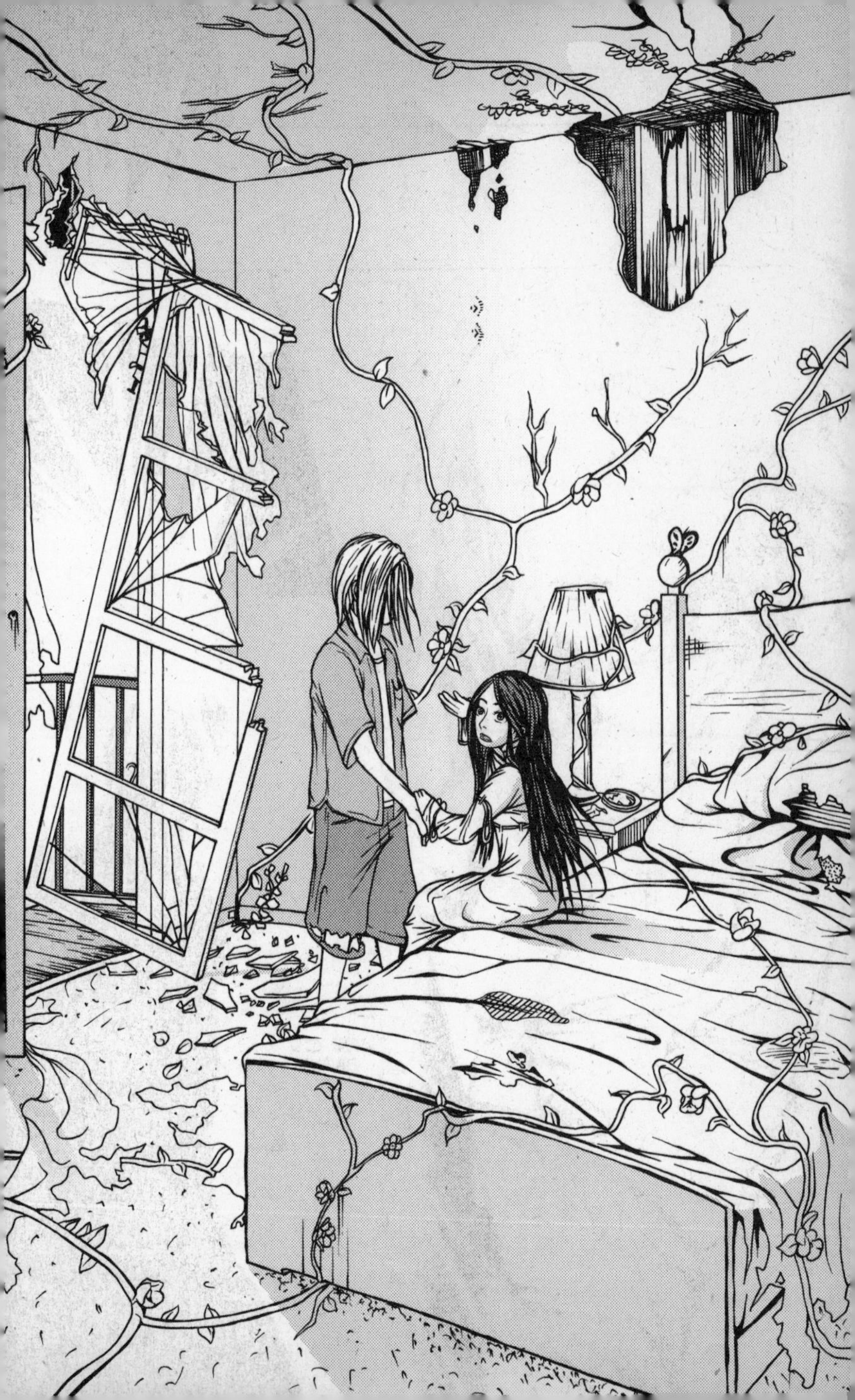

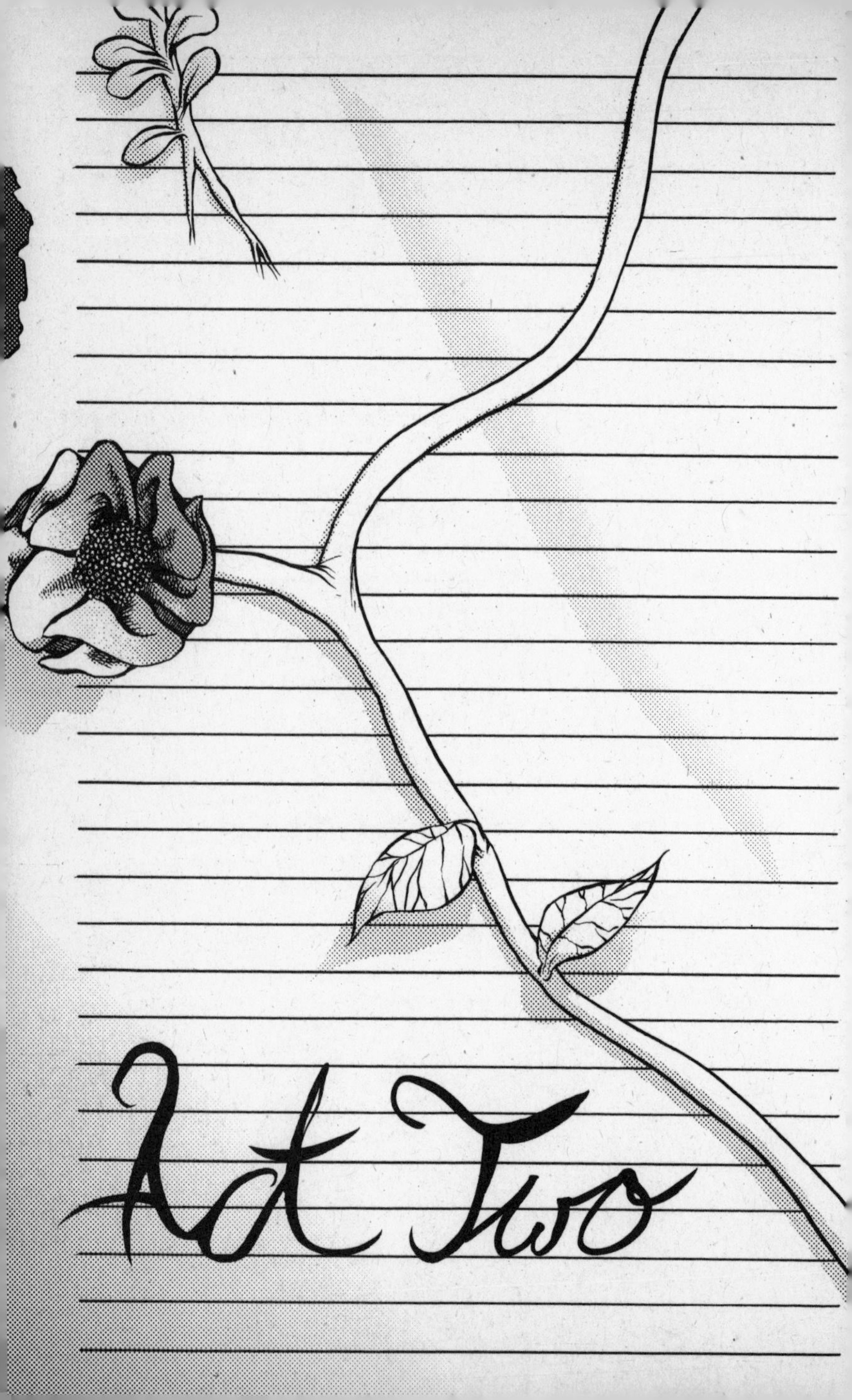

Act Two

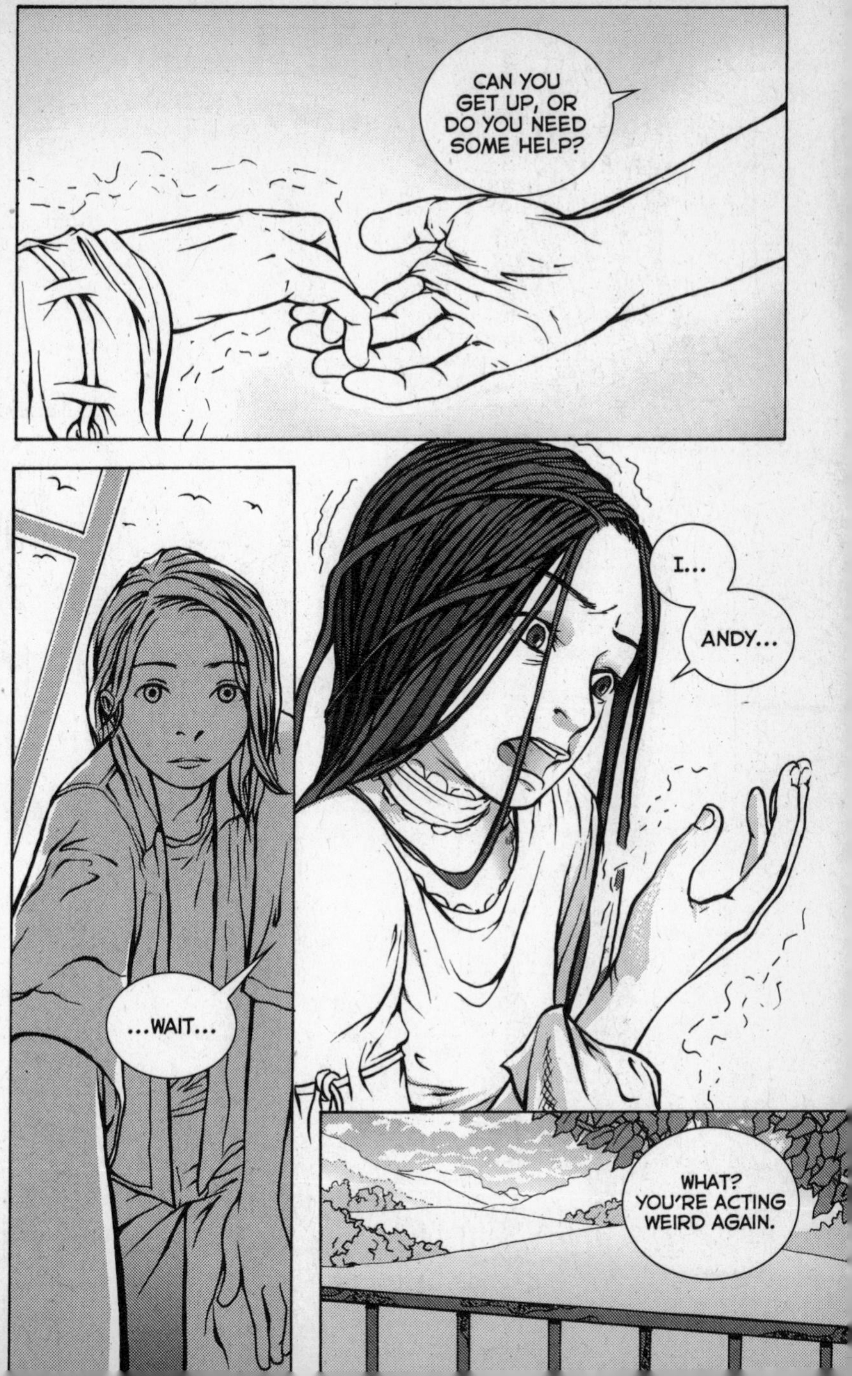
CAN YOU GET UP, OR DO YOU NEED SOME HELP?
I...
ANDY...
...WAIT...
WHAT? YOU'RE ACTING WEIRD AGAIN.

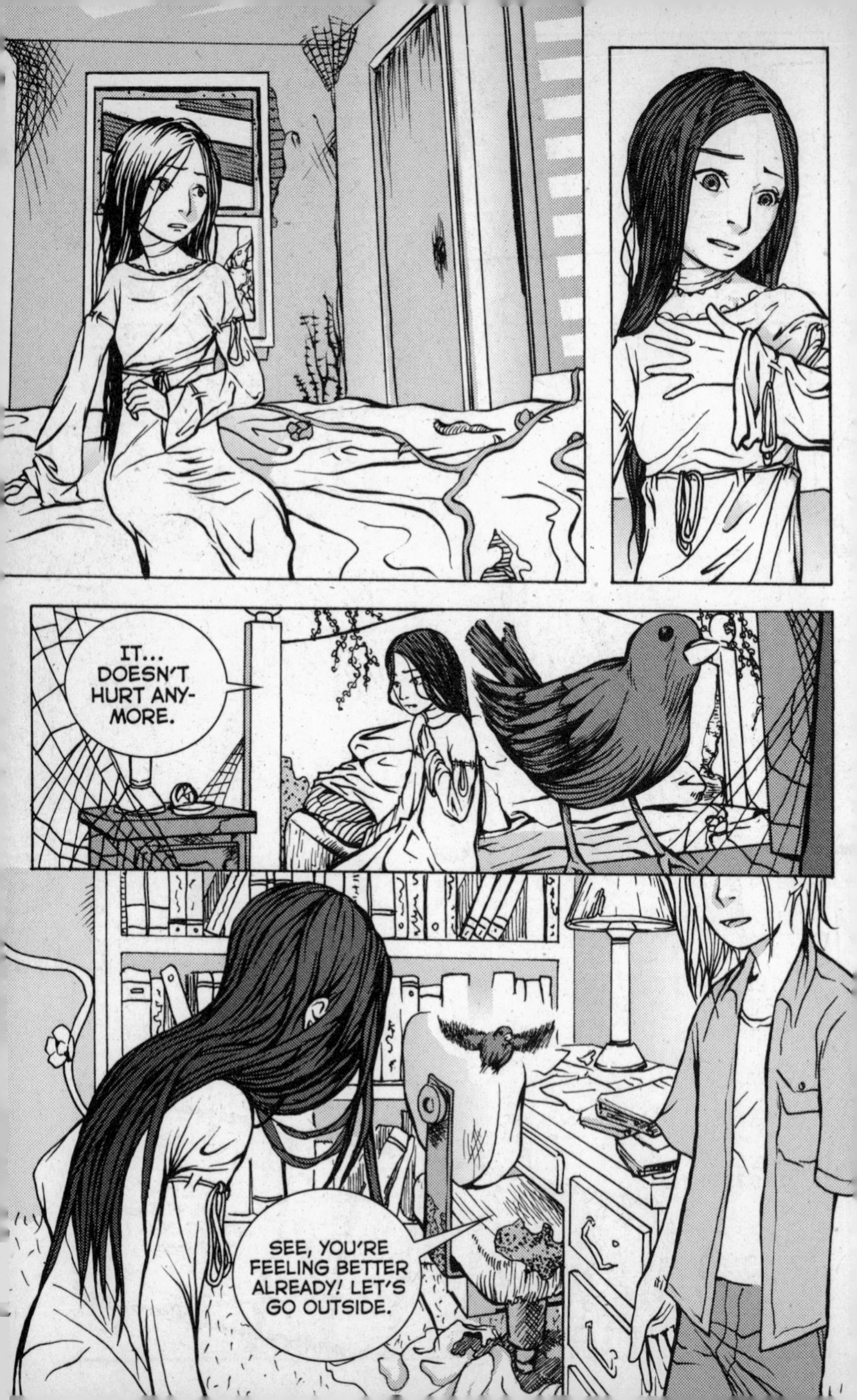
IT... DOESN'T HURT ANY-MORE.
SEE, YOU'RE FEELING BETTER ALREADY! LET'S GO OUTSIDE.

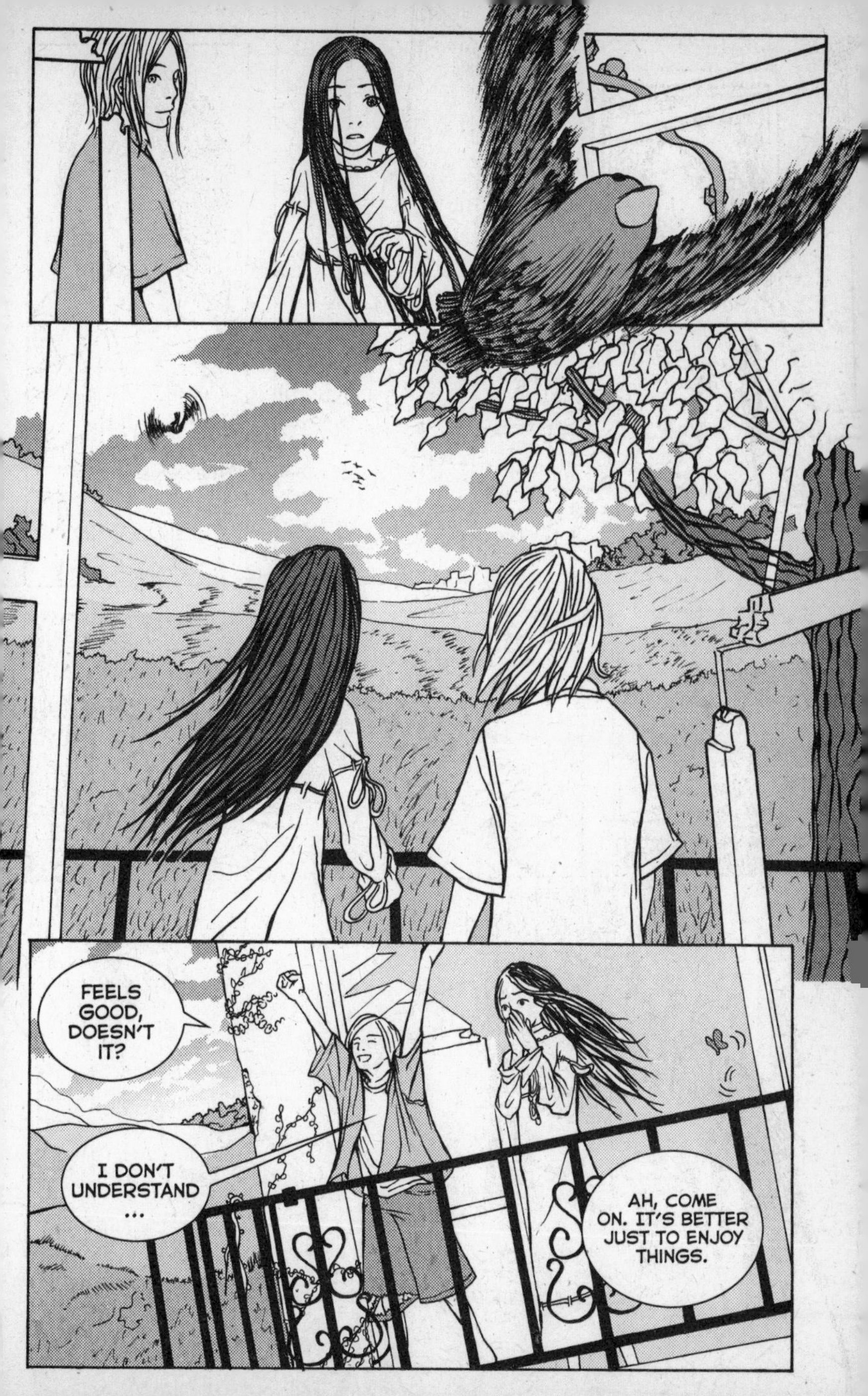
FEELS GOOD, DOESN'T IT?
I DON'T UNDERSTAND ...
AH, COME ON. IT'S BETTER JUST TO ENJOY THINGS.

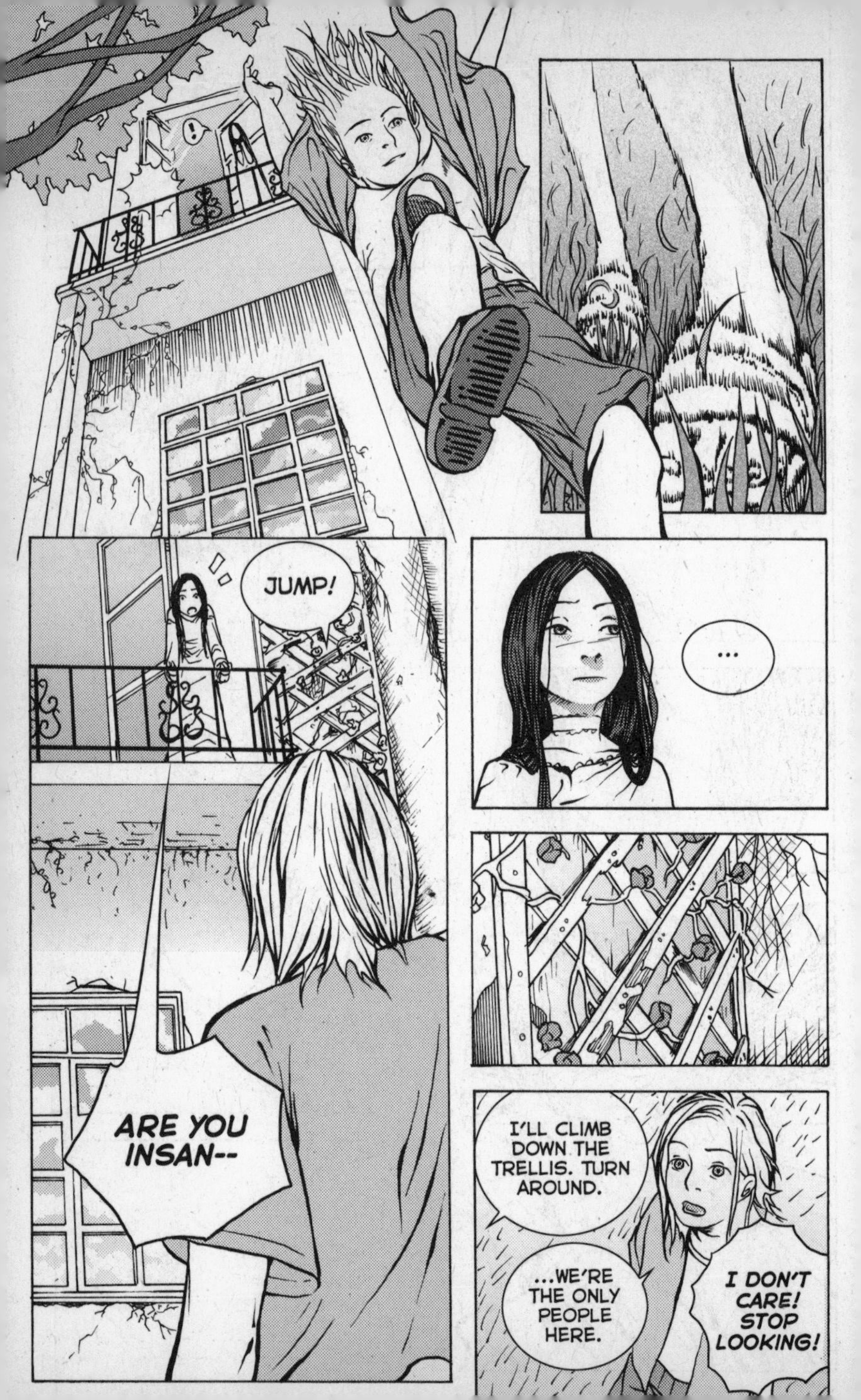
!
JUMP!
...
ARE YOU INSAN--
I'LL CLIMB DOWN THE TRELLIS. TURN AROUND.
...WE'RE THE ONLY PEOPLE HERE.
I DON'T CARE! STOP LOOKING!

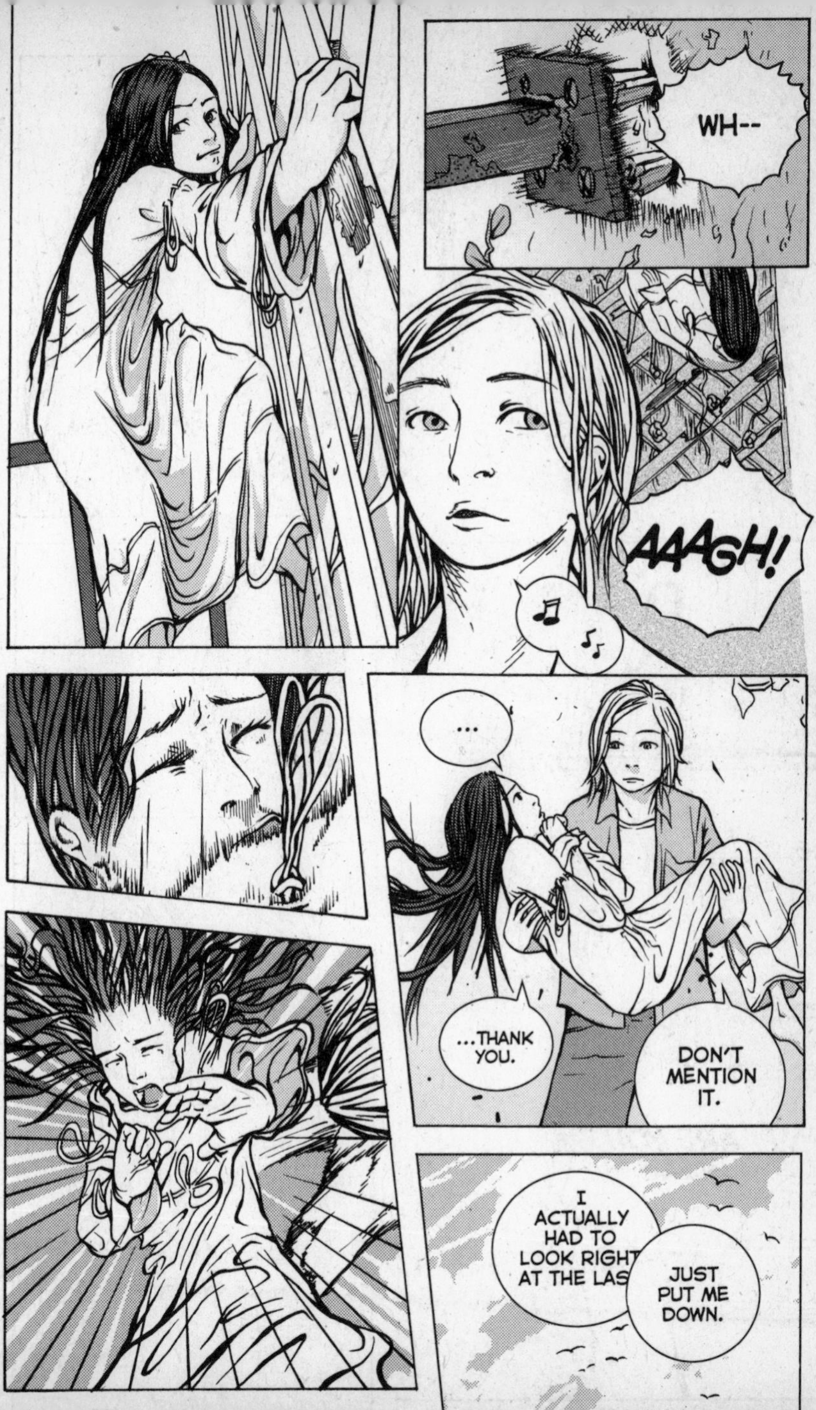
WH--
AAAGH!
...
...THANK YOU.
DON'T MENTION IT.
I ACTUALLY HAD TO LOOK RIGHT AT THE LAS
JUST PUT ME DOWN.

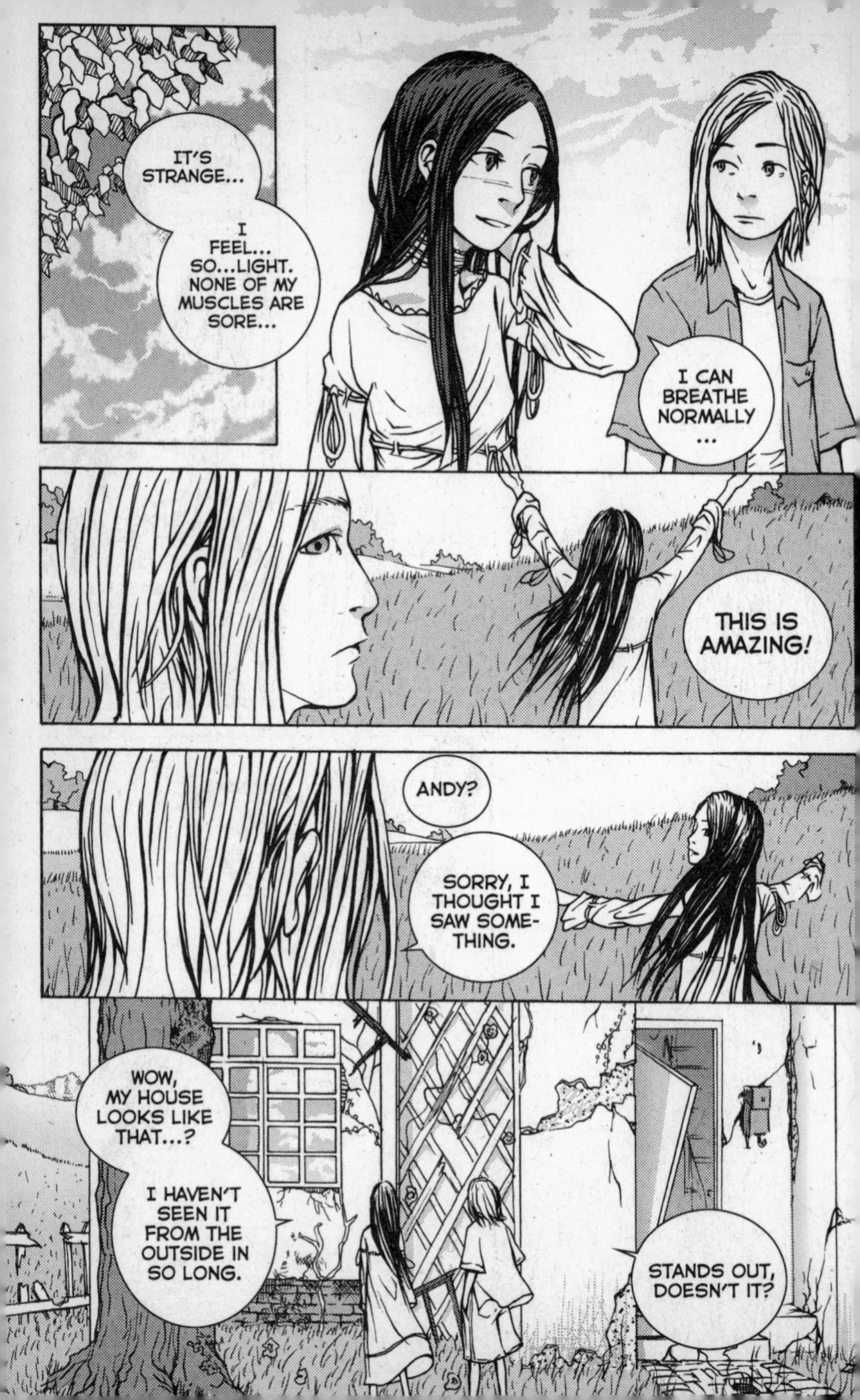
IT'S STRANGE...
I FEEL... SO...LIGHT. NONE OF MY MUSCLES ARE SORE...
I CAN BREATHE NORMALLY ...
THIS IS AMAZING!
ANDY?
SORRY, I THOUGHT I SAW SOME-THING.
WOW, MY HOUSE LOOKS LIKE THAT...?
I HAVEN'T SEEN IT FROM THE OUTSIDE IN SO LONG.
STANDS OUT, DOESN'T IT?

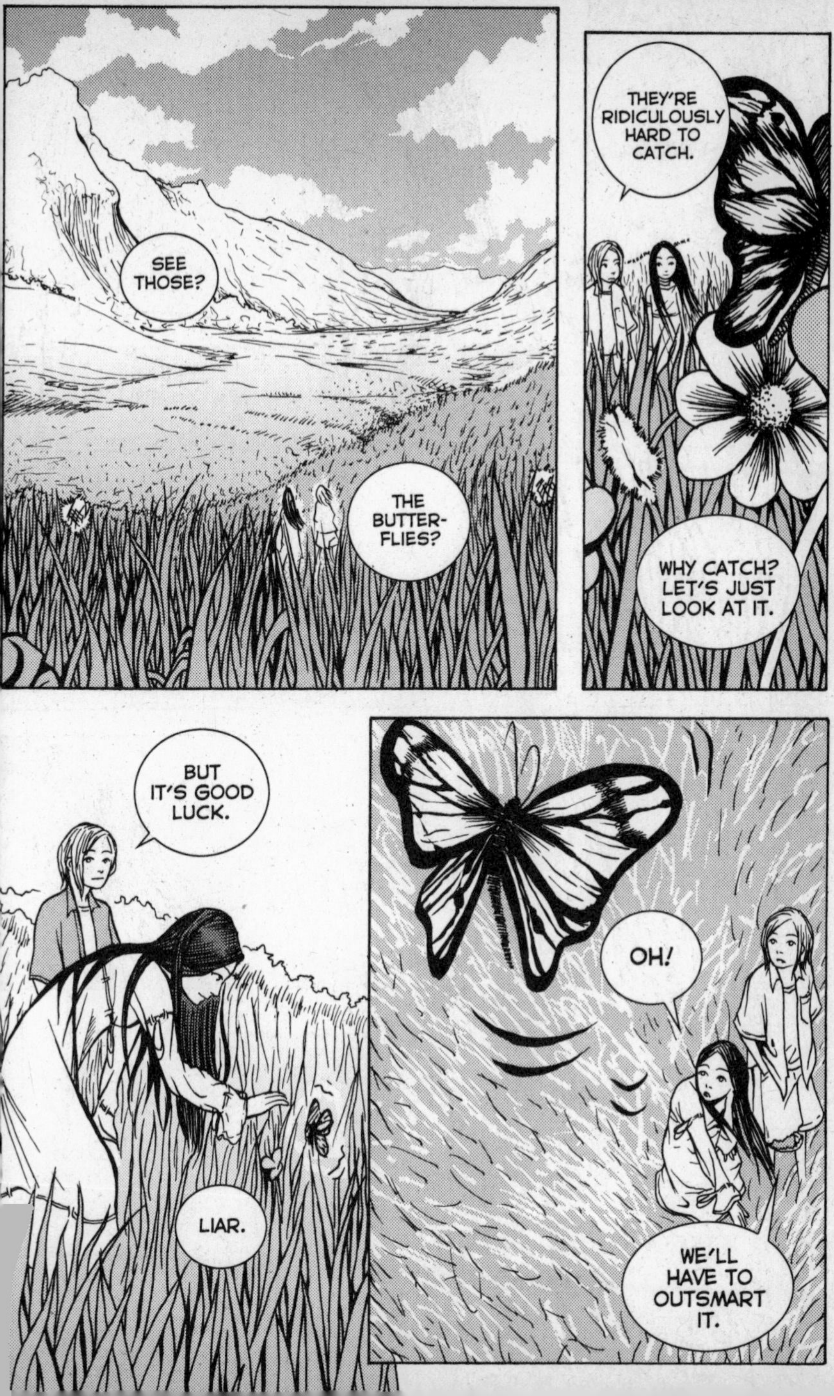
SEE THOSE?
THE BUTTER-FLIES?
THEY'RE RIDICULOUSLY HARD TO CATCH.
WHY CATCH? LET'S JUST LOOK AT IT.
BUT IT'S GOOD LUCK.
LIAR.
OH!
WE'LL HAVE TO OUTSMART IT.

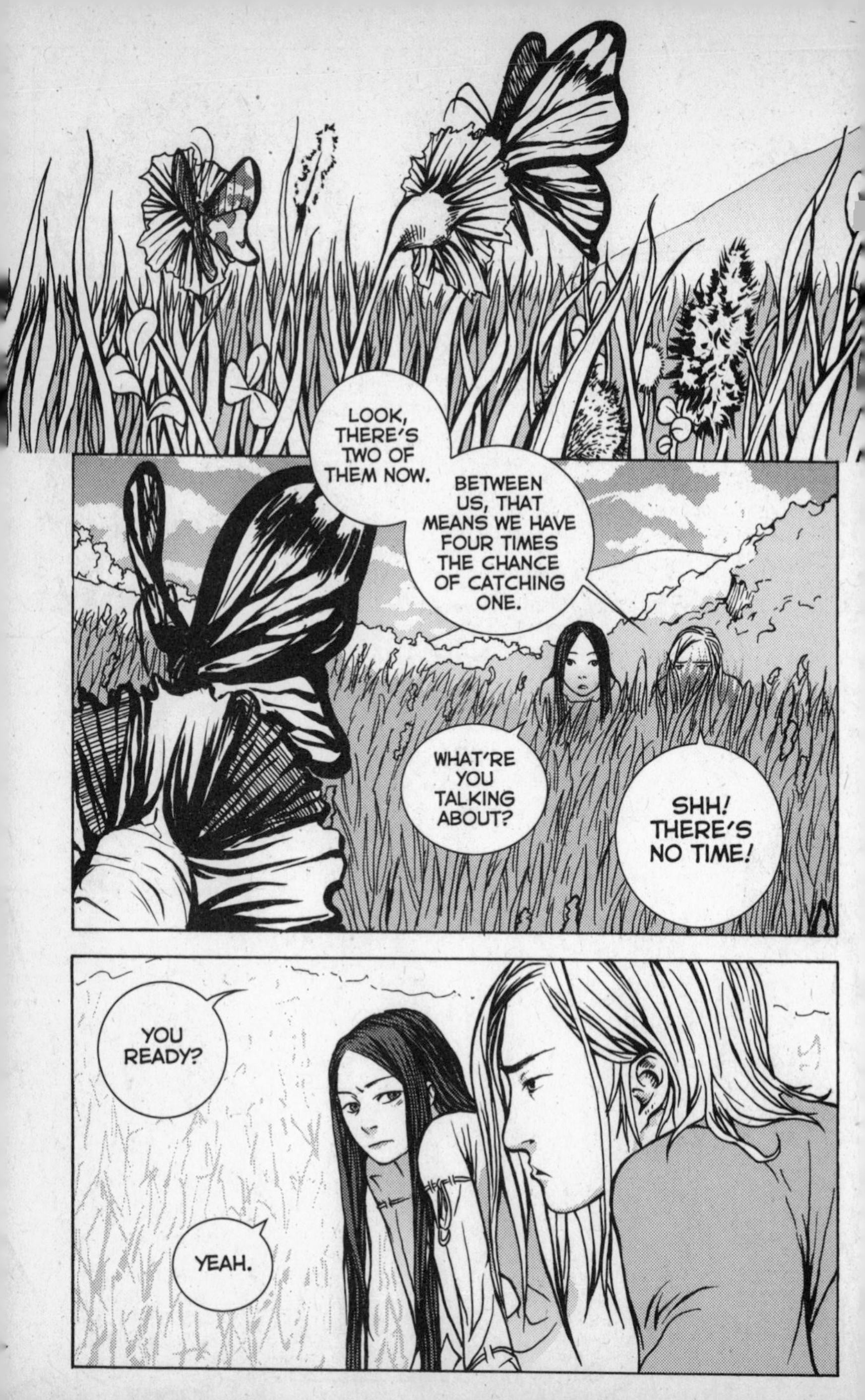

LOOK, THERE'S TWO OF THEM NOW.
BETWEEN US, THAT MEANS WE HAVE FOUR TIMES THE CHANCE OF CATCHING ONE.
WHAT'RE YOU TALKING ABOUT?
SHH! THERE'S NO TIME!
YOU READY?
YEAH.

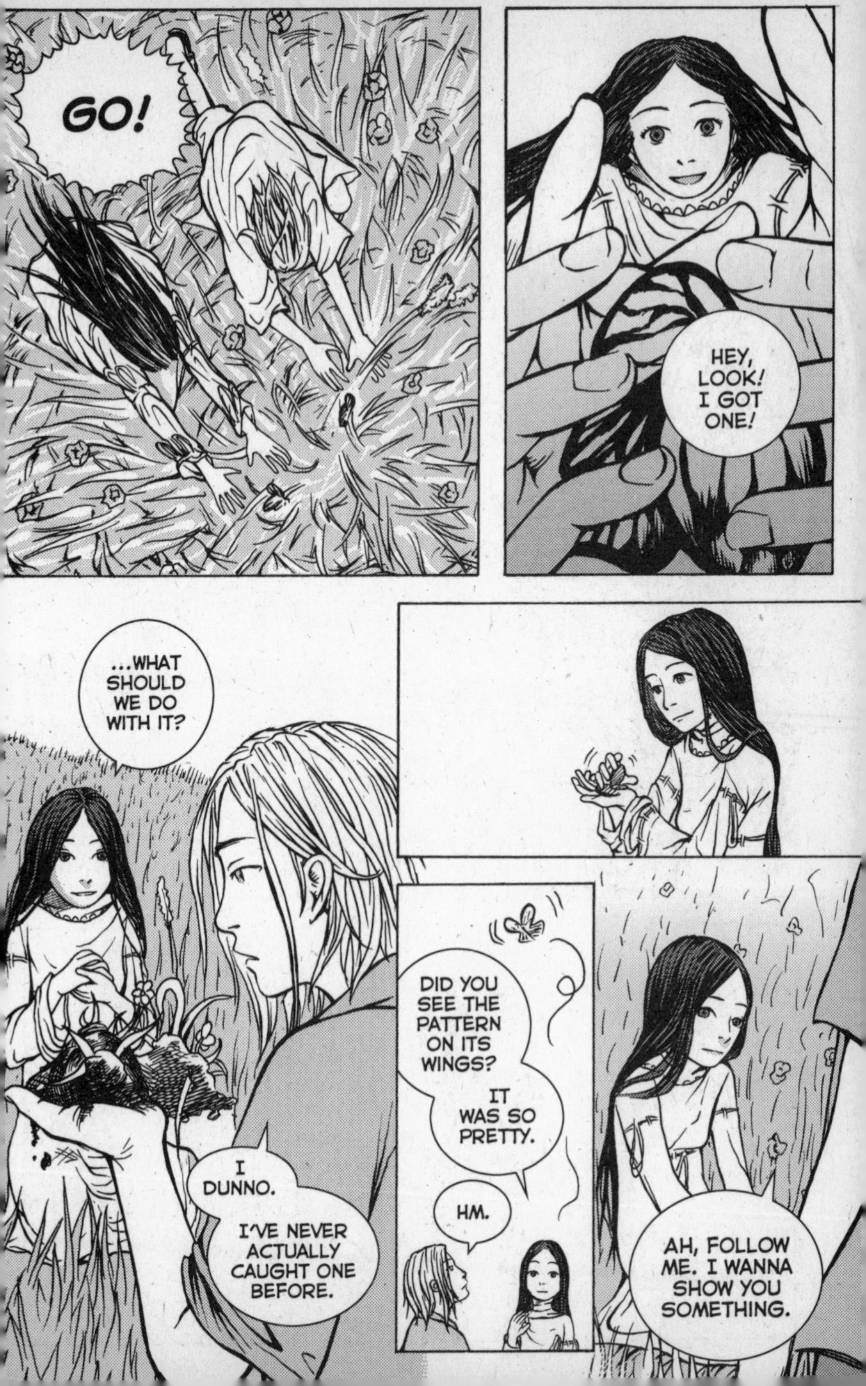
GO!
HEY, LOOK! I GOT ONE!
...WHAT SHOULD WE DO WITH IT?
I DUNNO.
I'VE NEVER ACTUALLY CAUGHT ONE BEFORE.
DID YOU SEE THE PATTERN ON ITS WINGS?
IT WAS SO PRETTY.
HM.
AH, FOLLOW ME. I WANNA SHOW YOU SOMETHING.

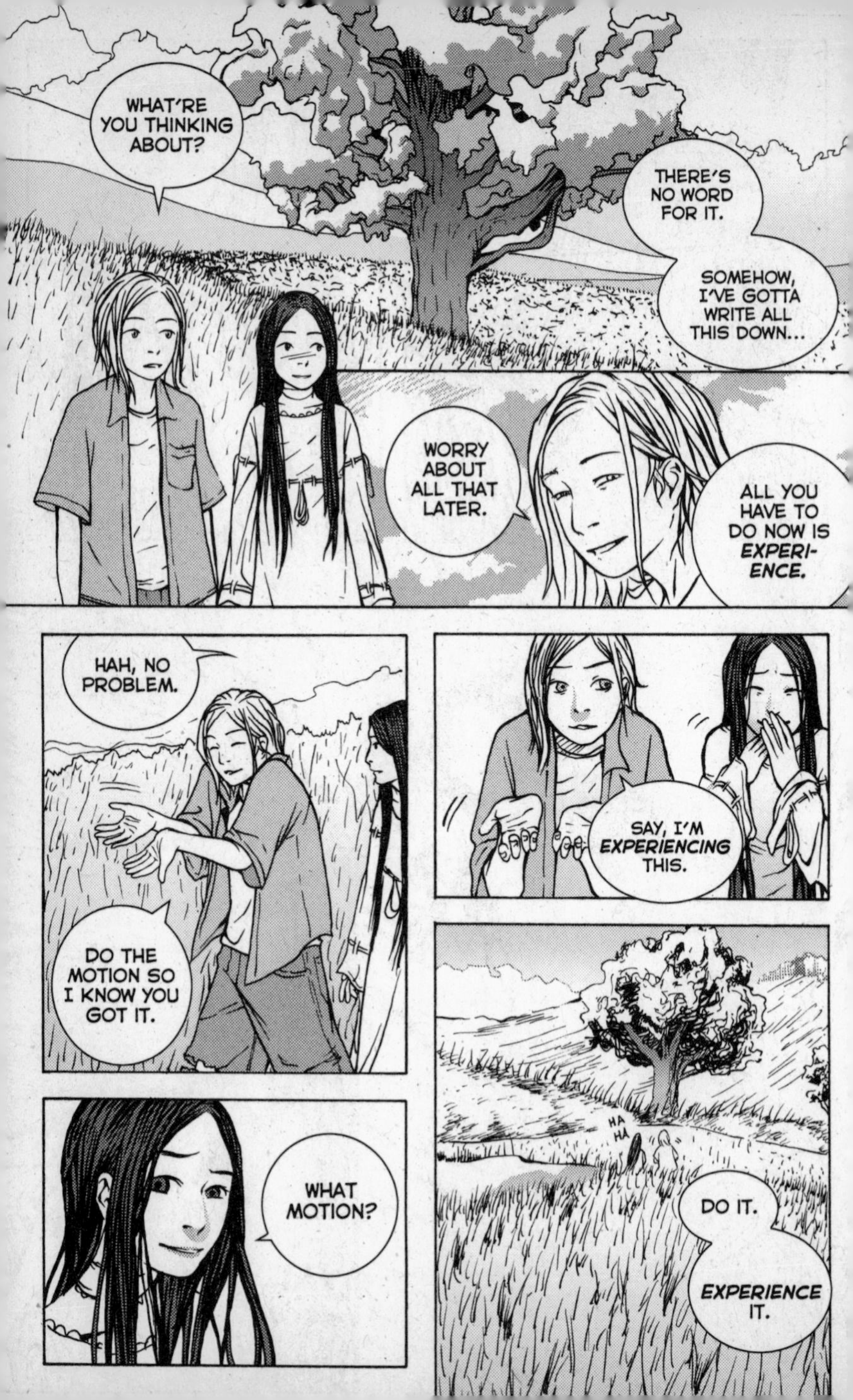
WHAT'RE YOU THINKING ABOUT?
THERE'S NO WORD FOR IT.
SOMEHOW, I'VE GOTTA WRITE ALL THIS DOWN...
WORRY ABOUT ALL THAT LATER.
ALL YOU HAVE TO DO NOW IS *EXPERIENCE*.
HAH, NO PROBLEM.
DO THE MOTION SO I KNOW YOU GOT IT.
SAY, I'M *EXPERIENCING* THIS.
WHAT MOTION?
HA HA
DO IT.
EXPERIENCE IT.

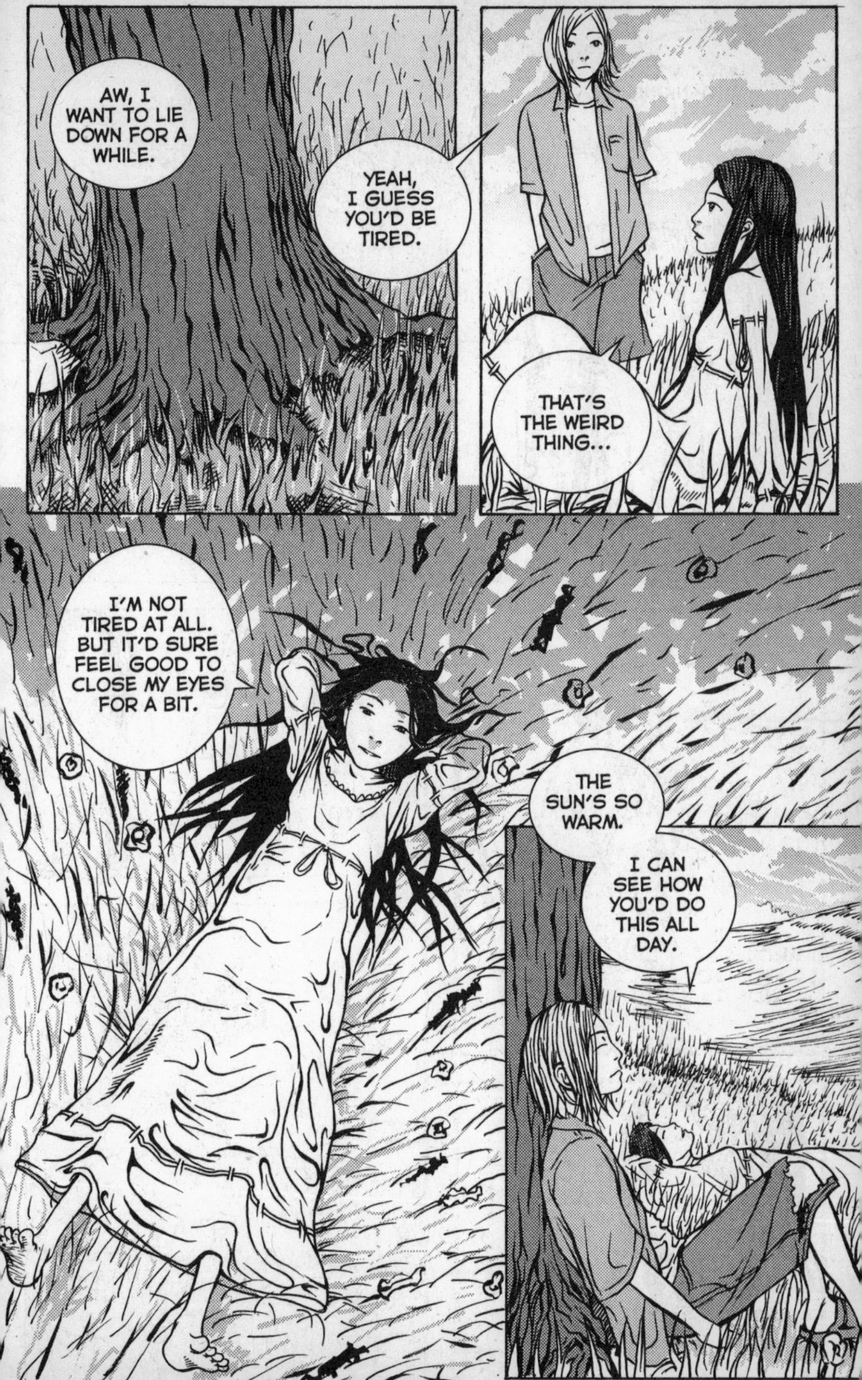
AW, I WANT TO LIE DOWN FOR A WHILE.
YEAH, I GUESS YOU'D BE TIRED.
THAT'S THE WEIRD THING...
I'M NOT TIRED AT ALL. BUT IT'D SURE FEEL GOOD TO CLOSE MY EYES FOR A BIT.
THE SUN'S SO WARM.
I CAN SEE HOW YOU'D DO THIS ALL DAY.

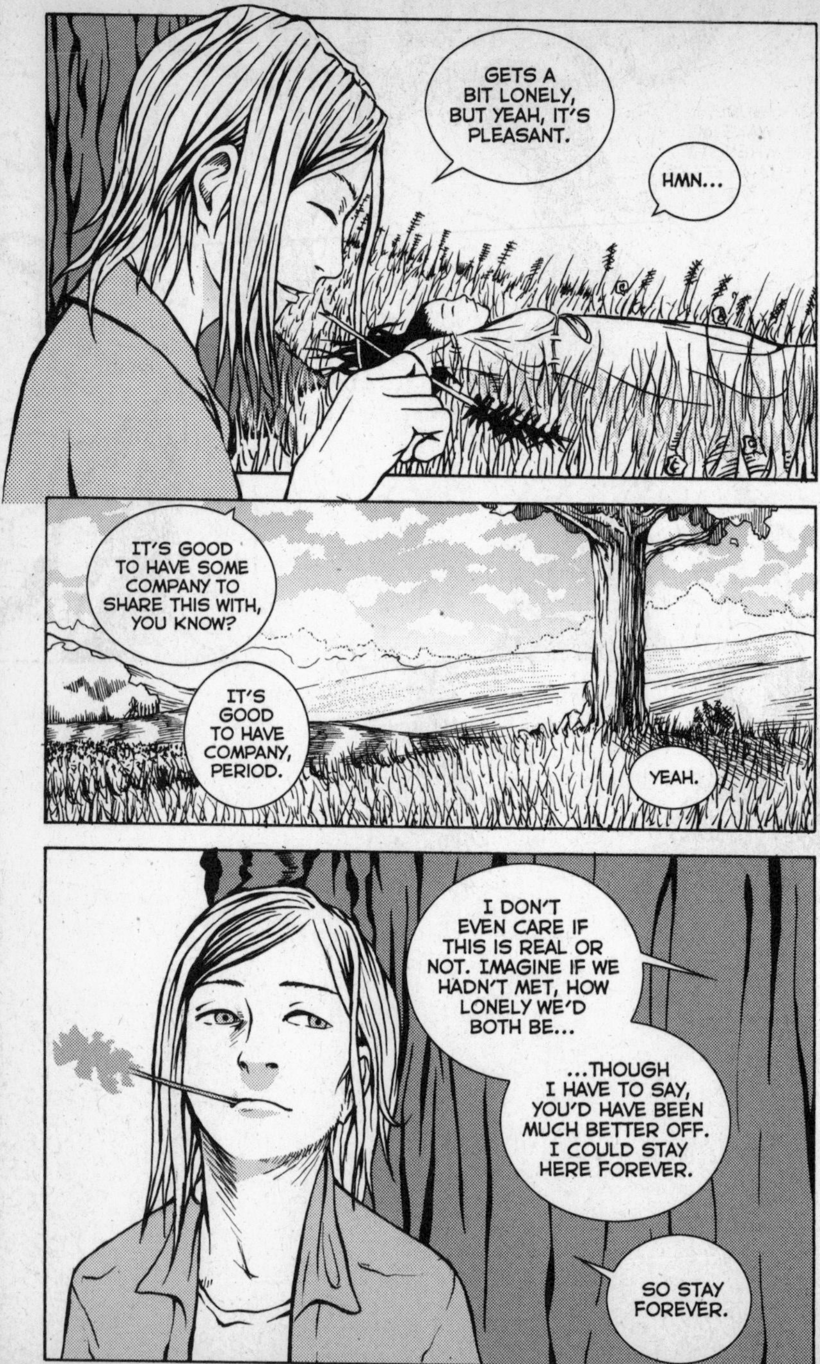
GETS A BIT LONELY, BUT YEAH, IT'S PLEASANT.
HMN...
IT'S GOOD TO HAVE SOME COMPANY TO SHARE THIS WITH, YOU KNOW?
IT'S GOOD TO HAVE COMPANY, PERIOD.
YEAH.
I DON'T EVEN CARE IF THIS IS REAL OR NOT. IMAGINE IF WE HADN'T MET, HOW LONELY WE'D BOTH BE...
...THOUGH I HAVE TO SAY, YOU'D HAVE BEEN MUCH BETTER OFF. I COULD STAY HERE FOREVER.
SO STAY FOREVER.

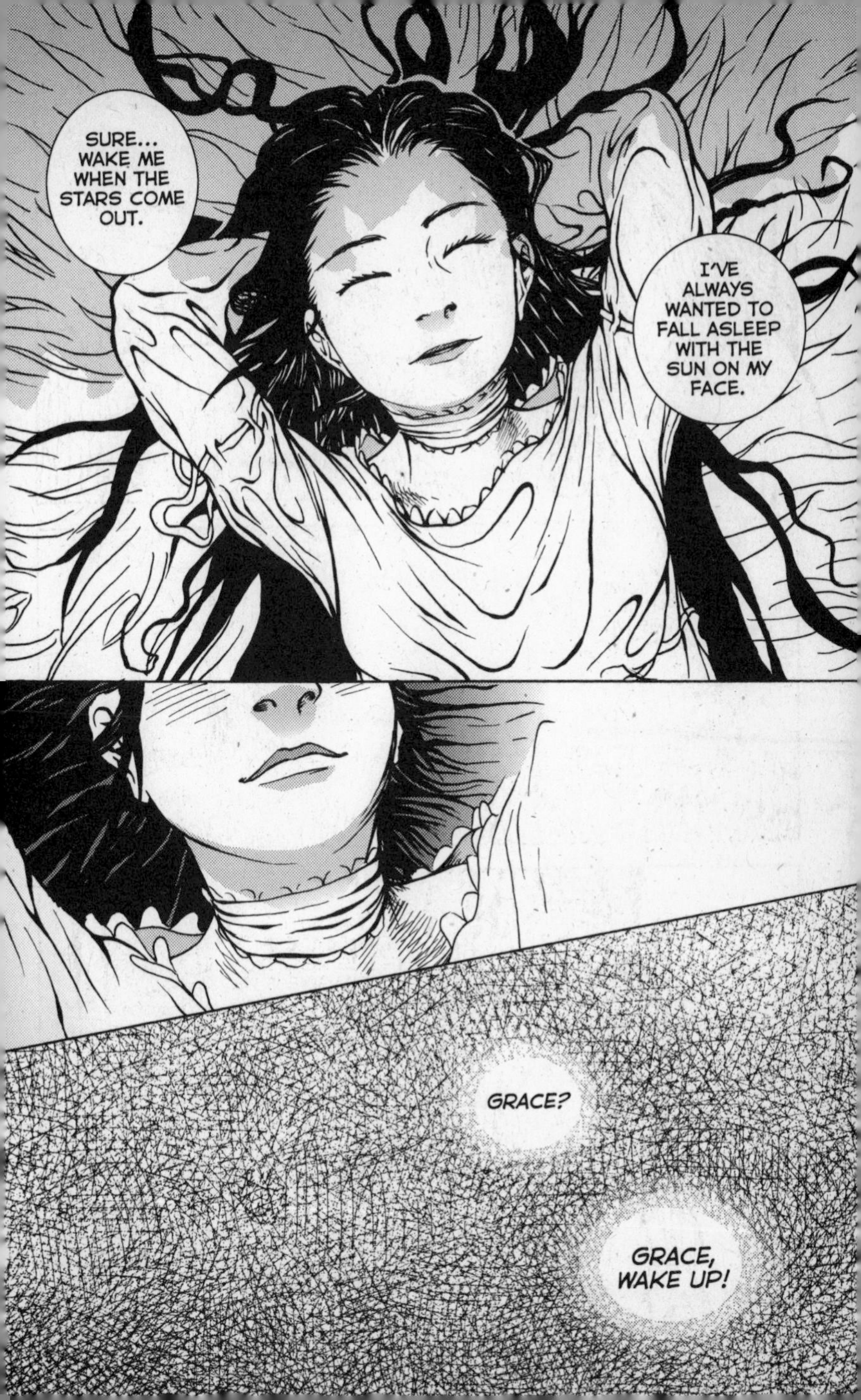
SURE... WAKE ME WHEN THE STARS COME OUT.
I'VE ALWAYS WANTED TO FALL ASLEEP WITH THE SUN ON MY FACE.
GRACE?
GRACE, WAKE UP!

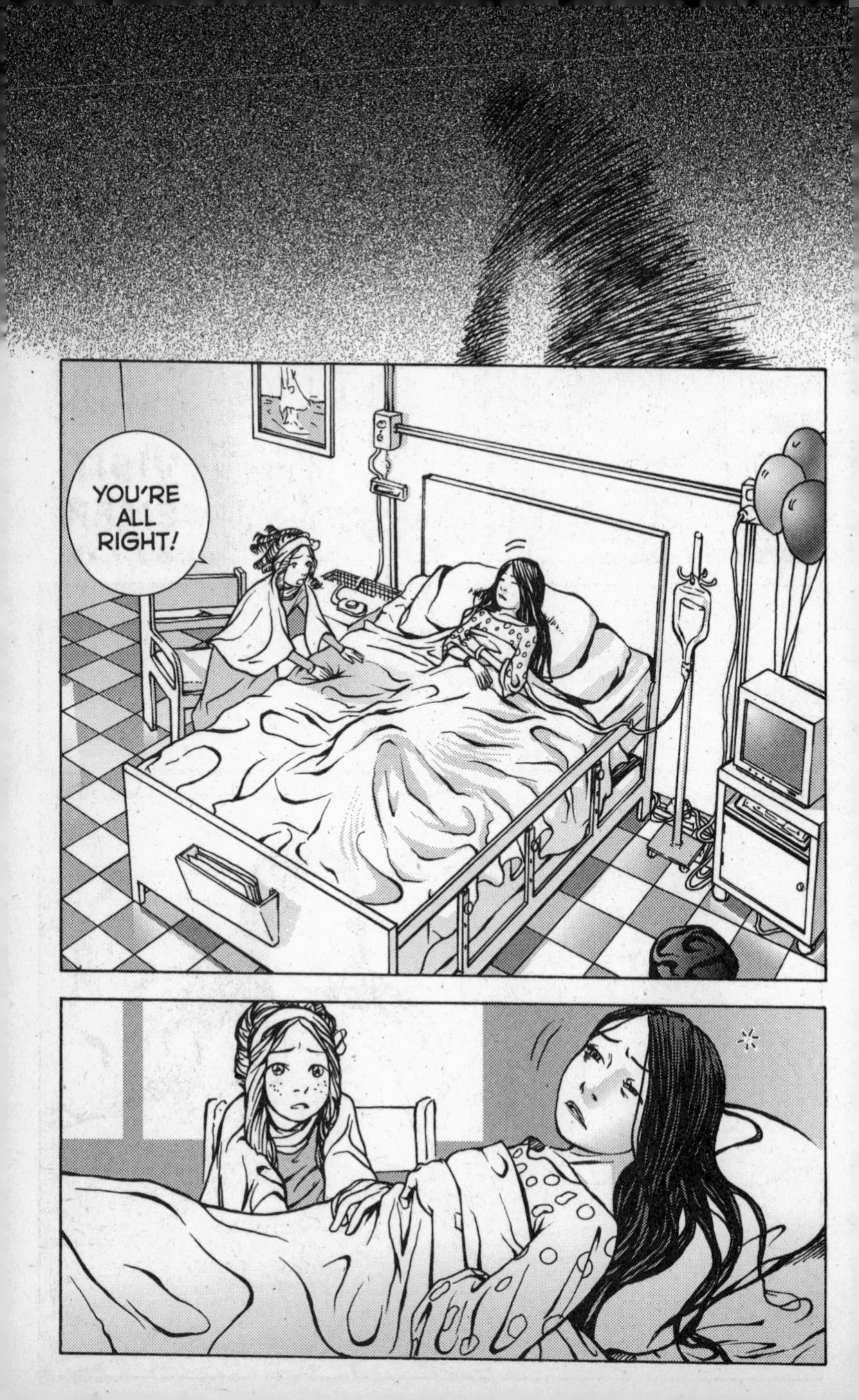
YOU'RE ALL RIGHT!

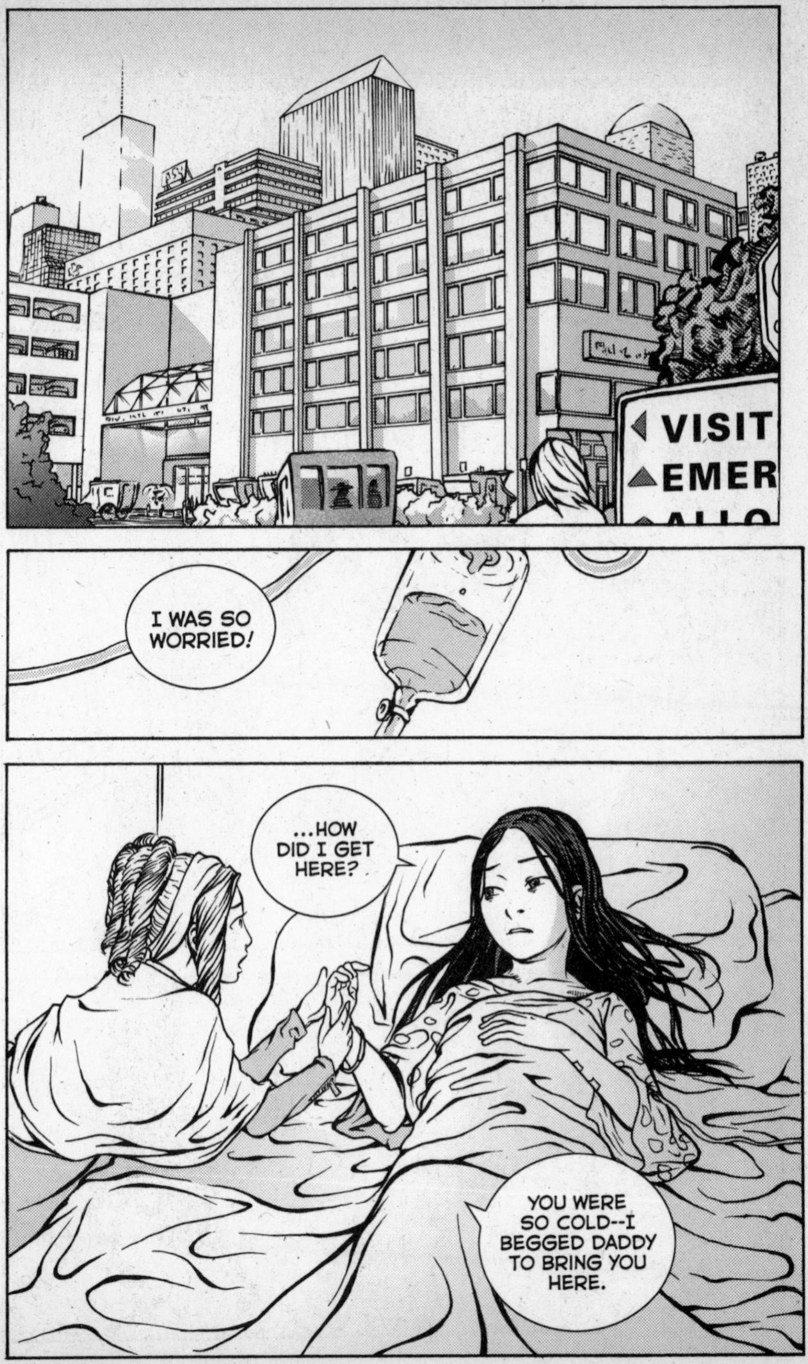
VISIT
EMER
I WAS SO WORRIED!
...HOW DID I GET HERE?
YOU WERE SO COLD--I BEGGED DADDY TO BRING YOU HERE.

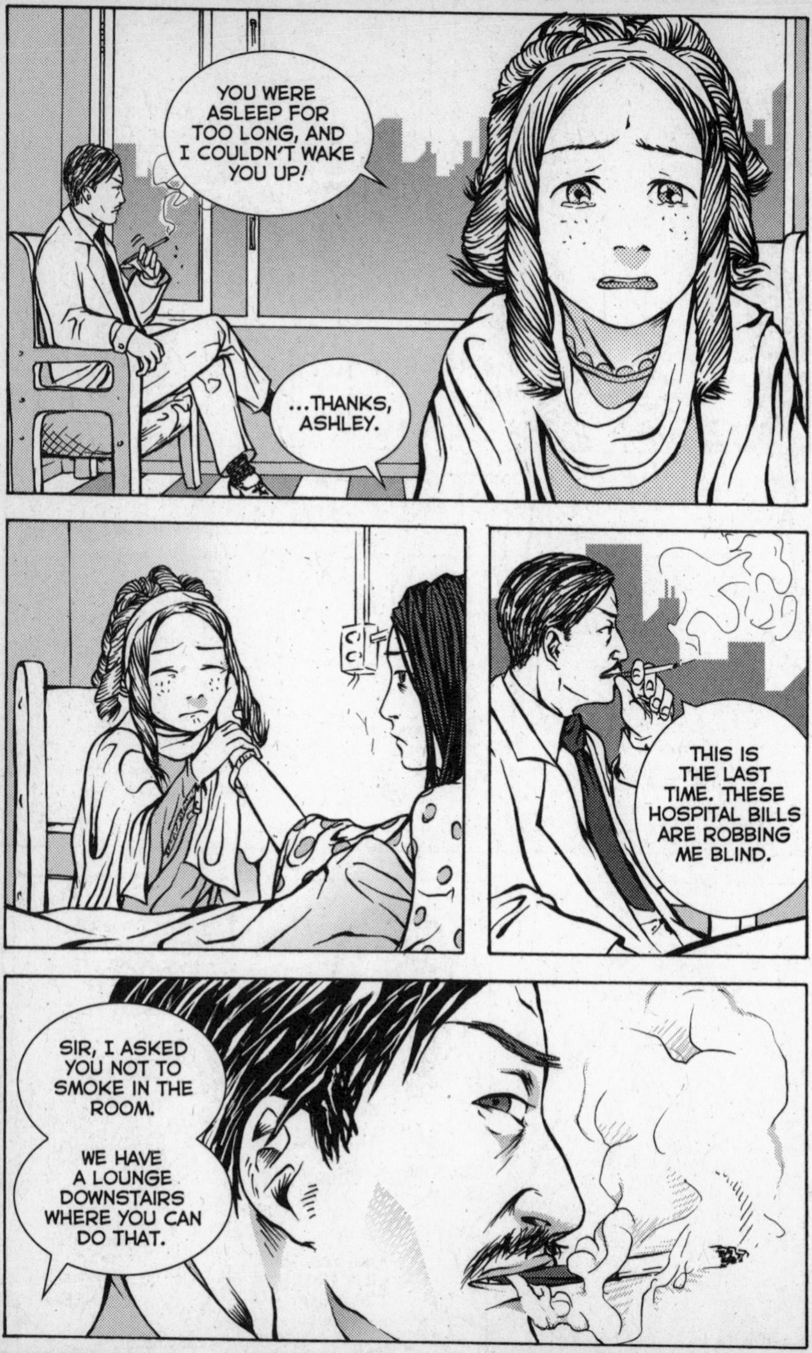
YOU WERE ASLEEP FOR TOO LONG, AND I COULDN'T WAKE YOU UP!
...THANKS, ASHLEY.
THIS IS THE LAST TIME. THESE HOSPITAL BILLS ARE ROBBING ME BLIND.
SIR, I ASKED YOU NOT TO SMOKE IN THE ROOM.
WE HAVE A LOUNGE DOWNSTAIRS WHERE YOU CAN DO THAT.

DON'T WORRY ABOUT THE SMOKING. WHAT'S THE DAMAGE?

BILLS DON'T MATTER AT THE MOMENT.

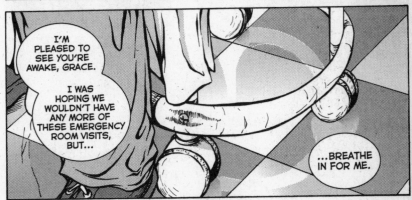

I'M PLEASED TO SEE YOU'RE AWAKE, GRACE.

I WAS HOPING WE WOULDN'T HAVE ANY MORE OF THESE EMERGENCY ROOM VISITS, BUT...

...BREATHE IN FOR ME.

HAVE YOU BEEN FEELING WORSE LATELY?

ACTUALLY, NO...I'VE BEEN MUCH BETTER.

I CAN MOVE AROUND A BIT MORE.

MAYBE YOU'RE MOVING AROUND TOO MUCH, THEN.

YOU'RE LUCKY TO HAVE YOUR SISTER AND FATHER TO WORRY ABOUT YOU...

YOU SHOULD ASK THEM FOR HELP WHENEVER YOU NEED IT.

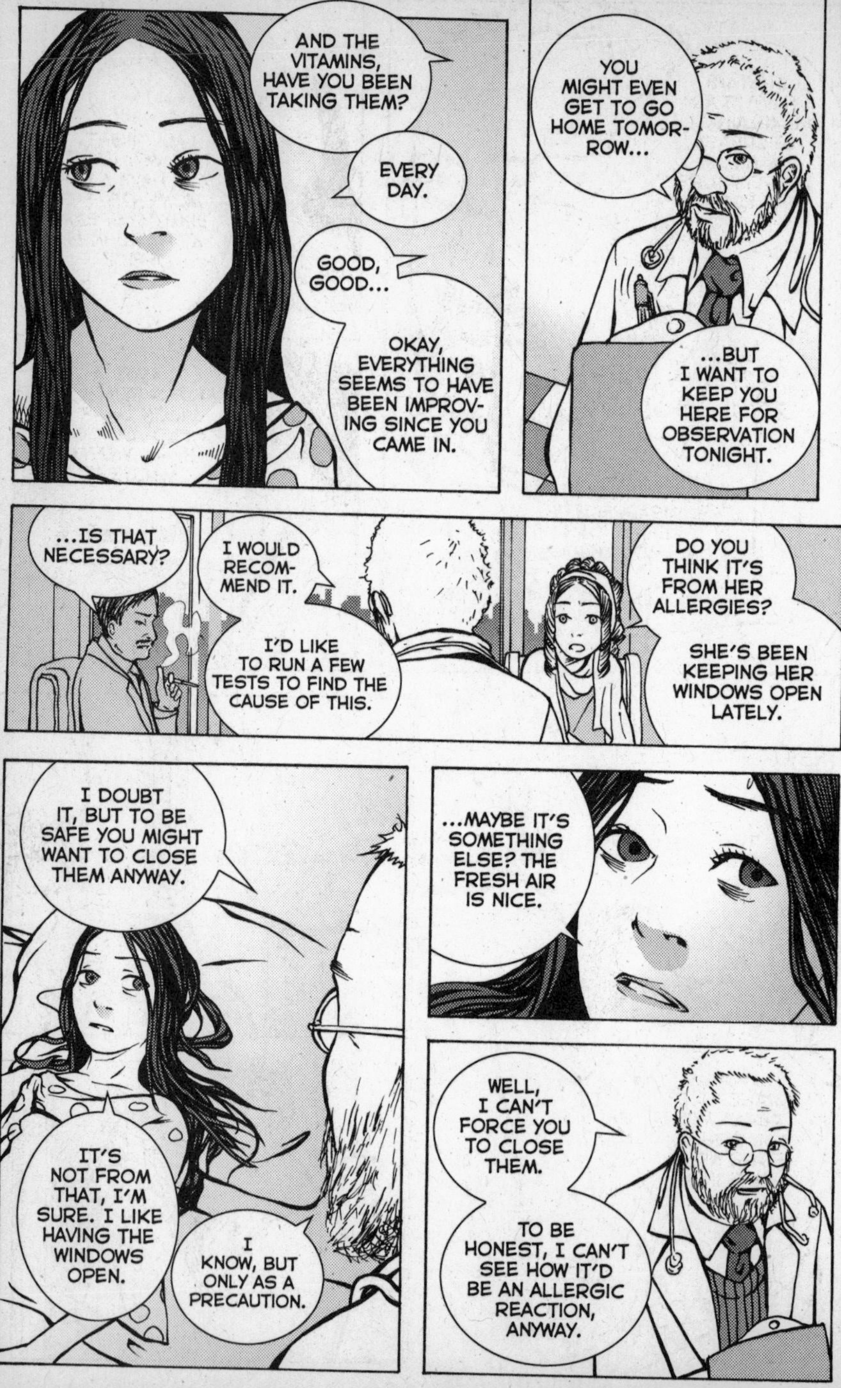
AND THE VITAMINS, HAVE YOU BEEN TAKING THEM?
EVERY DAY.
GOOD, GOOD...
OKAY, EVERYTHING SEEMS TO HAVE BEEN IMPROVING SINCE YOU CAME IN.
YOU MIGHT EVEN GET TO GO HOME TOMORROW...
...BUT I WANT TO KEEP YOU HERE FOR OBSERVATION TONIGHT.
...IS THAT NECESSARY?
I WOULD RECOMMEND IT.
I'D LIKE TO RUN A FEW TESTS TO FIND THE CAUSE OF THIS.
DO YOU THINK IT'S FROM HER ALLERGIES?
SHE'S BEEN KEEPING HER WINDOWS OPEN LATELY.
I DOUBT IT, BUT TO BE SAFE YOU MIGHT WANT TO CLOSE THEM ANYWAY.
IT'S NOT FROM THAT, I'M SURE. I LIKE HAVING THE WINDOWS OPEN.
I KNOW, BUT ONLY AS A PRECAUTION.
...MAYBE IT'S SOMETHING ELSE? THE FRESH AIR IS NICE.
WELL, I CAN'T FORCE YOU TO CLOSE THEM.
TO BE HONEST, I CAN'T SEE HOW IT'D BE AN ALLERGIC REACTION, ANYWAY.

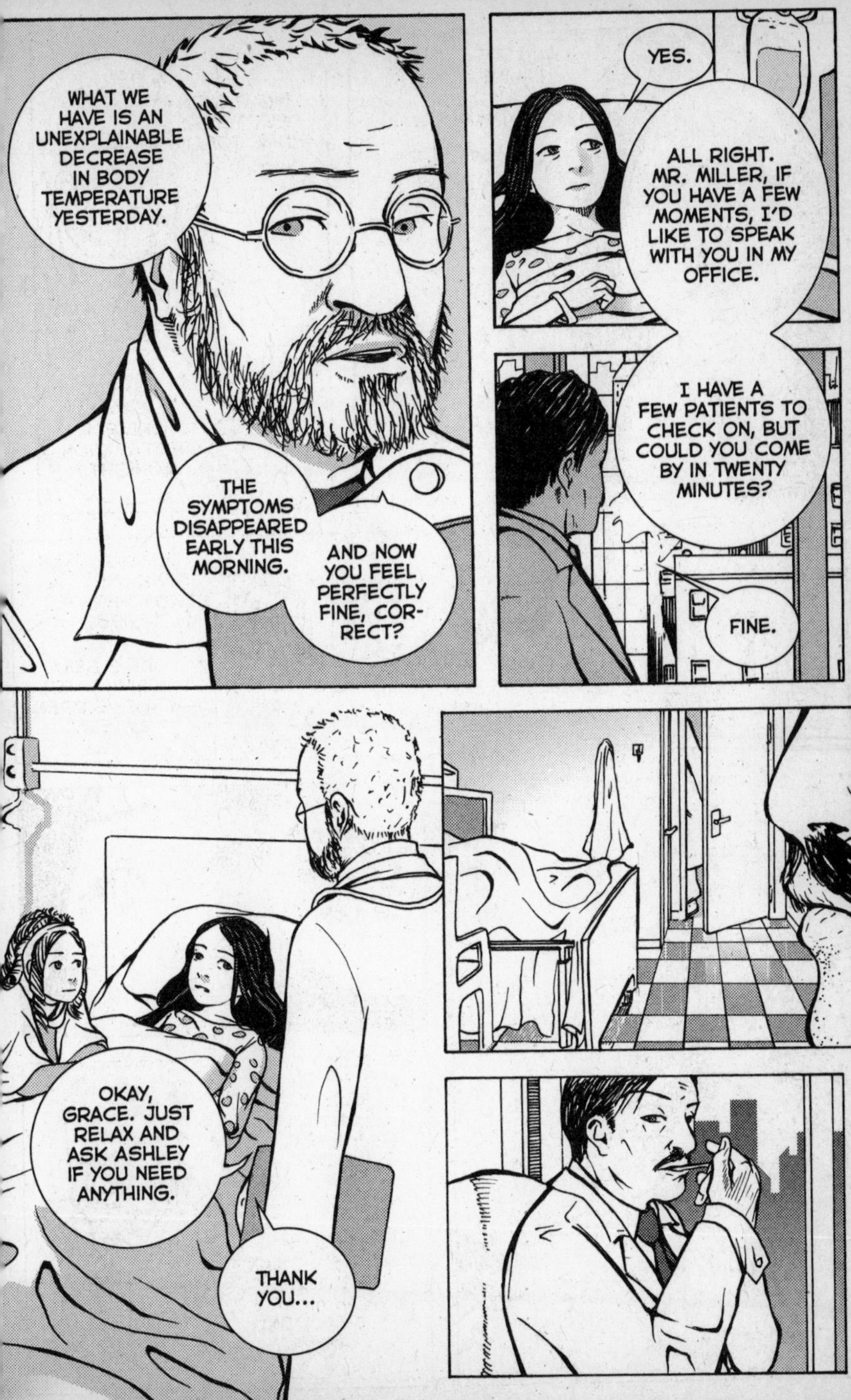
WHAT WE HAVE IS AN UNEXPLAINABLE DECREASE IN BODY TEMPERATURE YESTERDAY.
THE SYMPTOMS DISAPPEARED EARLY THIS MORNING.
AND NOW YOU FEEL PERFECTLY FINE, COR-RECT?
YES.
ALL RIGHT. MR. MILLER, IF YOU HAVE A FEW MOMENTS, I'D LIKE TO SPEAK WITH YOU IN MY OFFICE.
I HAVE A FEW PATIENTS TO CHECK ON, BUT COULD YOU COME BY IN TWENTY MINUTES?
FINE.
OKAY, GRACE. JUST RELAX AND ASK ASHLEY IF YOU NEED ANYTHING.
THANK YOU...

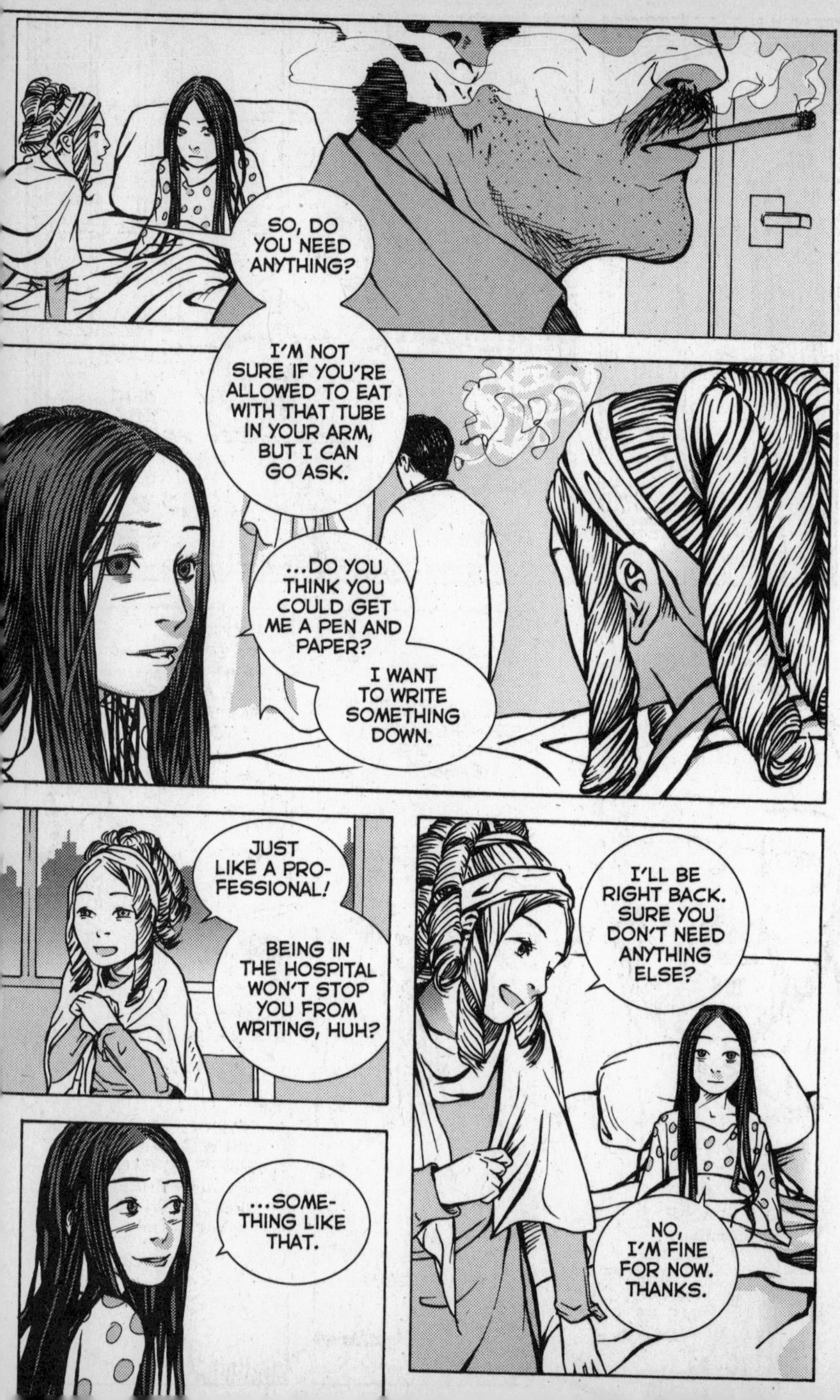
SO, DO YOU NEED ANYTHING?
I'M NOT SURE IF YOU'RE ALLOWED TO EAT WITH THAT TUBE IN YOUR ARM, BUT I CAN GO ASK.
...DO YOU THINK YOU COULD GET ME A PEN AND PAPER?
I WANT TO WRITE SOMETHING DOWN.
JUST LIKE A PRO-FESSIONAL!
BEING IN THE HOSPITAL WON'T STOP YOU FROM WRITING, HUH?
...SOME-THING LIKE THAT.
I'LL BE RIGHT BACK. SURE YOU DON'T NEED ANYTHING ELSE?
NO, I'M FINE FOR NOW. THANKS.

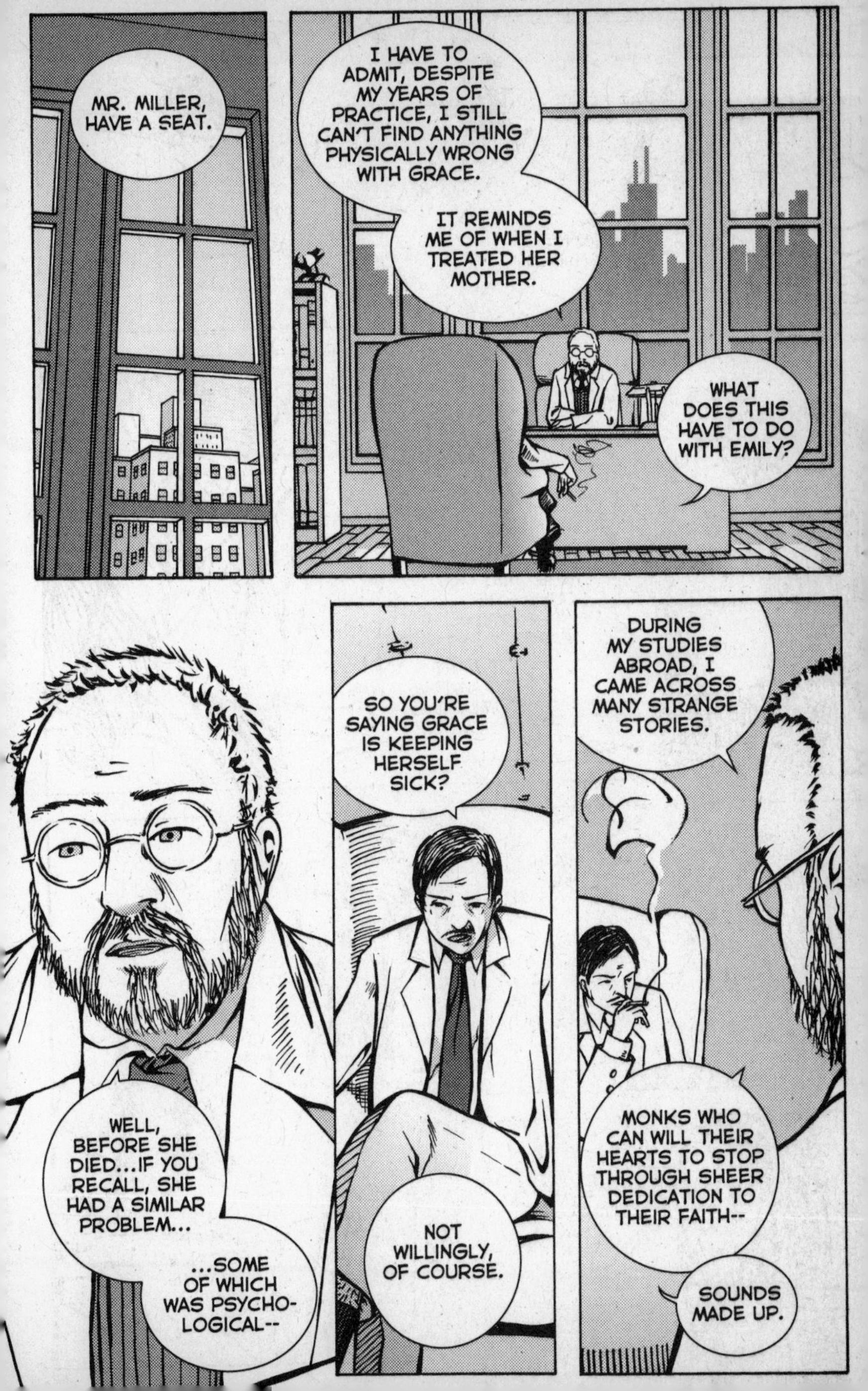
MR. MILLER, HAVE A SEAT.
I HAVE TO ADMIT, DESPITE MY YEARS OF PRACTICE, I STILL CAN'T FIND ANYTHING PHYSICALLY WRONG WITH GRACE.
IT REMINDS ME OF WHEN I TREATED HER MOTHER.
WHAT DOES THIS HAVE TO DO WITH EMILY?
WELL, BEFORE SHE DIED...IF YOU RECALL, SHE HAD A SIMILAR PROBLEM...
...SOME OF WHICH WAS PSYCHO-LOGICAL--
SO YOU'RE SAYING GRACE IS KEEPING HERSELF SICK?
NOT WILLINGLY, OF COURSE.
DURING MY STUDIES ABROAD, I CAME ACROSS MANY STRANGE STORIES.
MONKS WHO CAN WILL THEIR HEARTS TO STOP THROUGH SHEER DEDICATION TO THEIR FAITH--
SOUNDS MADE UP.

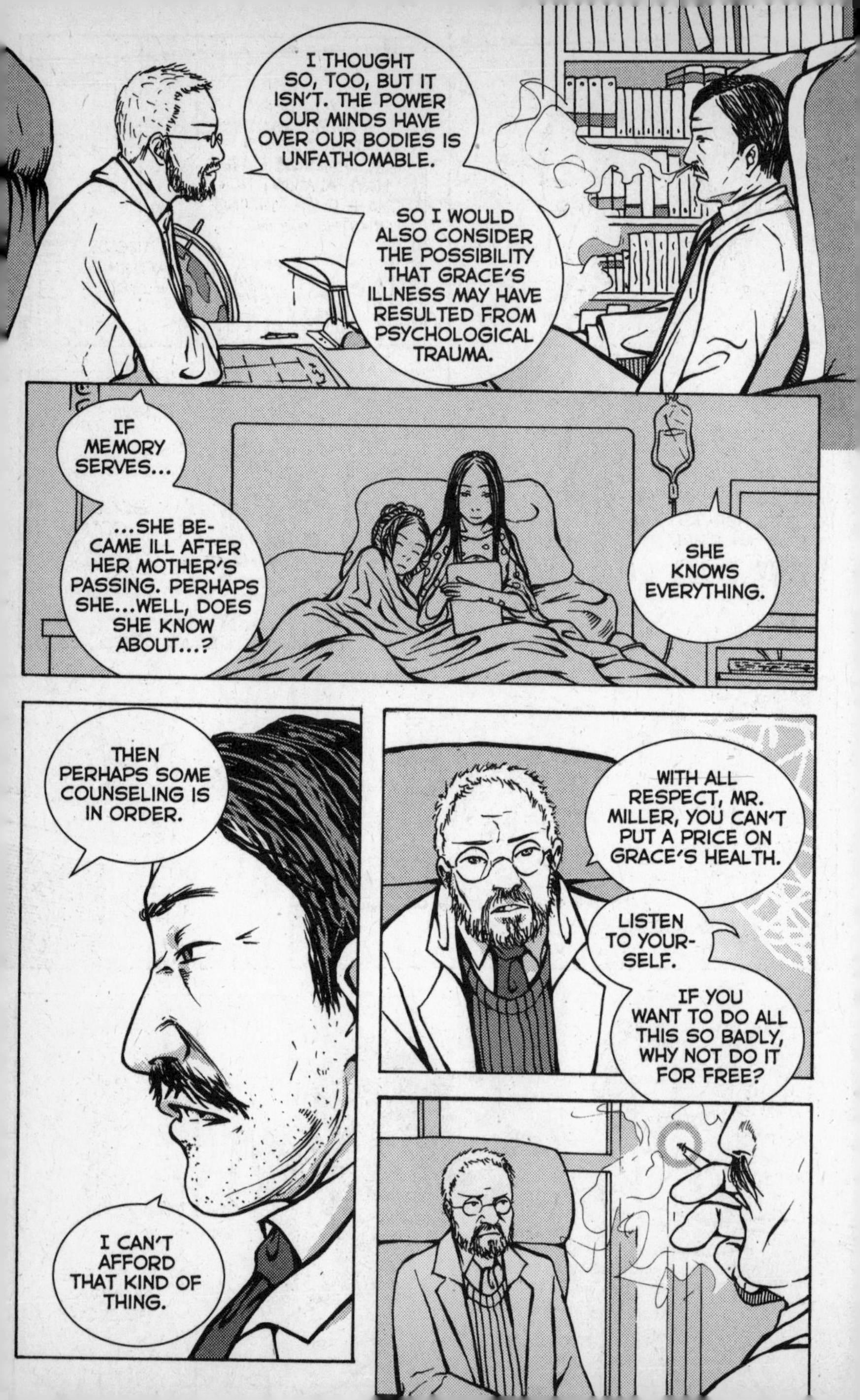
I THOUGHT SO, TOO, BUT IT ISN'T. THE POWER OUR MINDS HAVE OVER OUR BODIES IS UNFATHOMABLE.
SO I WOULD ALSO CONSIDER THE POSSIBILITY THAT GRACE'S ILLNESS MAY HAVE RESULTED FROM PSYCHOLOGICAL TRAUMA.
IF MEMORY SERVES...
...SHE BE-CAME ILL AFTER HER MOTHER'S PASSING. PERHAPS SHE...WELL, DOES SHE KNOW ABOUT...?
SHE KNOWS EVERYTHING.
THEN PERHAPS SOME COUNSELING IS IN ORDER.
I CAN'T AFFORD THAT KIND OF THING.
WITH ALL RESPECT, MR. MILLER, YOU CAN'T PUT A PRICE ON GRACE'S HEALTH.
LISTEN TO YOUR-SELF.
IF YOU WANT TO DO ALL THIS SO BADLY, WHY NOT DO IT FOR FREE?

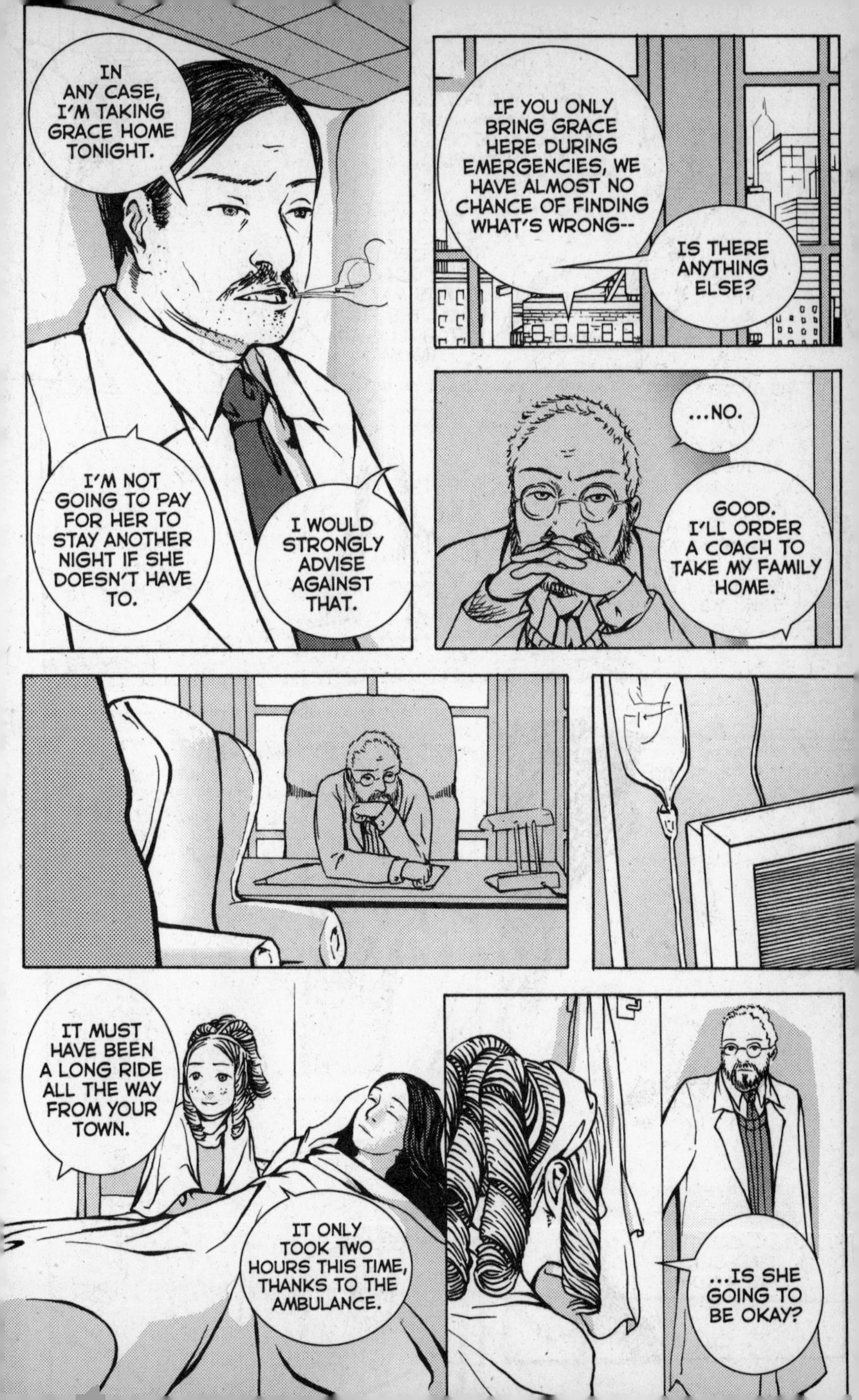
IN ANY CASE, I'M TAKING GRACE HOME TONIGHT.
I'M NOT GOING TO PAY FOR HER TO STAY ANOTHER NIGHT IF SHE DOESN'T HAVE TO.
I WOULD STRONGLY ADVISE AGAINST THAT.
IF YOU ONLY BRING GRACE HERE DURING EMERGENCIES, WE HAVE ALMOST NO CHANCE OF FINDING WHAT'S WRONG--
IS THERE ANYTHING ELSE?
...NO.
GOOD. I'LL ORDER A COACH TO TAKE MY FAMILY HOME.
IT MUST HAVE BEEN A LONG RIDE ALL THE WAY FROM YOUR TOWN.
IT ONLY TOOK TWO HOURS THIS TIME, THANKS TO THE AMBULANCE.
...IS SHE GOING TO BE OKAY?

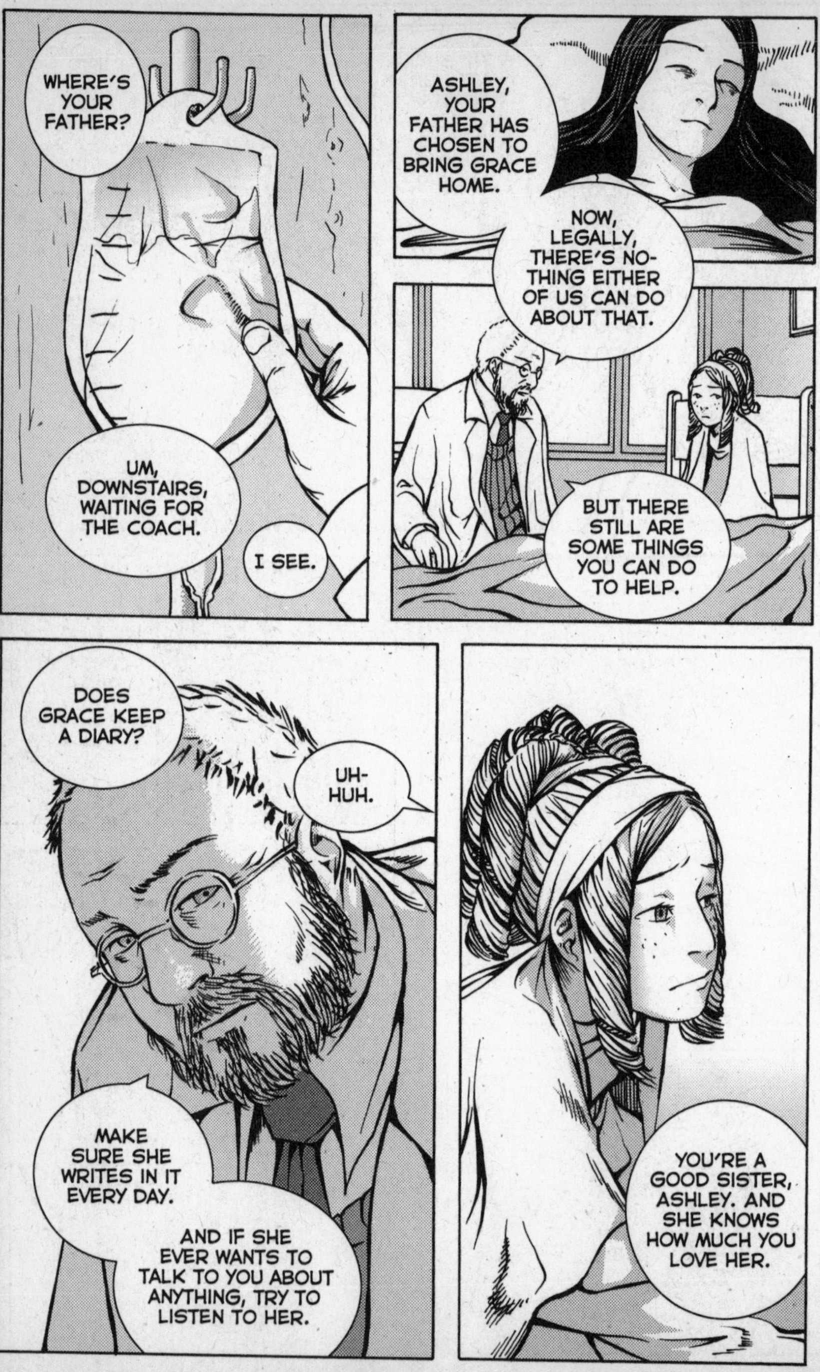
WHERE'S YOUR FATHER?
UM, DOWNSTAIRS, WAITING FOR THE COACH.
I SEE.
ASHLEY, YOUR FATHER HAS CHOSEN TO BRING GRACE HOME.
NOW, LEGALLY, THERE'S NO-THING EITHER OF US CAN DO ABOUT THAT.
BUT THERE STILL ARE SOME THINGS YOU CAN DO TO HELP.
DOES GRACE KEEP A DIARY?
UH-HUH.
MAKE SURE SHE WRITES IN IT EVERY DAY.
AND IF SHE EVER WANTS TO TALK TO YOU ABOUT ANYTHING, TRY TO LISTEN TO HER.
YOU'RE A GOOD SISTER, ASHLEY. AND SHE KNOWS HOW MUCH YOU LOVE HER.

MAKE SURE SHE TAKES HER VITAMINS AS WELL, AND EATS PROPERLY.

IF THERE'S ANYTHING WRONG, OR IF YOU HAVE A QUESTION, YOU HAVE BOTH MY NUMBERS.

CALL ME ANYTIME, AND I'LL DO MY BEST TO HELP.

THANK YOU SO MUCH...!

AND TRY NOT TO FOCUS TOO MUCH ON THESE SAD THINGS, OKAY?

THE COACH IS HERE.

ASHLEY, WAKE YOUR SISTER UP AND BRING HER DOWNSTAIRS. I'LL BE WAITING OUTSIDE.

OKAY.

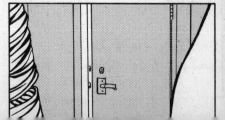

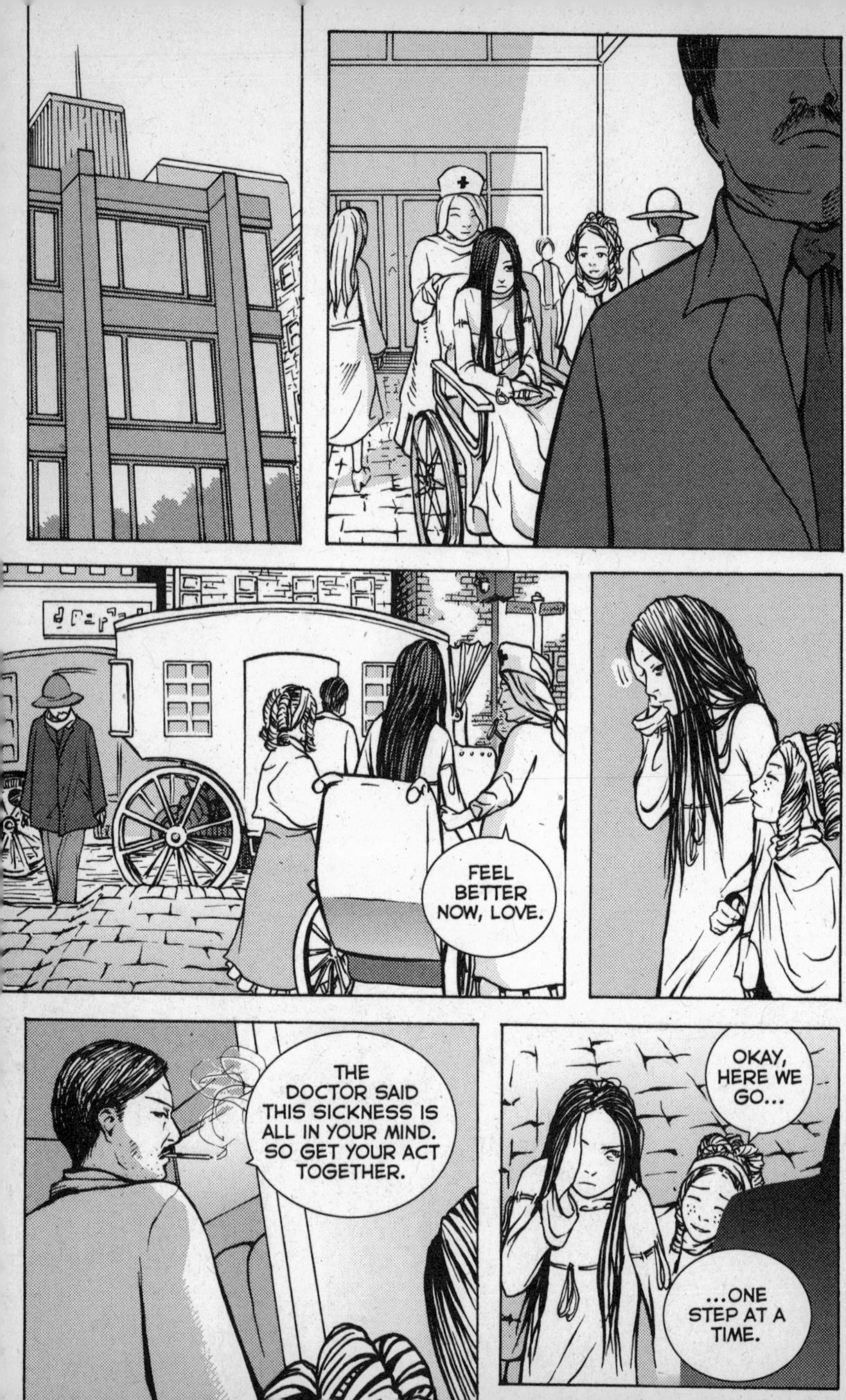
FEEL BETTER NOW, LOVE.
THE DOCTOR SAID THIS SICKNESS IS ALL IN YOUR MIND. SO GET YOUR ACT TOGETHER.
OKAY, HERE WE GO...
...ONE STEP AT A TIME.

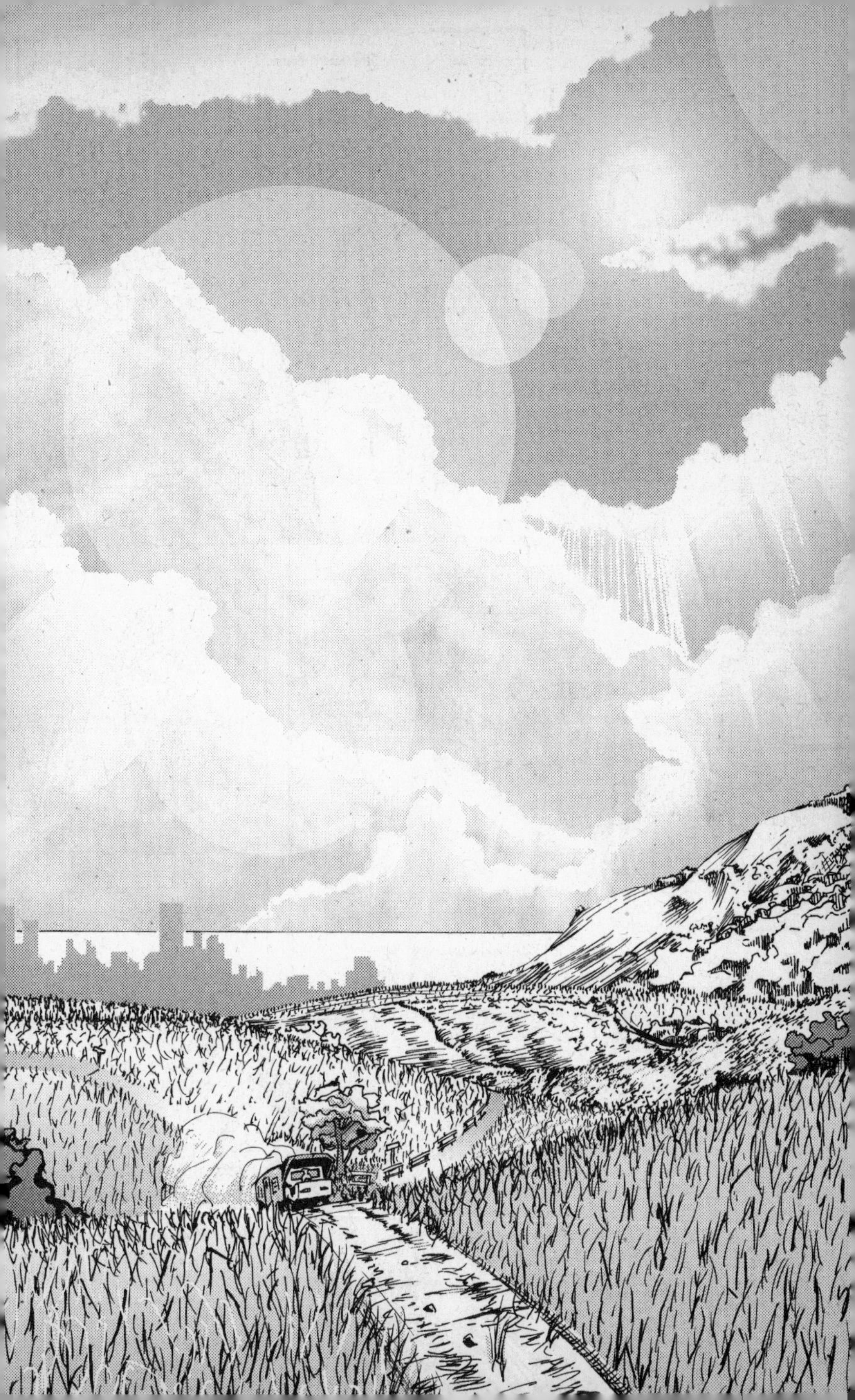

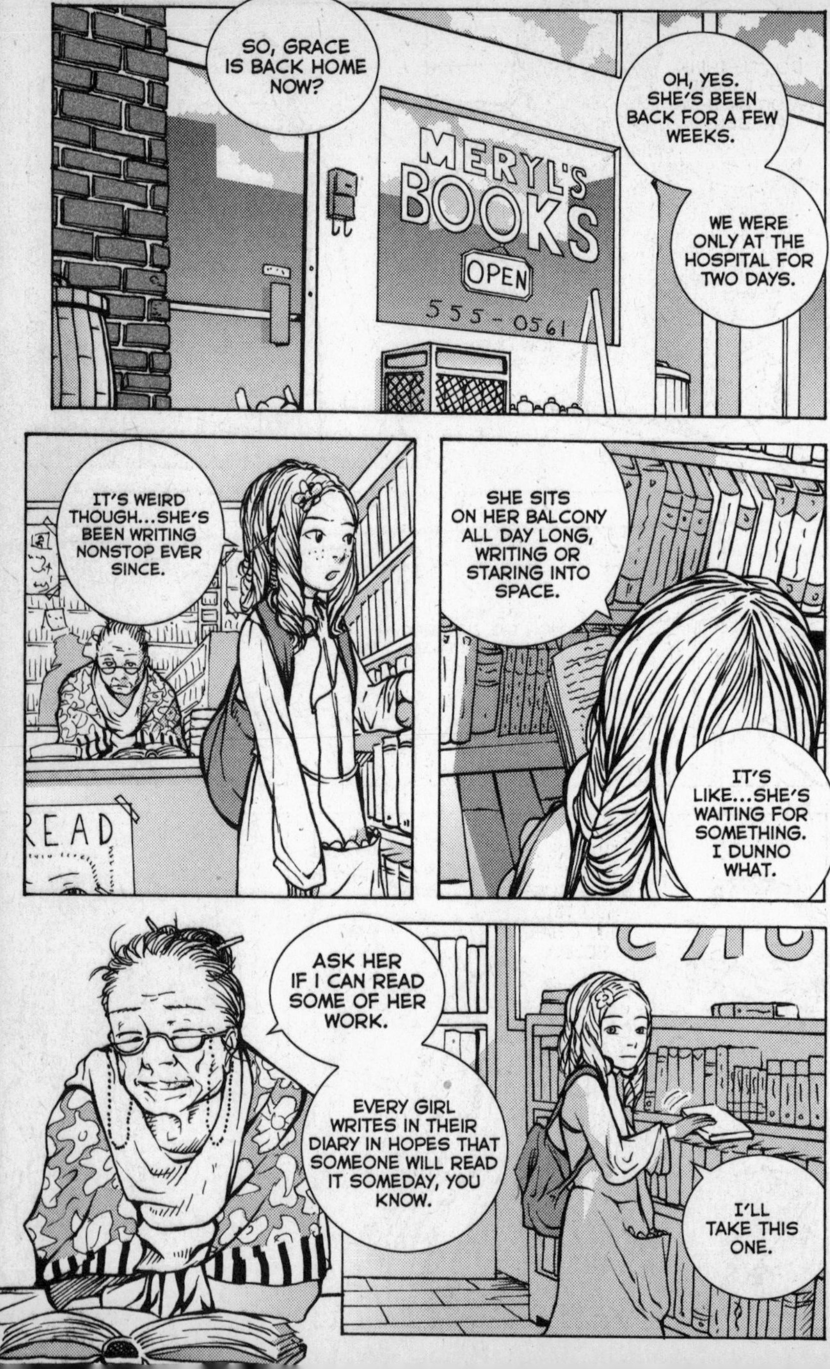
SO, GRACE IS BACK HOME NOW?
MERYL'S BOOKS
OPEN
555-0561
OH, YES. SHE'S BEEN BACK FOR A FEW WEEKS.
WE WERE ONLY AT THE HOSPITAL FOR TWO DAYS.
IT'S WEIRD THOUGH...SHE'S BEEN WRITING NONSTOP EVER SINCE.
READ
SHE SITS ON HER BALCONY ALL DAY LONG, WRITING OR STARING INTO SPACE.
IT'S LIKE...SHE'S WAITING FOR SOMETHING. I DUNNO WHAT.
ASK HER IF I CAN READ SOME OF HER WORK.
EVERY GIRL WRITES IN THEIR DIARY IN HOPES THAT SOMEONE WILL READ IT SOMEDAY, YOU KNOW.
I'LL TAKE THIS ONE.

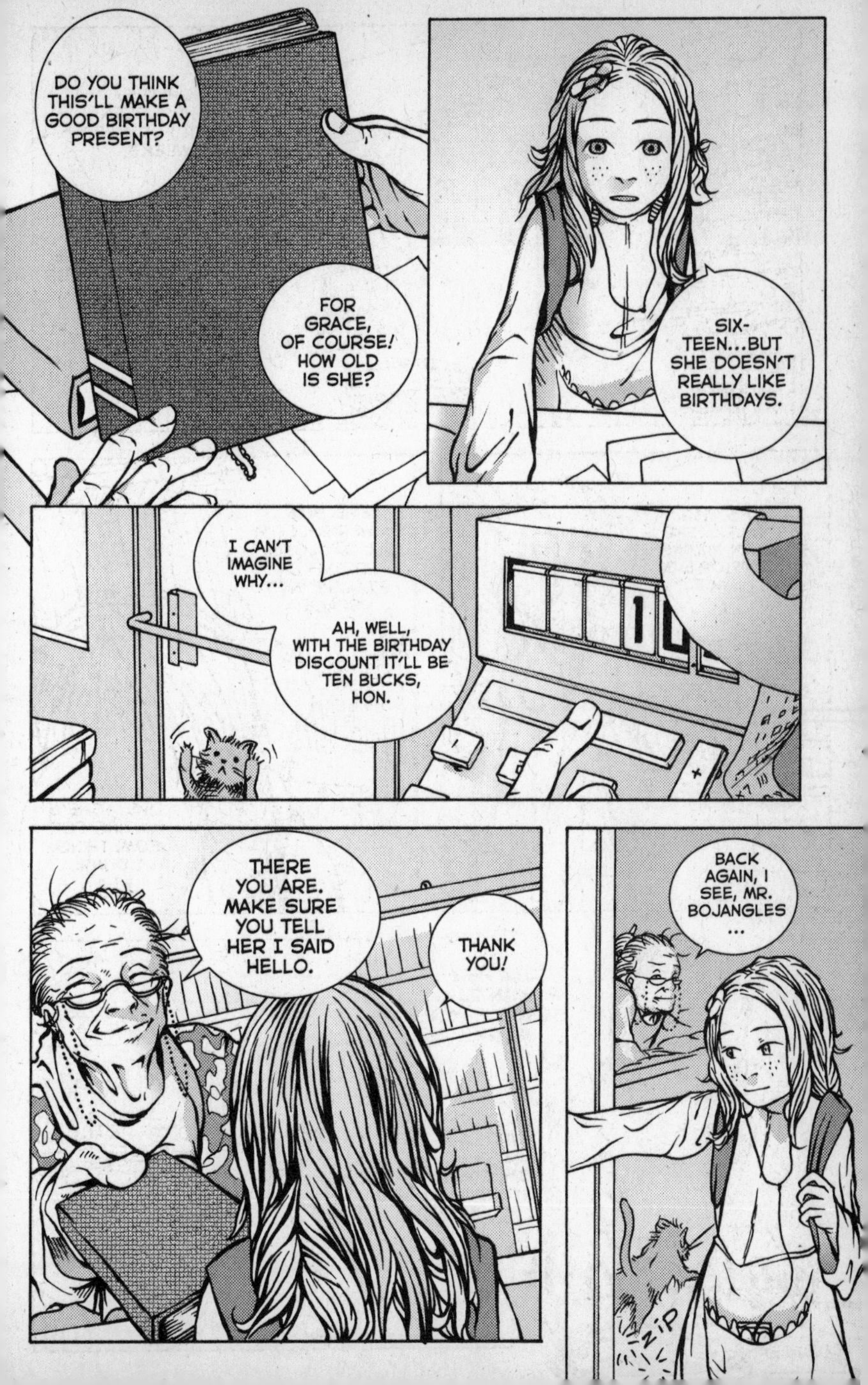
DO YOU THINK THIS'LL MAKE A GOOD BIRTHDAY PRESENT?
FOR GRACE, OF COURSE! HOW OLD IS SHE?
SIX-TEEN...BUT SHE DOESN'T REALLY LIKE BIRTHDAYS.
I CAN'T IMAGINE WHY...
AH, WELL, WITH THE BIRTHDAY DISCOUNT IT'LL BE TEN BUCKS, HON.
THERE YOU ARE. MAKE SURE YOU TELL HER I SAID HELLO.
THANK YOU!
BACK AGAIN, I SEE, MR. BOJANGLES ...
ZIP

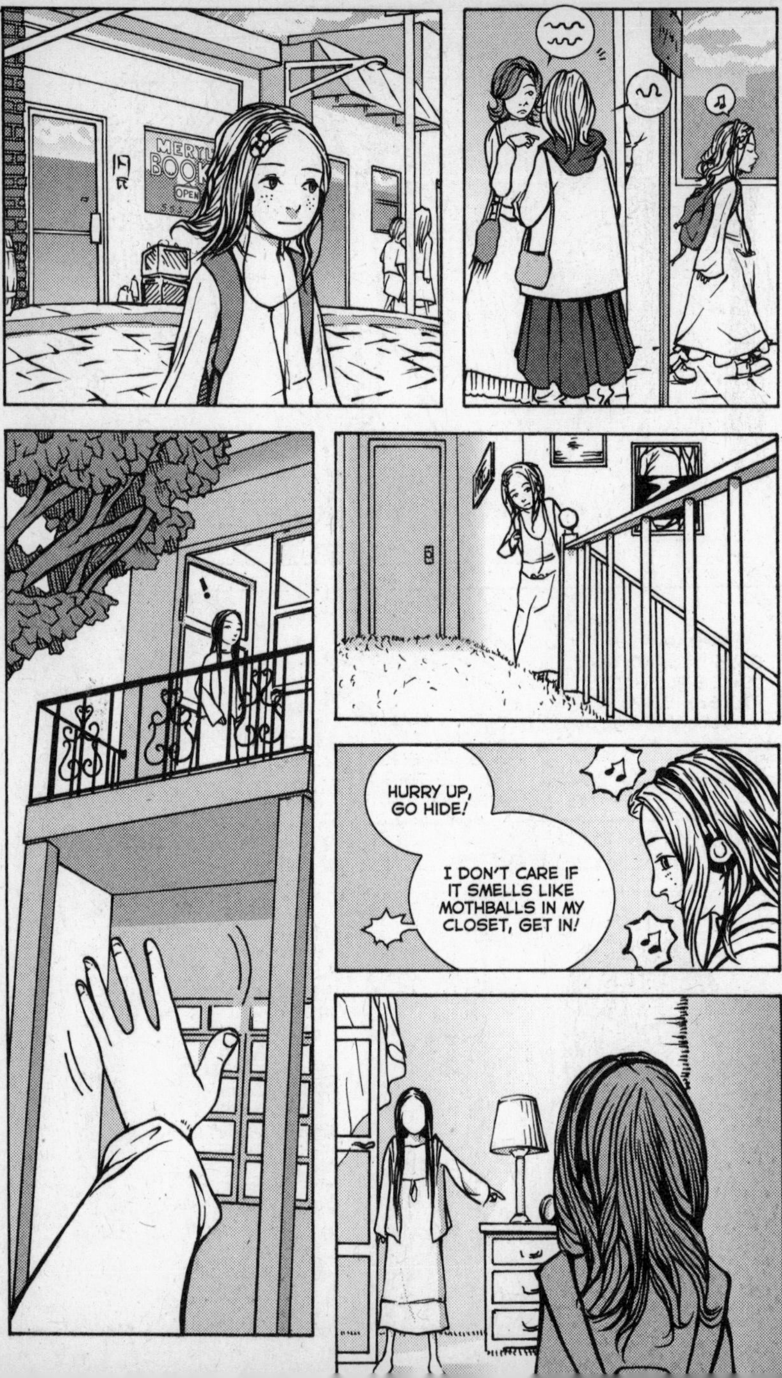
OPEN
HURRY UP, GO HIDE!
I DON'T CARE IF IT SMELLS LIKE MOTHBALLS IN MY CLOSET, GET IN!

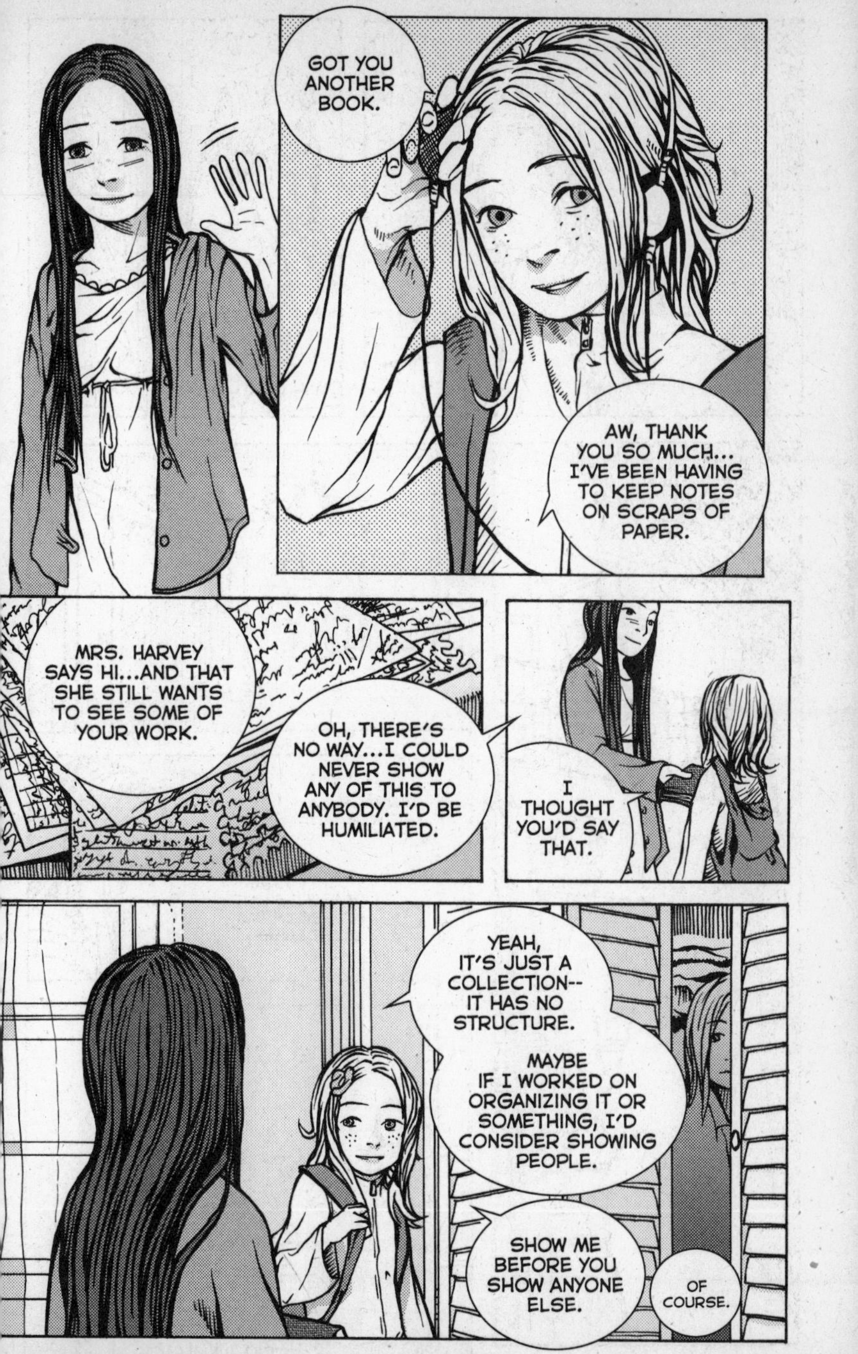
GOT YOU ANOTHER BOOK.
AW, THANK YOU SO MUCH... I'VE BEEN HAVING TO KEEP NOTES ON SCRAPS OF PAPER.
MRS. HARVEY SAYS HI...AND THAT SHE STILL WANTS TO SEE SOME OF YOUR WORK.
OH, THERE'S NO WAY...I COULD NEVER SHOW ANY OF THIS TO ANYBODY. I'D BE HUMILIATED.
I THOUGHT YOU'D SAY THAT.
YEAH, IT'S JUST A COLLECTION-- IT HAS NO STRUCTURE.
MAYBE IF I WORKED ON ORGANIZING IT OR SOMETHING, I'D CONSIDER SHOWING PEOPLE.
SHOW ME BEFORE YOU SHOW ANYONE ELSE.
OF COURSE.

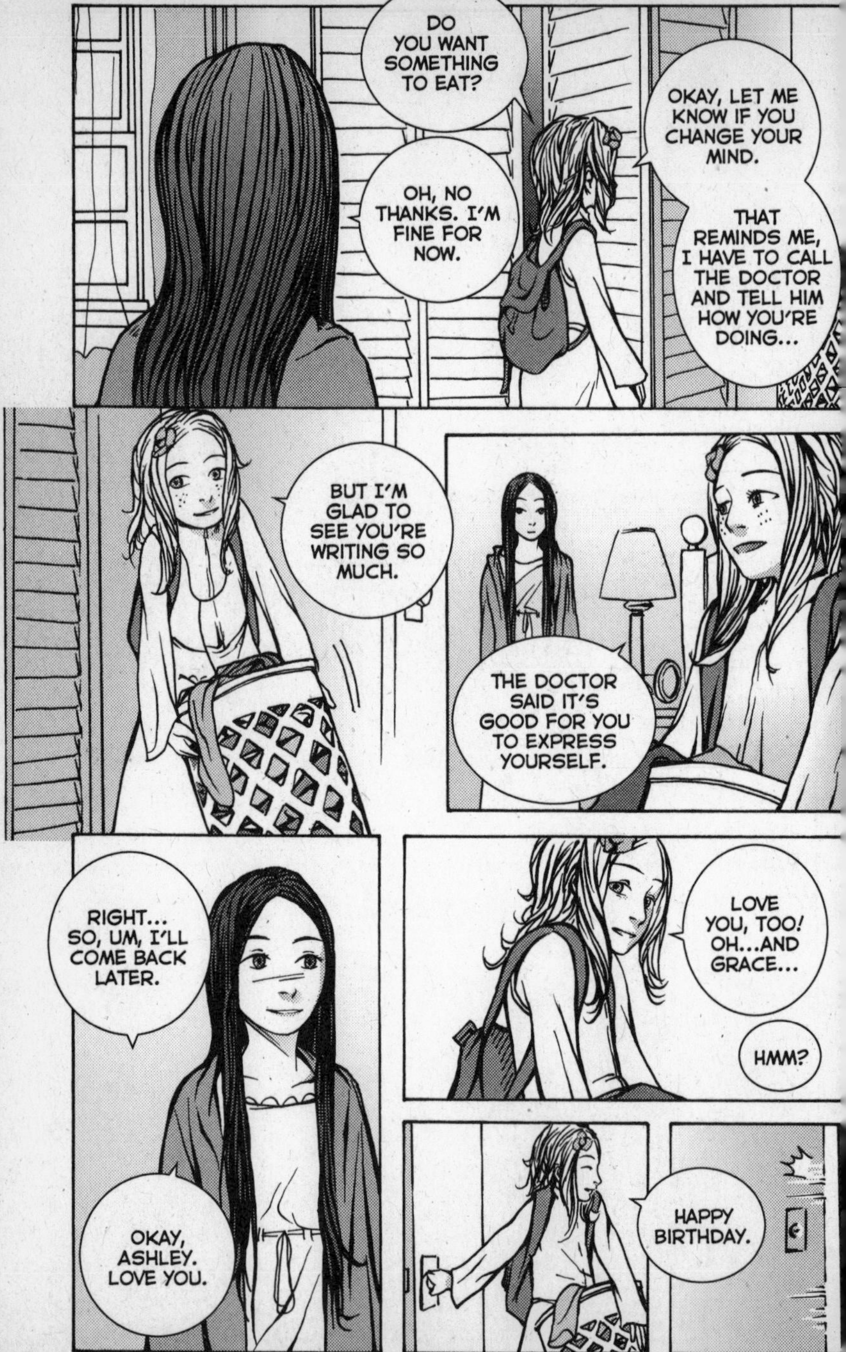
DO YOU WANT SOMETHING TO EAT?
OH, NO THANKS. I'M FINE FOR NOW.
OKAY, LET ME KNOW IF YOU CHANGE YOUR MIND.
THAT REMINDS ME, I HAVE TO CALL THE DOCTOR AND TELL HIM HOW YOU'RE DOING...
BUT I'M GLAD TO SEE YOU'RE WRITING SO MUCH.
THE DOCTOR SAID IT'S GOOD FOR YOU TO EXPRESS YOURSELF.
RIGHT... SO, UM, I'LL COME BACK LATER.
OKAY, ASHLEY. LOVE YOU.
LOVE YOU, TOO! OH...AND GRACE...
HMM?
HAPPY BIRTHDAY.

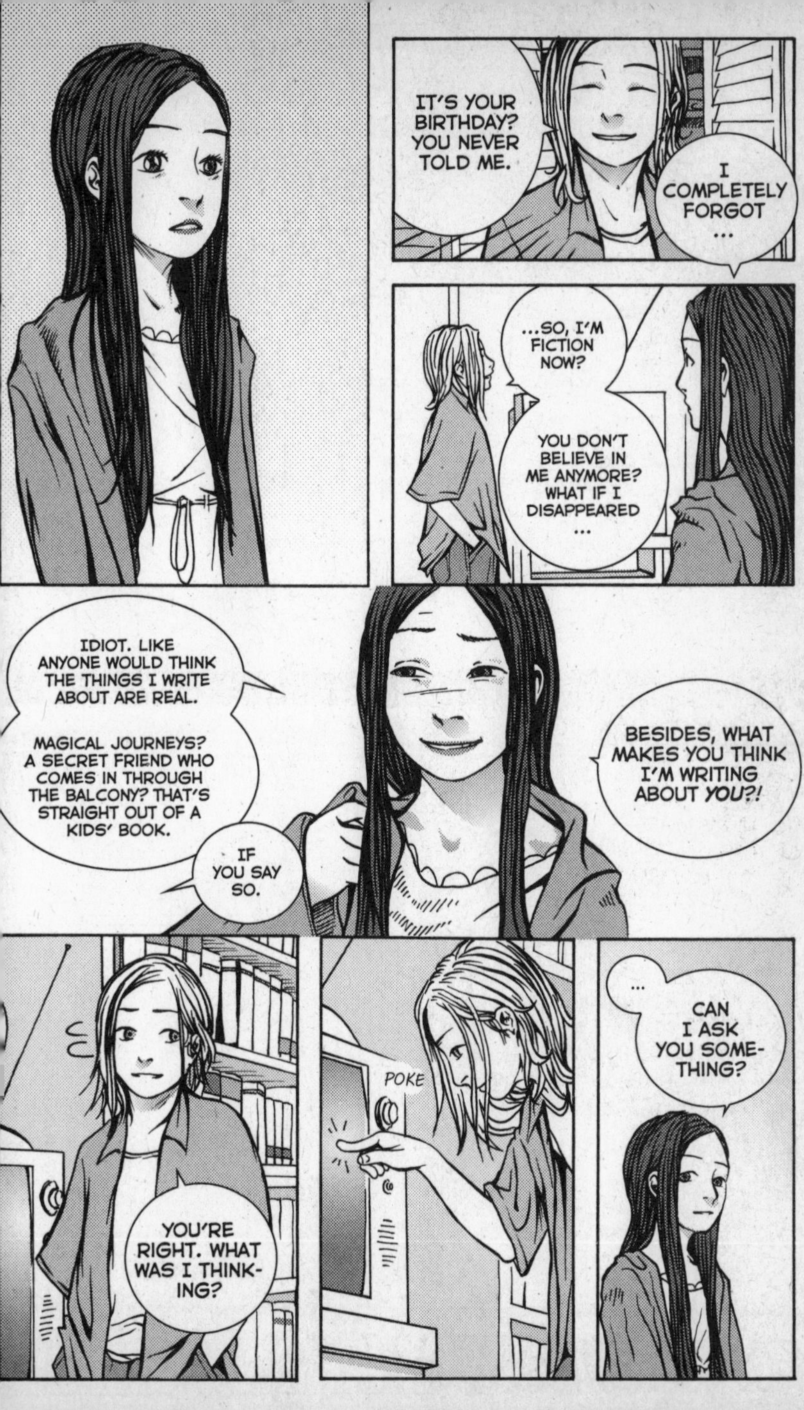
IT'S YOUR BIRTHDAY? YOU NEVER TOLD ME.
I COMPLETELY FORGOT ...
...SO, I'M FICTION NOW?
YOU DON'T BELIEVE IN ME ANYMORE? WHAT IF I DISAPPEARED ...
IDIOT. LIKE ANYONE WOULD THINK THE THINGS I WRITE ABOUT ARE REAL.
MAGICAL JOURNEYS? A SECRET FRIEND WHO COMES IN THROUGH THE BALCONY? THAT'S STRAIGHT OUT OF A KIDS' BOOK.
IF YOU SAY SO.
BESIDES, WHAT MAKES YOU THINK I'M WRITING ABOUT *YOU*?!
YOU'RE RIGHT. WHAT WAS I THINK-ING?
POKE
...
CAN I ASK YOU SOME-THING?

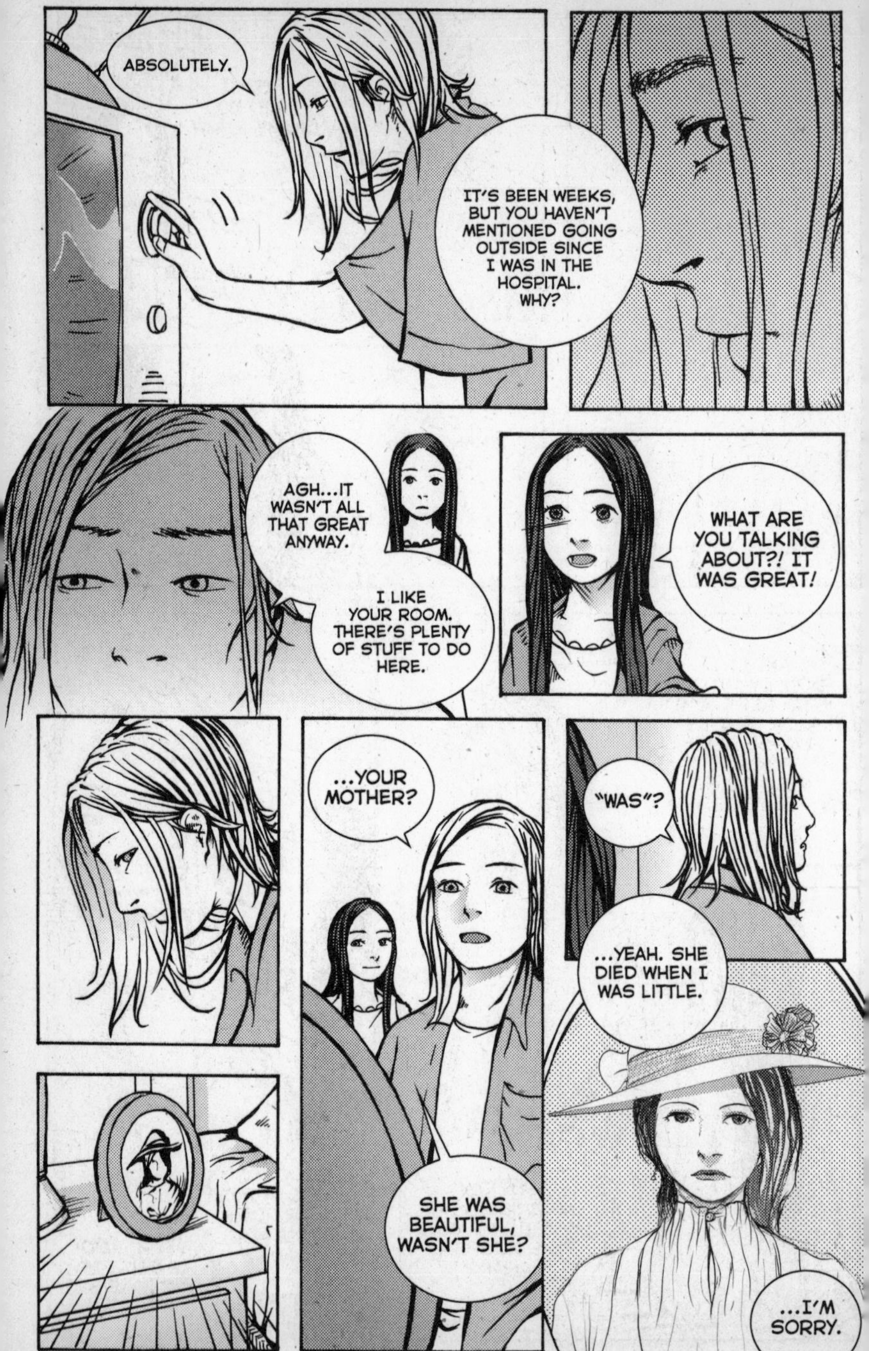
ABSOLUTELY.
IT'S BEEN WEEKS, BUT YOU HAVEN'T MENTIONED GOING OUTSIDE SINCE I WAS IN THE HOSPITAL. WHY?
AGH...IT WASN'T ALL THAT GREAT ANYWAY.
I LIKE YOUR ROOM. THERE'S PLENTY OF STUFF TO DO HERE.
WHAT ARE YOU TALKING ABOUT?! IT WAS GREAT!
...YOUR MOTHER?
"WAS"?
...YEAH. SHE DIED WHEN I WAS LITTLE.
SHE WAS BEAUTIFUL, WASN'T SHE?
...I'M SORRY.

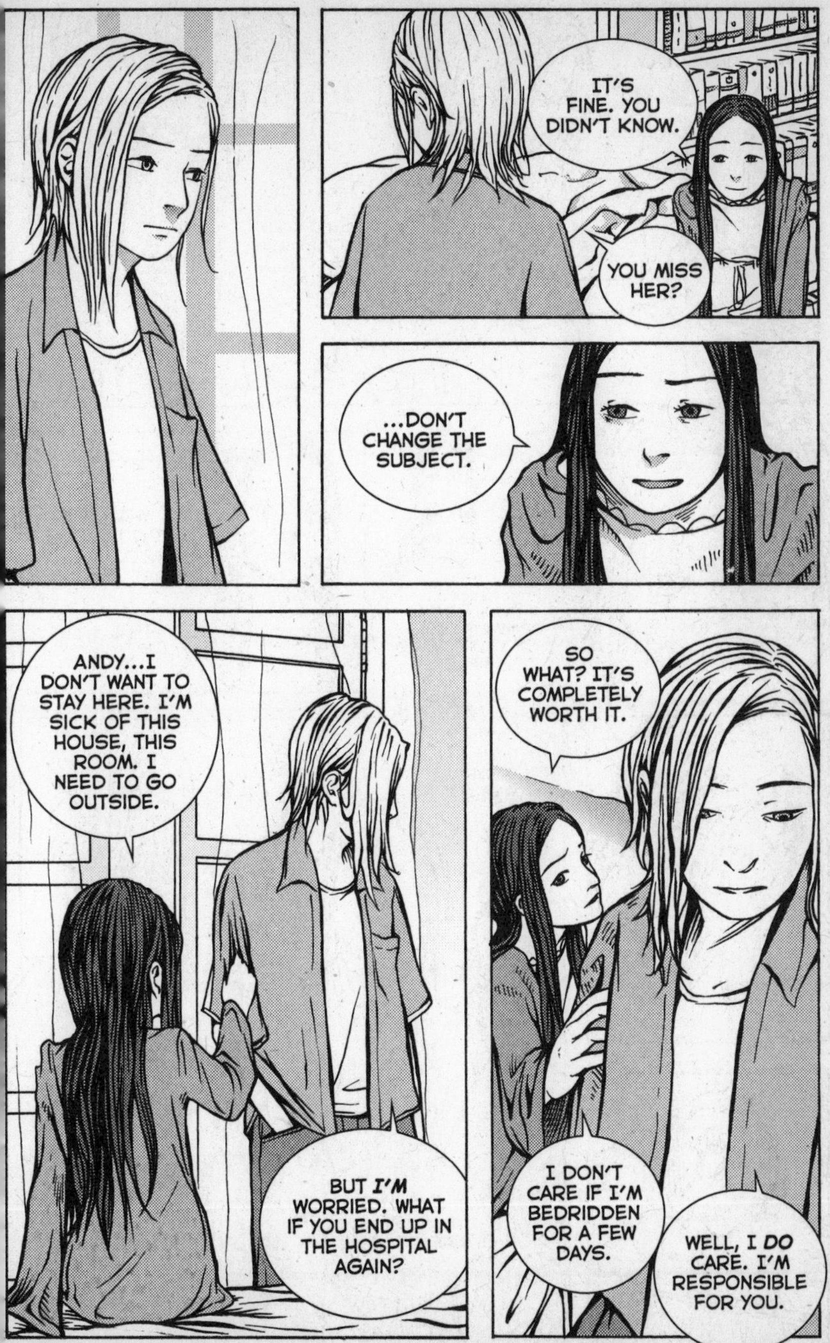
IT'S FINE. YOU DIDN'T KNOW.
YOU MISS HER?
...DON'T CHANGE THE SUBJECT.
ANDY...I DON'T WANT TO STAY HERE. I'M SICK OF THIS HOUSE, THIS ROOM. I NEED TO GO OUTSIDE.
BUT *I'M* WORRIED. WHAT IF YOU END UP IN THE HOSPITAL AGAIN?
SO WHAT? IT'S COMPLETELY WORTH IT.
I DON'T CARE IF I'M BEDRIDDEN FOR A FEW DAYS.
WELL, I *DO* CARE. I'M RESPONSIBLE FOR YOU.

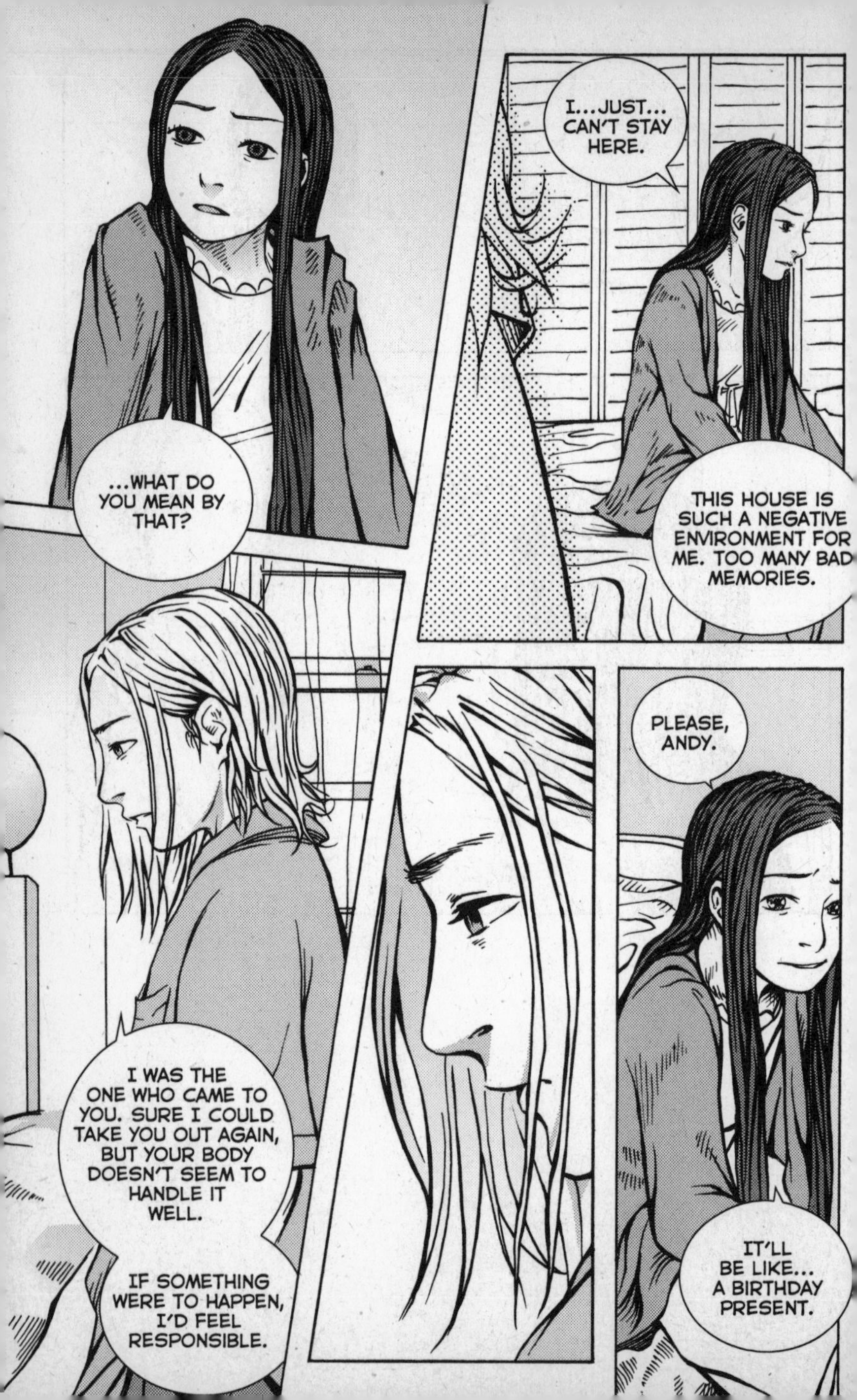
...WHAT DO YOU MEAN BY THAT?
I...JUST... CAN'T STAY HERE.
THIS HOUSE IS SUCH A NEGATIVE ENVIRONMENT FOR ME. TOO MANY BAD MEMORIES.
I WAS THE ONE WHO CAME TO YOU. SURE I COULD TAKE YOU OUT AGAIN, BUT YOUR BODY DOESN'T SEEM TO HANDLE IT WELL.
IF SOMETHING WERE TO HAPPEN, I'D FEEL RESPONSIBLE.
PLEASE, ANDY.
IT'LL BE LIKE... A BIRTHDAY PRESENT.

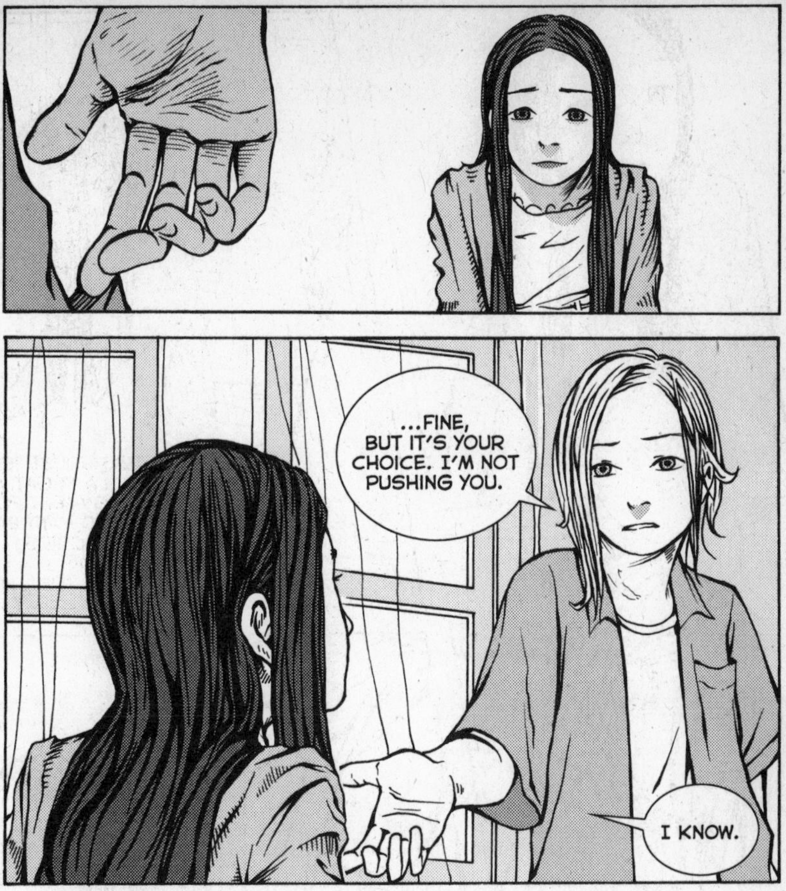
...FINE, BUT IT'S YOUR CHOICE. I'M NOT PUSHING YOU.
I KNOW.

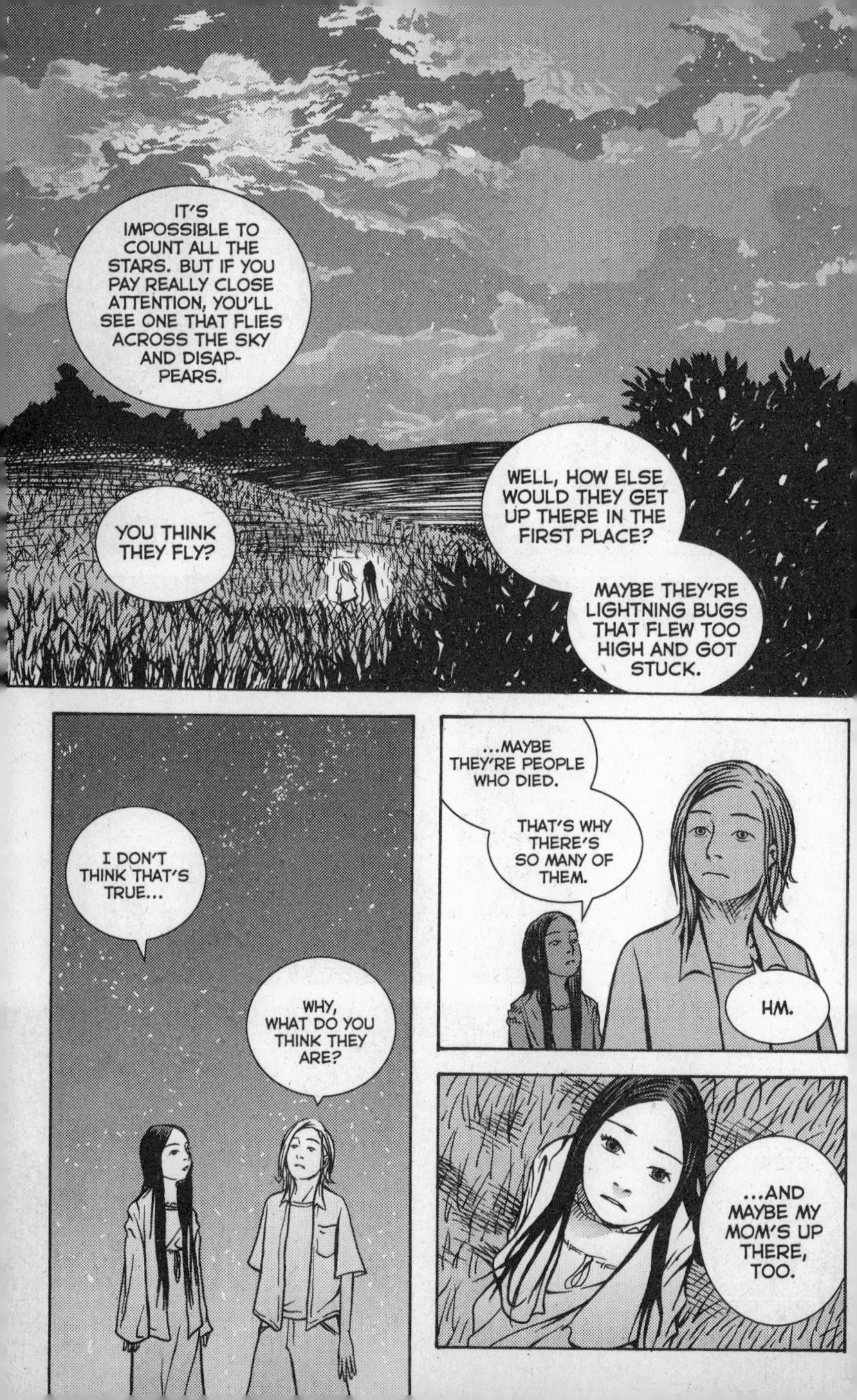
IT'S IMPOSSIBLE TO COUNT ALL THE STARS. BUT IF YOU PAY REALLY CLOSE ATTENTION, YOU'LL SEE ONE THAT FLIES ACROSS THE SKY AND DISAP-PEARS.
YOU THINK THEY FLY?
WELL, HOW ELSE WOULD THEY GET UP THERE IN THE FIRST PLACE?
MAYBE THEY'RE LIGHTNING BUGS THAT FLEW TOO HIGH AND GOT STUCK.
I DON'T THINK THAT'S TRUE...
WHY, WHAT DO YOU THINK THEY ARE?
...MAYBE THEY'RE PEOPLE WHO DIED.
THAT'S WHY THERE'S SO MANY OF THEM.
HM.
...AND MAYBE MY MOM'S UP THERE, TOO.

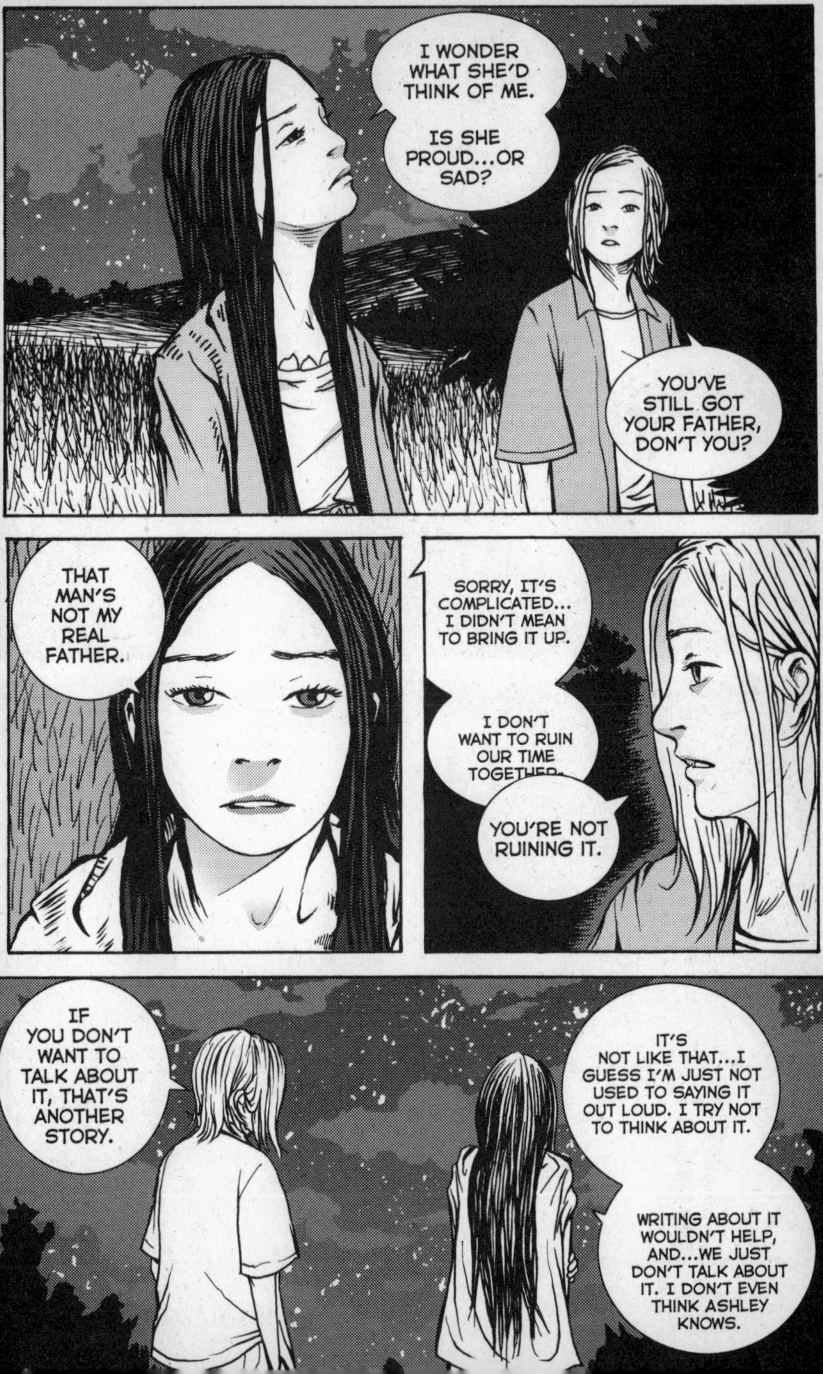
I WONDER WHAT SHE'D THINK OF ME.
IS SHE PROUD...OR SAD?
YOU'VE STILL GOT YOUR FATHER, DON'T YOU?
THAT MAN'S NOT MY REAL FATHER.
SORRY, IT'S COMPLICATED... I DIDN'T MEAN TO BRING IT UP.
I DON'T WANT TO RUIN OUR TIME TOGETHER.
YOU'RE NOT RUINING IT.
IF YOU DON'T WANT TO TALK ABOUT IT, THAT'S ANOTHER STORY.
IT'S NOT LIKE THAT...I GUESS I'M JUST NOT USED TO SAYING IT OUT LOUD. I TRY NOT TO THINK ABOUT IT.
WRITING ABOUT IT WOULDN'T HELP, AND...WE JUST DON'T TALK ABOUT IT. I DON'T EVEN THINK ASHLEY KNOWS.

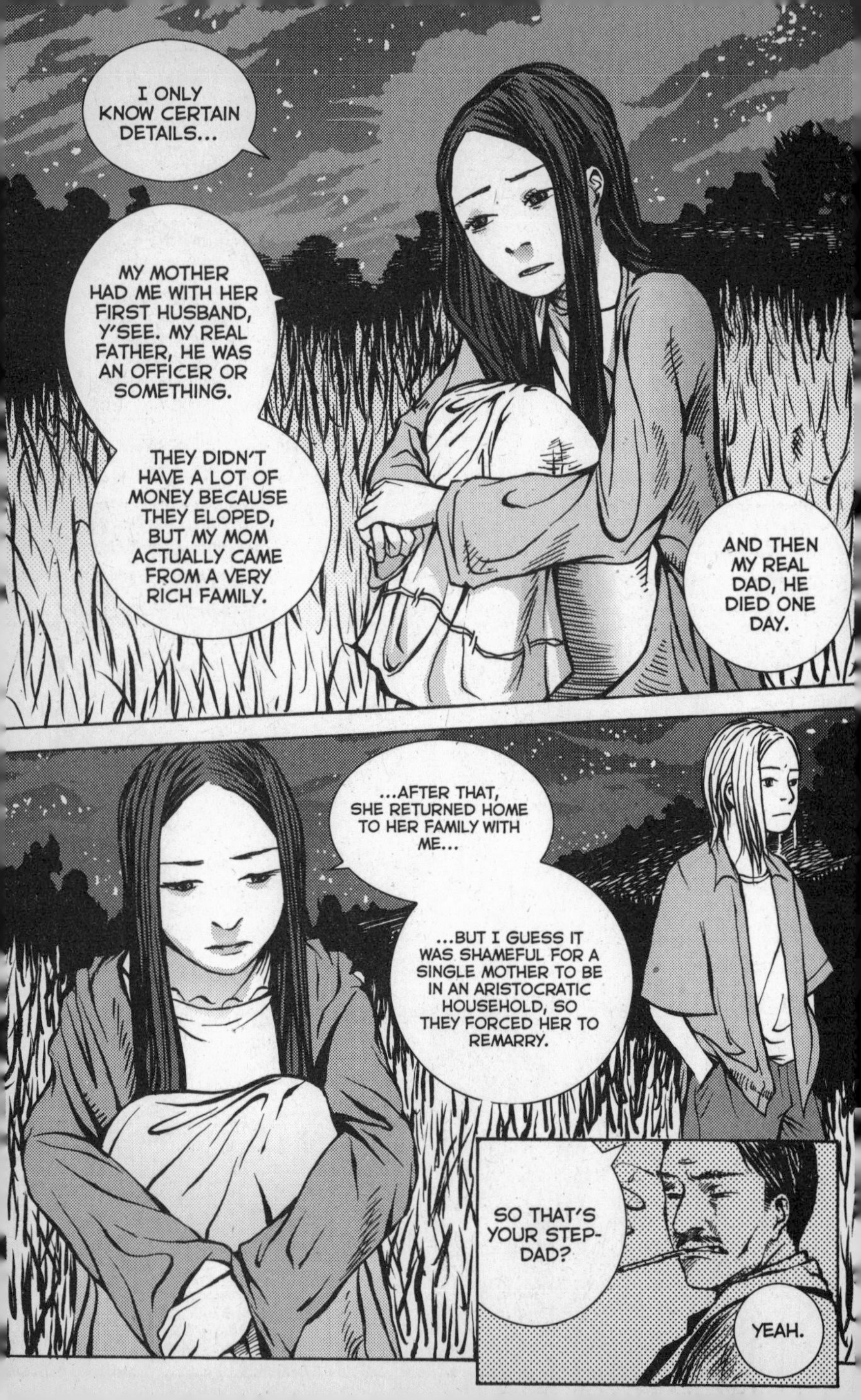
I ONLY KNOW CERTAIN DETAILS...
MY MOTHER HAD ME WITH HER FIRST HUSBAND, Y'SEE. MY REAL FATHER, HE WAS AN OFFICER OR SOMETHING.
THEY DIDN'T HAVE A LOT OF MONEY BECAUSE THEY ELOPED, BUT MY MOM ACTUALLY CAME FROM A VERY RICH FAMILY.
AND THEN MY REAL DAD, HE DIED ONE DAY.
...AFTER THAT, SHE RETURNED HOME TO HER FAMILY WITH ME...
...BUT I GUESS IT WAS SHAMEFUL FOR A SINGLE MOTHER TO BE IN AN ARISTOCRATIC HOUSEHOLD, SO THEY FORCED HER TO REMARRY.
SO THAT'S YOUR STEP-DAD?
YEAH.

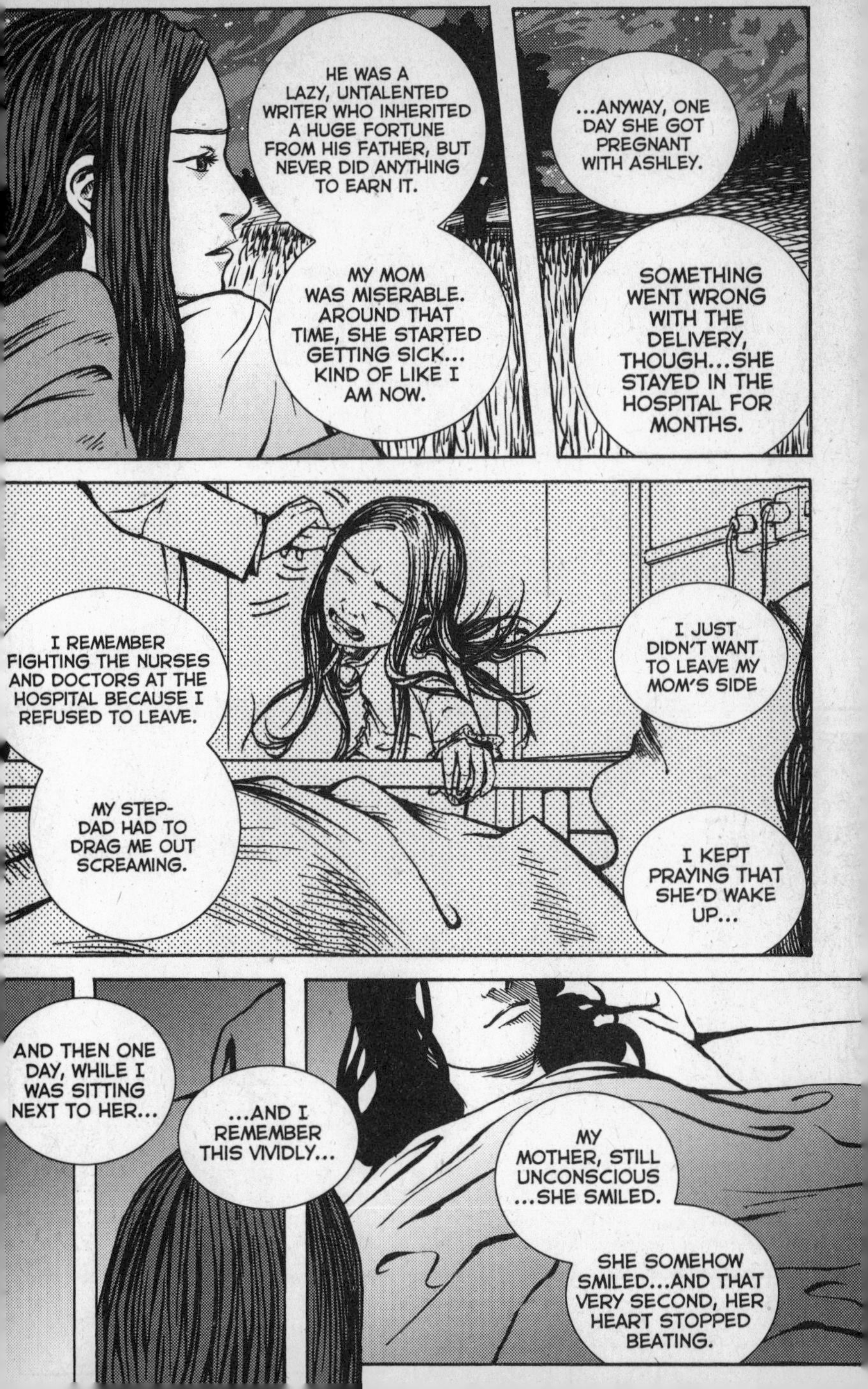
HE WAS A LAZY, UNTALENTED WRITER WHO INHERITED A HUGE FORTUNE FROM HIS FATHER, BUT NEVER DID ANYTHING TO EARN IT.
MY MOM WAS MISERABLE. AROUND THAT TIME, SHE STARTED GETTING SICK... KIND OF LIKE I AM NOW.
...ANYWAY, ONE DAY SHE GOT PREGNANT WITH ASHLEY.
SOMETHING WENT WRONG WITH THE DELIVERY, THOUGH...SHE STAYED IN THE HOSPITAL FOR MONTHS.
I REMEMBER FIGHTING THE NURSES AND DOCTORS AT THE HOSPITAL BECAUSE I REFUSED TO LEAVE.
MY STEP-DAD HAD TO DRAG ME OUT SCREAMING.
I JUST DIDN'T WANT TO LEAVE MY MOM'S SIDE
I KEPT PRAYING THAT SHE'D WAKE UP...
AND THEN ONE DAY, WHILE I WAS SITTING NEXT TO HER...
...AND I REMEMBER THIS VIVIDLY...
MY MOTHER, STILL UNCONSCIOUS ...SHE SMILED.
SHE SOMEHOW SMILED...AND THAT VERY SECOND, HER HEART STOPPED BEATING.

I NEVER UNDERSTOOD WHY, THOUGH.

THE DOCTORS SAID SHE WAS HAVING A PLEASANT DREAM AND THAT SHE DIED PEACEFULLY...BUT IT JUST DIDN'T MAKE SENSE.

AND THEN I BECAME SICK, TOO.

SO MY STEP-DAD INHERITED TONS OF MONEY AFTER HER DEATH, AND I'VE BEEN SICK EVER SINCE.

THE REST OF THE FAMILY AVOIDS US BECAUSE THEY THINK THEY'LL CATCH IT, TOO.

ASHLEY'S THE ONLY ONE WHO COMES NEAR ME THESE DAYS.

SHE DOESN'T EVEN KNOW I'M ONLY HER HALF-SISTER.

I DON'T THINK SHE WOULD CARE.

...YOU'RE PROBABLY RIGHT.

SHE'S TOO SWEET FOR HER OWN GOOD.

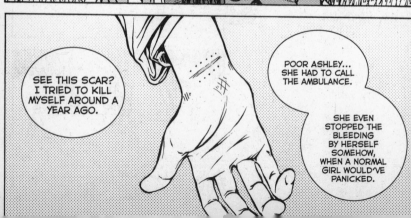

SEE THIS SCAR? I TRIED TO KILL MYSELF AROUND A YEAR AGO.

POOR ASHLEY... SHE HAD TO CALL THE AMBULANCE.

SHE EVEN STOPPED THE BLEEDING BY HERSELF SOMEHOW, WHEN A NORMAL GIRL WOULD'VE PANICKED.

...AND I'VE BEEN STUCK IN MY ROOM EVER SINCE, WITH ALL THESE MEMORIES HAUNTING ME.

I HAVE EVERY DETAIL OF THAT ROOM MEMORIZED.

I WRITE TO DISTRACT MYSELF...

...SOMETIMES IT'S BETTER NOT TO RUN AWAY, THOUGH.

I'M WORRIED MY VISITS WILL DO MORE HARM THAN GOOD.

YOU SEE WHY I WANT TO BE OUT HERE WITH YOU?

ANDY, YOU'VE GIVEN ME SUCH AN AMAZING GIFT.

THERE'S NO NEGATIVE TO THIS.

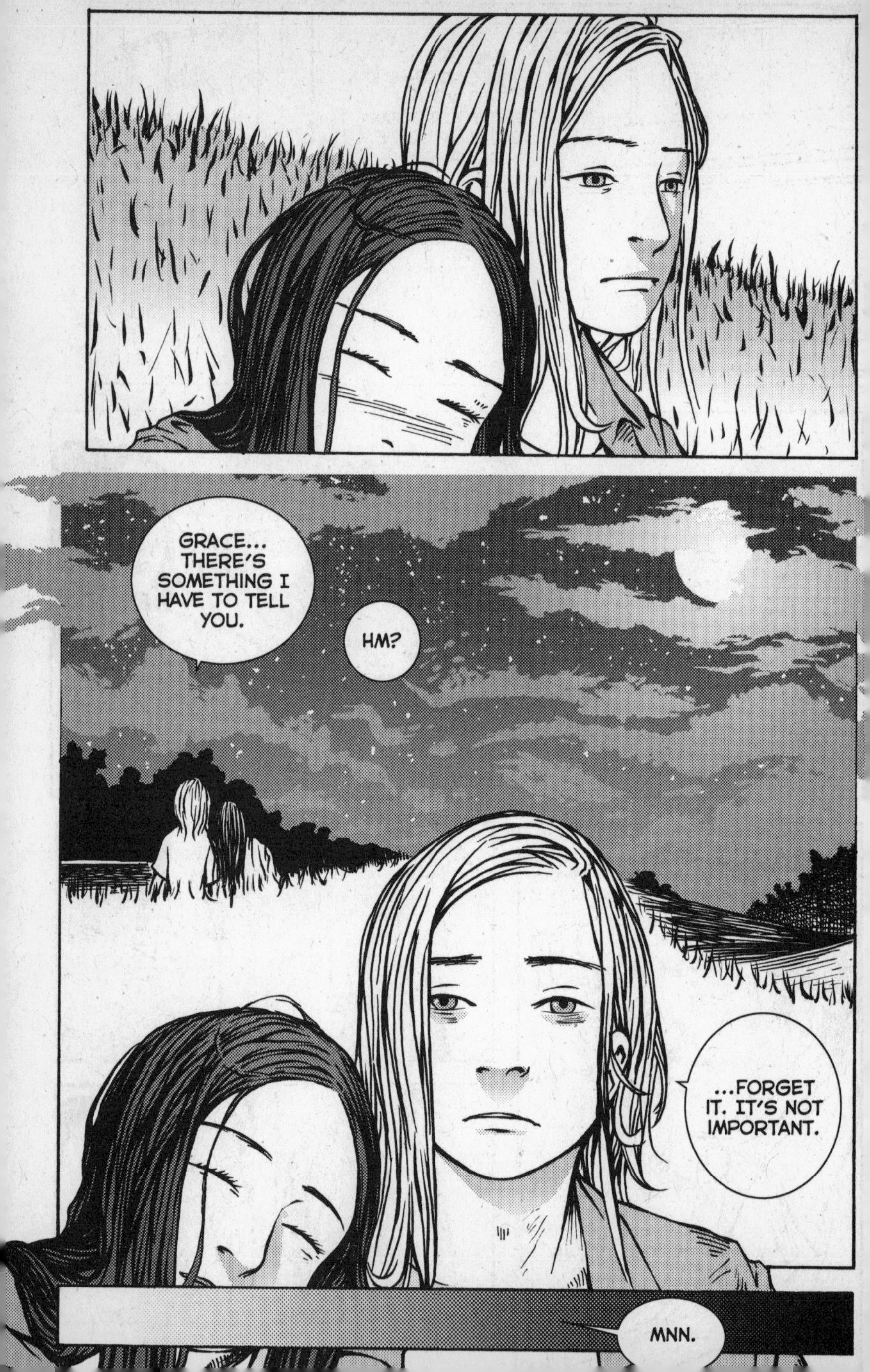
GRACE... THERE'S SOMETHING I HAVE TO TELL YOU.
HM?
...FORGET IT. IT'S NOT IMPORTANT.
MNN.

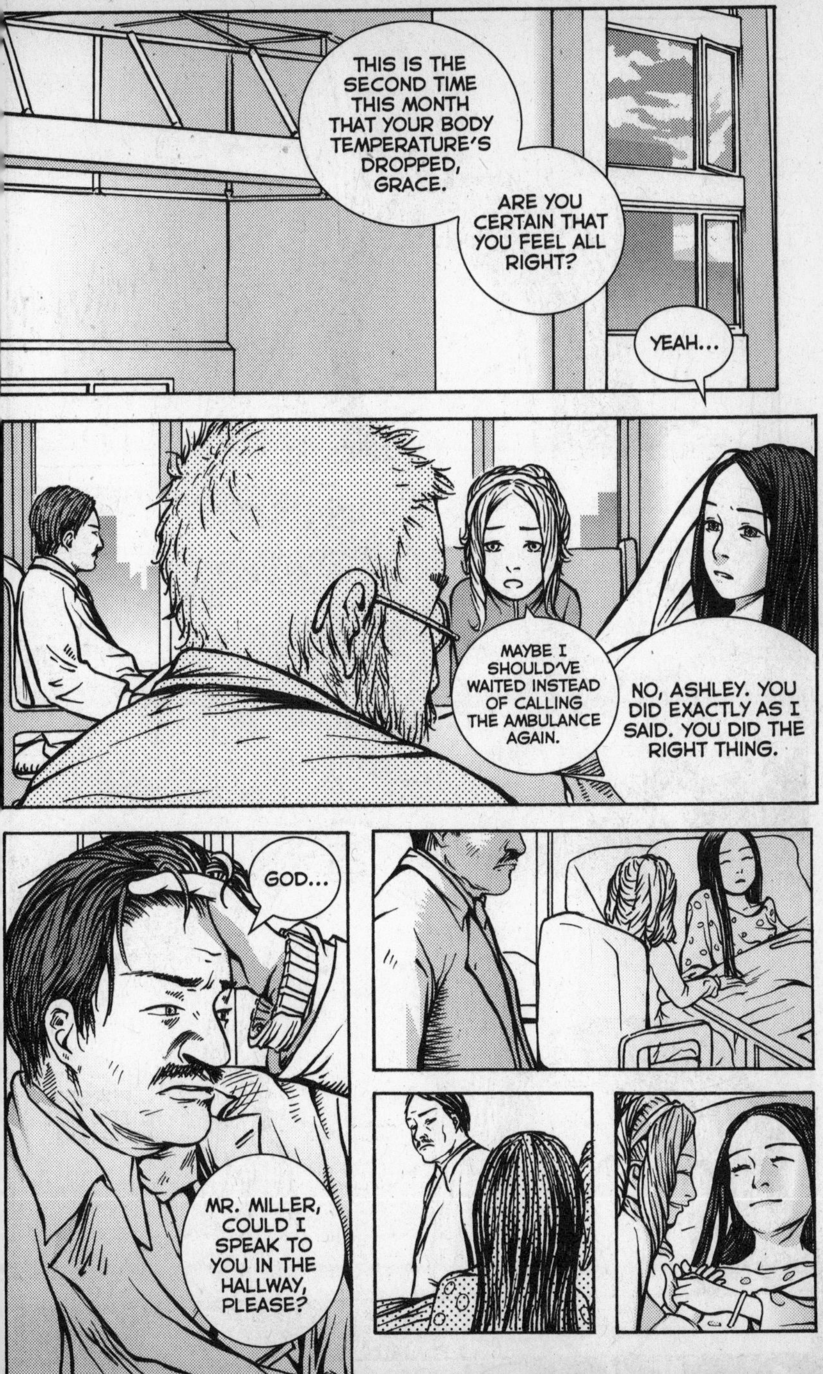
THIS IS THE SECOND TIME THIS MONTH THAT YOUR BODY TEMPERATURE'S DROPPED, GRACE.
ARE YOU CERTAIN THAT YOU FEEL ALL RIGHT?
YEAH...
MAYBE I SHOULD'VE WAITED INSTEAD OF CALLING THE AMBULANCE AGAIN.
NO, ASHLEY. YOU DID EXACTLY AS I SAID. YOU DID THE RIGHT THING.
GOD...
MR. MILLER, COULD I SPEAK TO YOU IN THE HALLWAY, PLEASE?

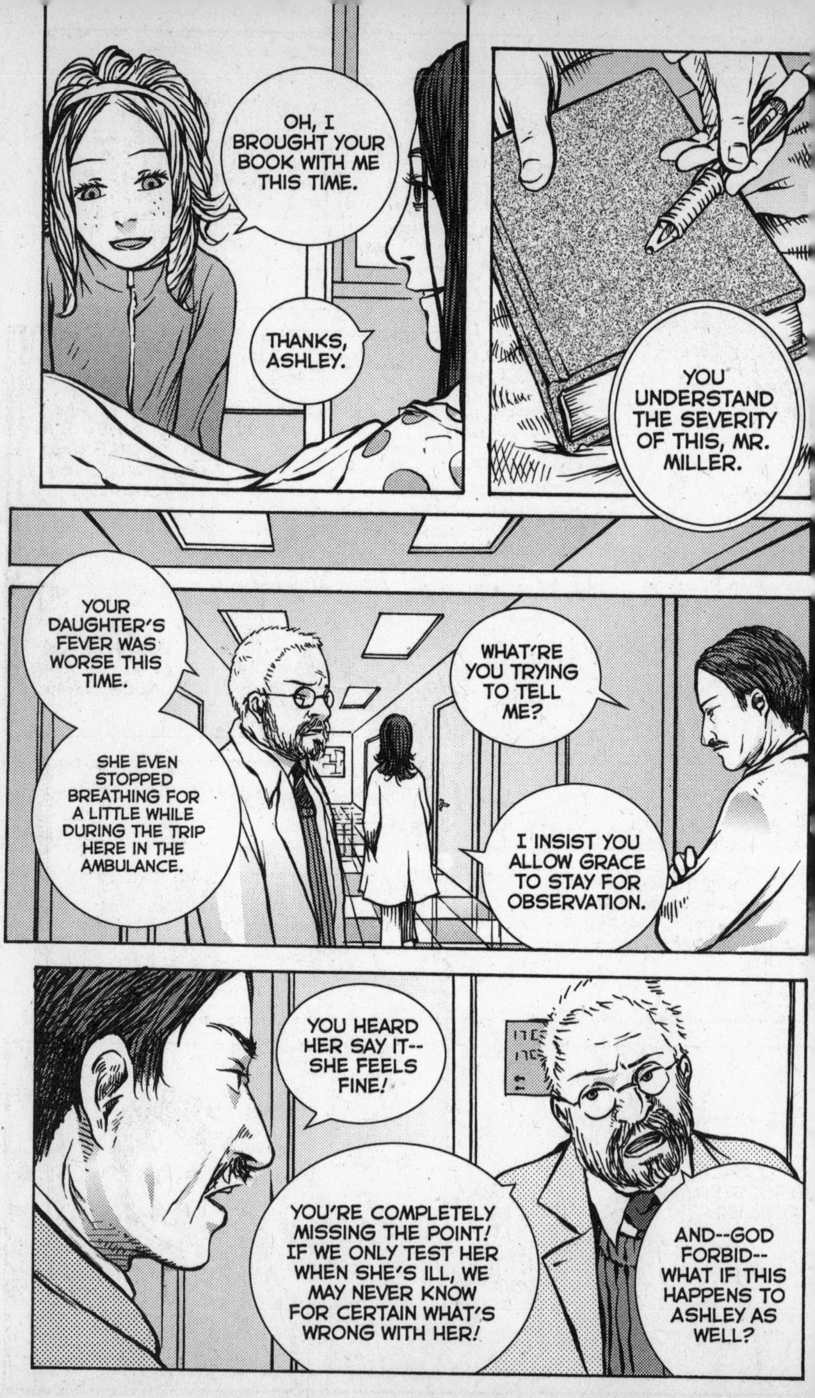
OH, I BROUGHT YOUR BOOK WITH ME THIS TIME.
THANKS, ASHLEY.
YOU UNDERSTAND THE SEVERITY OF THIS, MR. MILLER.
YOUR DAUGHTER'S FEVER WAS WORSE THIS TIME.
SHE EVEN STOPPED BREATHING FOR A LITTLE WHILE DURING THE TRIP HERE IN THE AMBULANCE.
WHAT'RE YOU TRYING TO TELL ME?
I INSIST YOU ALLOW GRACE TO STAY FOR OBSERVATION.
YOU HEARD HER SAY IT-- SHE FEELS FINE!
YOU'RE COMPLETELY MISSING THE POINT! IF WE ONLY TEST HER WHEN SHE'S ILL, WE MAY NEVER KNOW FOR CERTAIN WHAT'S WRONG WITH HER!
AND--GOD FORBID-- WHAT IF THIS HAPPENS TO ASHLEY AS WELL?

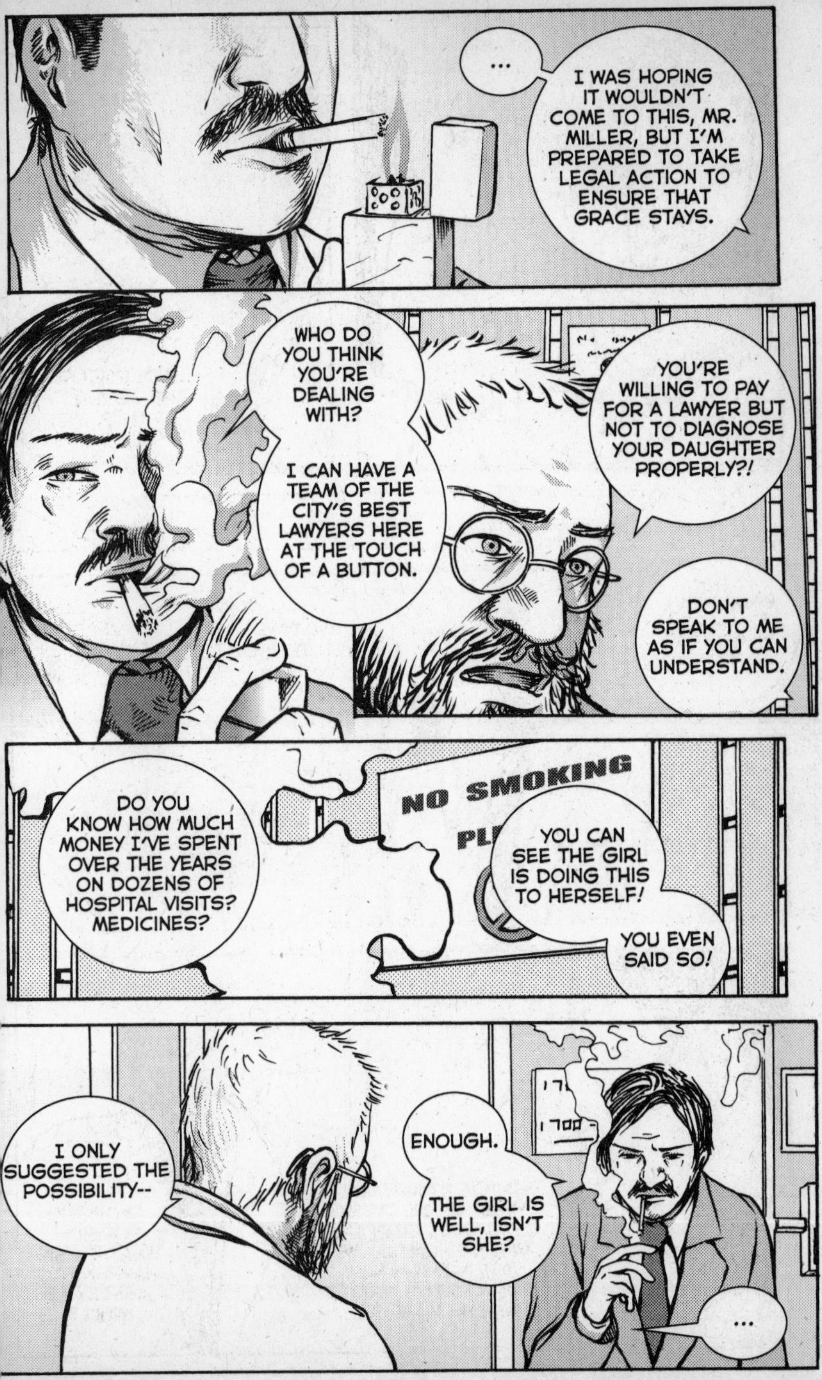
...
I WAS HOPING IT WOULDN'T COME TO THIS, MR. MILLER, BUT I'M PREPARED TO TAKE LEGAL ACTION TO ENSURE THAT GRACE STAYS.
WHO DO YOU THINK YOU'RE DEALING WITH?
I CAN HAVE A TEAM OF THE CITY'S BEST LAWYERS HERE AT THE TOUCH OF A BUTTON.
YOU'RE WILLING TO PAY FOR A LAWYER BUT NOT TO DIAGNOSE YOUR DAUGHTER PROPERLY?!
DON'T SPEAK TO ME AS IF YOU CAN UNDERSTAND.
DO YOU KNOW HOW MUCH MONEY I'VE SPENT OVER THE YEARS ON DOZENS OF HOSPITAL VISITS? MEDICINES?
NO SMOKING
YOU CAN SEE THE GIRL IS DOING THIS TO HERSELF!
YOU EVEN SAID SO!
I ONLY SUGGESTED THE POSSIBILITY--
ENOUGH.
THE GIRL IS WELL, ISN'T SHE?
...

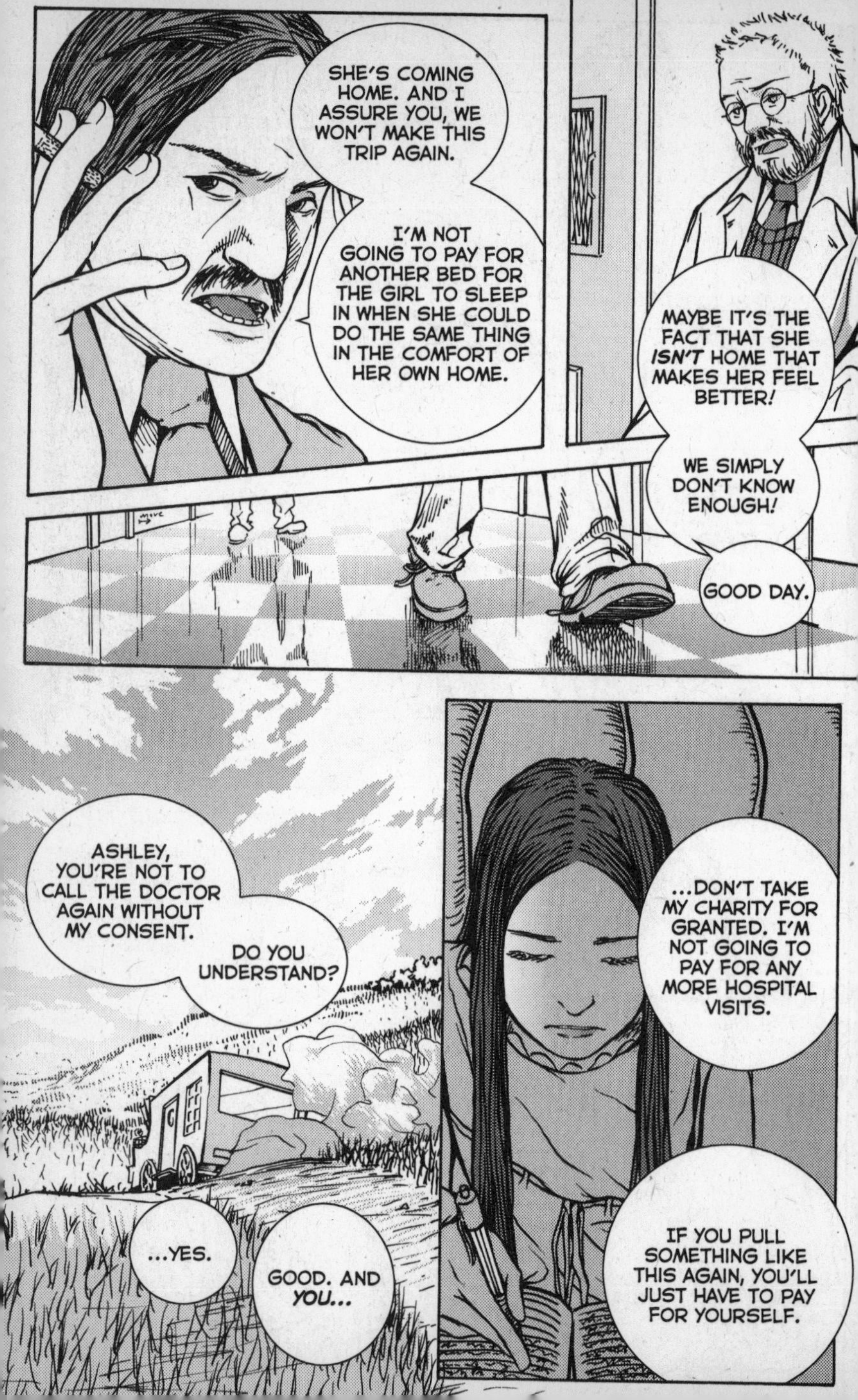
SHE'S COMING HOME. AND I ASSURE YOU, WE WON'T MAKE THIS TRIP AGAIN.
I'M NOT GOING TO PAY FOR ANOTHER BED FOR THE GIRL TO SLEEP IN WHEN SHE COULD DO THE SAME THING IN THE COMFORT OF HER OWN HOME.
MAYBE IT'S THE FACT THAT SHE *ISN'T* HOME THAT MAKES HER FEEL BETTER!
WE SIMPLY DON'T KNOW ENOUGH!
GOOD DAY.
ASHLEY, YOU'RE NOT TO CALL THE DOCTOR AGAIN WITHOUT MY CONSENT.
DO YOU UNDERSTAND?
...YES.
GOOD. AND *YOU*...
...DON'T TAKE MY CHARITY FOR GRANTED. I'M NOT GOING TO PAY FOR ANY MORE HOSPITAL VISITS.
IF YOU PULL SOMETHING LIKE THIS AGAIN, YOU'LL JUST HAVE TO PAY FOR YOURSELF.

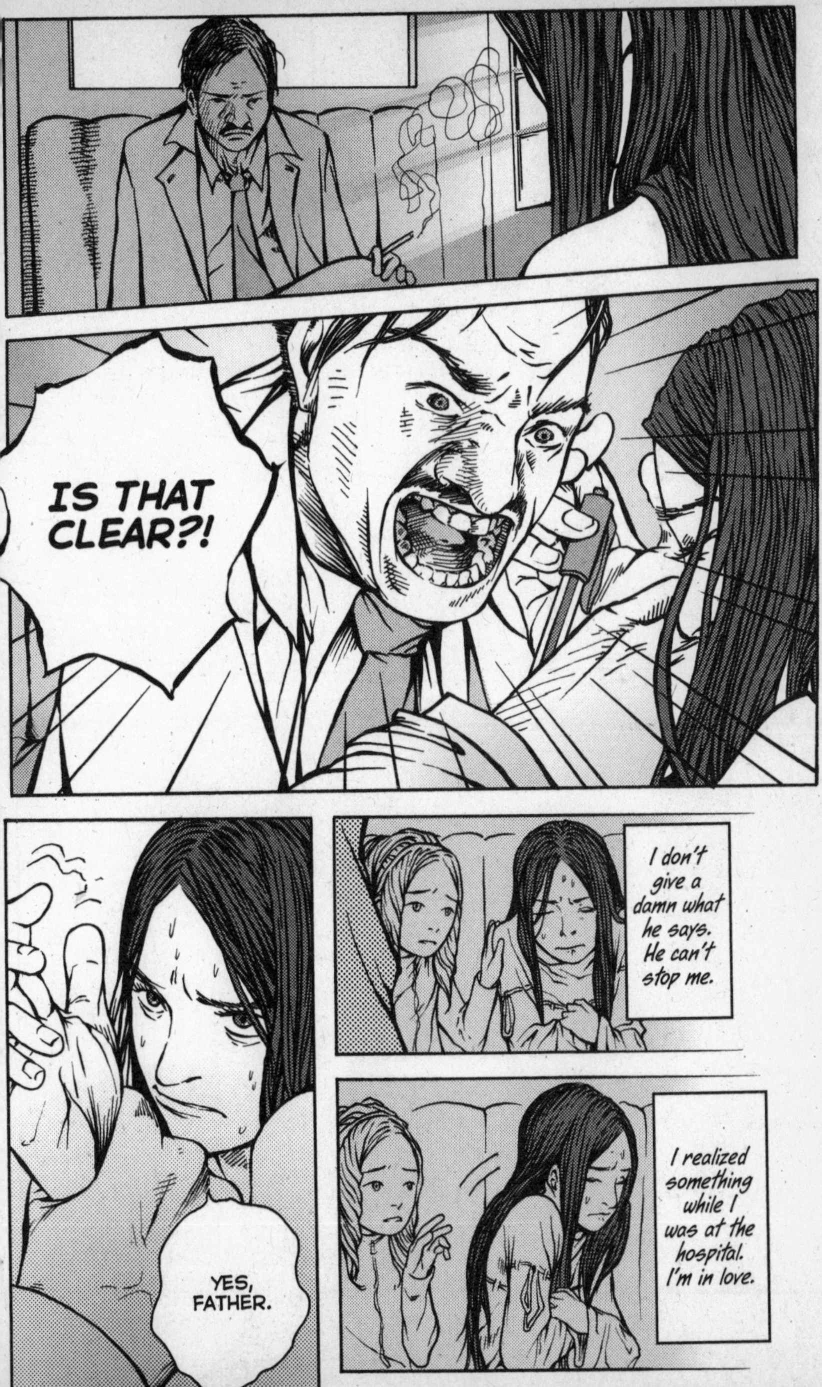
IS THAT CLEAR?!
YES, FATHER.
I don't give a damn what he says. He can't stop me.
I realized something while I was at the hospital. I'm in love.

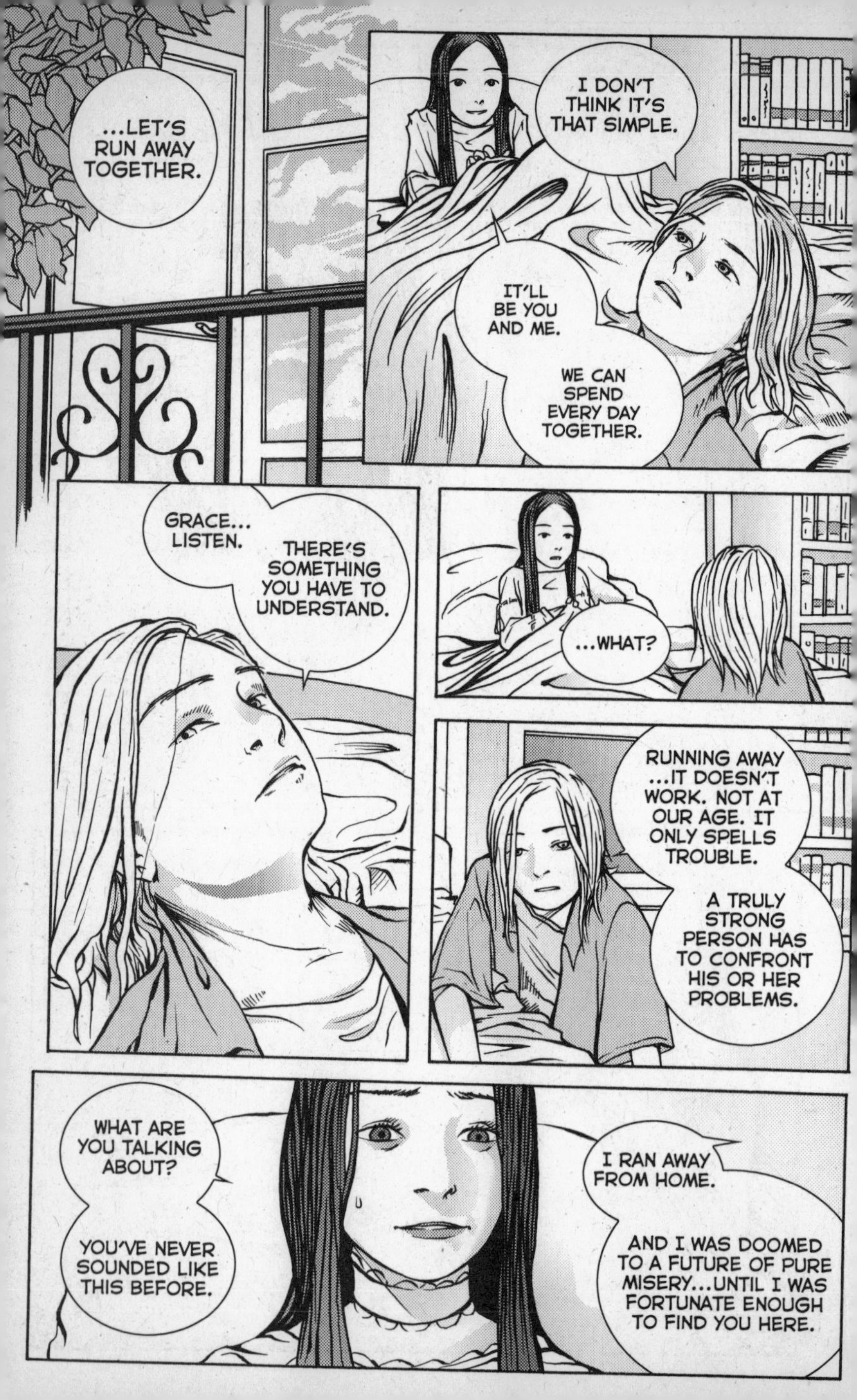
...LET'S RUN AWAY TOGETHER.
I DON'T THINK IT'S THAT SIMPLE.
IT'LL BE YOU AND ME.
WE CAN SPEND EVERY DAY TOGETHER.
GRACE... LISTEN.
THERE'S SOMETHING YOU HAVE TO UNDERSTAND.
...WHAT?
RUNNING AWAY ...IT DOESN'T WORK. NOT AT OUR AGE. IT ONLY SPELLS TROUBLE.
A TRULY STRONG PERSON HAS TO CONFRONT HIS OR HER PROBLEMS.
WHAT ARE YOU TALKING ABOUT?
YOU'VE NEVER SOUNDED LIKE THIS BEFORE.
I RAN AWAY FROM HOME.
AND I WAS DOOMED TO A FUTURE OF PURE MISERY...UNTIL I WAS FORTUNATE ENOUGH TO FIND YOU HERE.

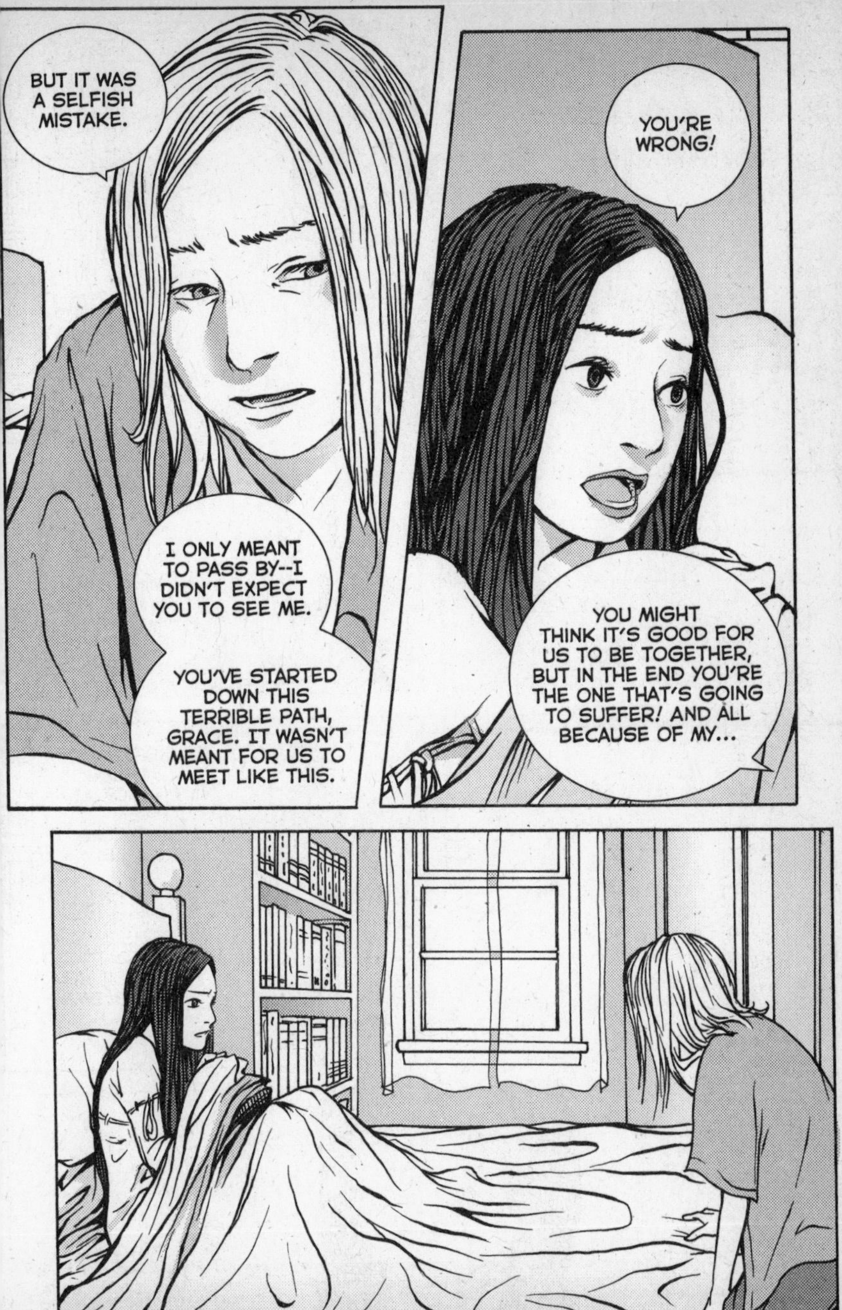
BUT IT WAS A SELFISH MISTAKE.
I ONLY MEANT TO PASS BY--I DIDN'T EXPECT YOU TO SEE ME.
YOU'VE STARTED DOWN THIS TERRIBLE PATH, GRACE. IT WASN'T MEANT FOR US TO MEET LIKE THIS.
YOU'RE WRONG!
YOU MIGHT THINK IT'S GOOD FOR US TO BE TOGETHER, BUT IN THE END YOU'RE THE ONE THAT'S GOING TO SUFFER! AND ALL BECAUSE OF MY...

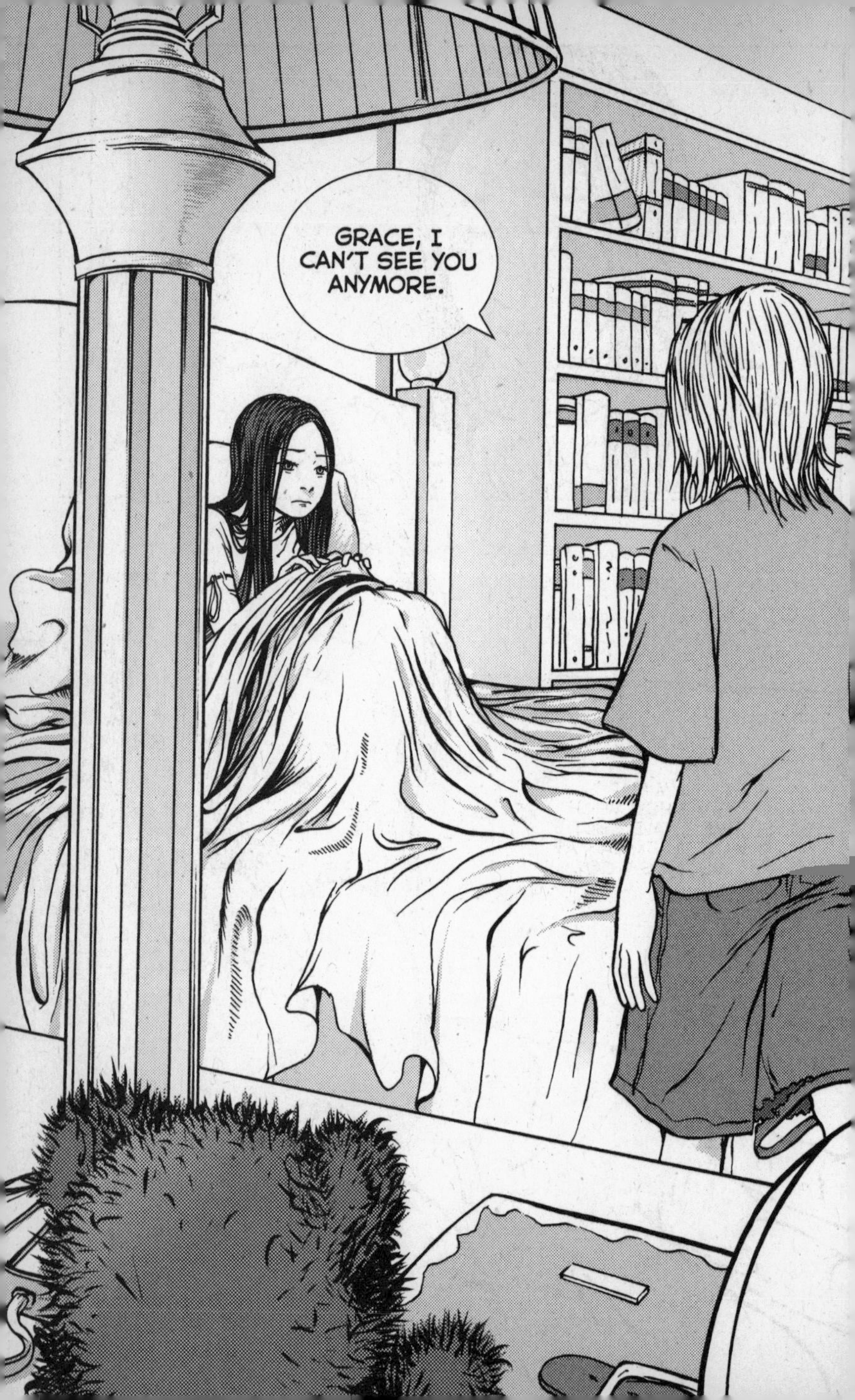
GRACE, I CAN'T SEE YOU ANYMORE.

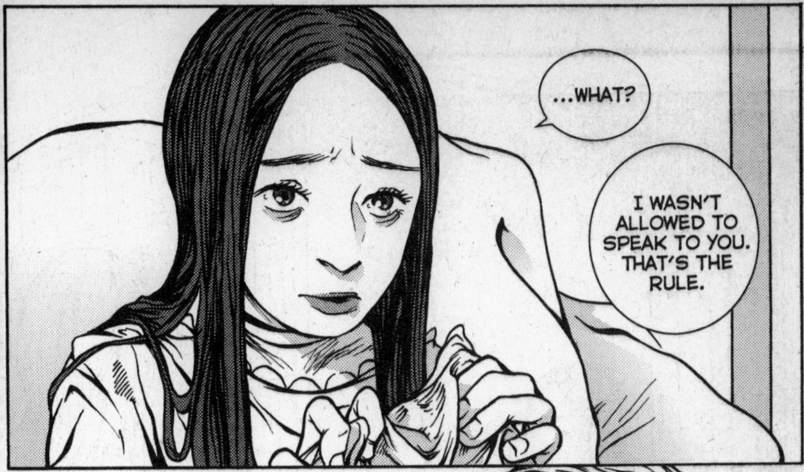
...WHAT?
I WASN'T ALLOWED TO SPEAK TO YOU. THAT'S THE RULE.
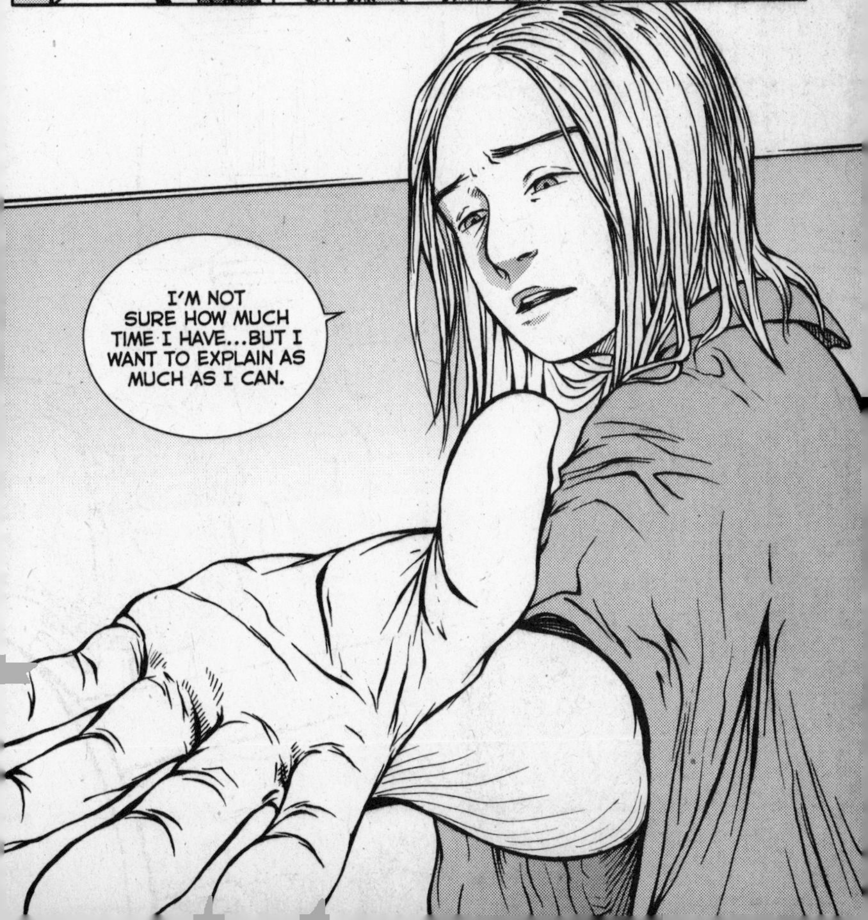
I'M NOT SURE HOW MUCH TIME I HAVE...BUT I WANT TO EXPLAIN AS MUCH AS I CAN.

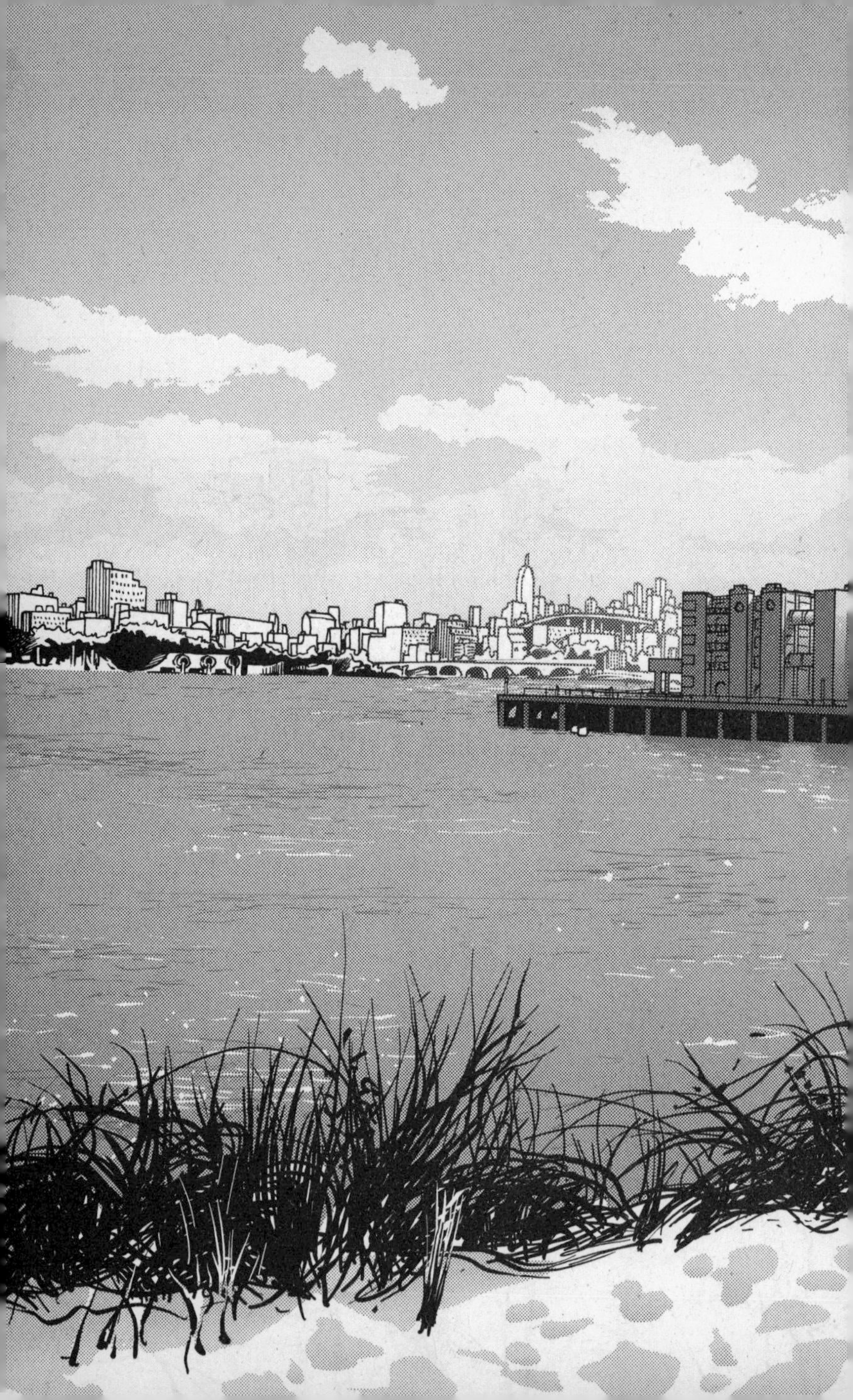

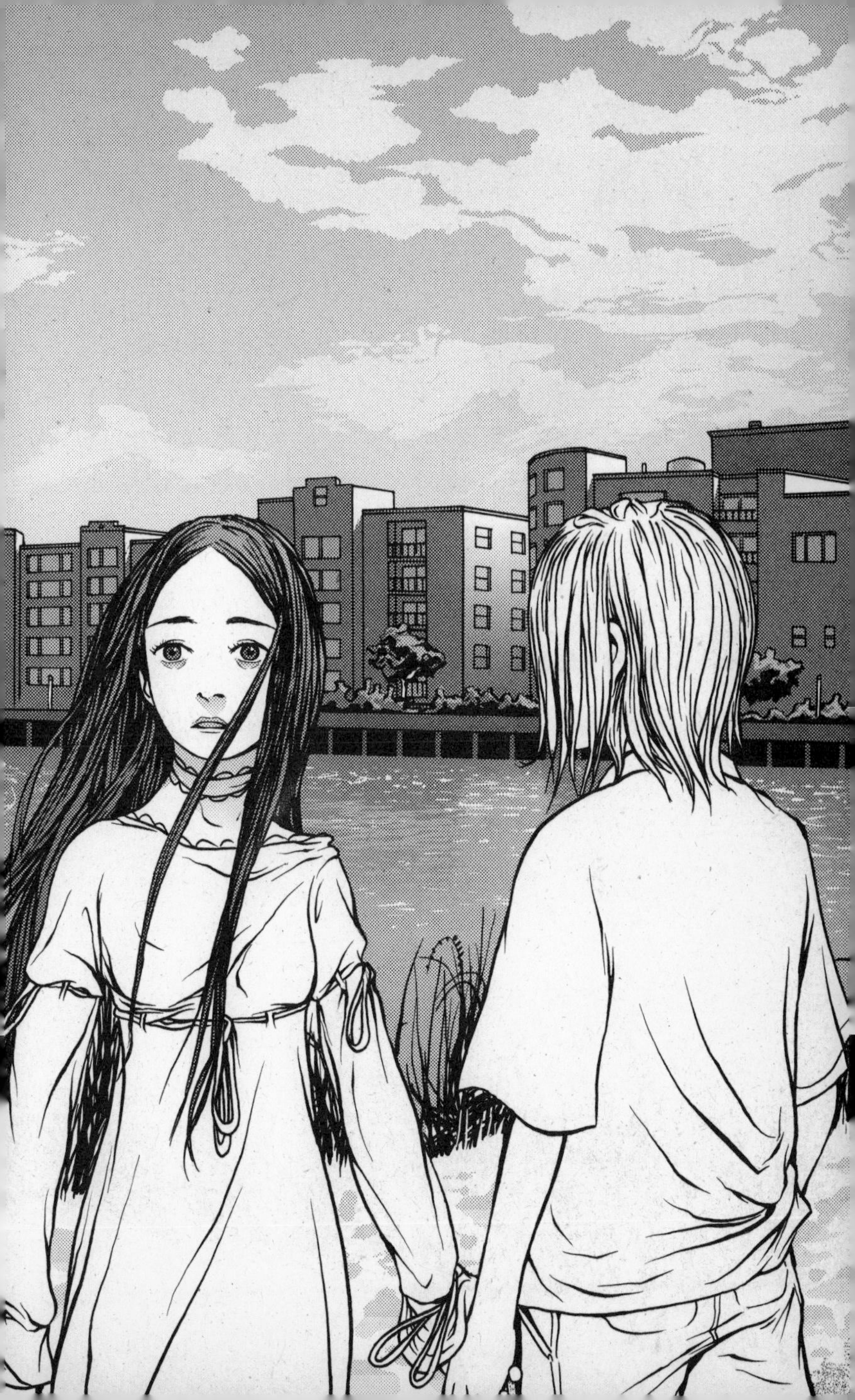

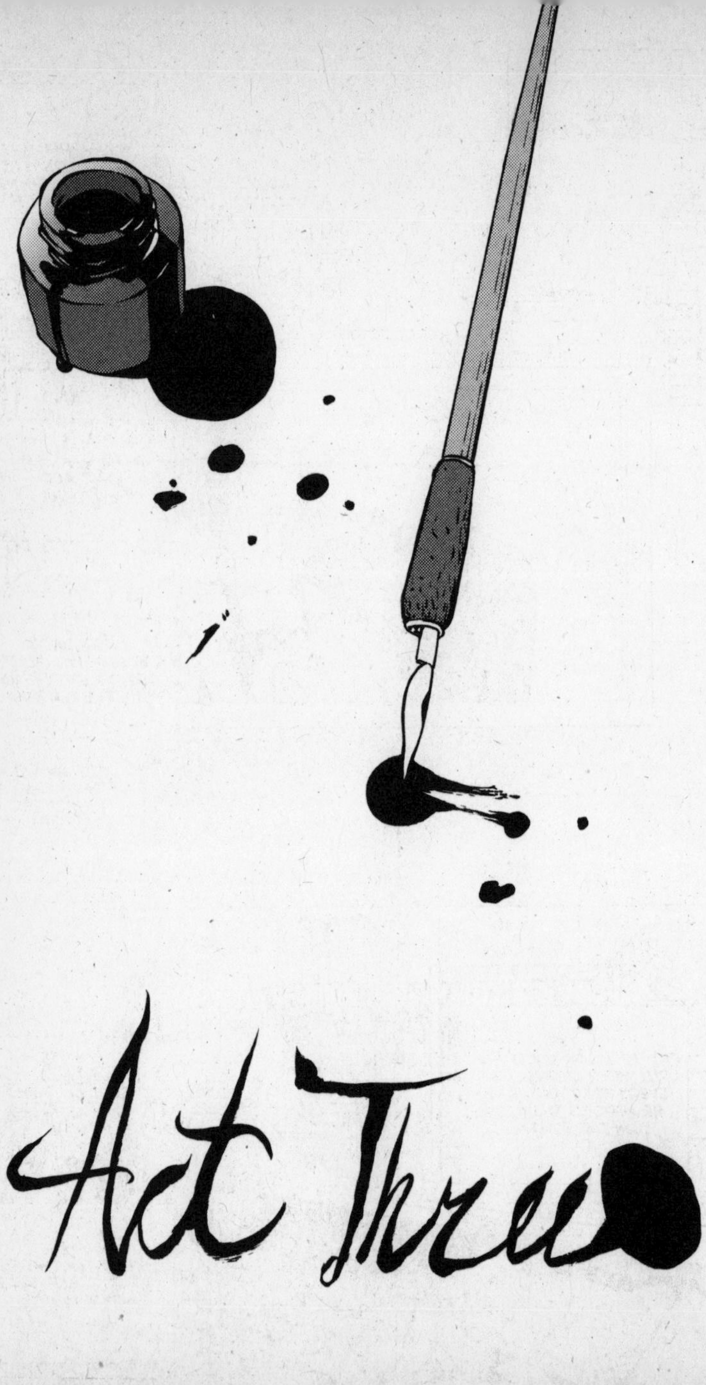

Act Three

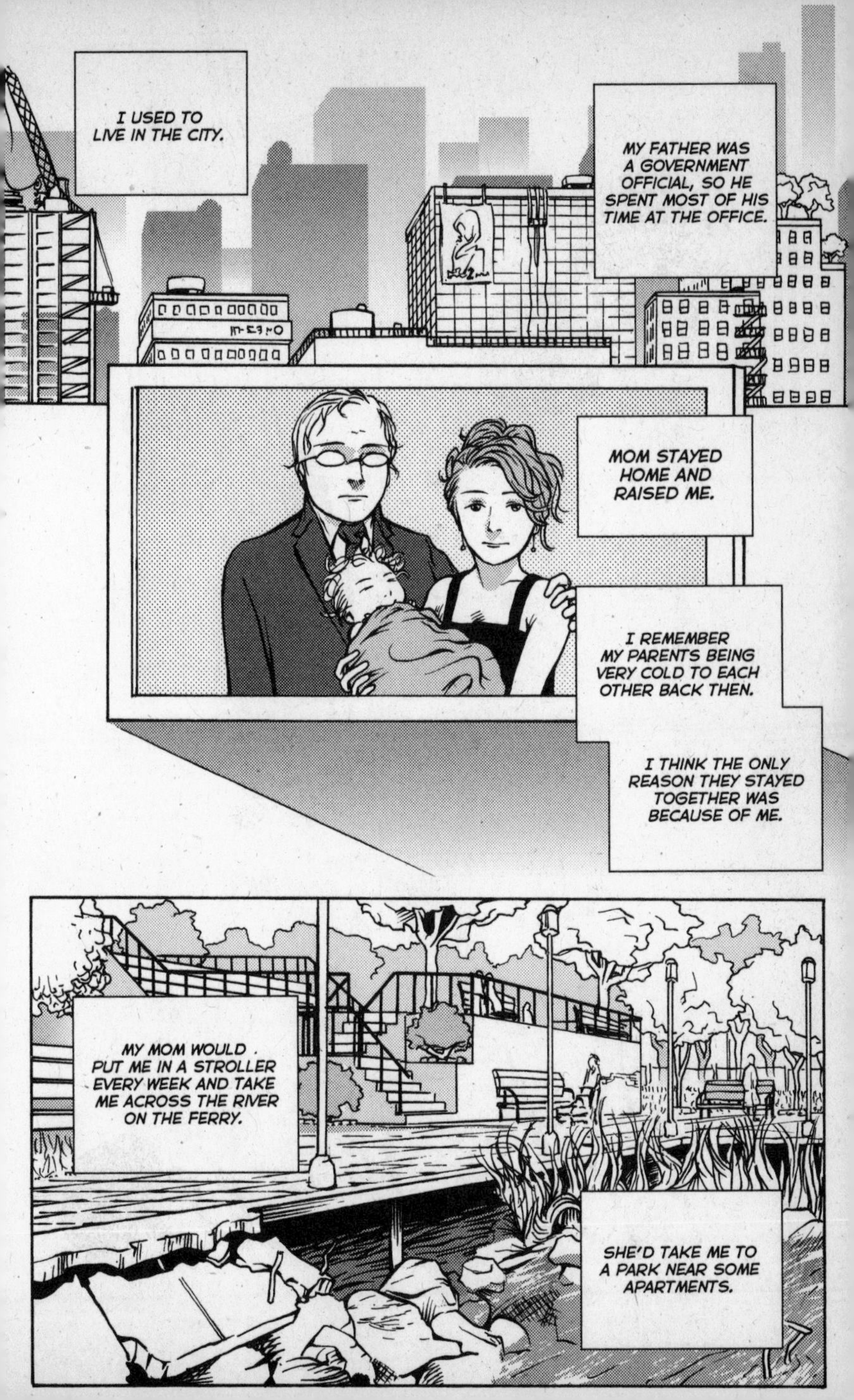
I USED TO LIVE IN THE CITY.
MY FATHER WAS A GOVERNMENT OFFICIAL, SO HE SPENT MOST OF HIS TIME AT THE OFFICE.
MOM STAYED HOME AND RAISED ME.
I REMEMBER MY PARENTS BEING VERY COLD TO EACH OTHER BACK THEN.
I THINK THE ONLY REASON THEY STAYED TOGETHER WAS BECAUSE OF ME.
MY MOM WOULD PUT ME IN A STROLLER EVERY WEEK AND TAKE ME ACROSS THE RIVER ON THE FERRY.
SHE'D TAKE ME TO A PARK NEAR SOME APARTMENTS.

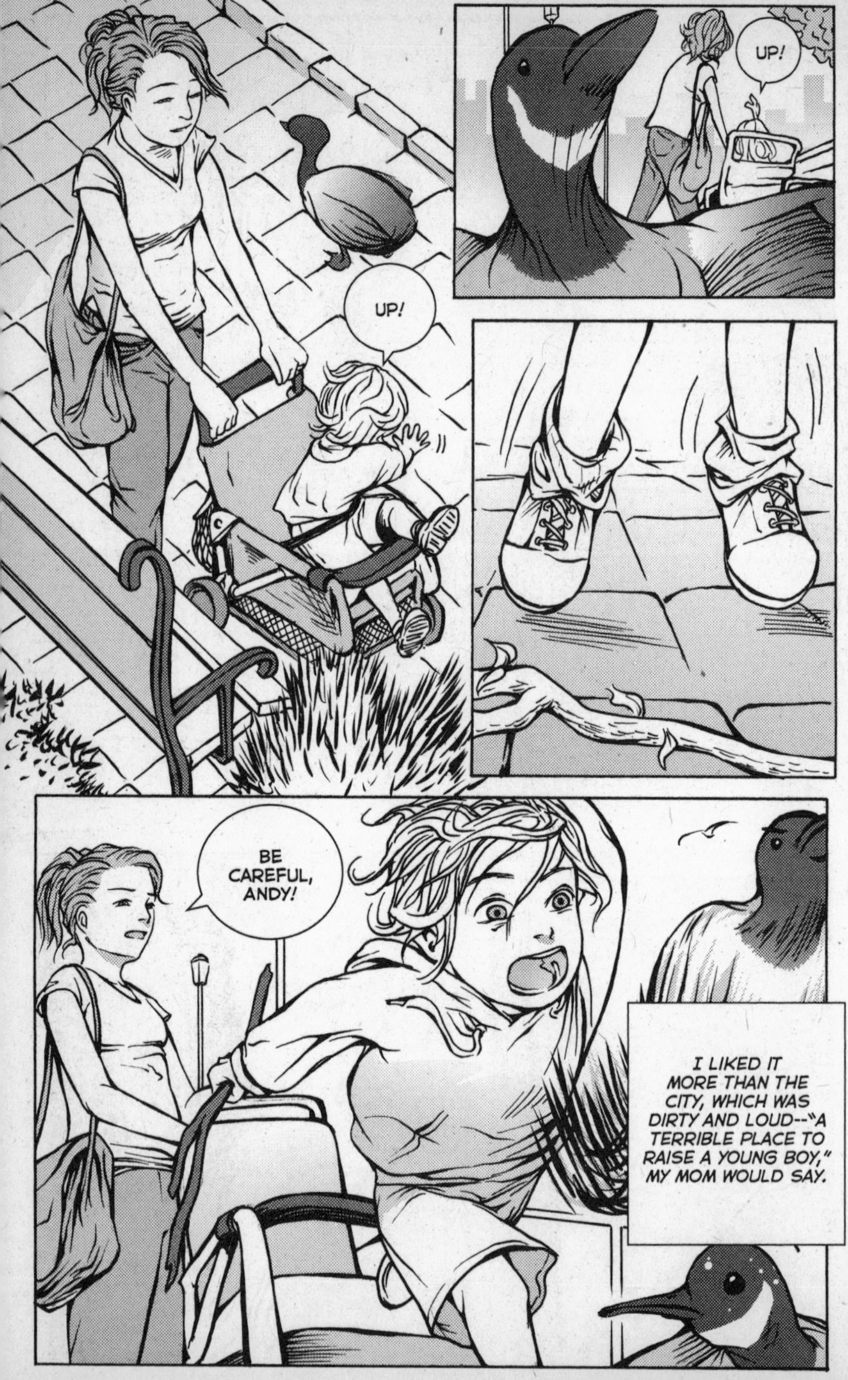
UP!
UP!
BE CAREFUL, ANDY!
I LIKED IT MORE THAN THE CITY, WHICH WAS DIRTY AND LOUD--"A TERRIBLE PLACE TO RAISE A YOUNG BOY," MY MOM WOULD SAY.

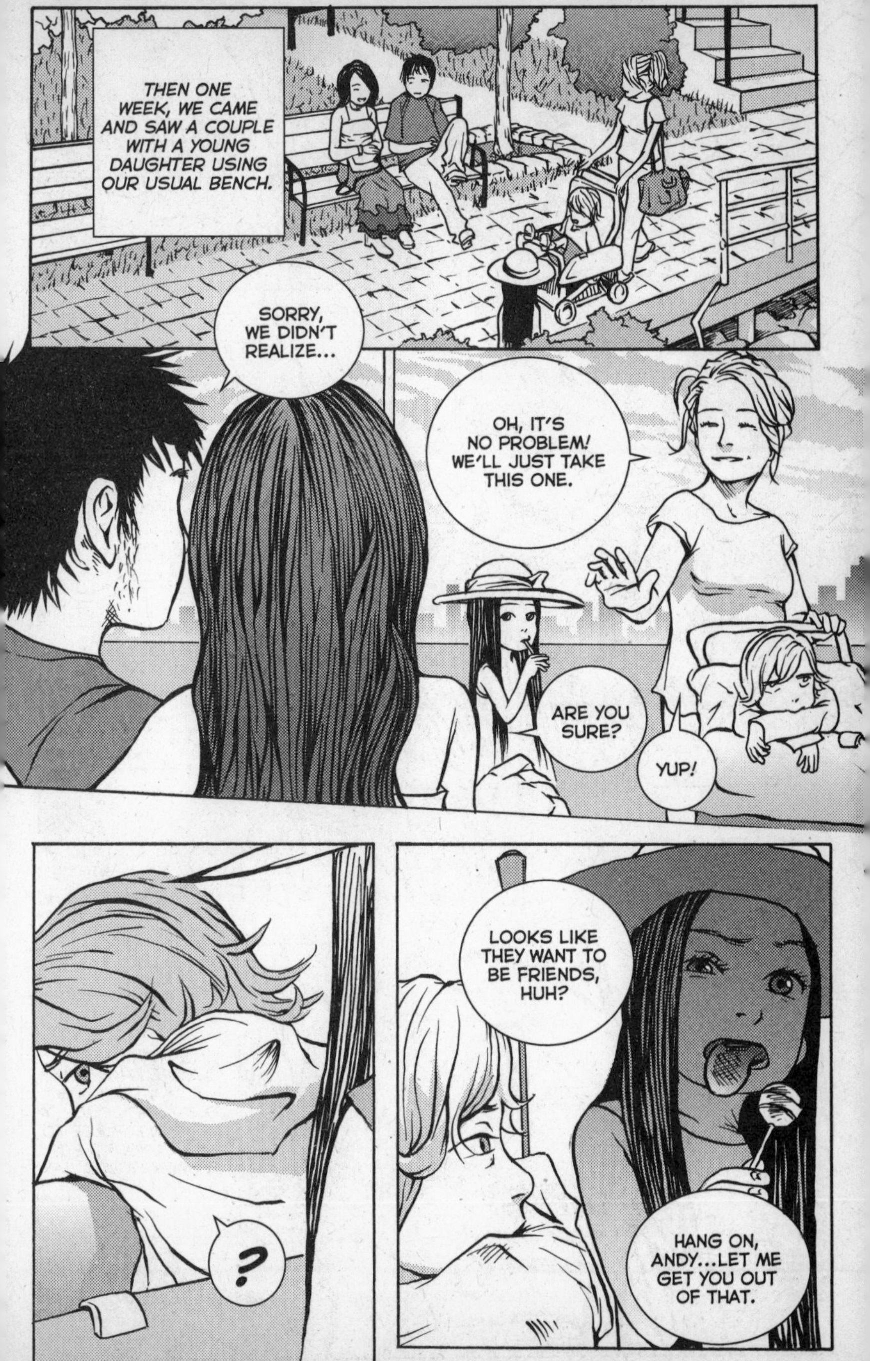
THEN ONE WEEK, WE CAME AND SAW A COUPLE WITH A YOUNG DAUGHTER USING OUR USUAL BENCH.
SORRY, WE DIDN'T REALIZE...
OH, IT'S NO PROBLEM! WE'LL JUST TAKE THIS ONE.
ARE YOU SURE?
YUP!
?
LOOKS LIKE THEY WANT TO BE FRIENDS, HUH?
HANG ON, ANDY...LET ME GET YOU OUT OF THAT.

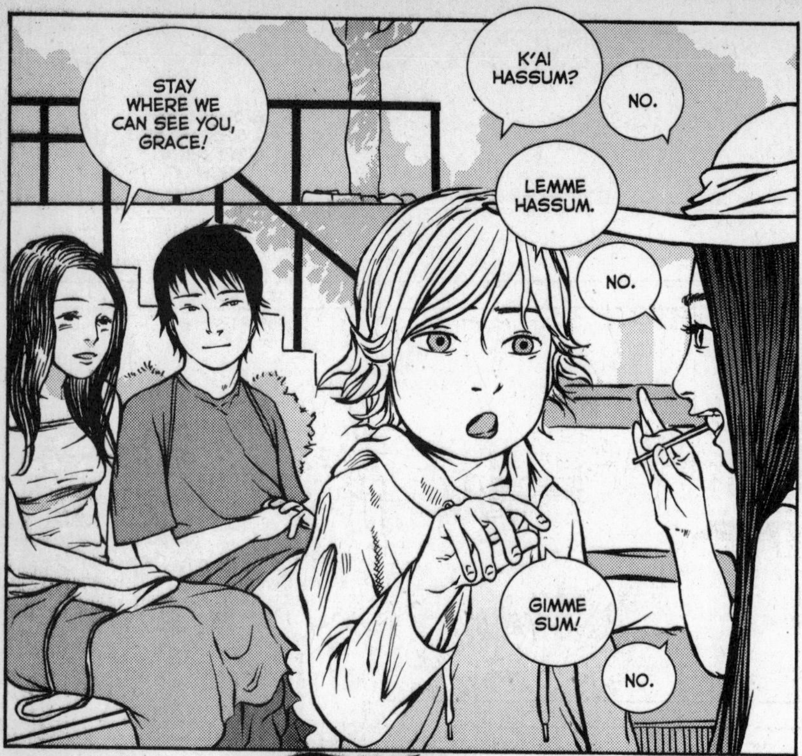
STAY WHERE WE CAN SEE YOU, GRACE!
K'AI HASSUM?
NO.
LEMME HASSUM.
NO.
GIMME SUM!
NO.

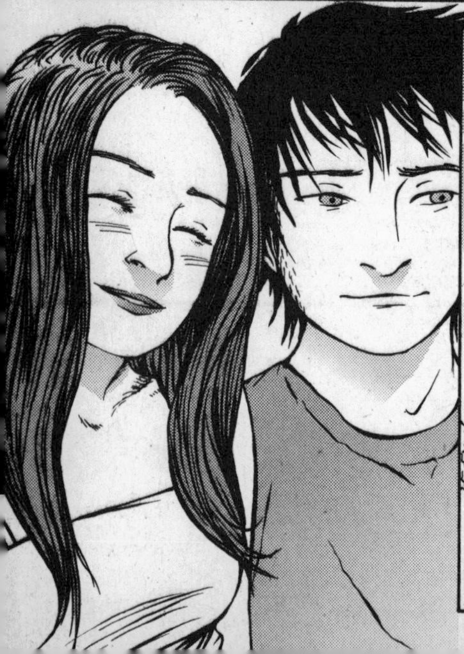

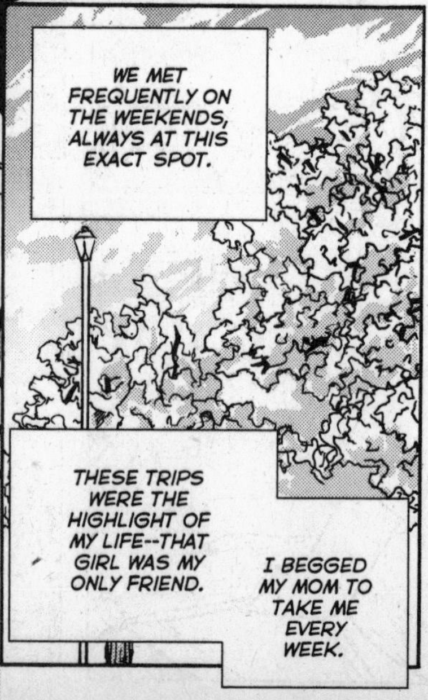
WE MET FREQUENTLY ON THE WEEKENDS, ALWAYS AT THIS EXACT SPOT.
THESE TRIPS WERE THE HIGHLIGHT OF MY LIFE--THAT GIRL WAS MY ONLY FRIEND.
I BEGGED MY MOM TO TAKE ME EVERY WEEK.

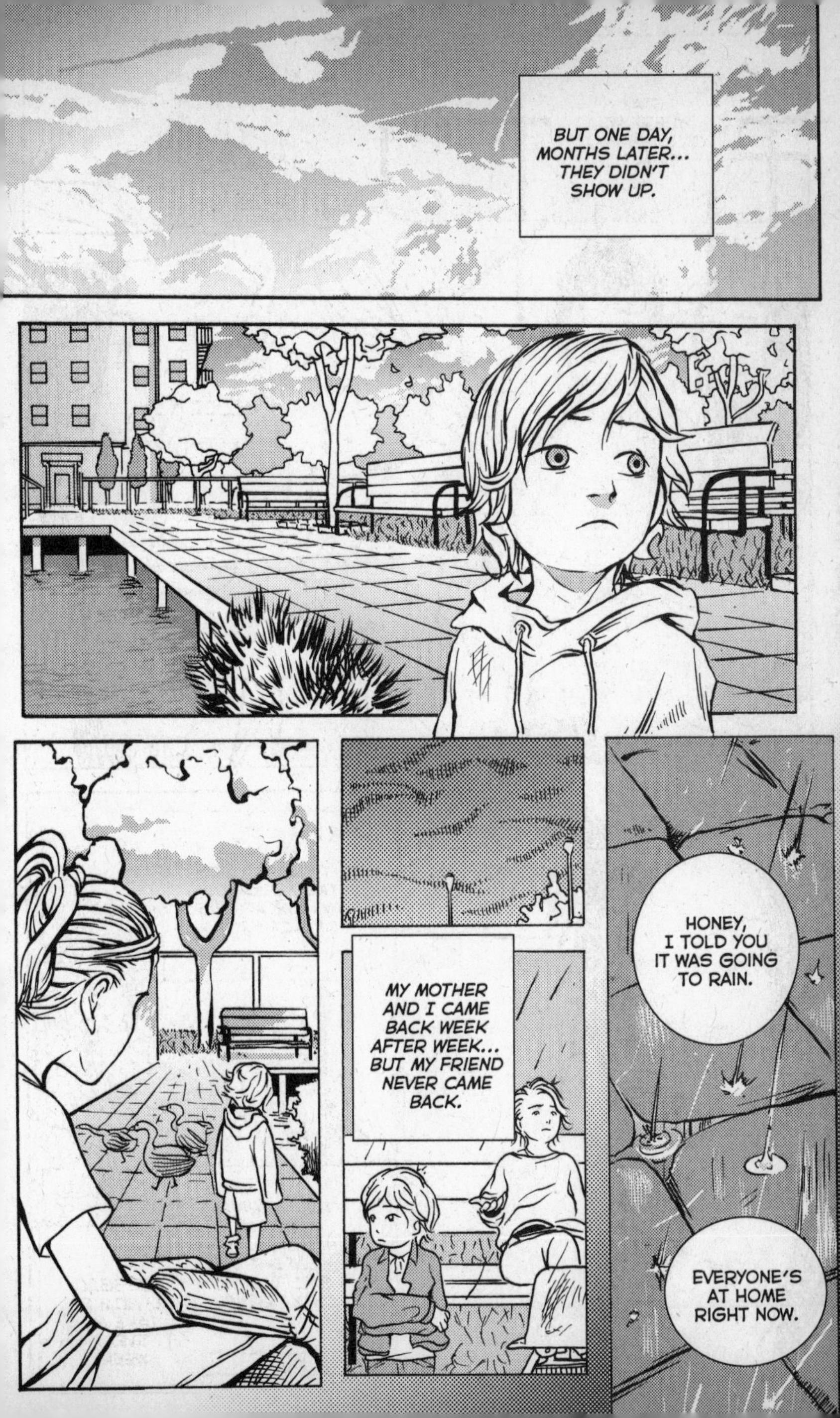
BUT ONE DAY, MONTHS LATER... THEY DIDN'T SHOW UP.
MY MOTHER AND I CAME BACK WEEK AFTER WEEK... BUT MY FRIEND NEVER CAME BACK.
HONEY, I TOLD YOU IT WAS GOING TO RAIN.
EVERYONE'S AT HOME RIGHT NOW.

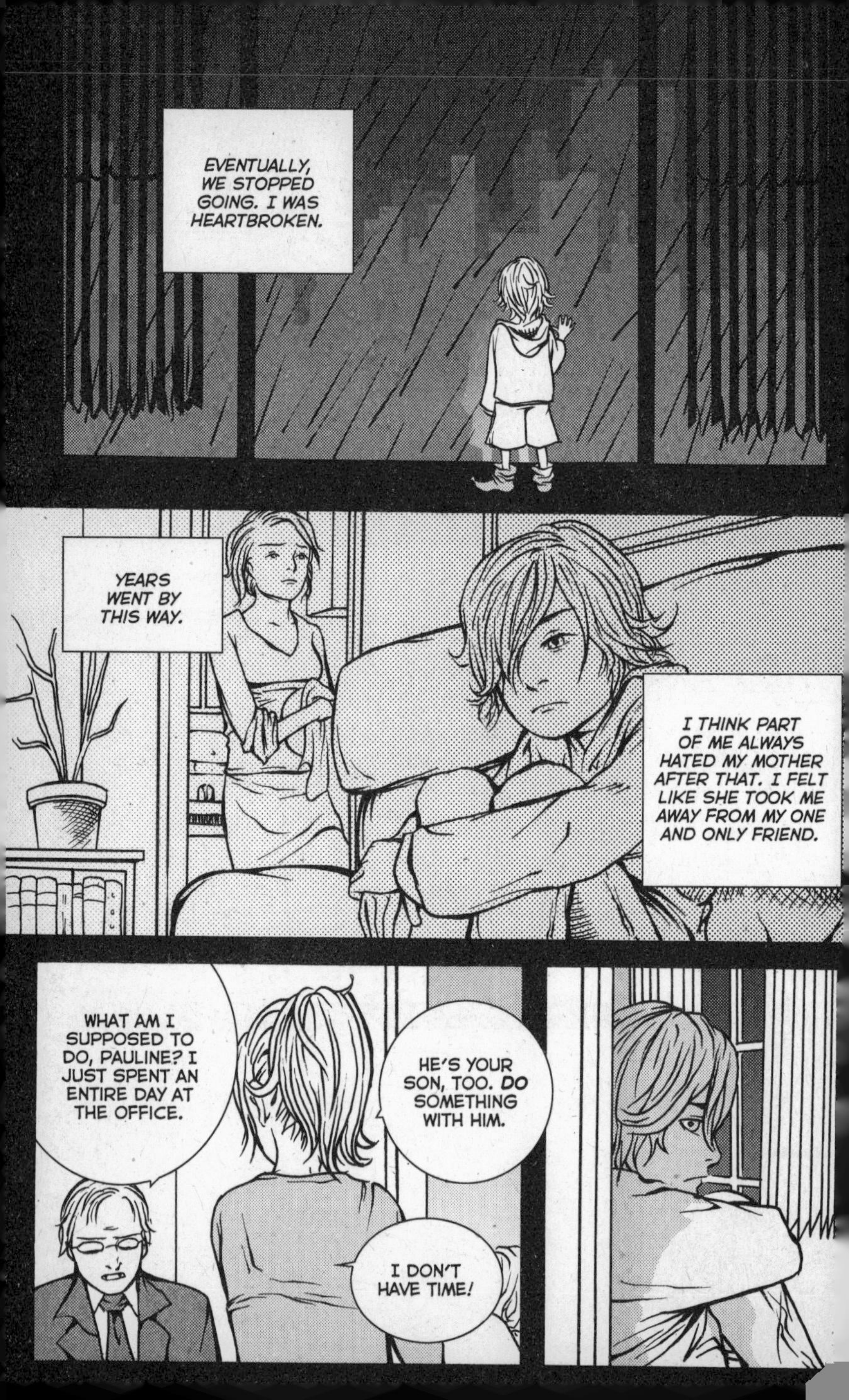
EVENTUALLY, WE STOPPED GOING. I WAS HEARTBROKEN.
YEARS WENT BY THIS WAY.
I THINK PART OF ME ALWAYS HATED MY MOTHER AFTER THAT. I FELT LIKE SHE TOOK ME AWAY FROM MY ONE AND ONLY FRIEND.
WHAT AM I SUPPOSED TO DO, PAULINE? I JUST SPENT AN ENTIRE DAY AT THE OFFICE.
HE'S YOUR SON, TOO. *DO* SOMETHING WITH HIM.
I DON'T HAVE TIME!

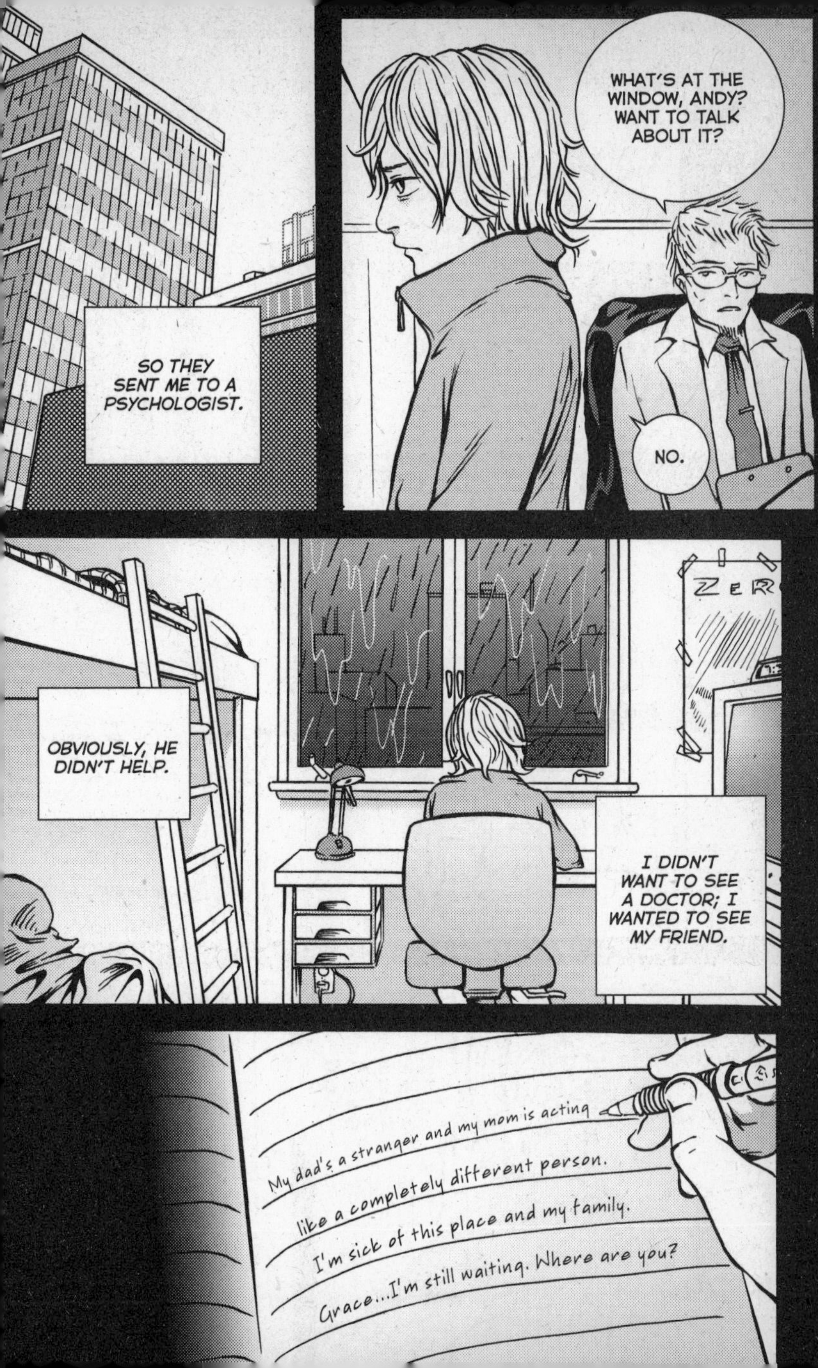
SO THEY SENT ME TO A PSYCHOLOGIST.
WHAT'S AT THE WINDOW, ANDY? WANT TO TALK ABOUT IT?
NO.
OBVIOUSLY, HE DIDN'T HELP.
I DIDN'T WANT TO SEE A DOCTOR; I WANTED TO SEE MY FRIEND.
My dad's a stranger and my mom is acting
like a completely different person.
I'm sick of this place and my family.
I'm still waiting. Where are you?
Grace...I'm still waiting. Where are you?

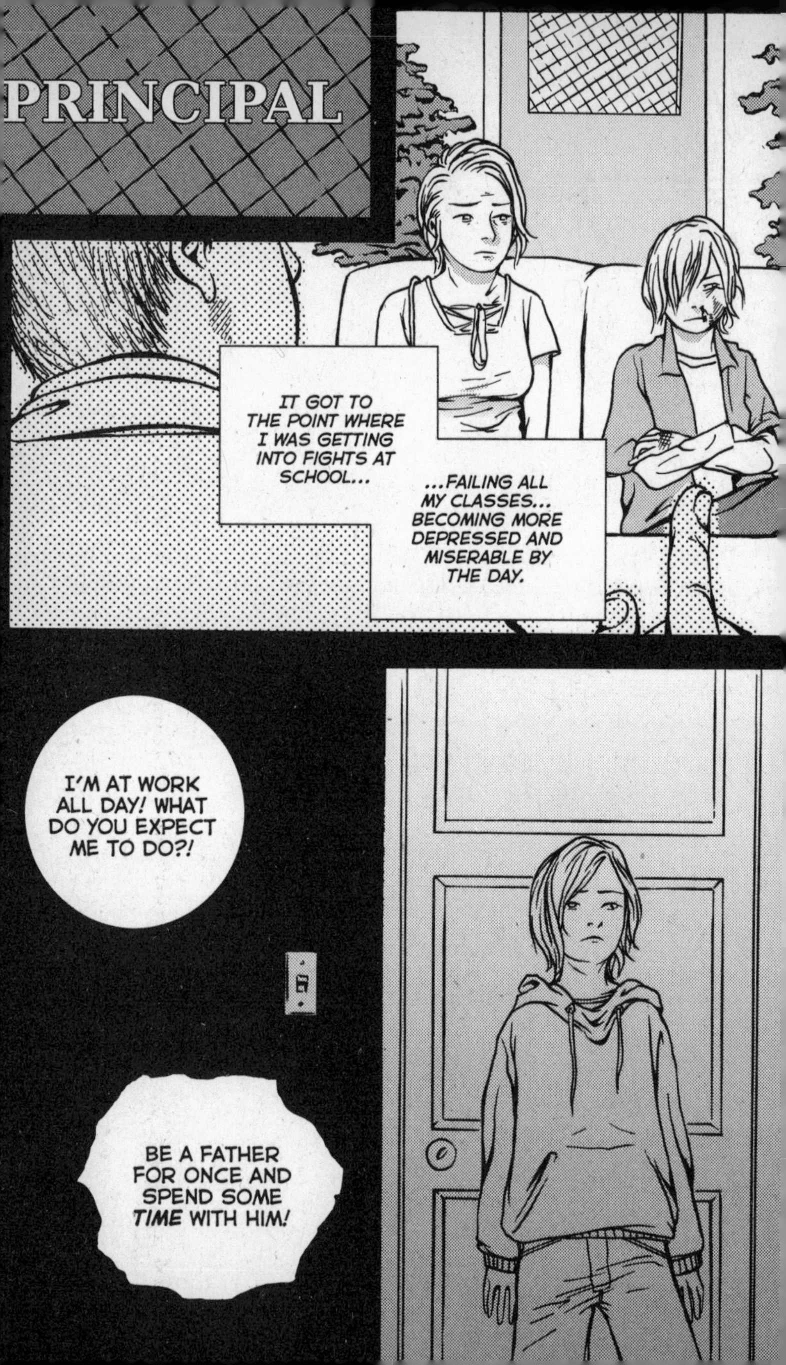
PRINCIPAL
IT GOT TO THE POINT WHERE I WAS GETTING INTO FIGHTS AT SCHOOL...
...FAILING ALL MY CLASSES... BECOMING MORE DEPRESSED AND MISERABLE BY THE DAY.
I'M AT WORK ALL DAY! WHAT DO YOU EXPECT ME TO DO?!
BE A FATHER FOR ONCE AND SPEND SOME *TIME* WITH HIM!

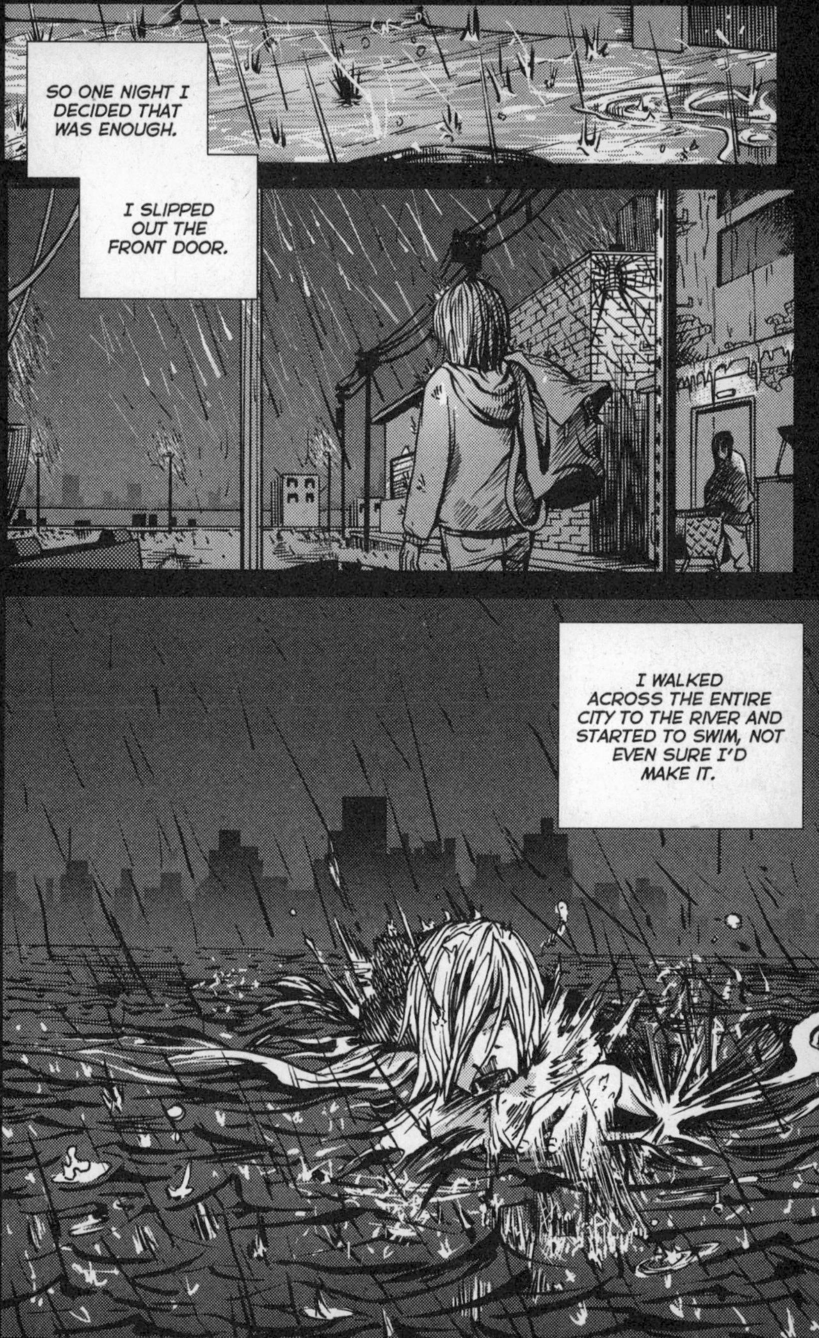
SO ONE NIGHT I DECIDED THAT WAS ENOUGH.
I SLIPPED OUT THE FRONT DOOR.
I WALKED ACROSS THE ENTIRE CITY TO THE RIVER AND STARTED TO SWIM, NOT EVEN SURE I'D MAKE IT.

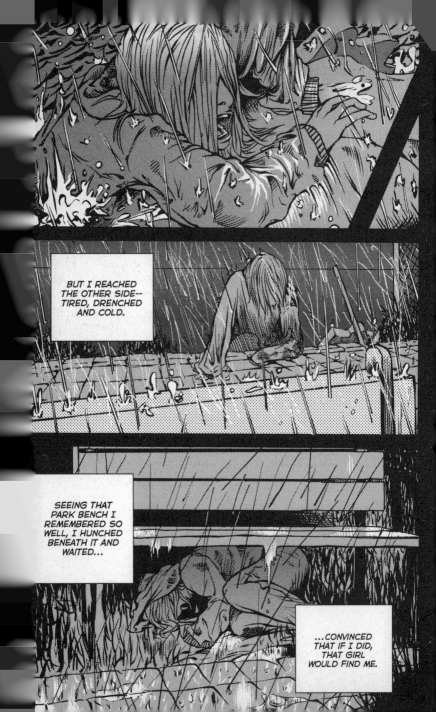

BUT I REACHED THE OTHER SIDE-- TIRED, DRENCHED AND COLD.

SEEING THAT PARK BENCH I REMEMBERED SO WELL, I HUNCHED BENEATH IT AND WAITED...

...CONVINCED THAT IF I DID, THAT GIRL WOULD FIND ME.

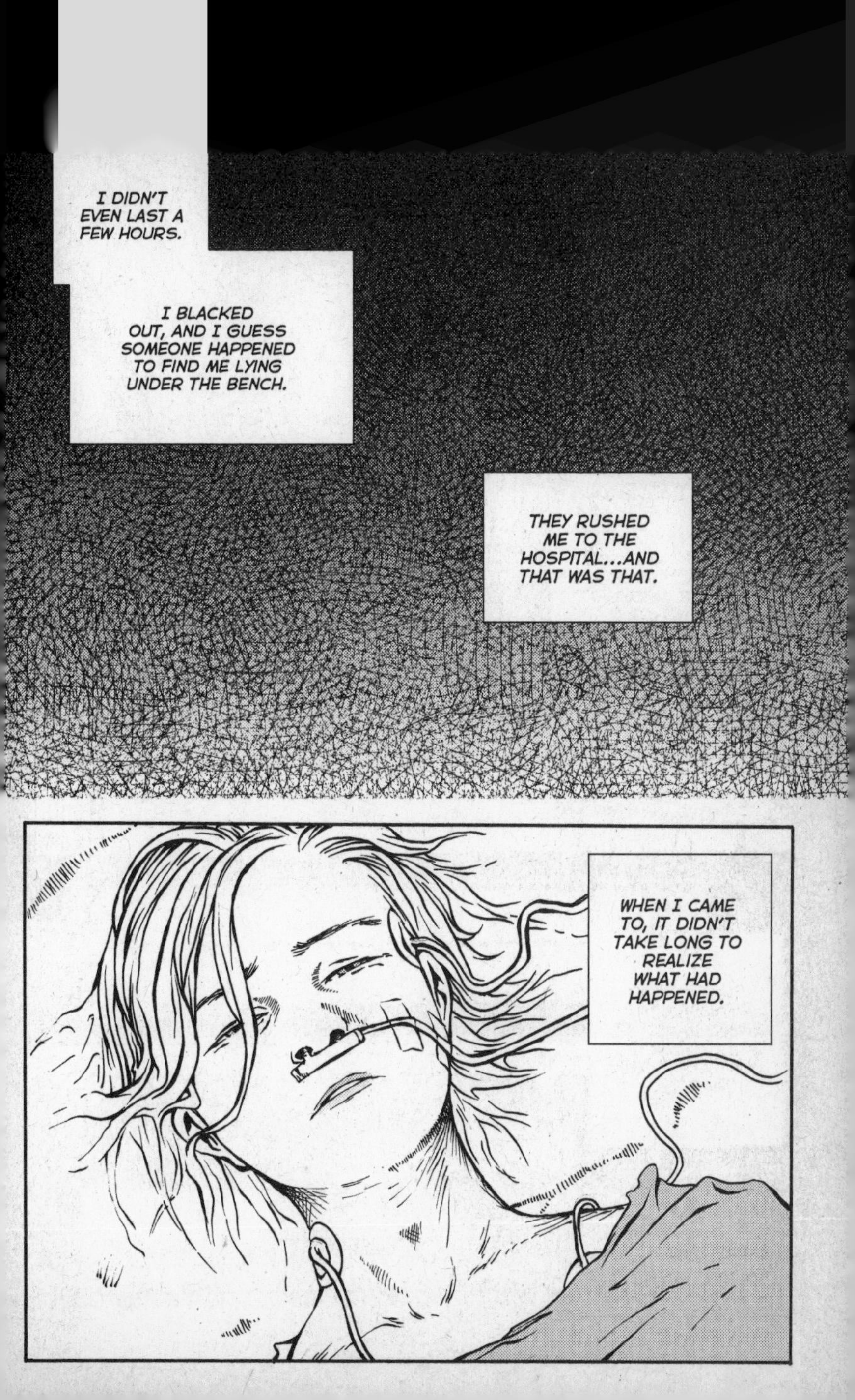
I DIDN'T EVEN LAST A FEW HOURS.
I BLACKED OUT, AND I GUESS SOMEONE HAPPENED TO FIND ME LYING UNDER THE BENCH.
THEY RUSHED ME TO THE HOSPITAL...AND THAT WAS THAT.
WHEN I CAME TO, IT DIDN'T TAKE LONG TO REALIZE WHAT HAD HAPPENED.

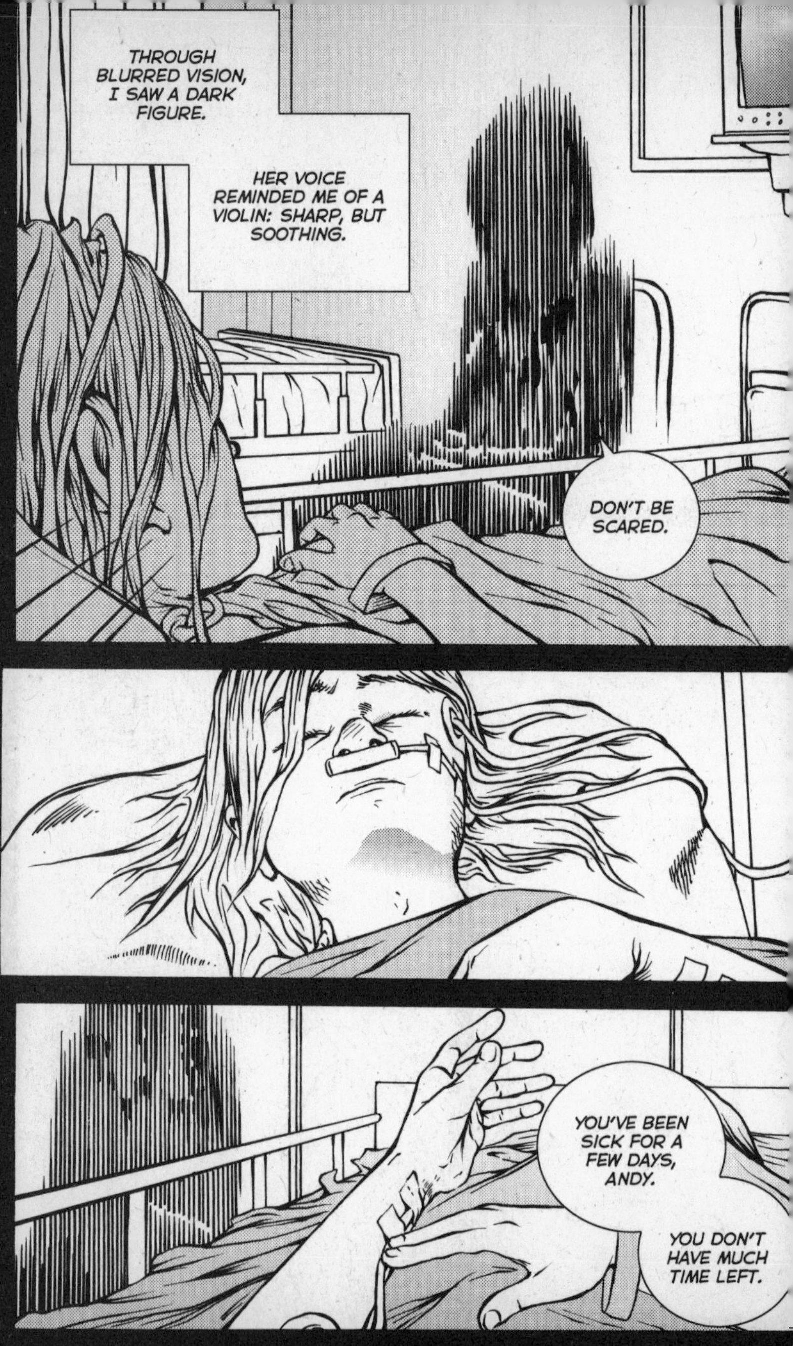
THROUGH BLURRED VISION, I SAW A DARK FIGURE.
HER VOICE REMINDED ME OF A VIOLIN: SHARP, BUT SOOTHING.
DON'T BE SCARED.
YOU'VE BEEN SICK FOR A FEW DAYS, ANDY.
YOU DON'T HAVE MUCH TIME LEFT.

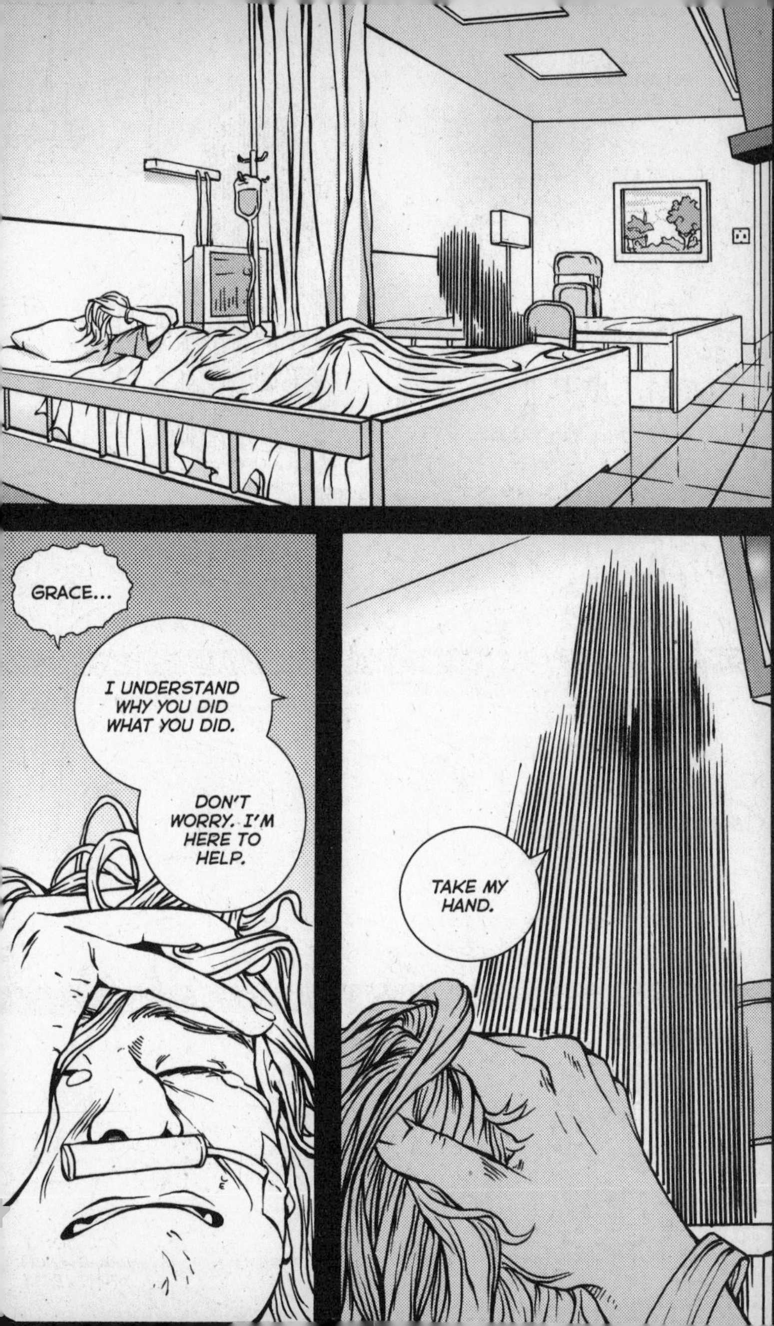
GRACE...
I UNDERSTAND WHY YOU DID WHAT YOU DID.
DON'T WORRY. I'M HERE TO HELP.
TAKE MY HAND.

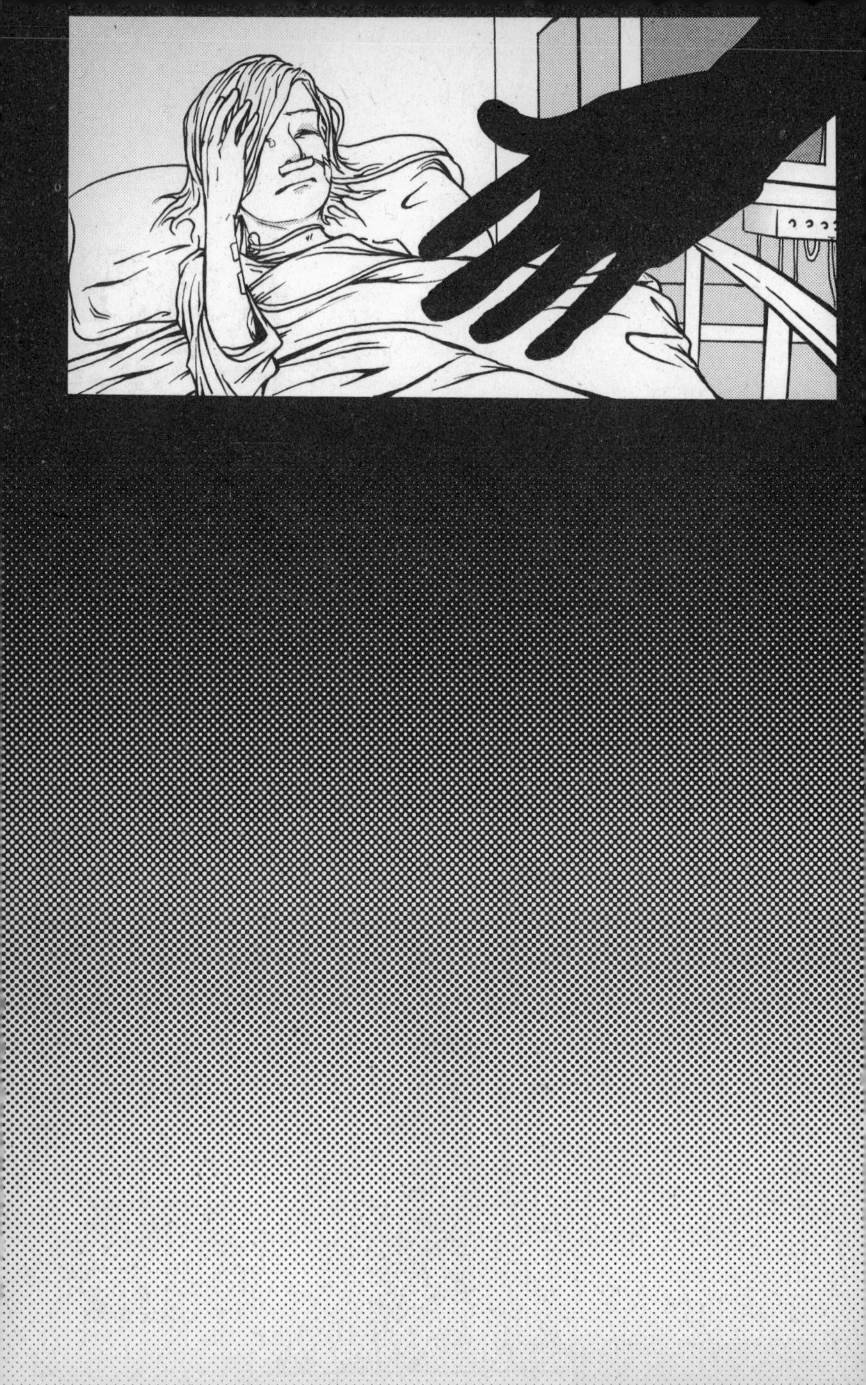

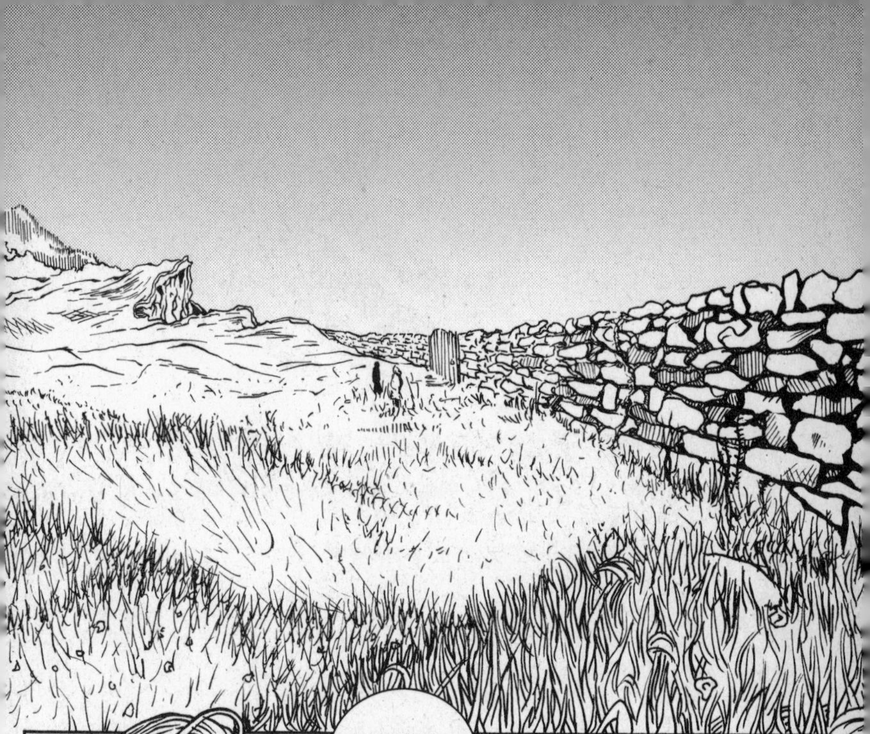

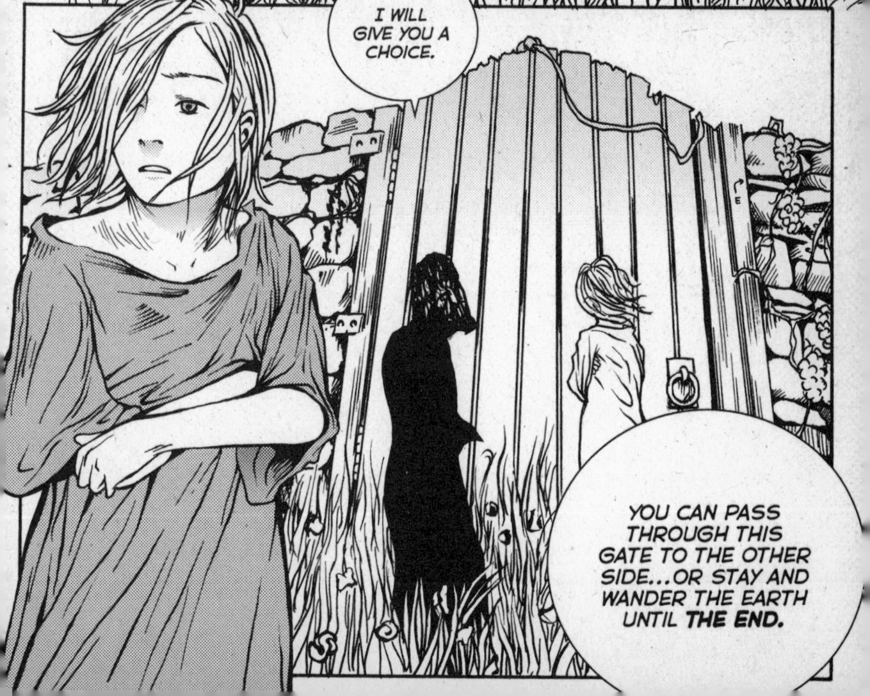
I WILL GIVE YOU A CHOICE.
YOU CAN PASS THROUGH THIS GATE TO THE OTHER SIDE...OR STAY AND WANDER THE EARTH UNTIL **THE END.**

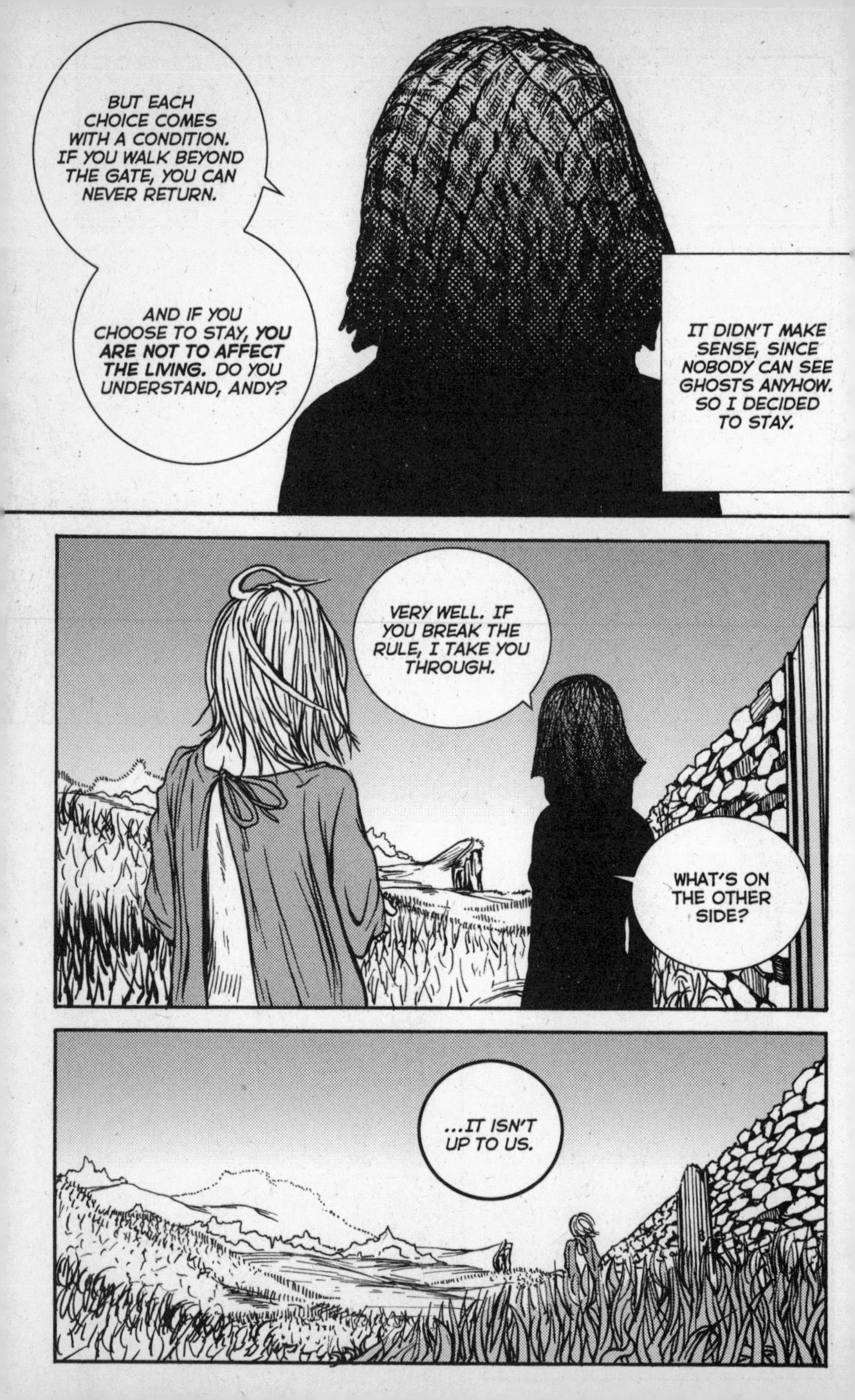
BUT EACH CHOICE COMES WITH A CONDITION. IF YOU WALK BEYOND THE GATE, YOU CAN NEVER RETURN.
AND IF YOU CHOOSE TO STAY, YOU ARE NOT TO AFFECT THE LIVING. DO YOU UNDERSTAND, ANDY?
IT DIDN'T MAKE SENSE, SINCE NOBODY CAN SEE GHOSTS ANYHOW. SO I DECIDED TO STAY.
VERY WELL. IF YOU BREAK THE RULE, I TAKE YOU THROUGH.
WHAT'S ON THE OTHER SIDE?
...IT ISN'T UP TO US.

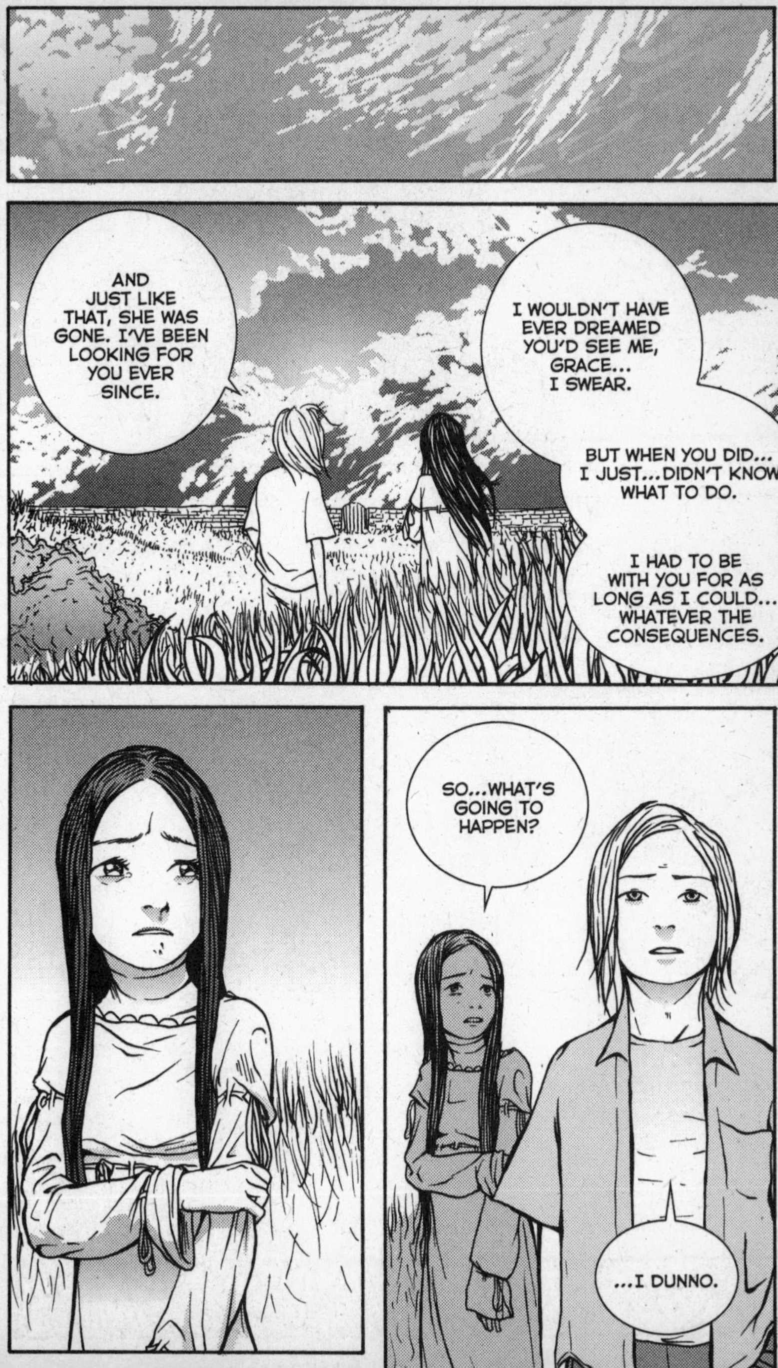
AND JUST LIKE THAT, SHE WAS GONE. I'VE BEEN LOOKING FOR YOU EVER SINCE.
I WOULDN'T HAVE EVER DREAMED YOU'D SEE ME, GRACE... I SWEAR.
BUT WHEN YOU DID... I JUST...DIDN'T KNOW WHAT TO DO.
I HAD TO BE WITH YOU FOR AS LONG AS I COULD... WHATEVER THE CONSEQUENCES.
SO...WHAT'S GOING TO HAPPEN?
...I DUNNO.

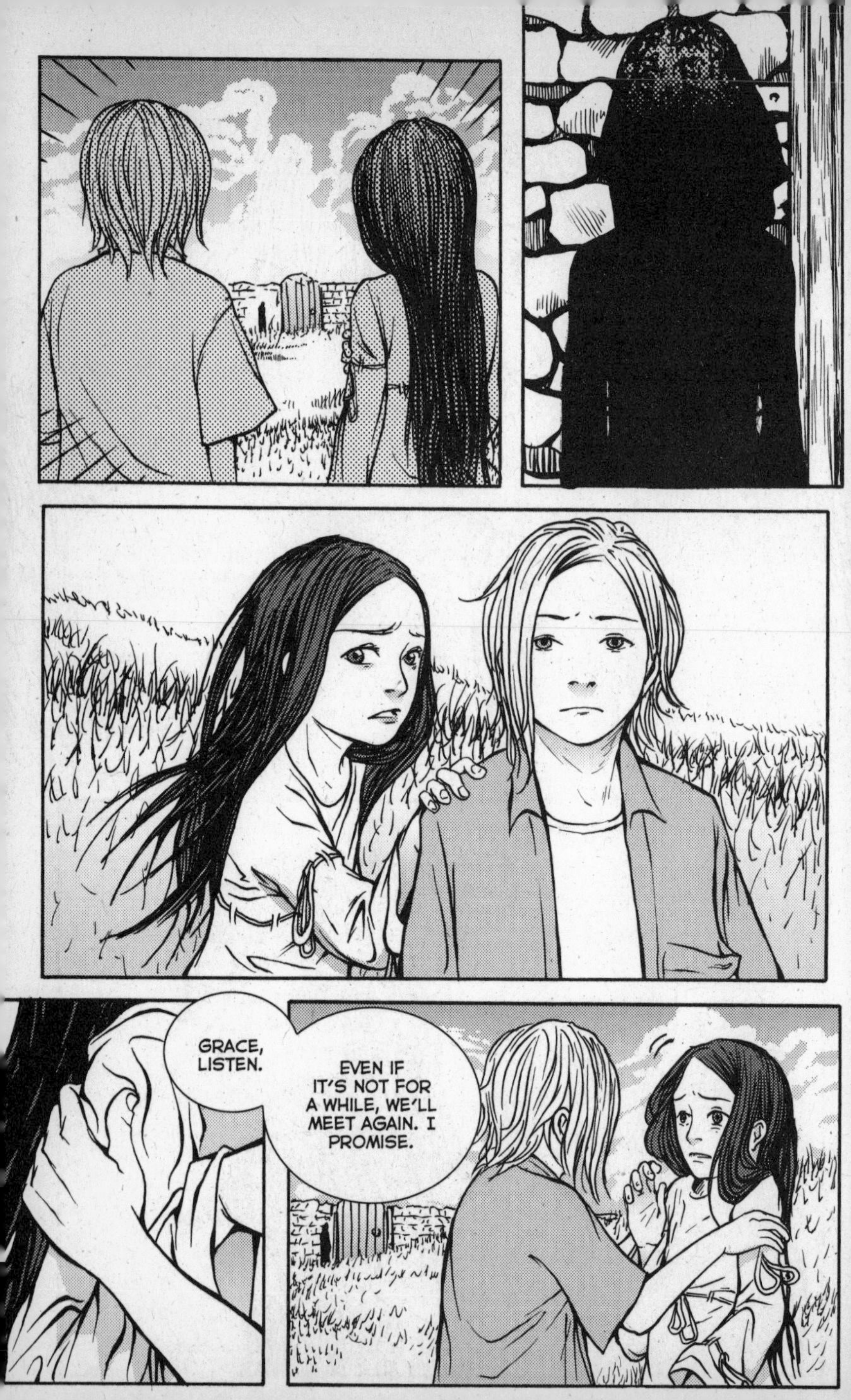
GRACE, LISTEN.
EVEN IF IT'S NOT FOR A WHILE, WE'LL MEET AGAIN. I PROMISE.

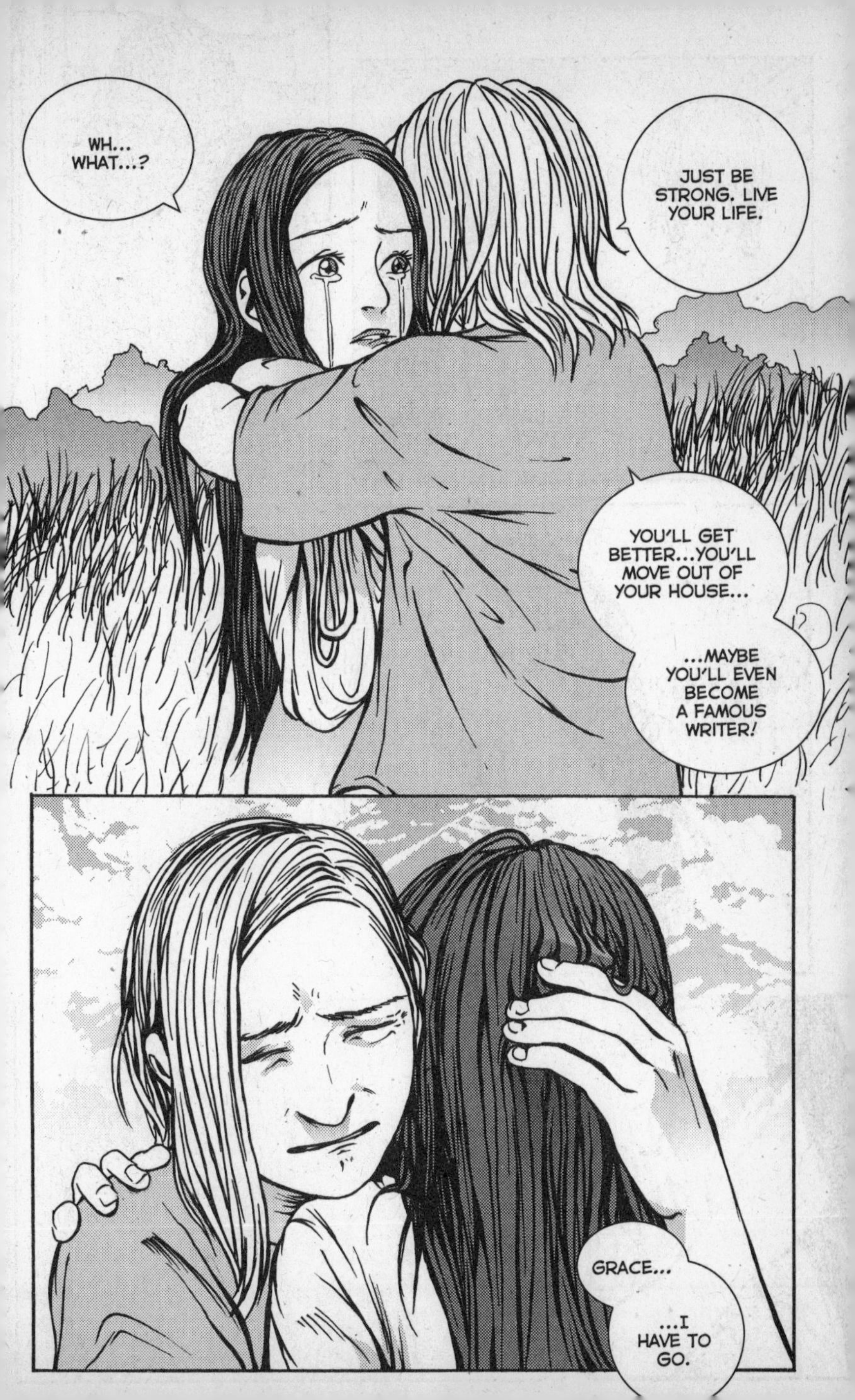
WH... WHAT...?
JUST BE STRONG. LIVE YOUR LIFE.
YOU'LL GET BETTER...YOU'LL MOVE OUT OF YOUR HOUSE...
...MAYBE YOU'LL EVEN BECOME A FAMOUS WRITER!
GRACE...
...I HAVE TO GO.

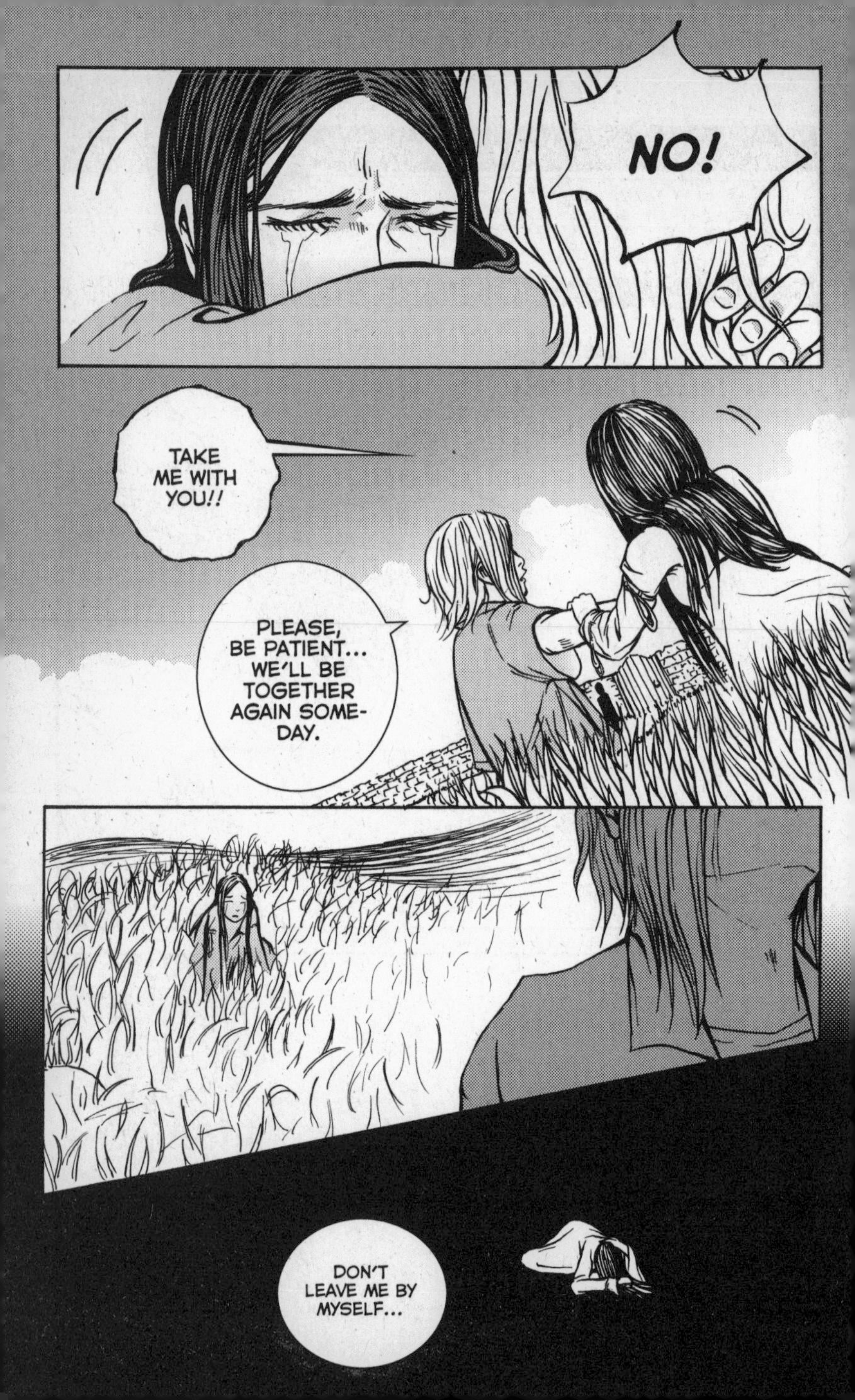
NO!
TAKE ME WITH YOU!!
PLEASE, BE PATIENT... WE'LL BE TOGETHER AGAIN SOME-DAY.
DON'T LEAVE ME BY MYSELF...

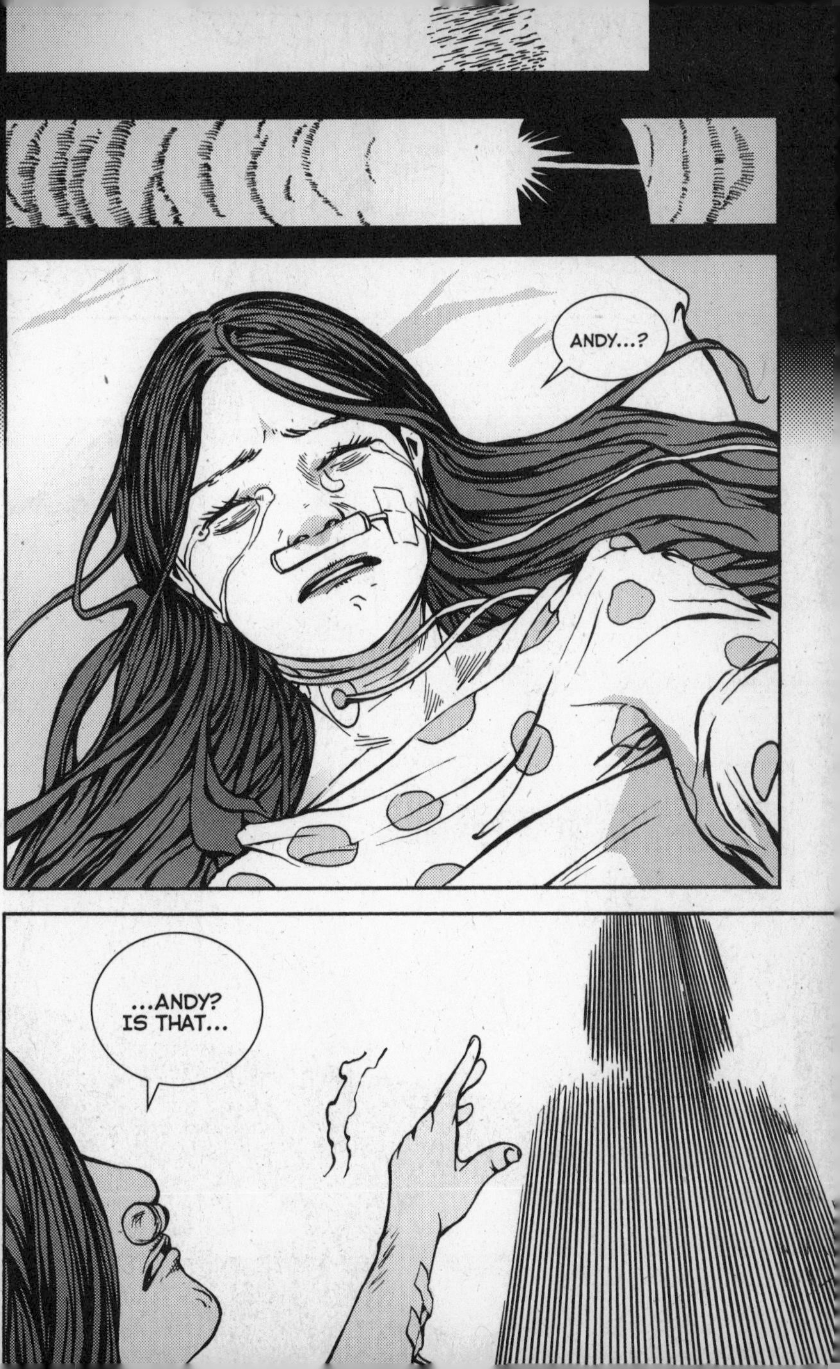
ANDY...?
...ANDY? IS THAT...

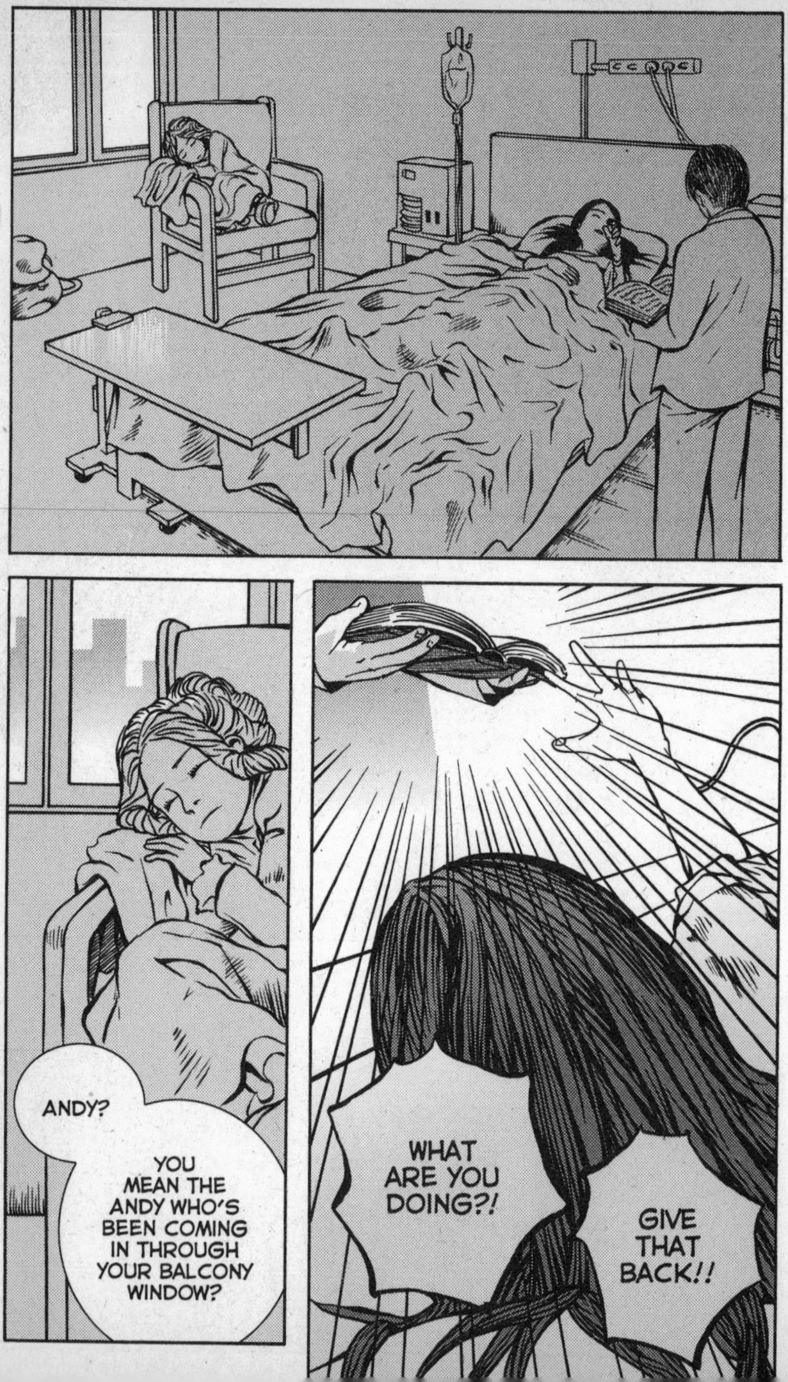
ANDY?
YOU MEAN THE ANDY WHO'S BEEN COMING IN THROUGH YOUR BALCONY WINDOW?
WHAT ARE YOU DOING?!
GIVE THAT BACK!!

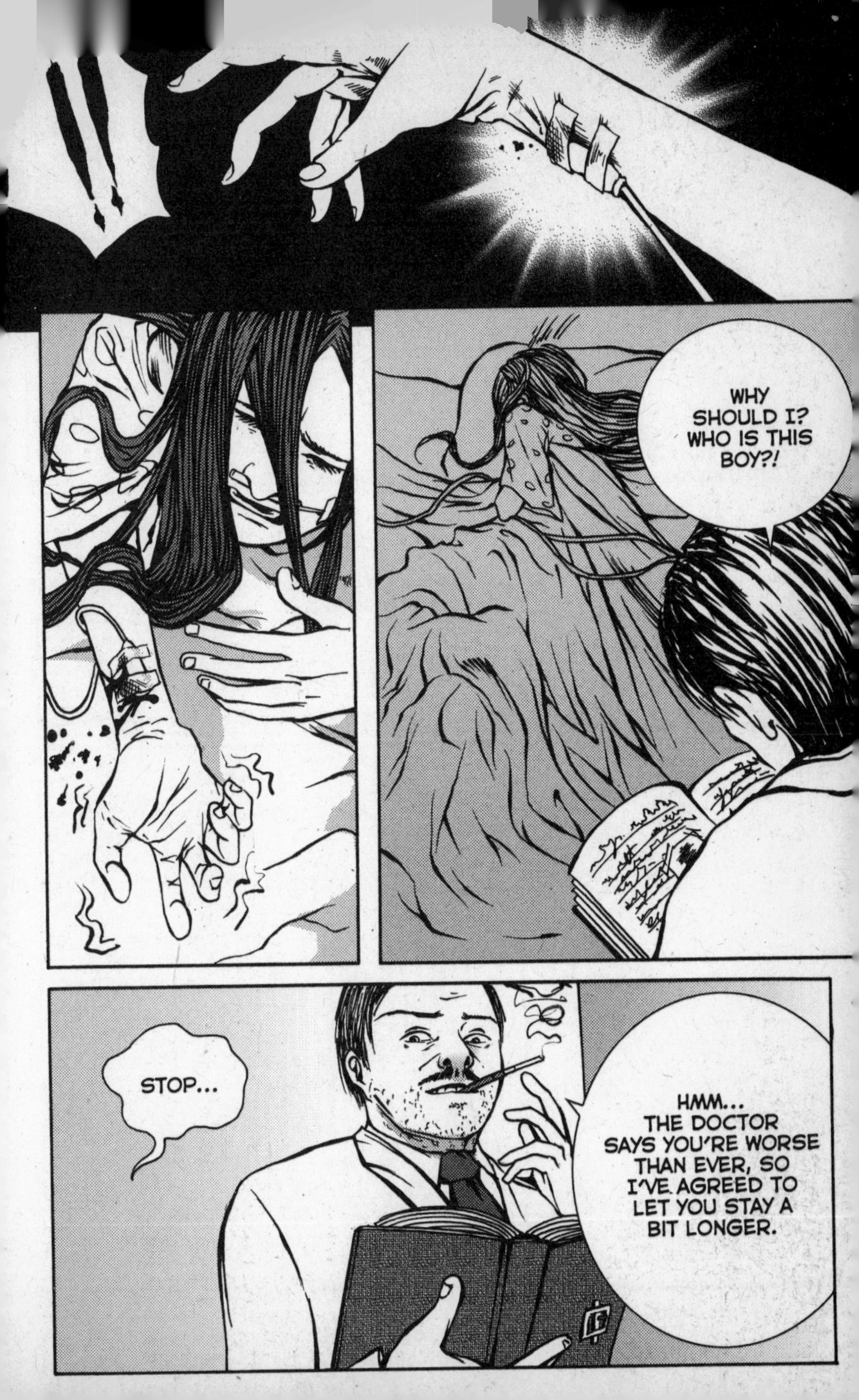
WHY SHOULD I? WHO IS THIS BOY?!
STOP...
HMM... THE DOCTOR SAYS YOU'RE WORSE THAN EVER, SO I'VE AGREED TO LET YOU STAY A BIT LONGER.

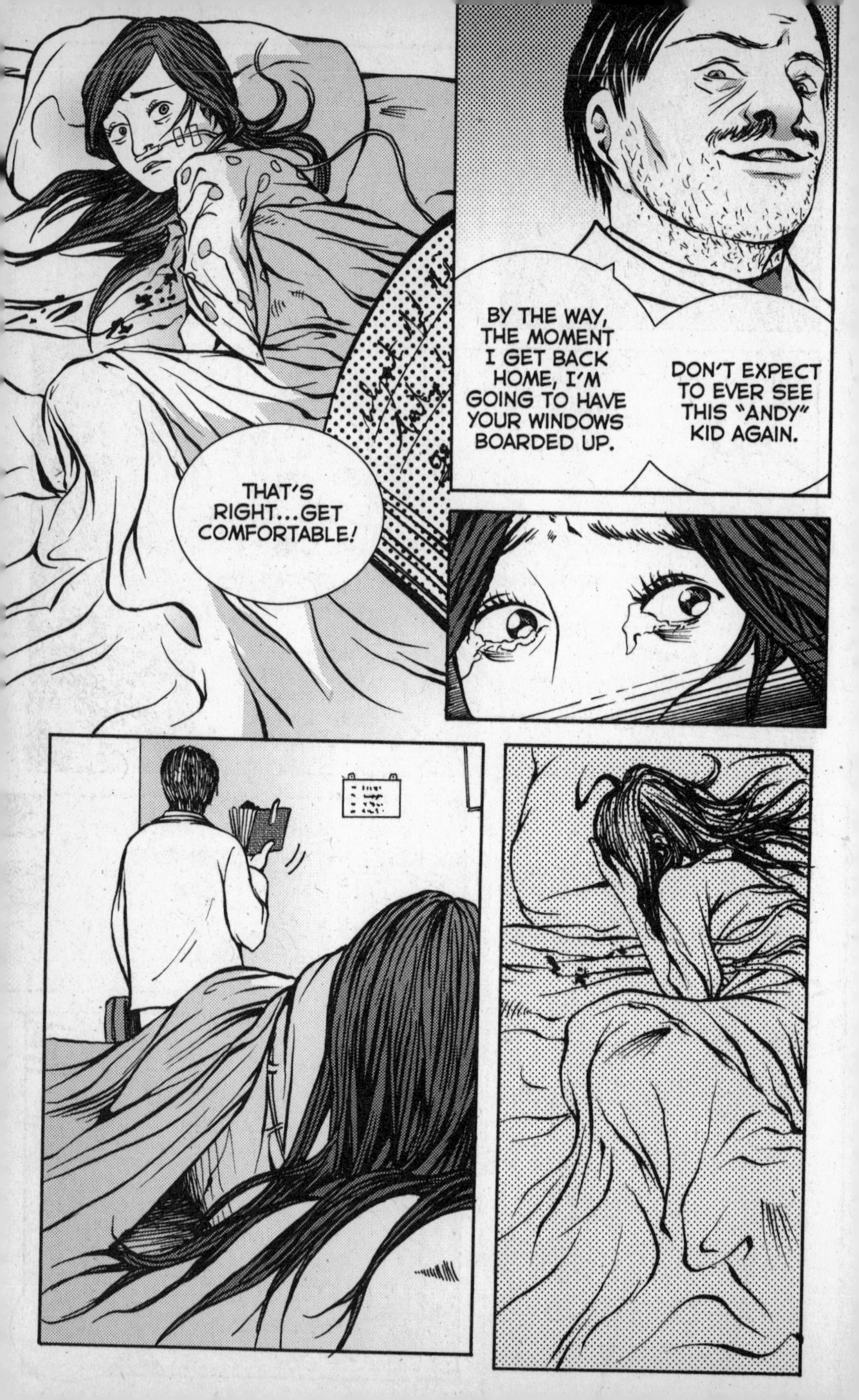
THAT'S RIGHT...GET COMFORTABLE!
BY THE WAY, THE MOMENT I GET BACK HOME, I'M GOING TO HAVE YOUR WINDOWS BOARDED UP.
DON'T EXPECT TO EVER SEE THIS "ANDY" KID AGAIN.

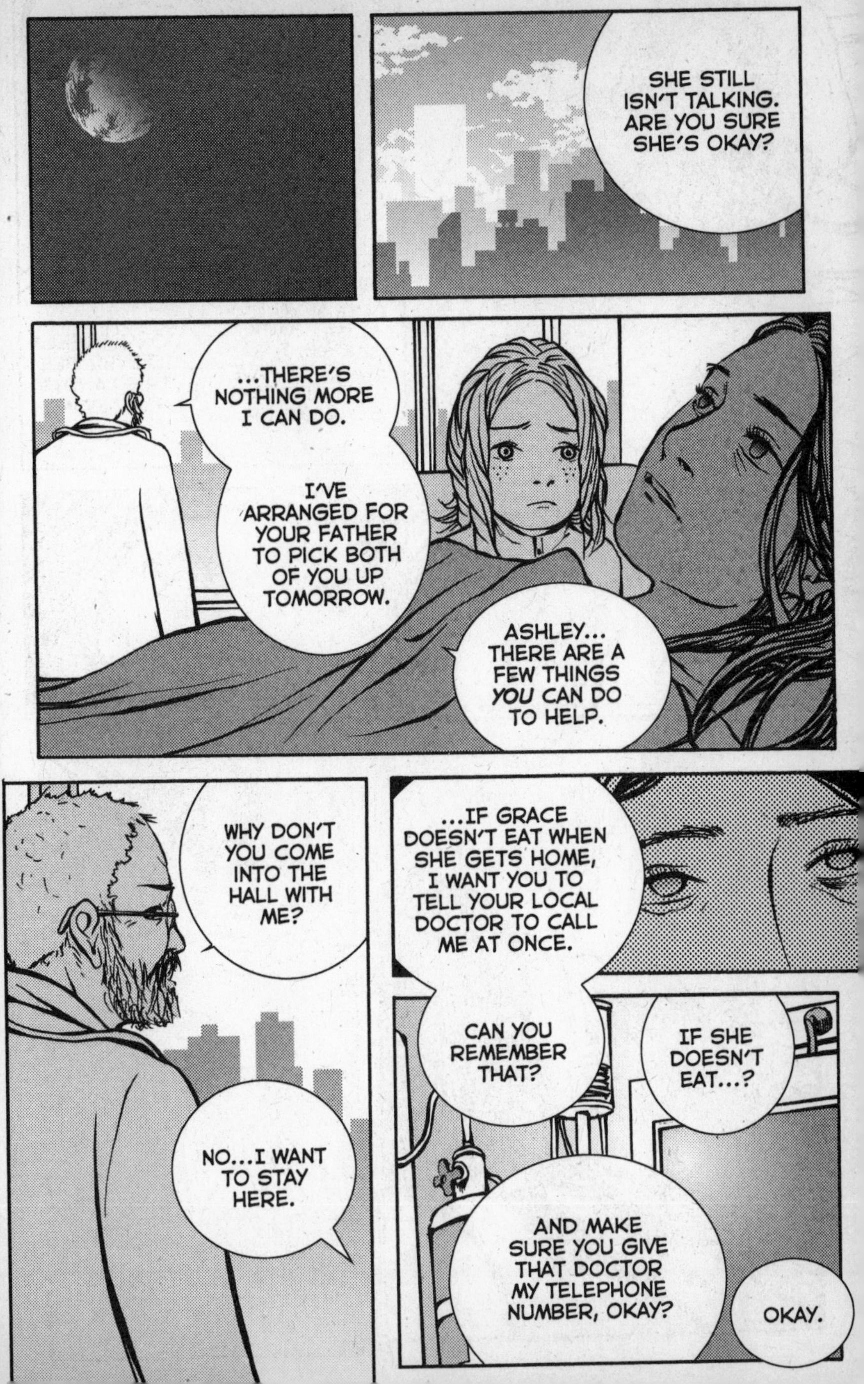
SHE STILL ISN'T TALKING. ARE YOU SURE SHE'S OKAY?
...THERE'S NOTHING MORE I CAN DO.
I'VE ARRANGED FOR YOUR FATHER TO PICK BOTH OF YOU UP TOMORROW.
ASHLEY... THERE ARE A FEW THINGS *YOU* CAN DO TO HELP.
WHY DON'T YOU COME INTO THE HALL WITH ME?
NO...I WANT TO STAY HERE.
...IF GRACE DOESN'T EAT WHEN SHE GETS HOME, I WANT YOU TO TELL YOUR LOCAL DOCTOR TO CALL ME AT ONCE.
CAN YOU REMEMBER THAT?
IF SHE DOESN'T EAT...?
AND MAKE SURE YOU GIVE THAT DOCTOR MY TELEPHONE NUMBER, OKAY?
OKAY.

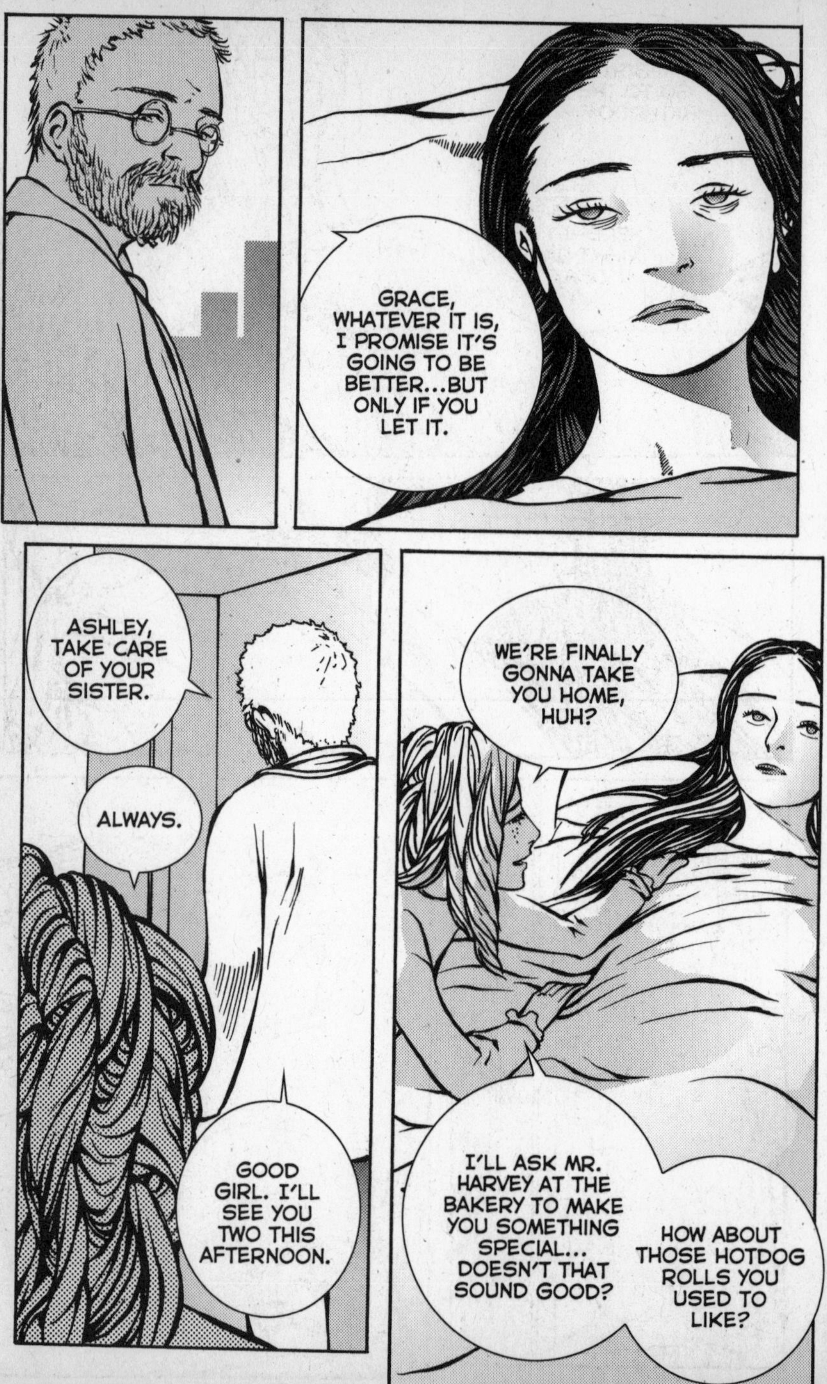
GRACE, WHATEVER IT IS, I PROMISE IT'S GOING TO BE BETTER...BUT ONLY IF YOU LET IT.
ASHLEY, TAKE CARE OF YOUR SISTER.
ALWAYS.
GOOD GIRL. I'LL SEE YOU TWO THIS AFTERNOON.
WE'RE FINALLY GONNA TAKE YOU HOME, HUH?
I'LL ASK MR. HARVEY AT THE BAKERY TO MAKE YOU SOMETHING SPECIAL... DOESN'T THAT SOUND GOOD?
HOW ABOUT THOSE HOTDOG ROLLS YOU USED TO LIKE?

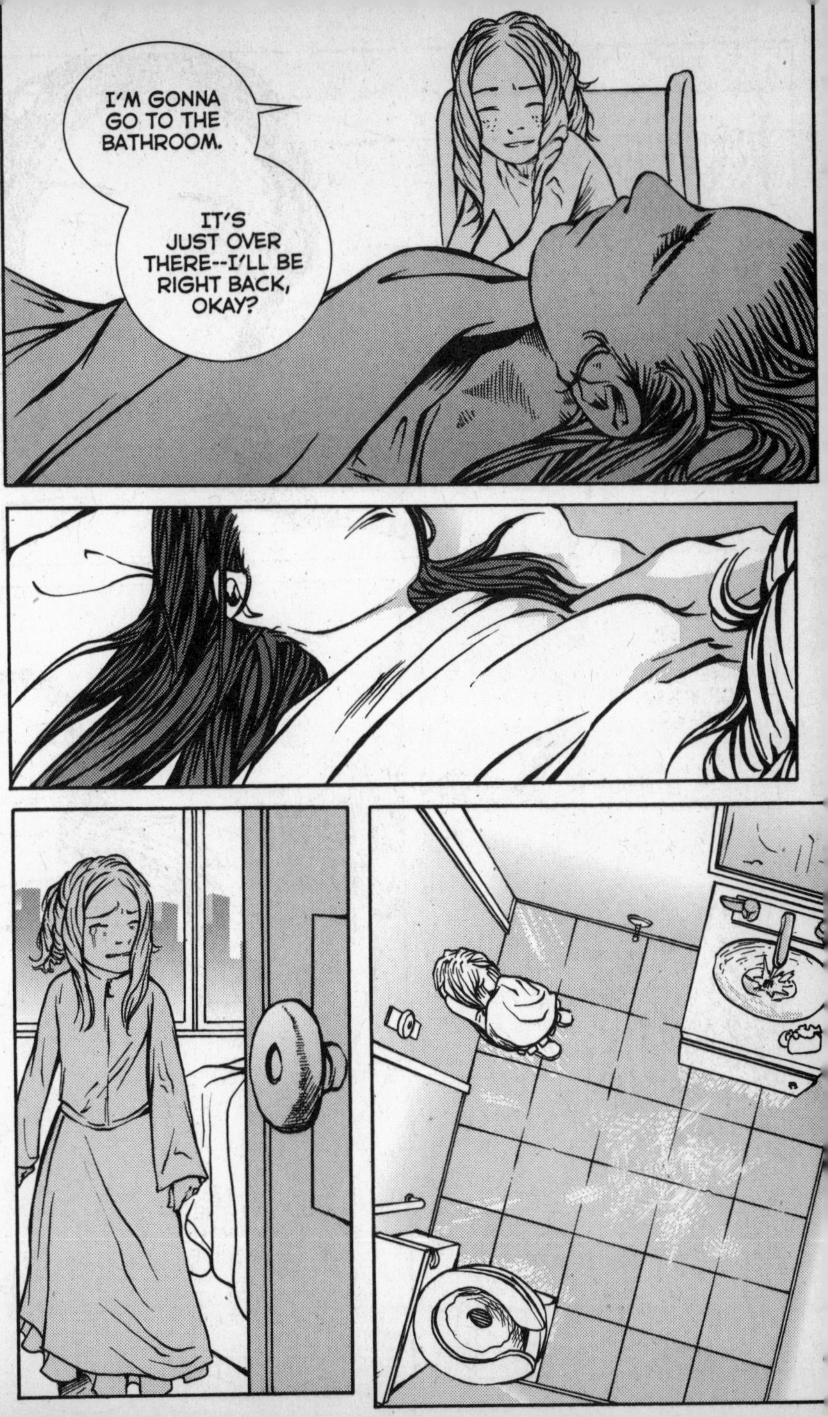
I'M GONNA GO TO THE BATHROOM.
IT'S JUST OVER THERE--I'LL BE RIGHT BACK, OKAY?

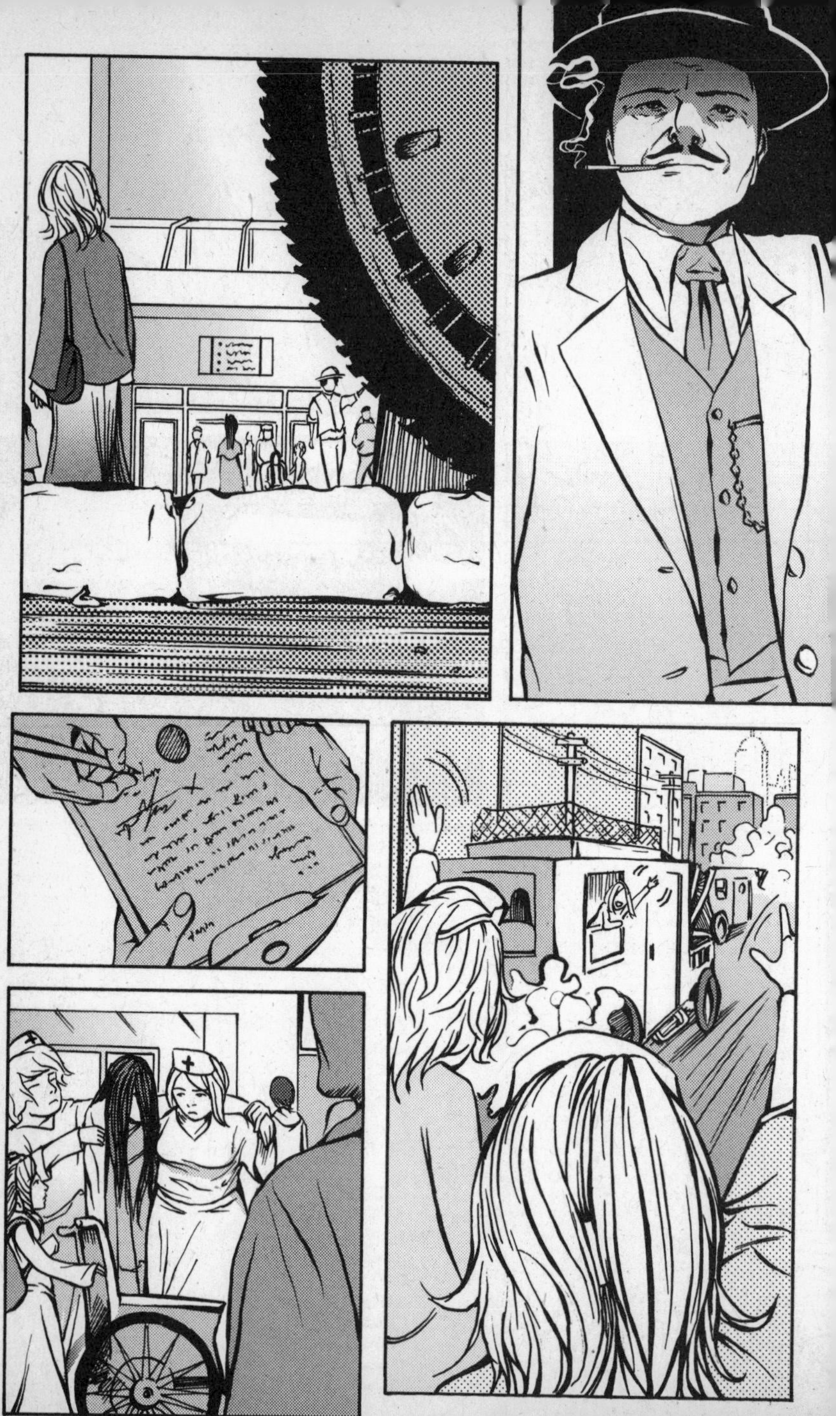

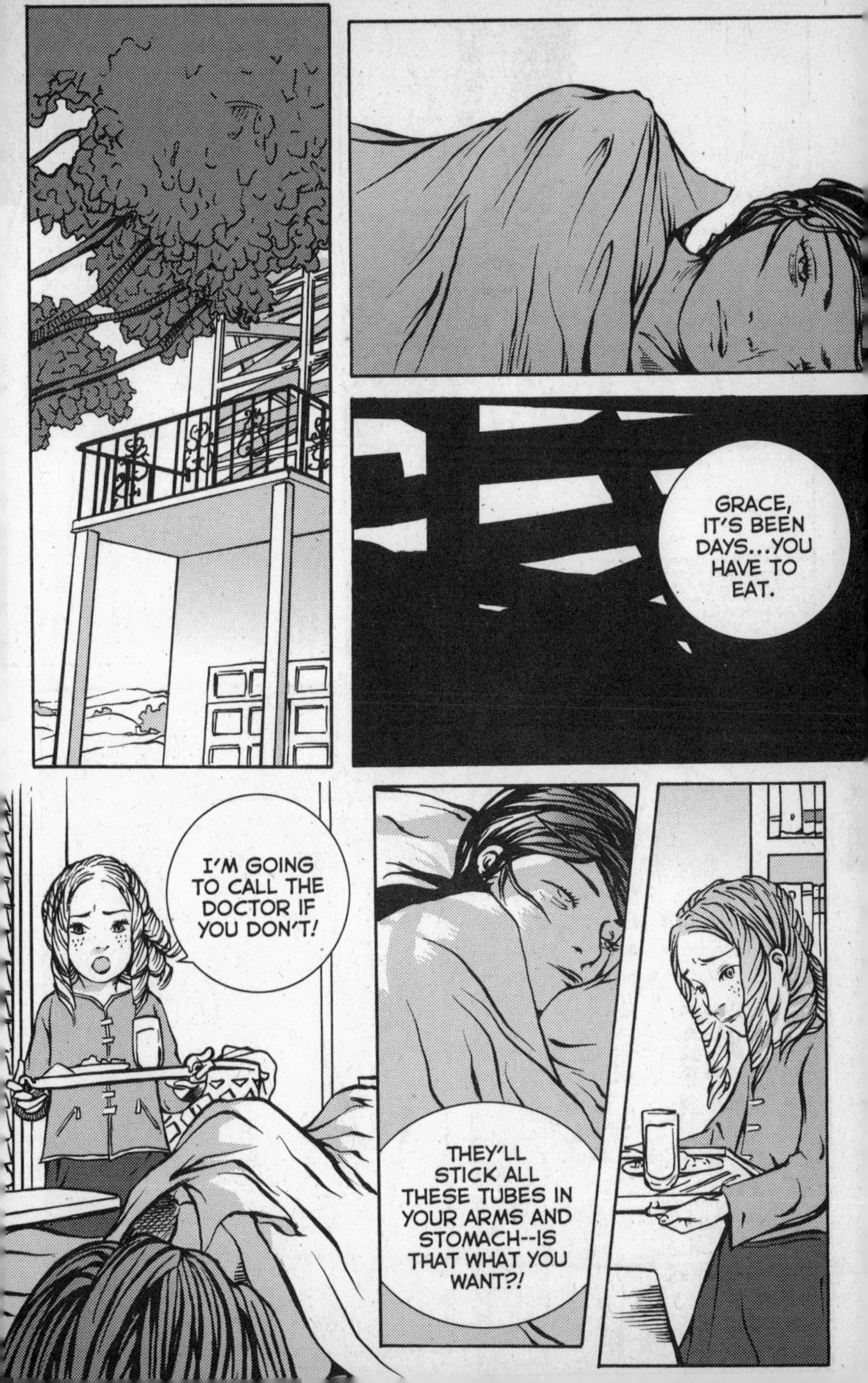
GRACE, IT'S BEEN DAYS...YOU HAVE TO EAT.
I'M GOING TO CALL THE DOCTOR IF YOU DON'T!
THEY'LL STICK ALL THESE TUBES IN YOUR ARMS AND STOMACH--IS THAT WHAT YOU WANT?!

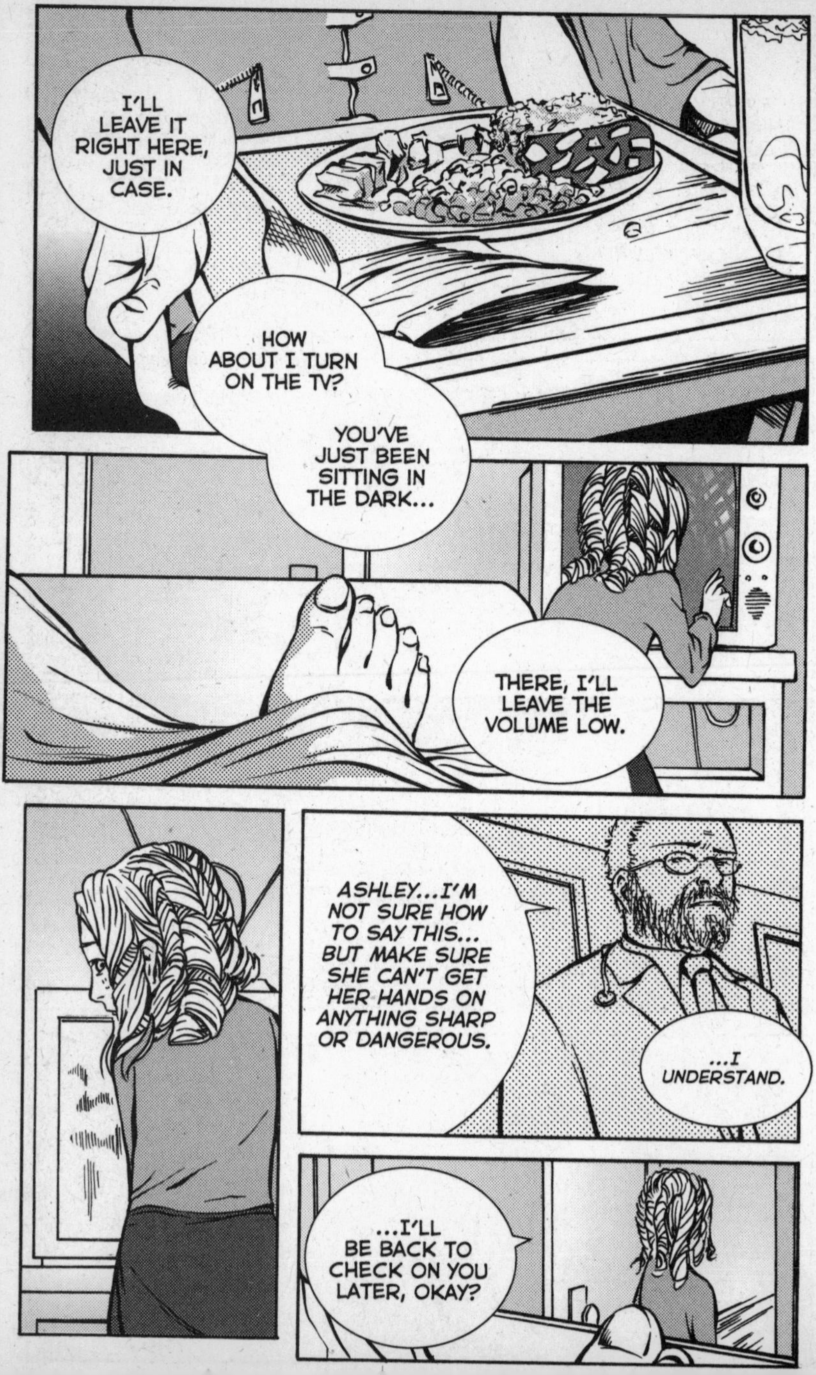
I'LL LEAVE IT RIGHT HERE, JUST IN CASE.
HOW ABOUT I TURN ON THE TV?
YOU'VE JUST BEEN SITTING IN THE DARK...
THERE, I'LL LEAVE THE VOLUME LOW.
ASHLEY...I'M NOT SURE HOW TO SAY THIS... BUT MAKE SURE SHE CAN'T GET HER HANDS ON ANYTHING SHARP OR DANGEROUS.
...I UNDERSTAND.
...I'LL BE BACK TO CHECK ON YOU LATER, OKAY?

...WITH TEMPERATURES IN THE LOW SEVENTIES FOR THE GREATER METROPOLITAN REGION. A PERFECT DAY TO TAKE THE FAMILY OUT FOR A PICNIC, WOULDN'T YOU SAY?

ABSOLUTELY, JOHN--THANKS FOR THE REPORT.

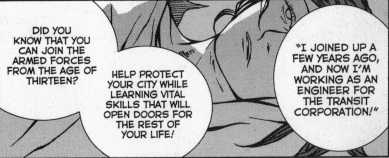

DID YOU KNOW THAT YOU CAN JOIN THE ARMED FORCES FROM THE AGE OF THIRTEEN?

HELP PROTECT YOUR CITY WHILE LEARNING VITAL SKILLS THAT WILL OPEN DOORS FOR THE REST OF YOUR LIFE!

"I JOINED UP A FEW YEARS AGO, AND NOW I'M WORKING AS AN ENGINEER FOR THE TRANSIT CORPORATION!"

CALL NOW FOR FREE INFORMATION ON HOW YOU CAN JOIN UP--AND EVEN EARN MONEY TOWARDS AN EDUCATION!

1-800-555-4444!

ONCE AGAIN...

WELCOME BACK.

WITH US IS OUR ASSOCIATE SCOTT JONES, WITH A REPORT SPECIAL ON THE NEW BOOK THAT'S BEEN GRIPPING READERS ACROSS THE NATION:

SICK GIRL.

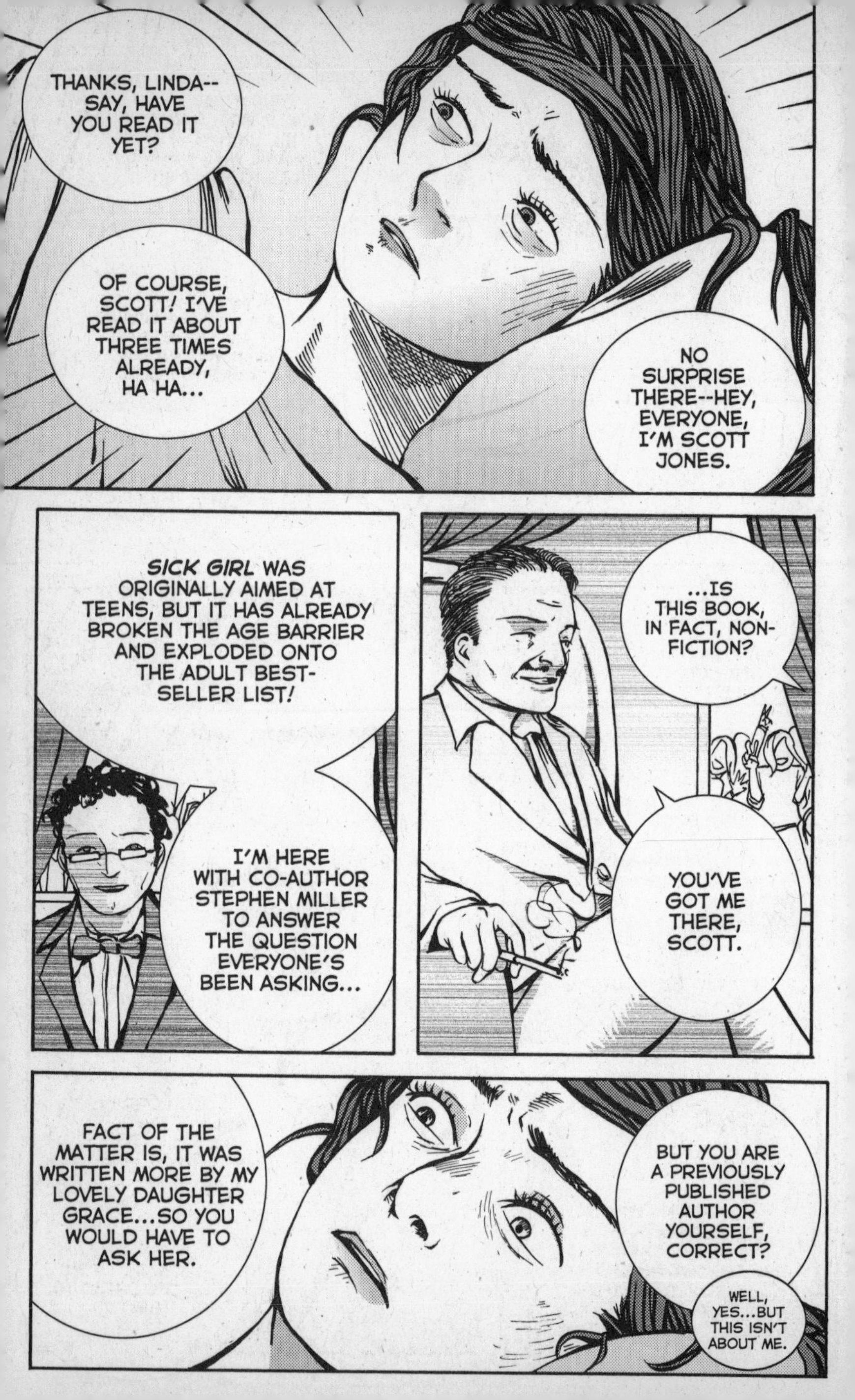
THANKS, LINDA--SAY, HAVE YOU READ IT YET?
OF COURSE, SCOTT! I'VE READ IT ABOUT THREE TIMES ALREADY, HA HA...
NO SURPRISE THERE--HEY, EVERYONE, I'M SCOTT JONES.
SICK GIRL WAS ORIGINALLY AIMED AT TEENS, BUT IT HAS ALREADY BROKEN THE AGE BARRIER AND EXPLODED ONTO THE ADULT BEST-SELLER LIST!
I'M HERE WITH CO-AUTHOR STEPHEN MILLER TO ANSWER THE QUESTION EVERYONE'S BEEN ASKING...
...IS THIS BOOK, IN FACT, NON-FICTION?
YOU'VE GOT ME THERE, SCOTT.
FACT OF THE MATTER IS, IT WAS WRITTEN MORE BY MY LOVELY DAUGHTER GRACE...SO YOU WOULD HAVE TO ASK HER.
BUT YOU ARE A PREVIOUSLY PUBLISHED AUTHOR YOURSELF, CORRECT?
WELL, YES...BUT THIS ISN'T ABOUT ME.

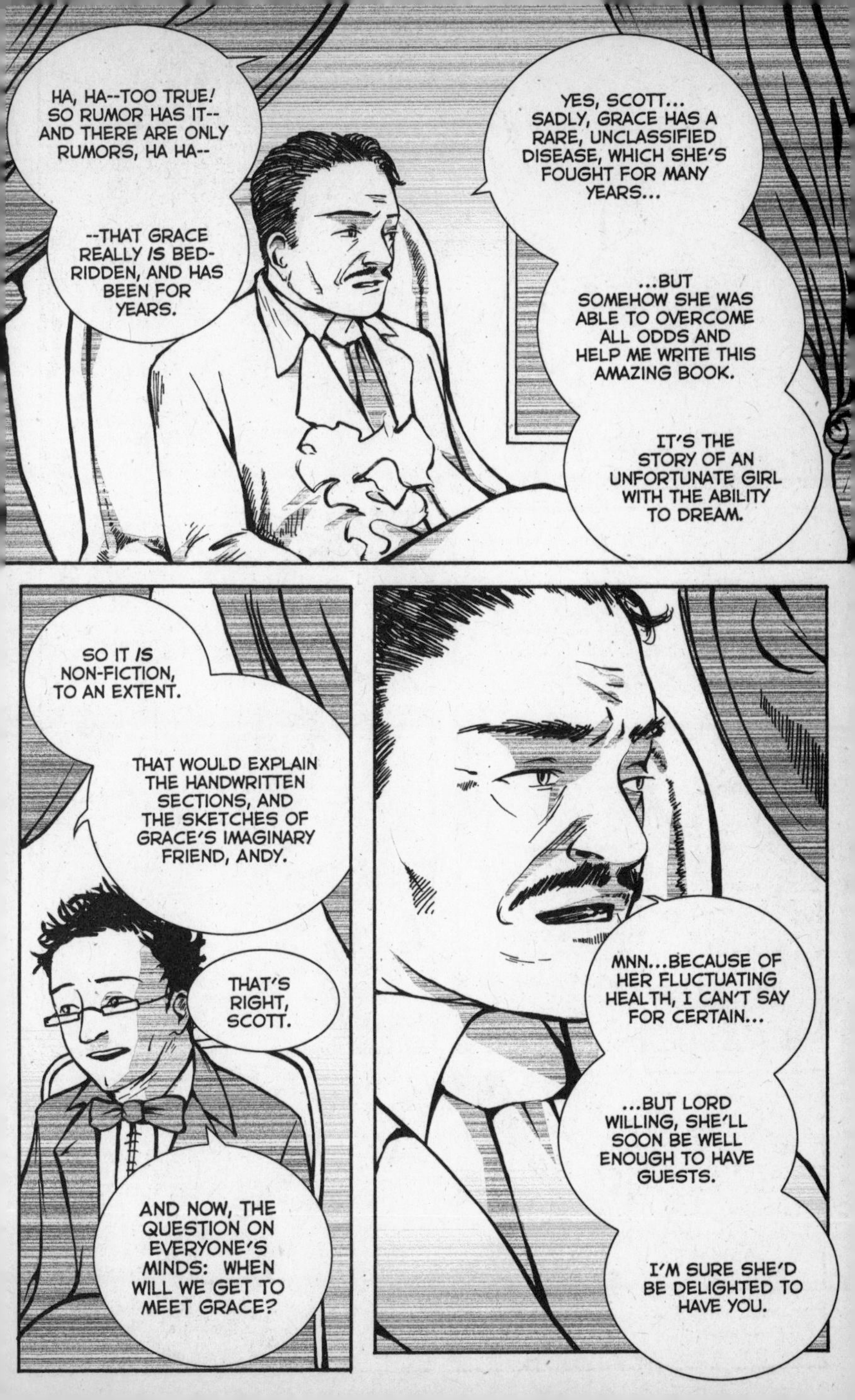
HA, HA--TOO TRUE! SO RUMOR HAS IT-- AND THERE ARE ONLY RUMORS, HA HA--
--THAT GRACE REALLY *IS* BED-RIDDEN, AND HAS BEEN FOR YEARS.
YES, SCOTT... SADLY, GRACE HAS A RARE, UNCLASSIFIED DISEASE, WHICH SHE'S FOUGHT FOR MANY YEARS...
...BUT SOMEHOW SHE WAS ABLE TO OVERCOME ALL ODDS AND HELP ME WRITE THIS AMAZING BOOK.
IT'S THE STORY OF AN UNFORTUNATE GIRL WITH THE ABILITY TO DREAM.
SO IT *IS* NON-FICTION, TO AN EXTENT.
THAT WOULD EXPLAIN THE HANDWRITTEN SECTIONS, AND THE SKETCHES OF GRACE'S IMAGINARY FRIEND, ANDY.
THAT'S RIGHT, SCOTT.
AND NOW, THE QUESTION ON EVERYONE'S MINDS: WHEN WILL WE GET TO MEET GRACE?
MNN...BECAUSE OF HER FLUCTUATING HEALTH, I CAN'T SAY FOR CERTAIN...
...BUT LORD WILLING, SHE'LL SOON BE WELL ENOUGH TO HAVE GUESTS.
I'M SURE SHE'D BE DELIGHTED TO HAVE YOU.

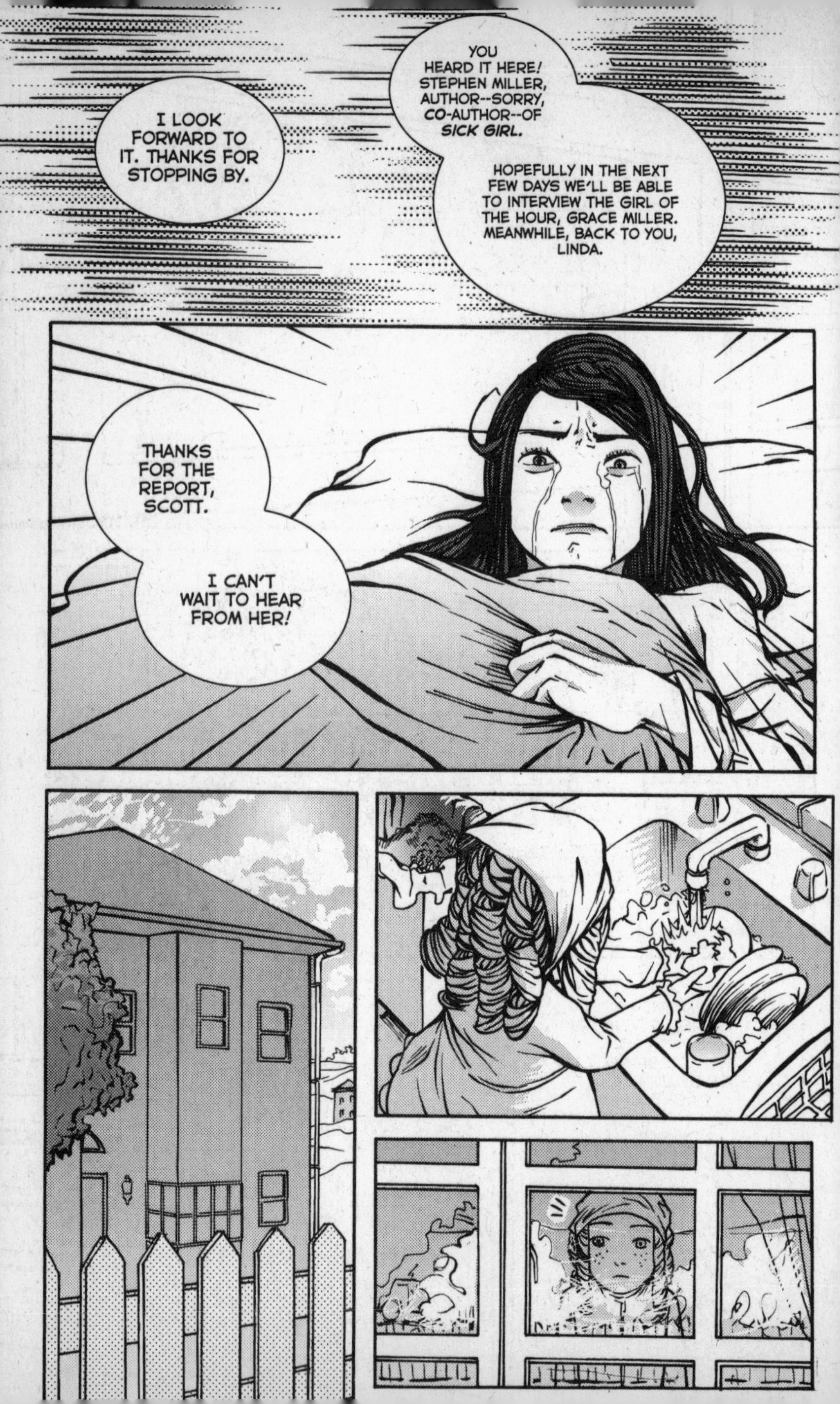
I LOOK FORWARD TO IT. THANKS FOR STOPPING BY.
YOU HEARD IT HERE! STEPHEN MILLER, AUTHOR--SORRY, CO-AUTHOR--OF SICK GIRL.
HOPEFULLY IN THE NEXT FEW DAYS WE'LL BE ABLE TO INTERVIEW THE GIRL OF THE HOUR, GRACE MILLER. MEANWHILE, BACK TO YOU, LINDA.
THANKS FOR THE REPORT, SCOTT.
I CAN'T WAIT TO HEAR FROM HER!

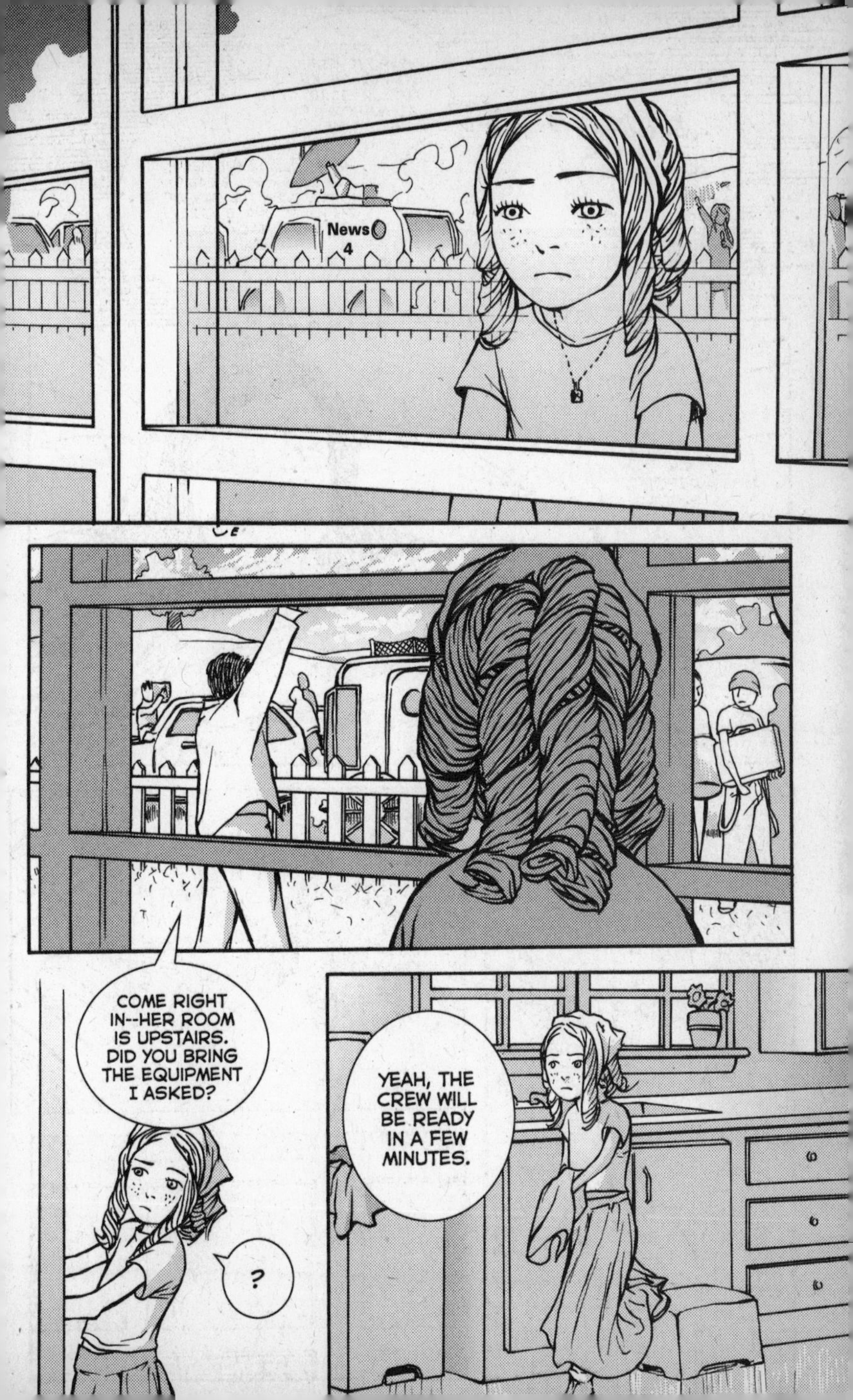
News 4
COME RIGHT IN--HER ROOM IS UPSTAIRS. DID YOU BRING THE EQUIPMENT I ASKED?
?
YEAH, THE CREW WILL BE READY IN A FEW MINUTES.

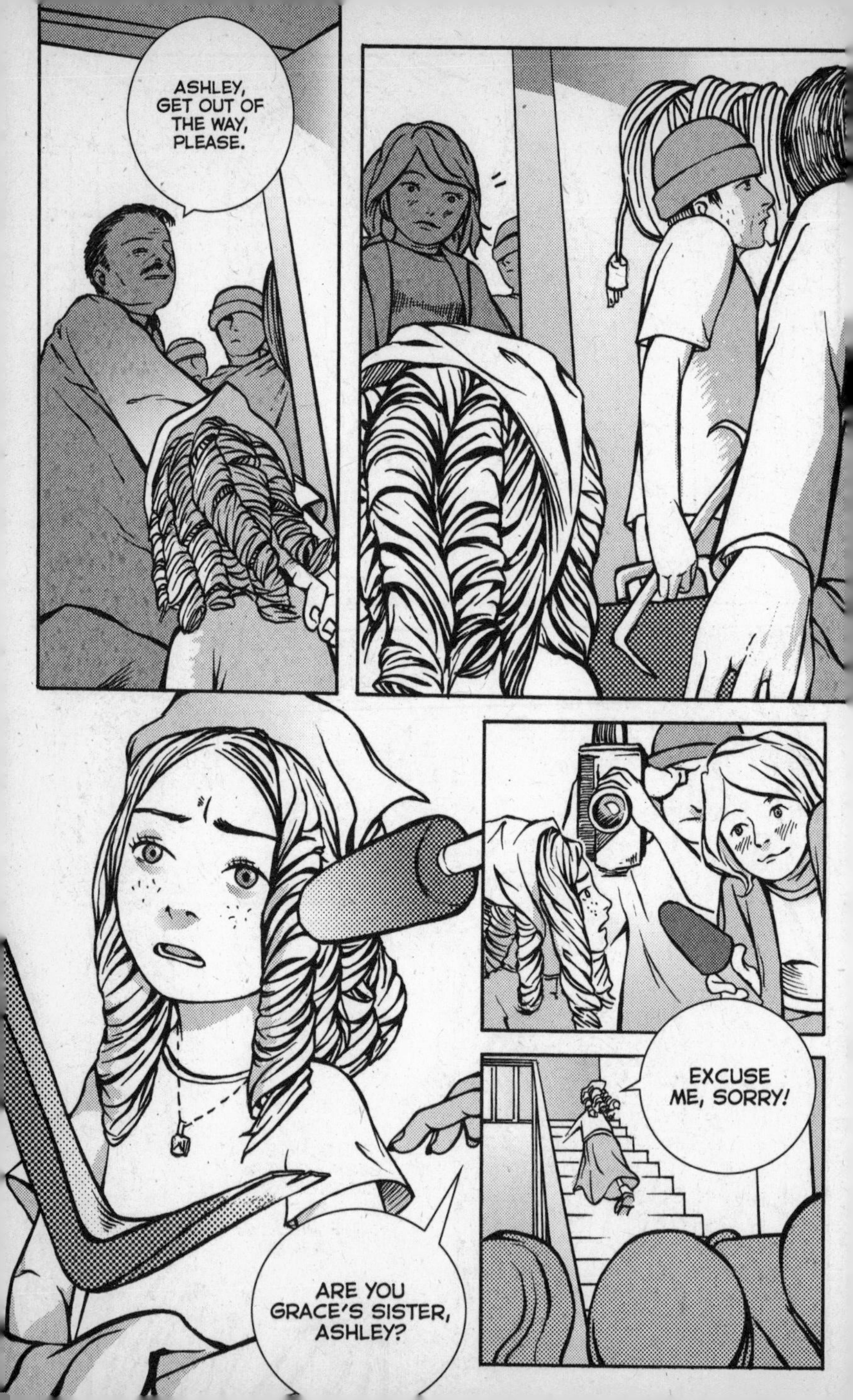
ASHLEY, GET OUT OF THE WAY, PLEASE.
EXCUSE ME, SORRY!
ARE YOU GRACE'S SISTER, ASHLEY?

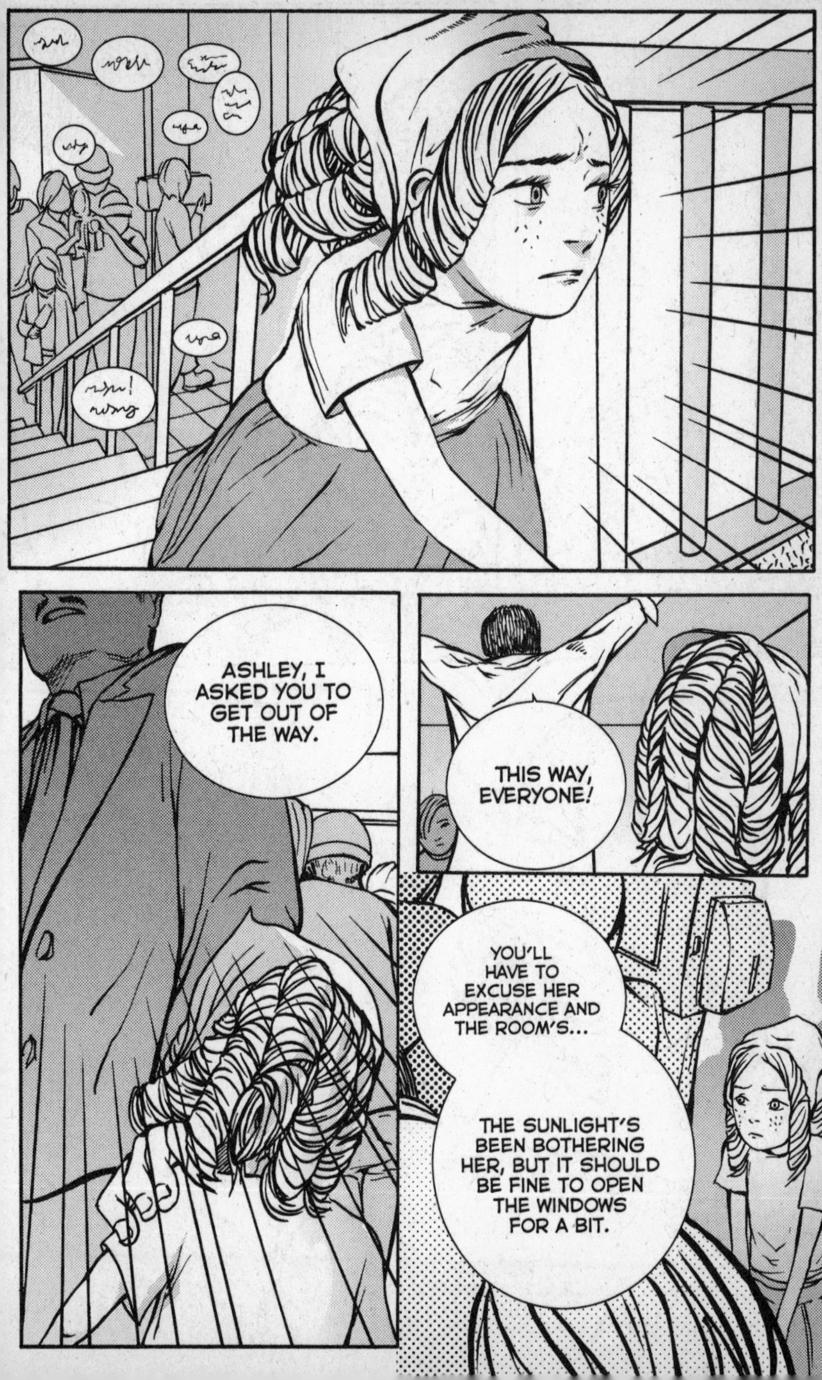
ASHLEY, I ASKED YOU TO GET OUT OF THE WAY.
THIS WAY, EVERYONE!
YOU'LL HAVE TO EXCUSE HER APPEARANCE AND THE ROOM'S...
THE SUNLIGHT'S BEEN BOTHERING HER, BUT IT SHOULD BE FINE TO OPEN THE WINDOWS FOR A BIT.

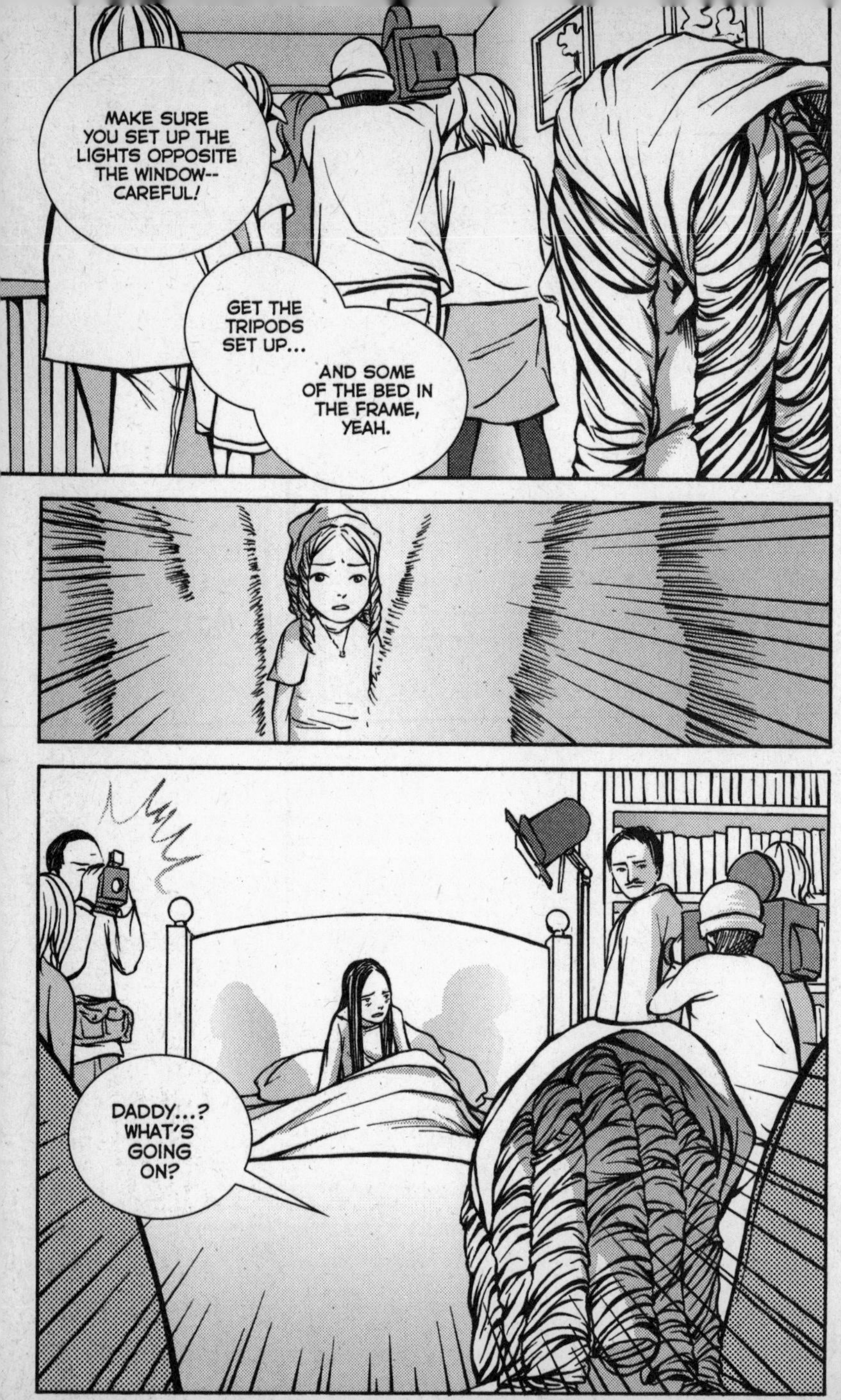
MAKE SURE YOU SET UP THE LIGHTS OPPOSITE THE WINDOW-- CAREFUL!
GET THE TRIPODS SET UP...
AND SOME OF THE BED IN THE FRAME, YEAH.
DADDY...? WHAT'S GOING ON?

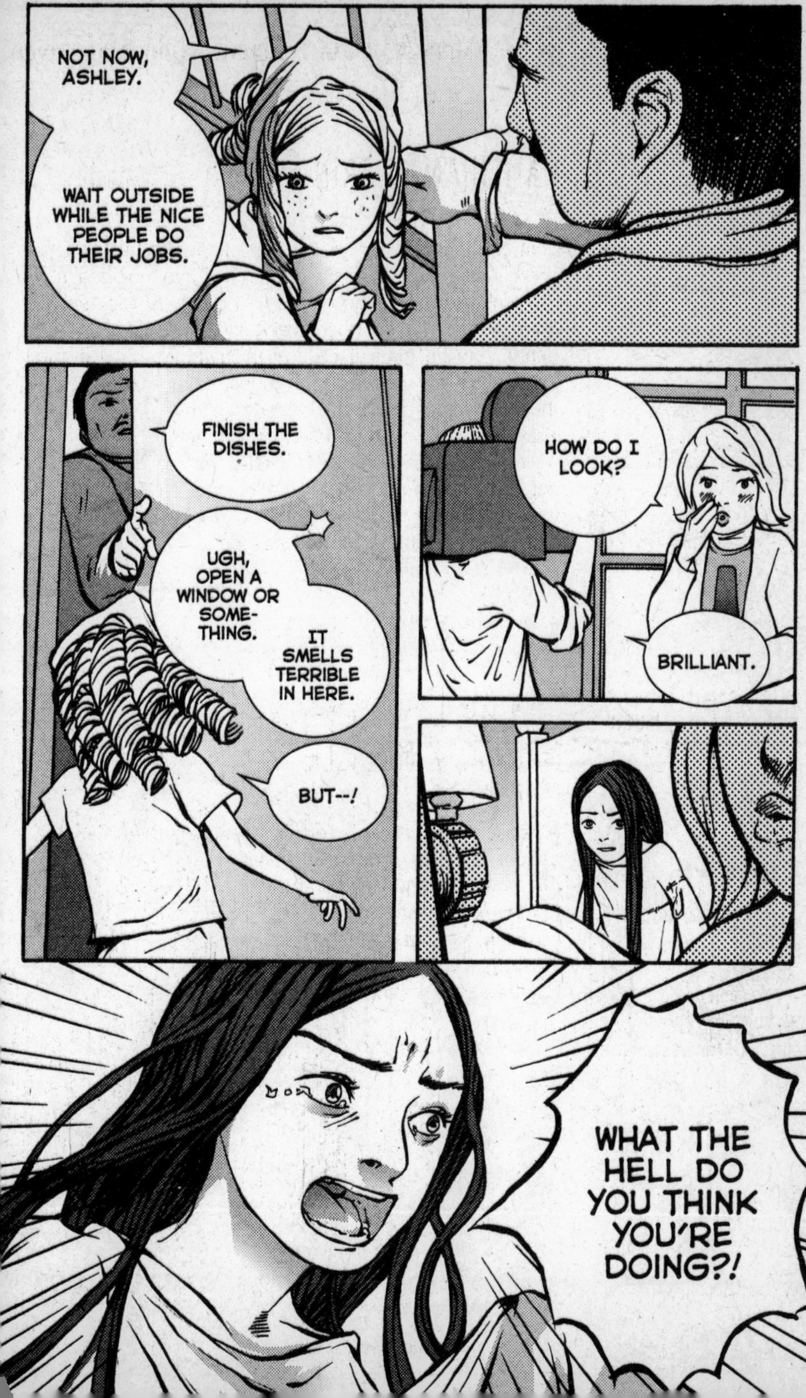
NOT NOW, ASHLEY.
WAIT OUTSIDE WHILE THE NICE PEOPLE DO THEIR JOBS.
FINISH THE DISHES.
UGH, OPEN A WINDOW OR SOME-THING.
IT SMELLS TERRIBLE IN HERE.
BUT--!
HOW DO I LOOK?
BRILLIANT.
WHAT THE HELL DO YOU THINK YOU'RE DOING?!

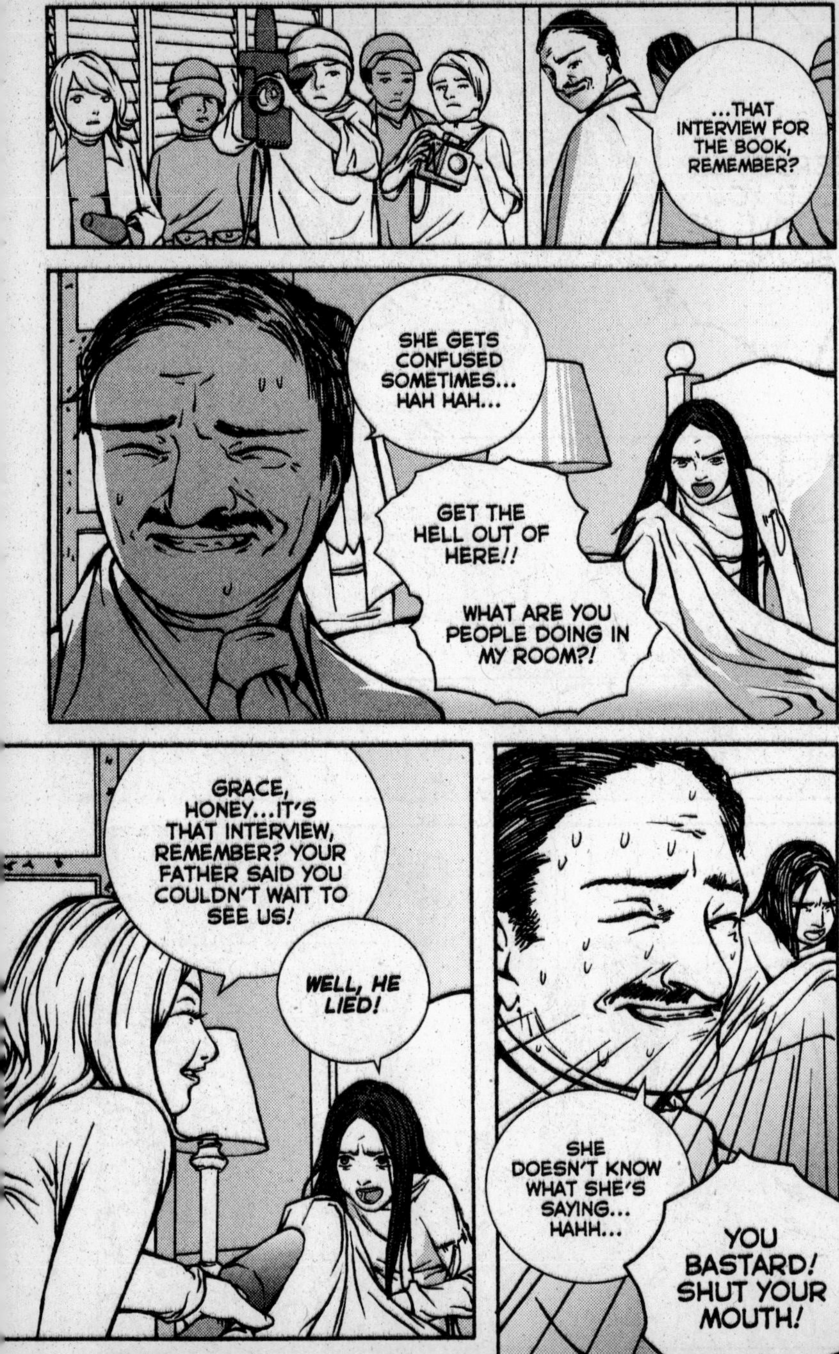
...THAT INTERVIEW FOR THE BOOK, REMEMBER?
SHE GETS CONFUSED SOMETIMES... HAH HAH...
GET THE HELL OUT OF HERE!!
WHAT ARE YOU PEOPLE DOING IN MY ROOM?!
GRACE, HONEY...IT'S THAT INTERVIEW, REMEMBER? YOUR FATHER SAID YOU COULDN'T WAIT TO SEE US!
WELL, HE LIED!
SHE DOESN'T KNOW WHAT SHE'S SAYING... HAHH...
YOU BASTARD! SHUT YOUR MOUTH!

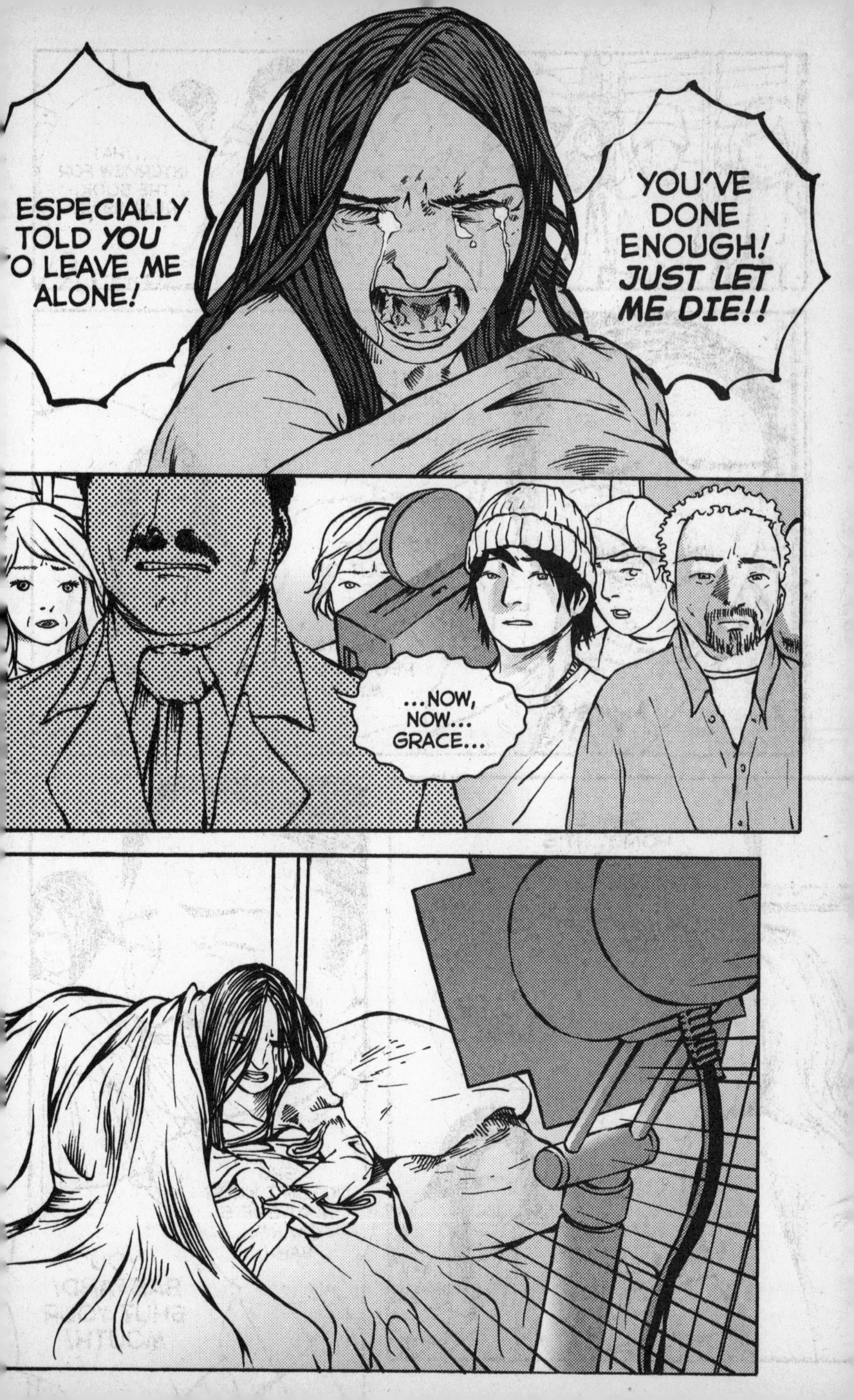
ESPECIALLY TOLD YOU 'O LEAVE ME ALONE!
YOU'VE DONE ENOUGH! JUST LET ME DIE!!
...NOW, NOW... GRACE...

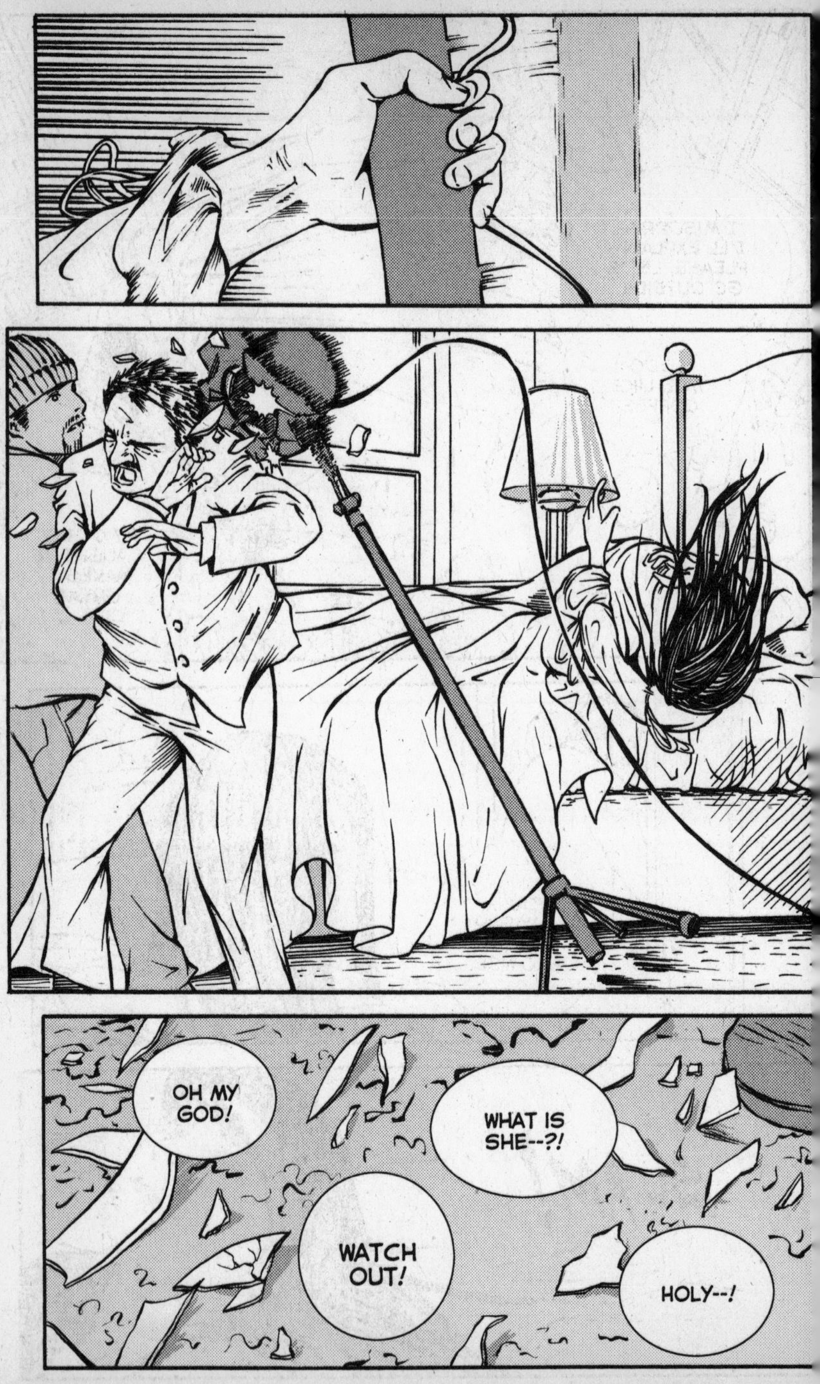
OH MY GOD!
WHAT IS SHE--?!
WATCH OUT!
HOLY--!

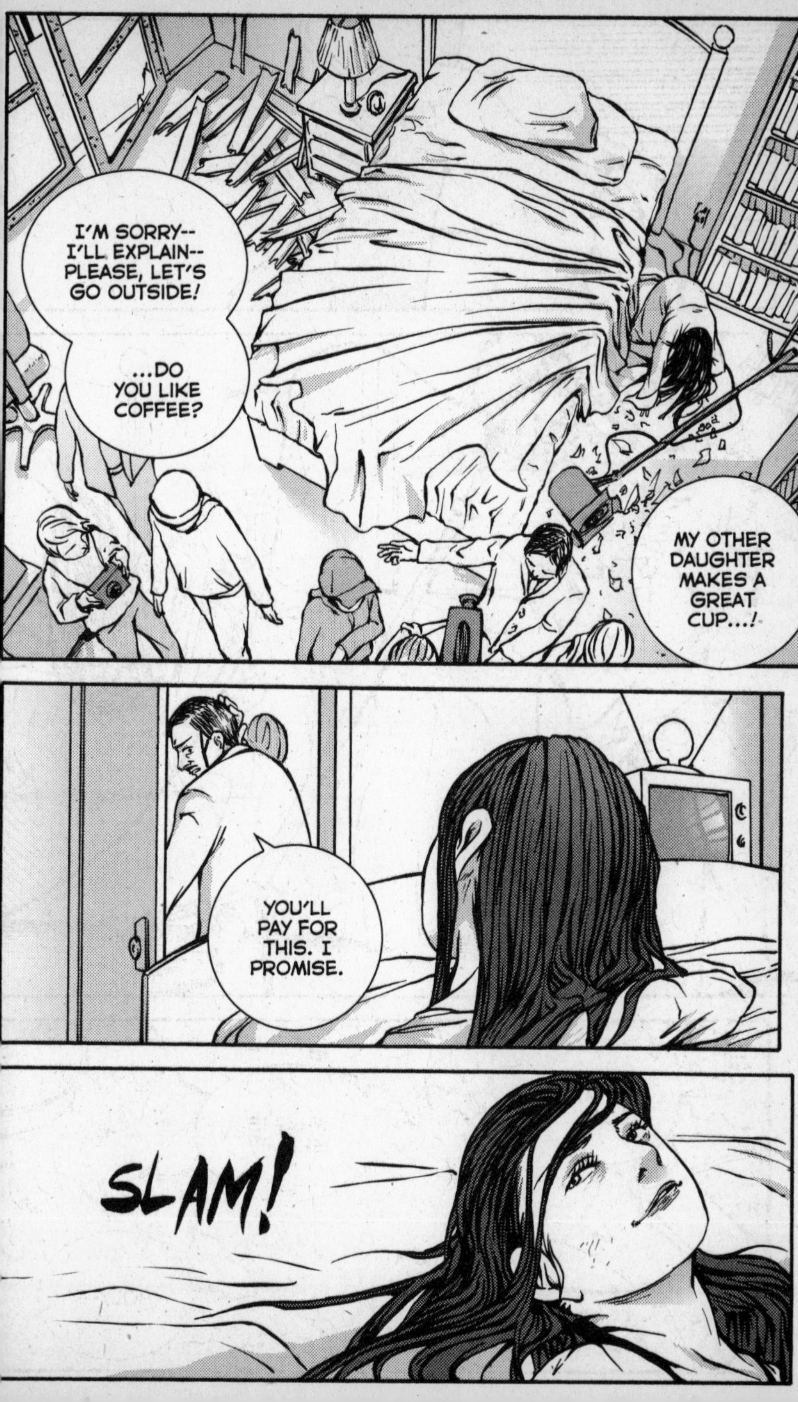
I'M SORRY-- I'LL EXPLAIN-- PLEASE, LET'S GO OUTSIDE!
...DO YOU LIKE COFFEE?
MY OTHER DAUGHTER MAKES A GREAT CUP...!
YOU'LL PAY FOR THIS. I PROMISE.
SLAM!

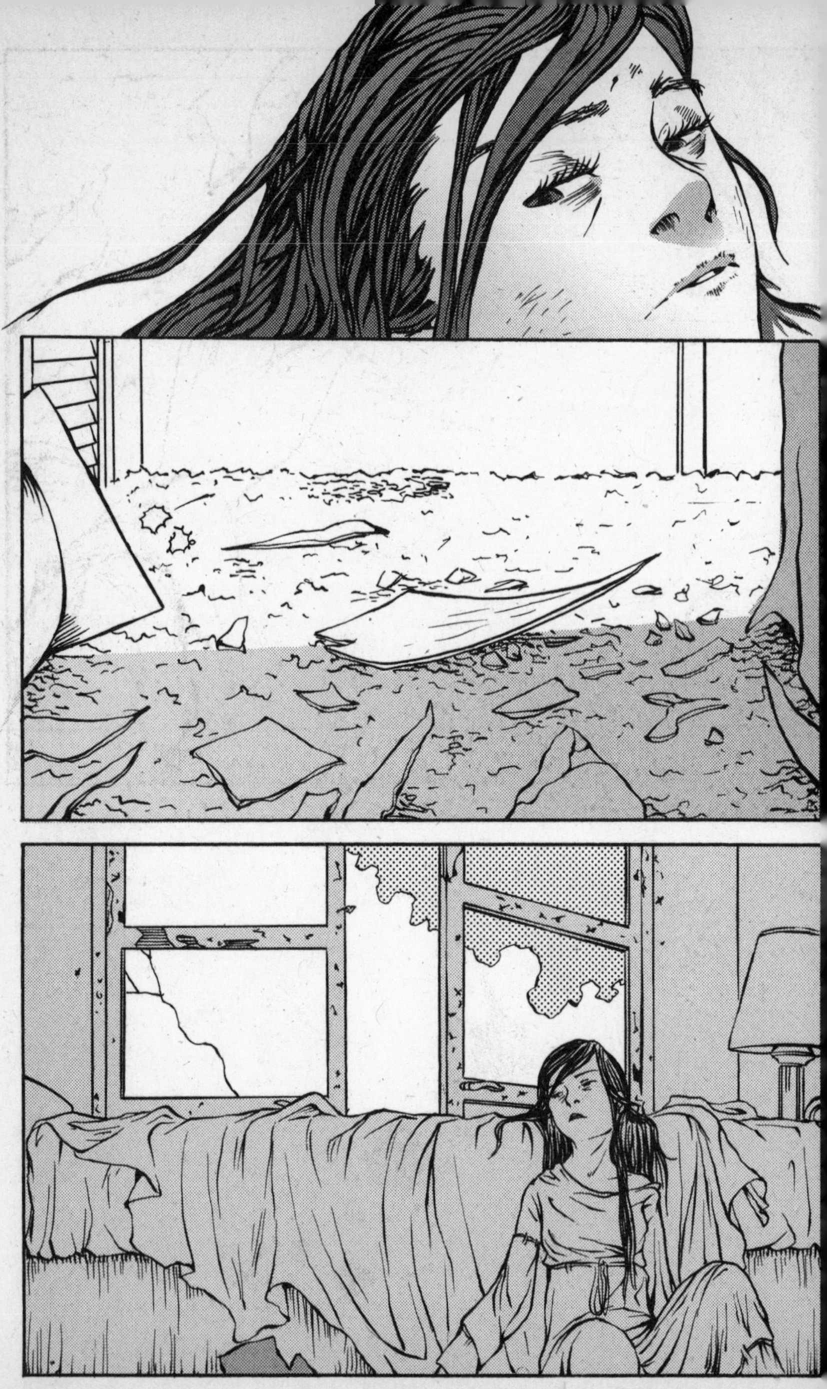

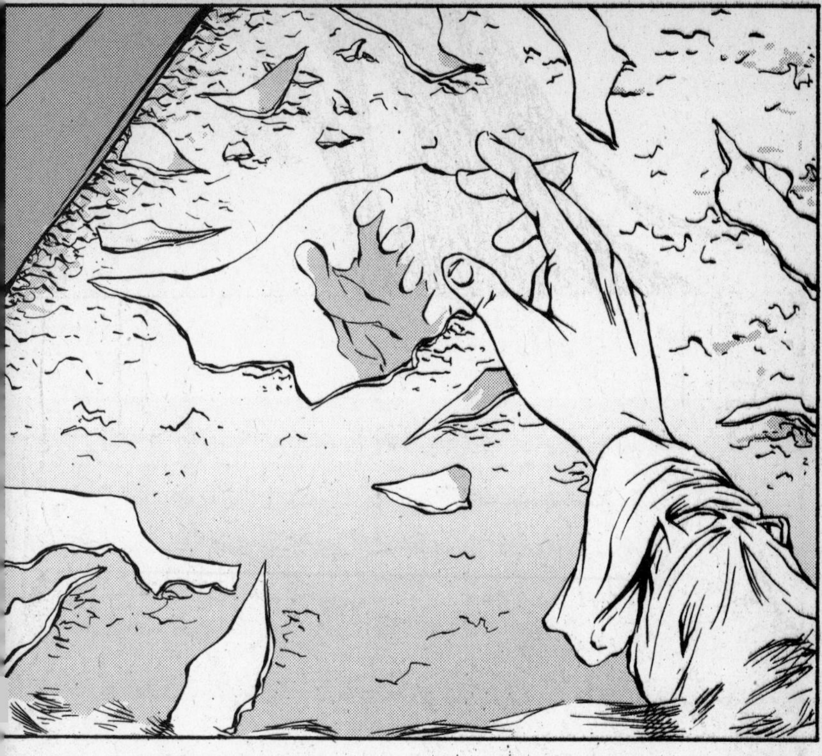

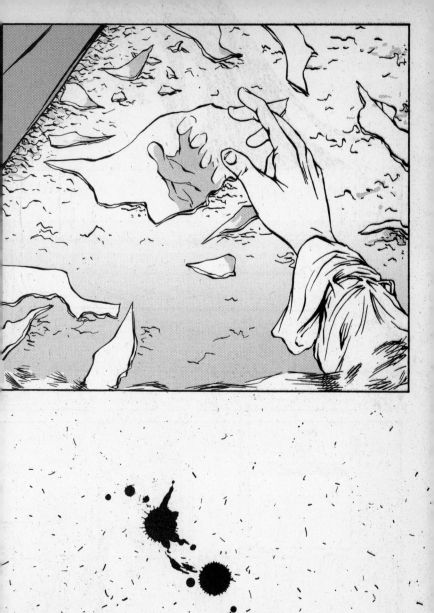

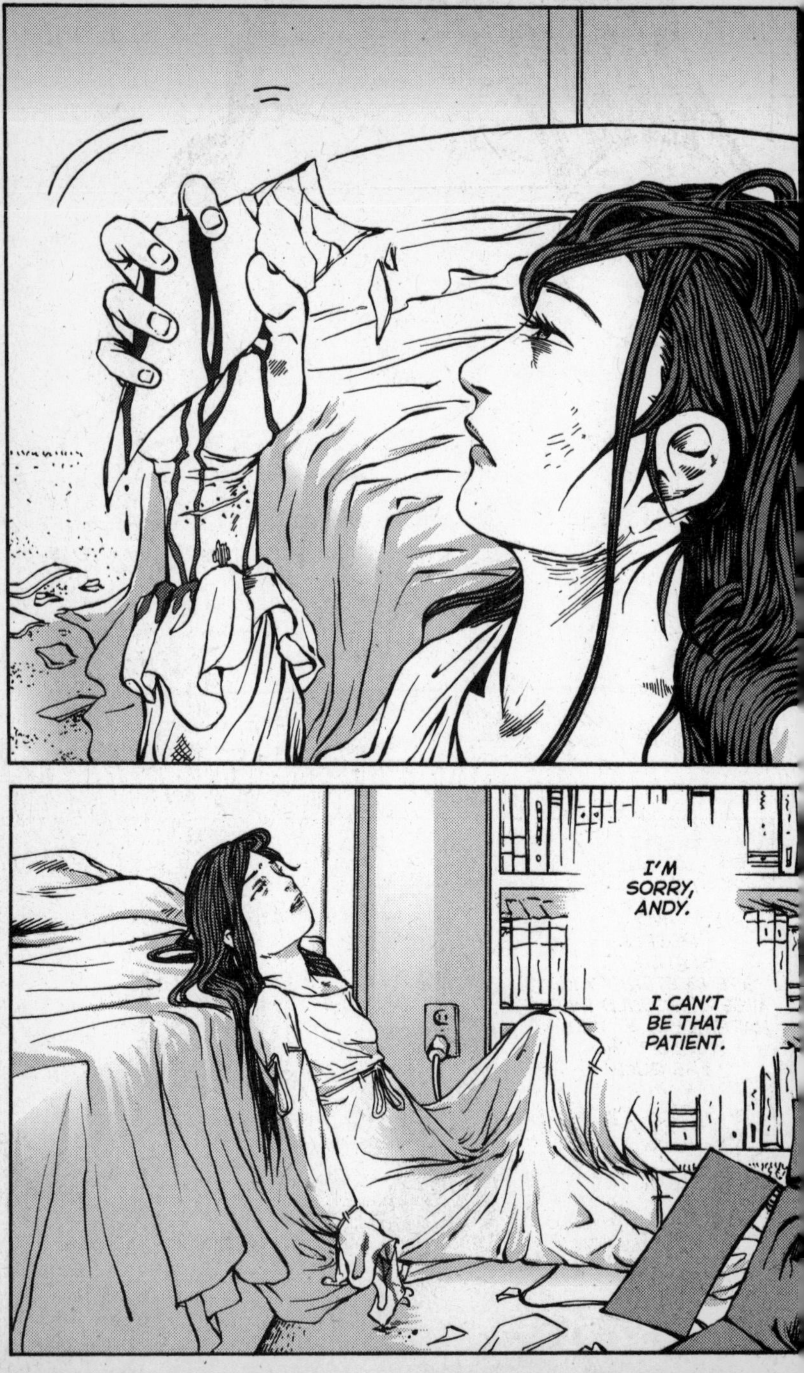
I'M SORRY, ANDY.
I CAN'T BE THAT PATIENT.

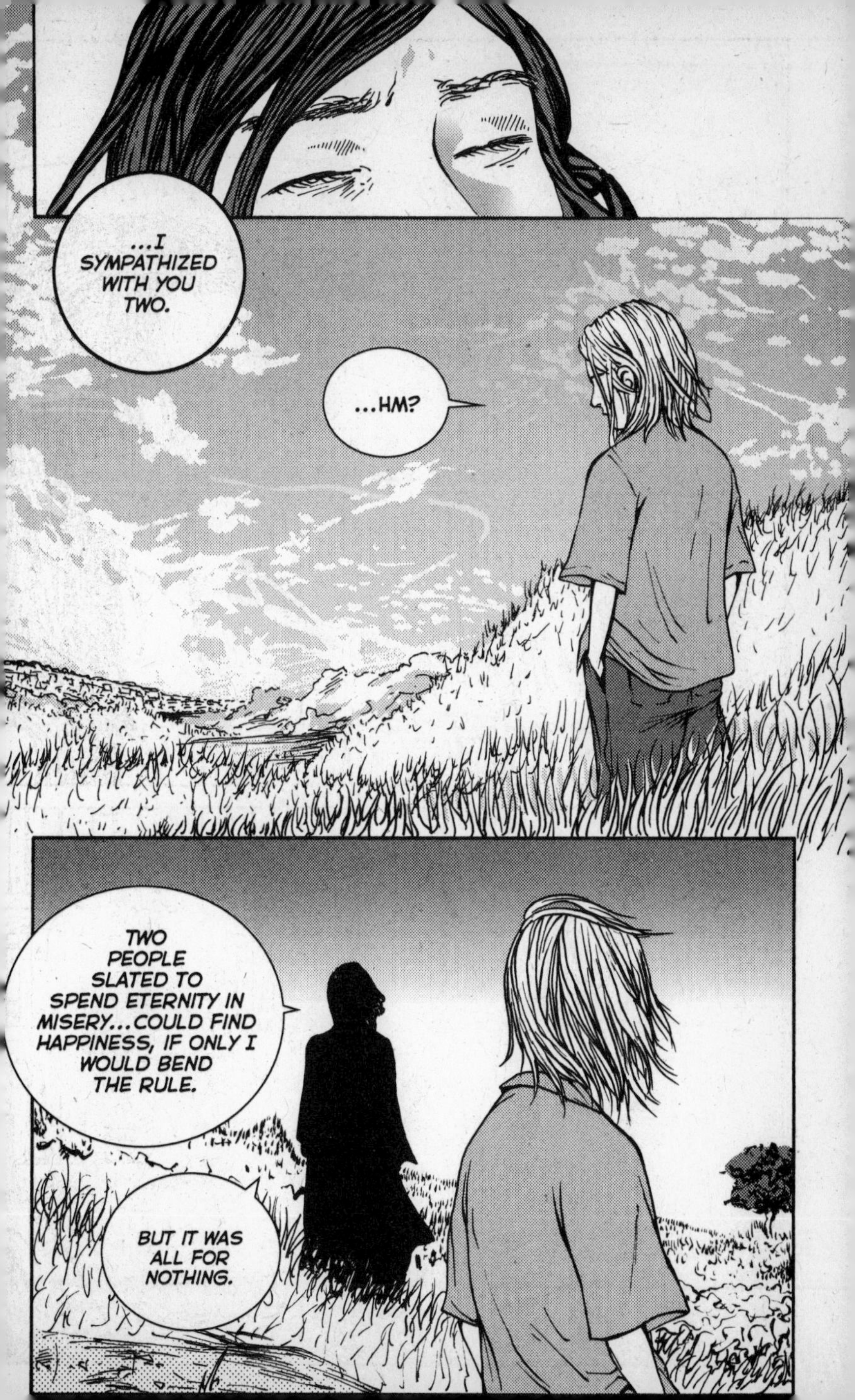
...I SYMPATHIZED WITH YOU TWO.
...HM?
TWO PEOPLE SLATED TO SPEND ETERNITY IN MISERY...COULD FIND HAPPINESS, IF ONLY I WOULD BEND THE RULE.
BUT IT WAS ALL FOR NOTHING.

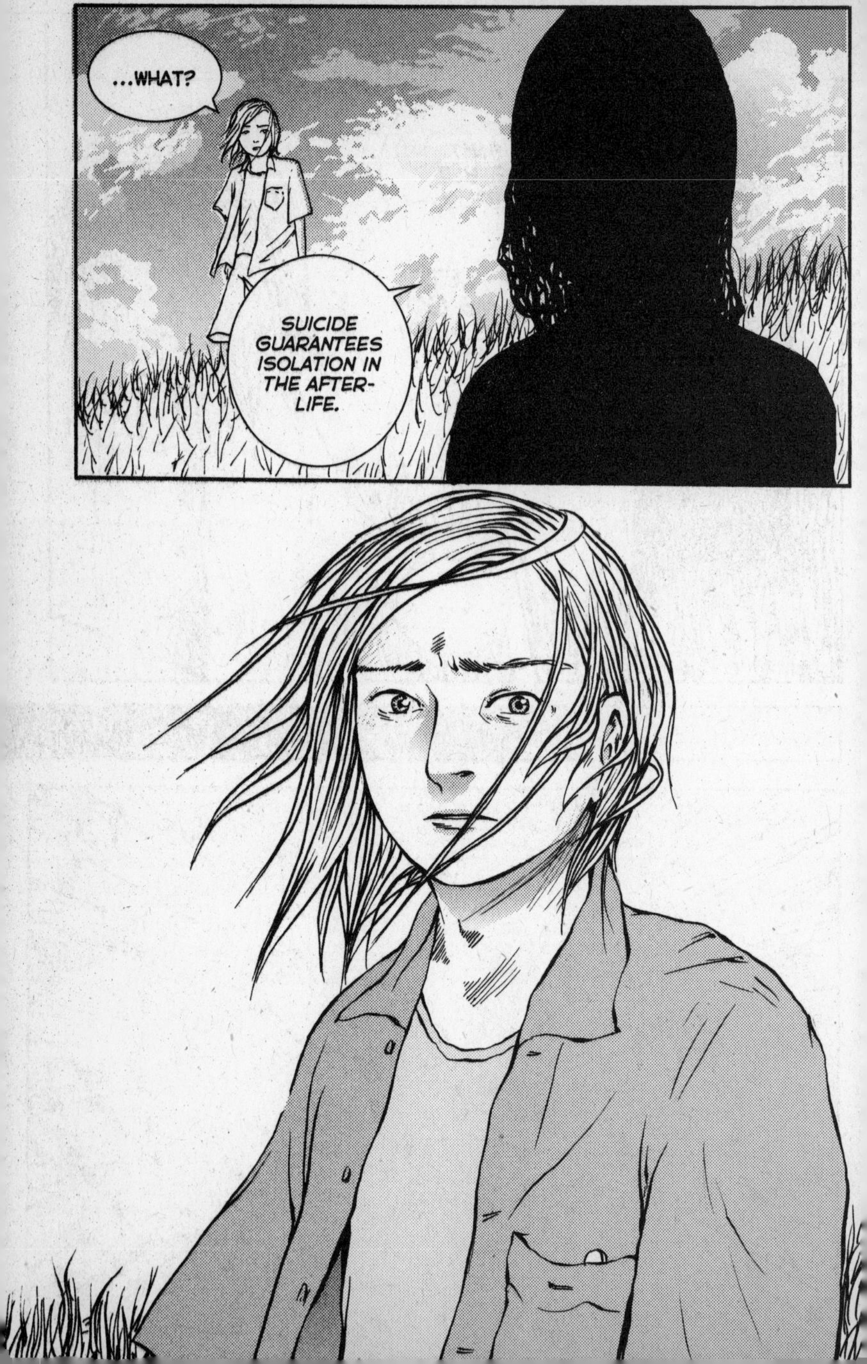
...WHAT?
SUICIDE GUARANTEES ISOLATION IN THE AFTER-LIFE.

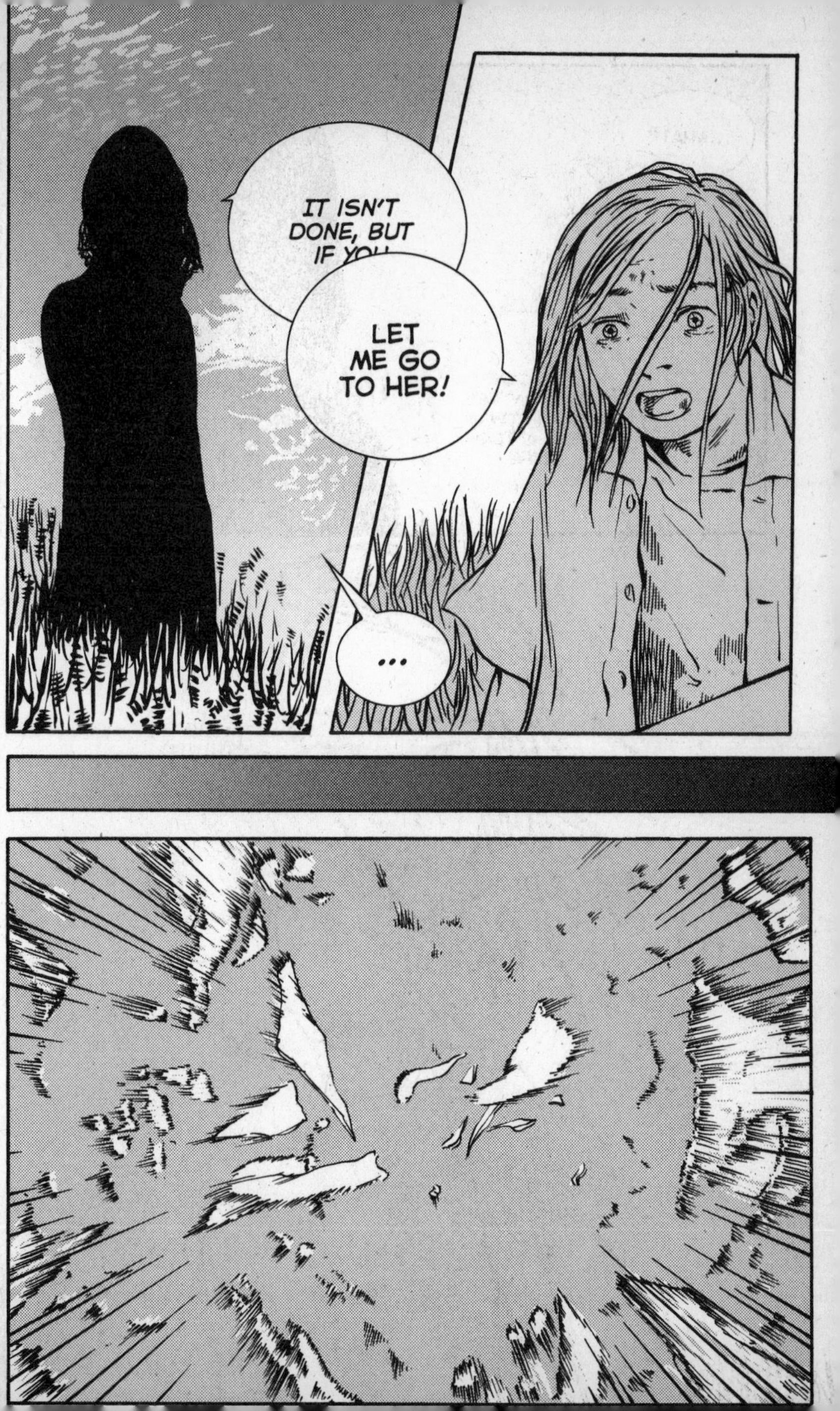
IT ISN'T DONE, BUT IF YOU
LET ME GO TO HER!
...

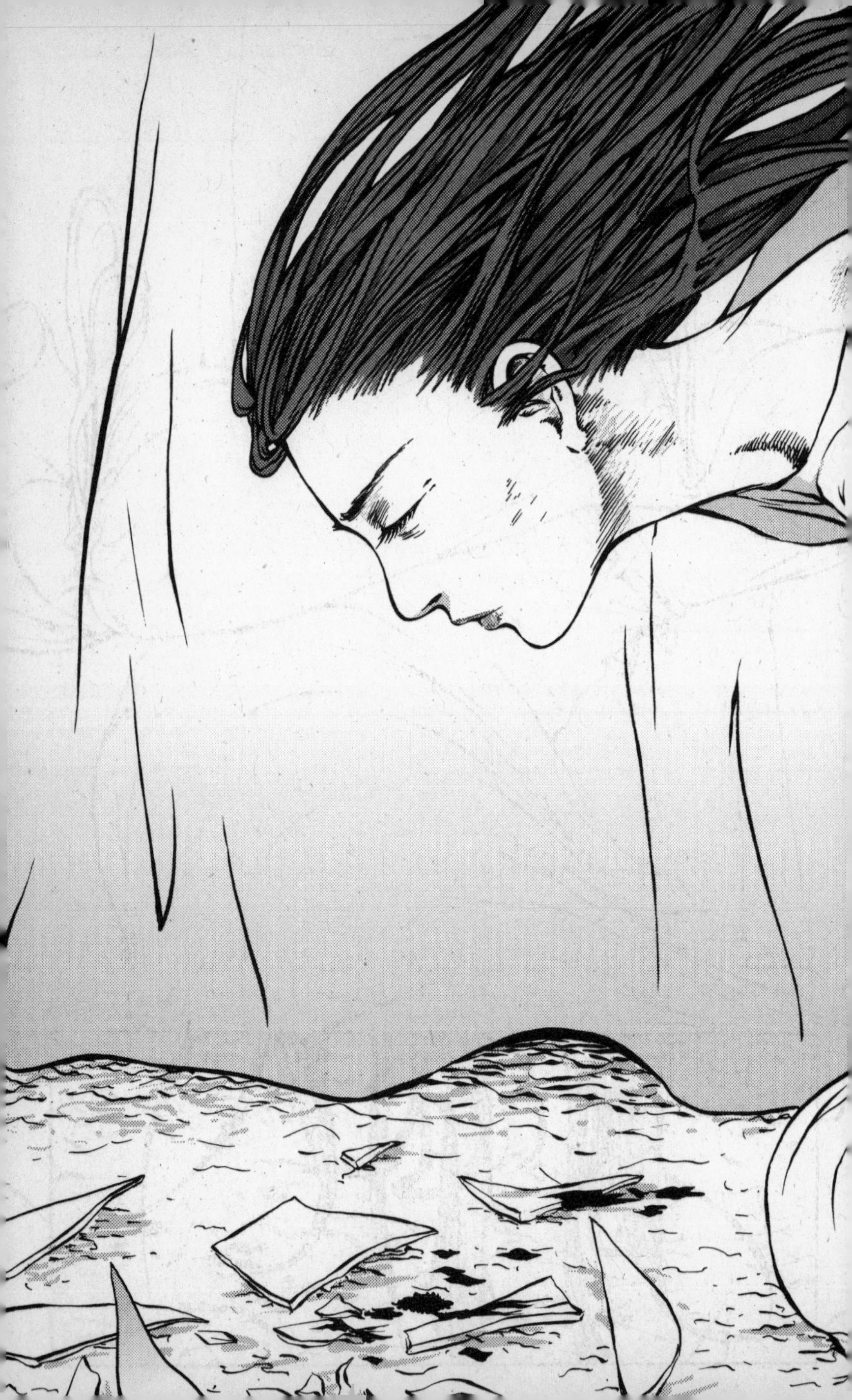

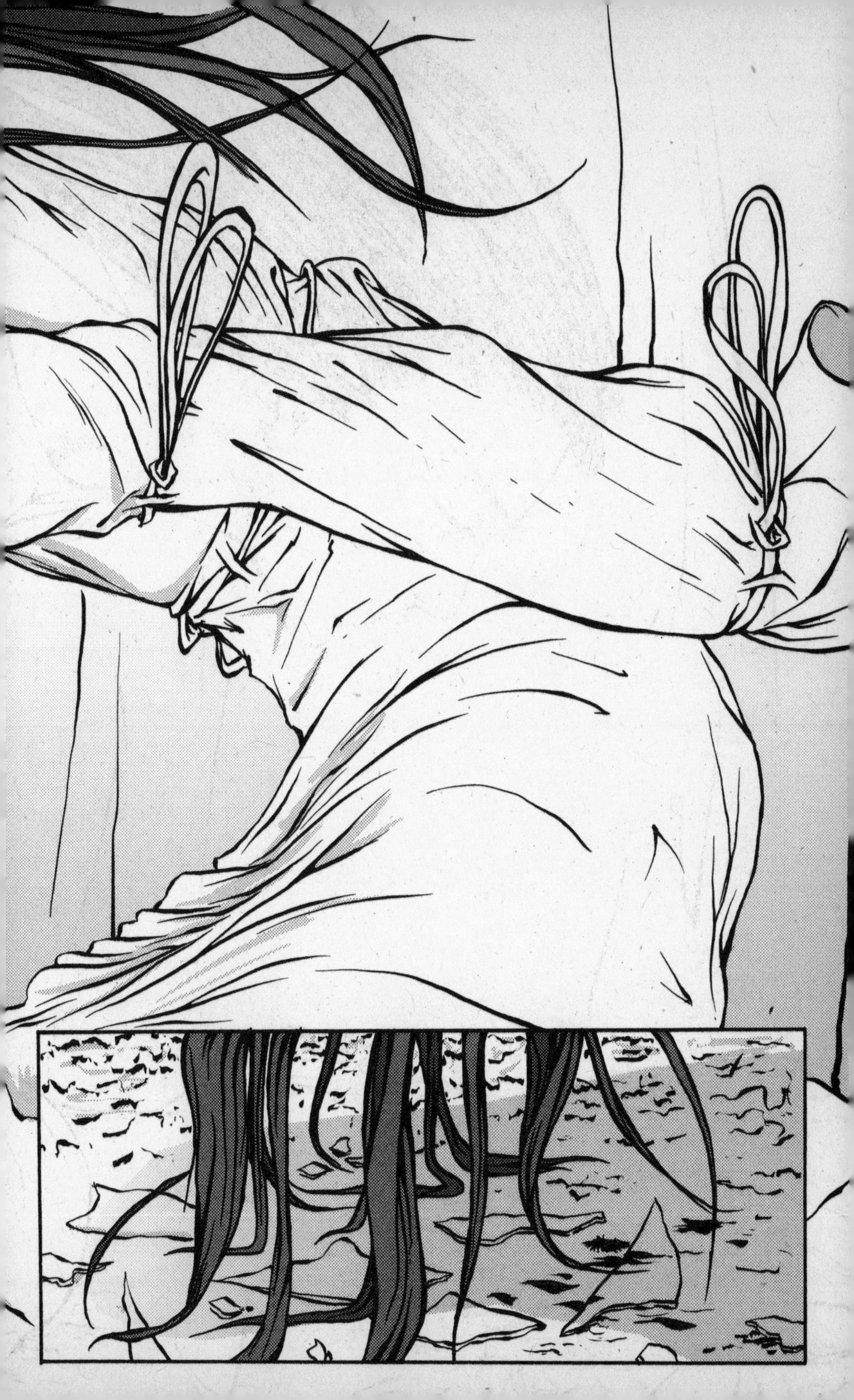

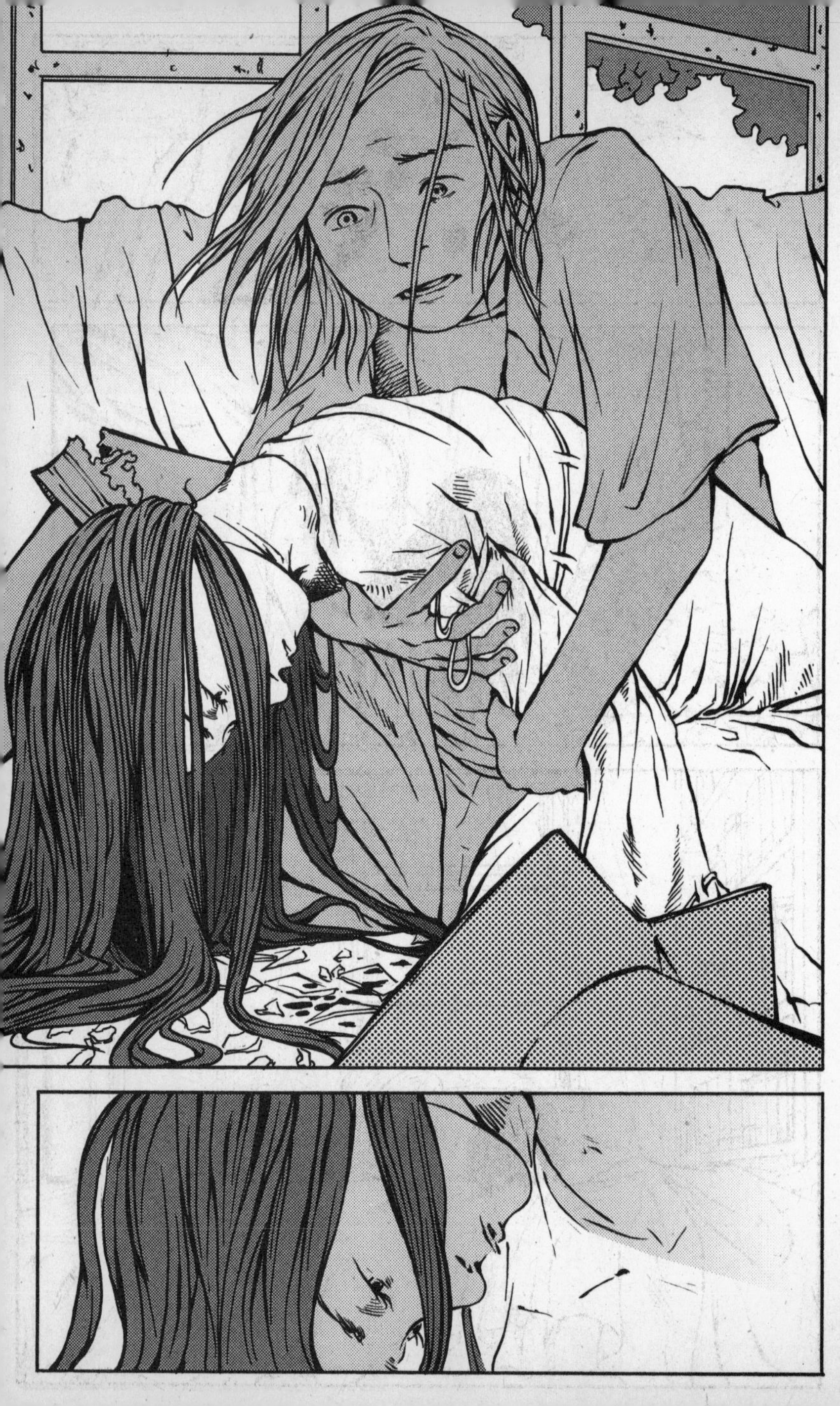

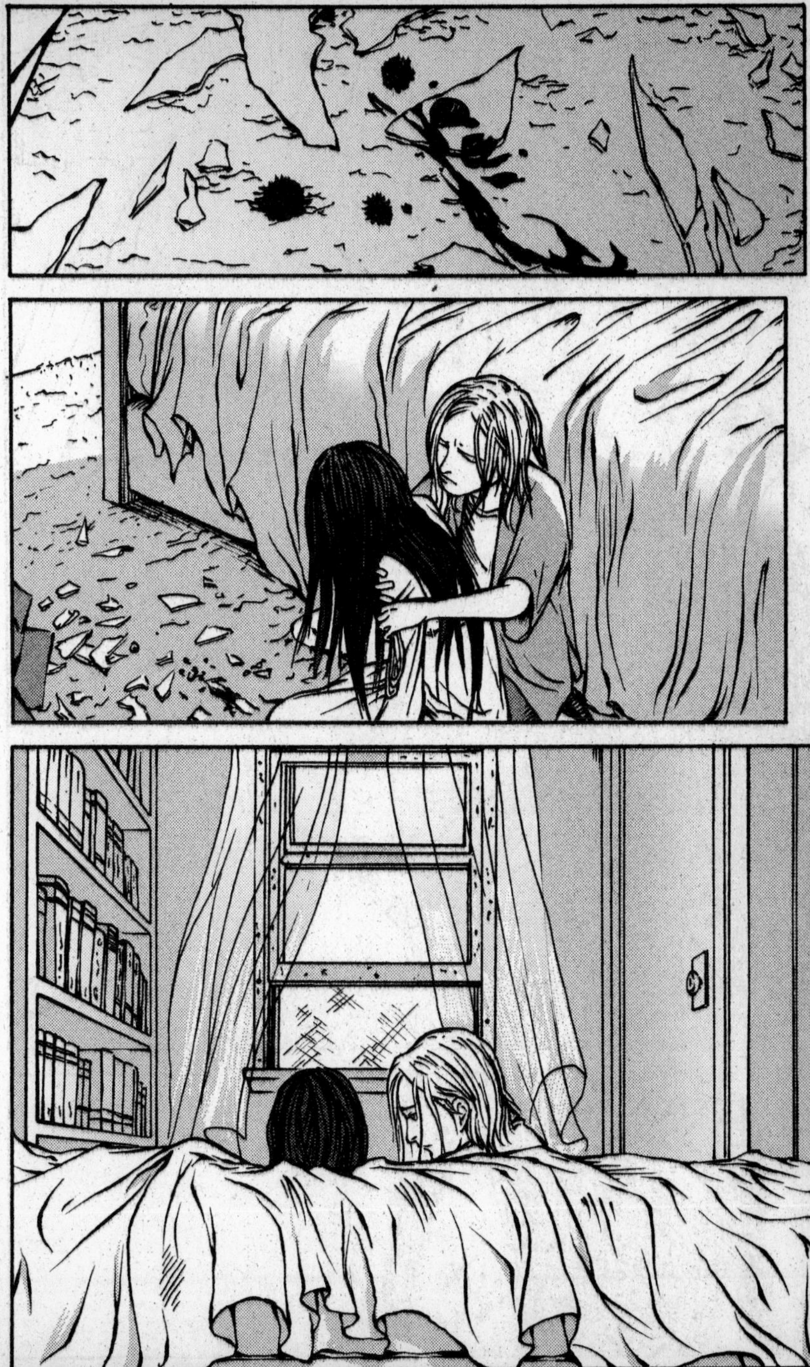

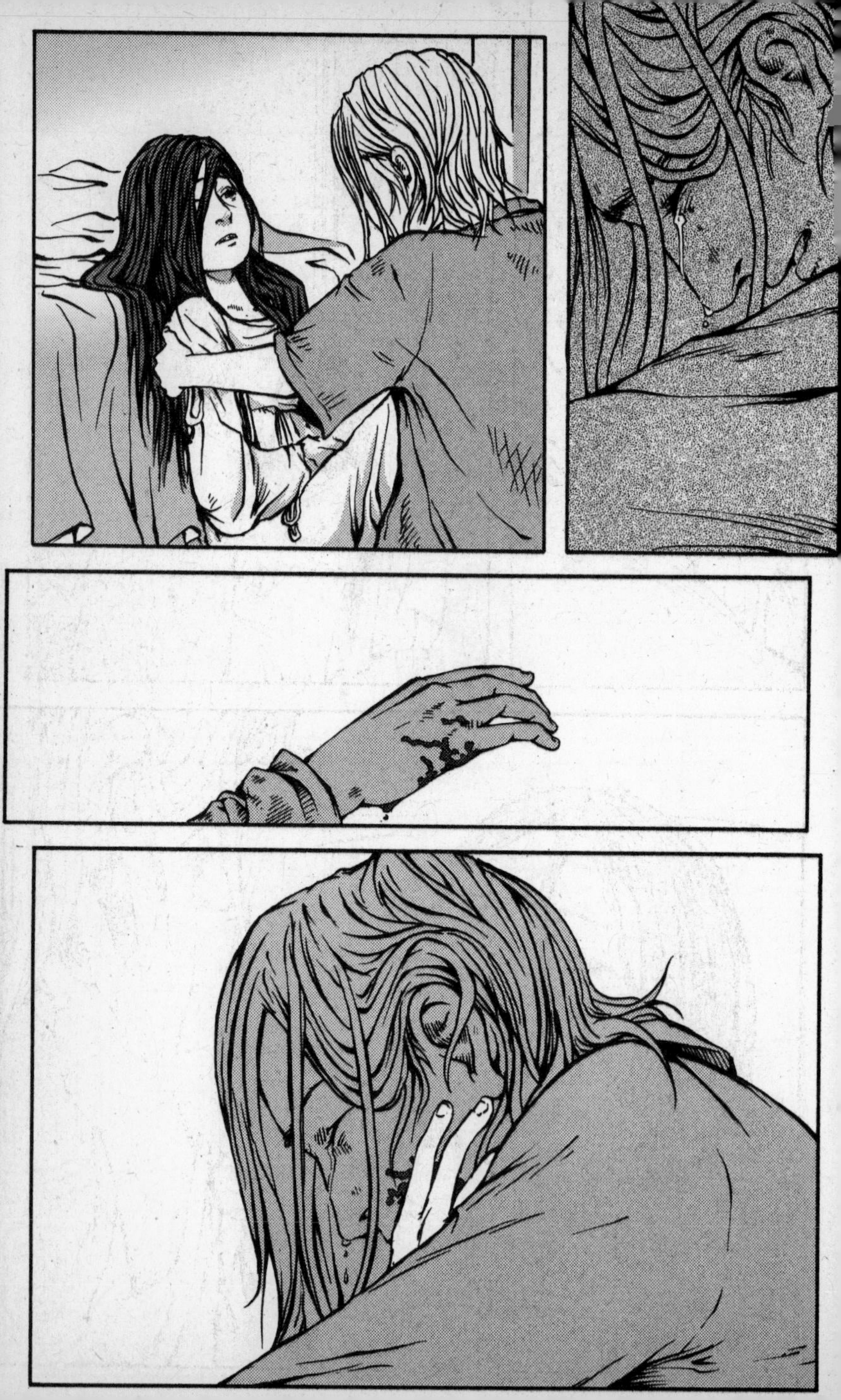

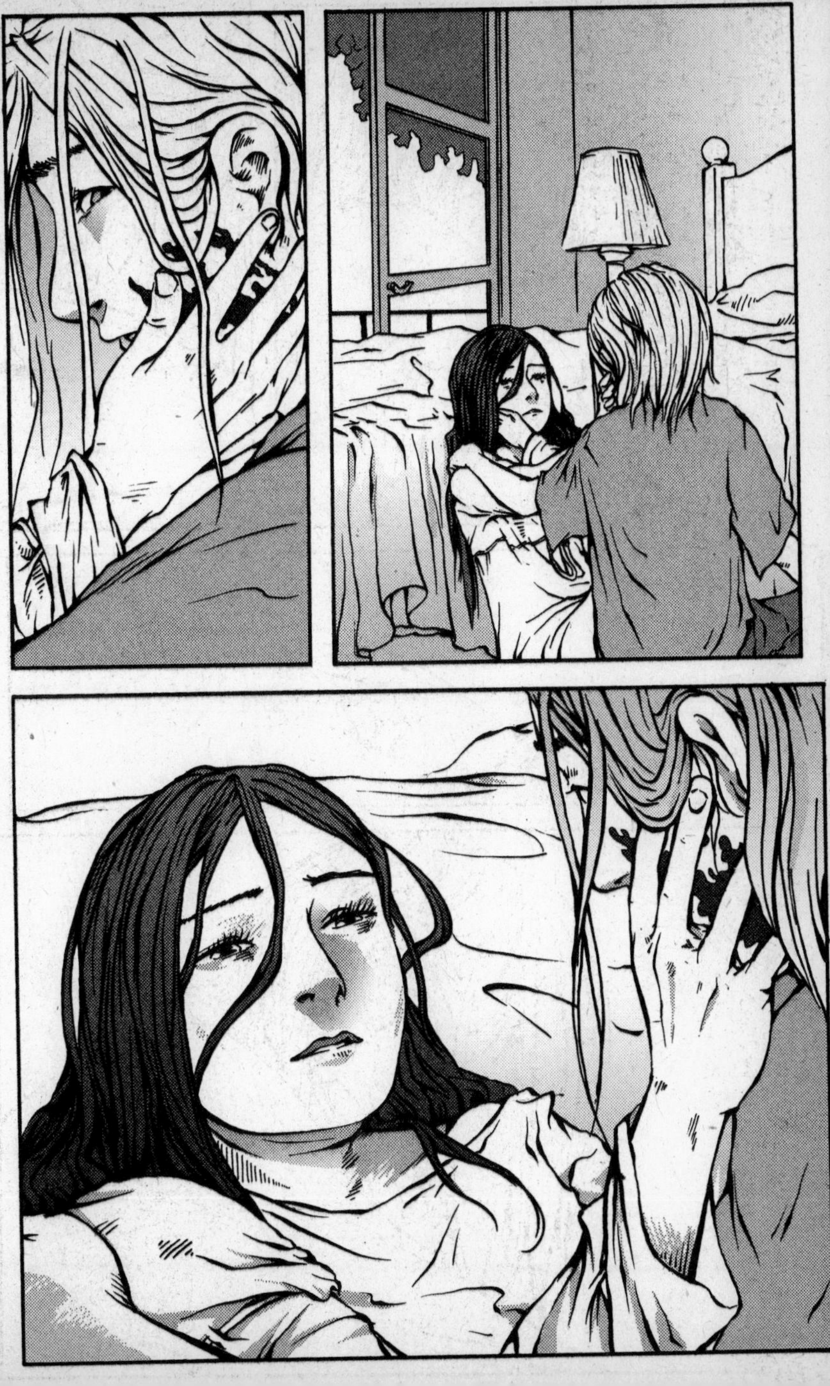

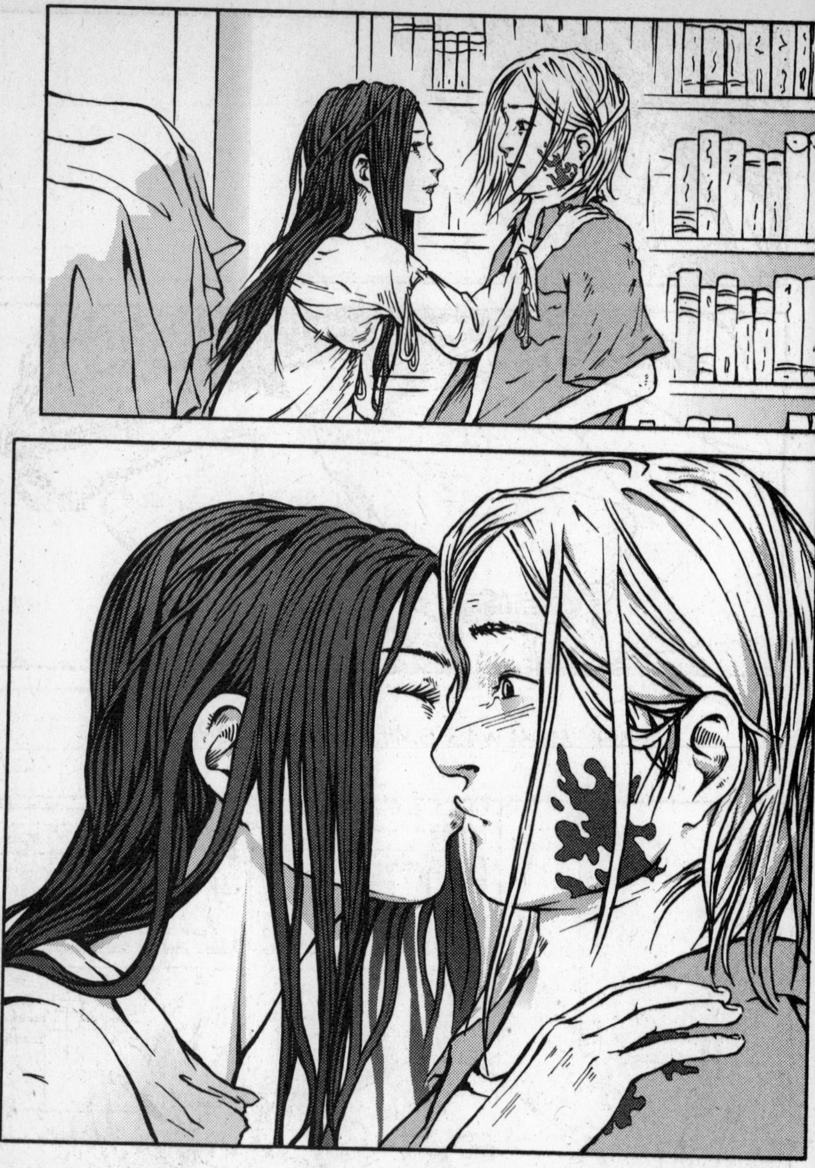

NOW I UNDERSTAND...

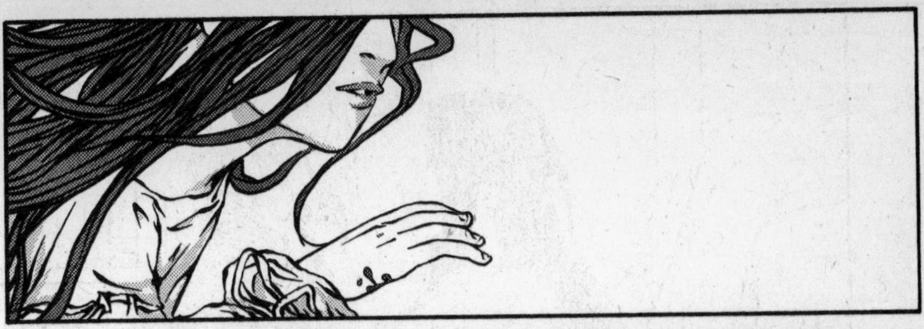

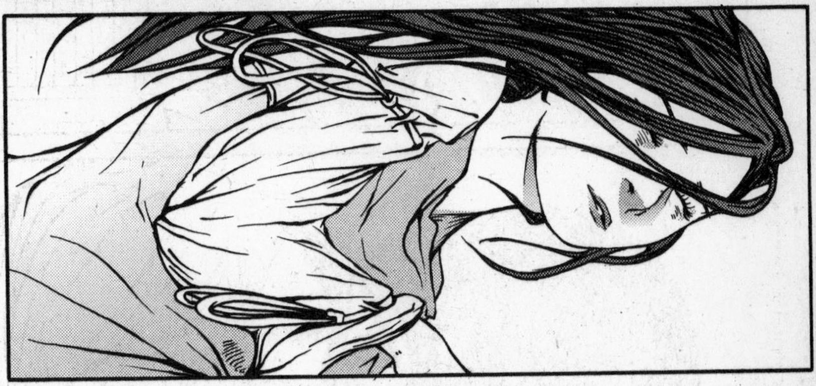

...WHY MOM WAS SMILING WHEN SHE DIED.

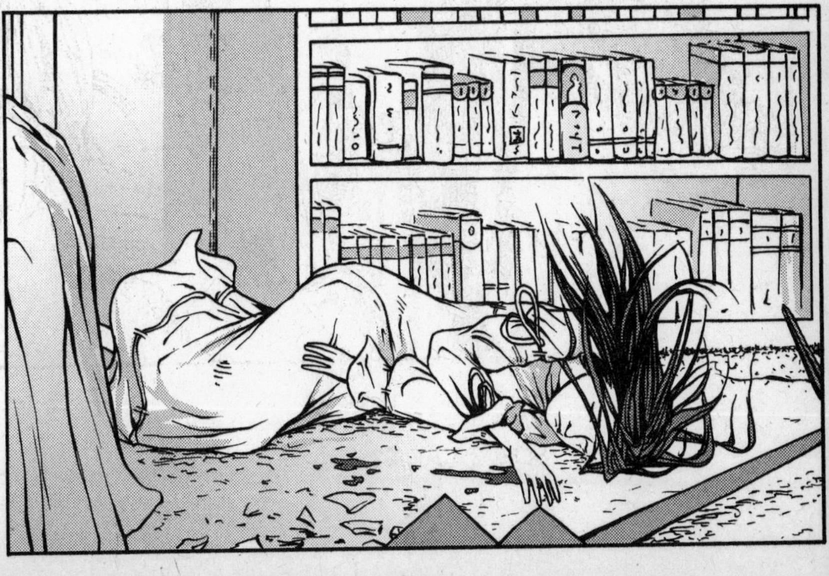

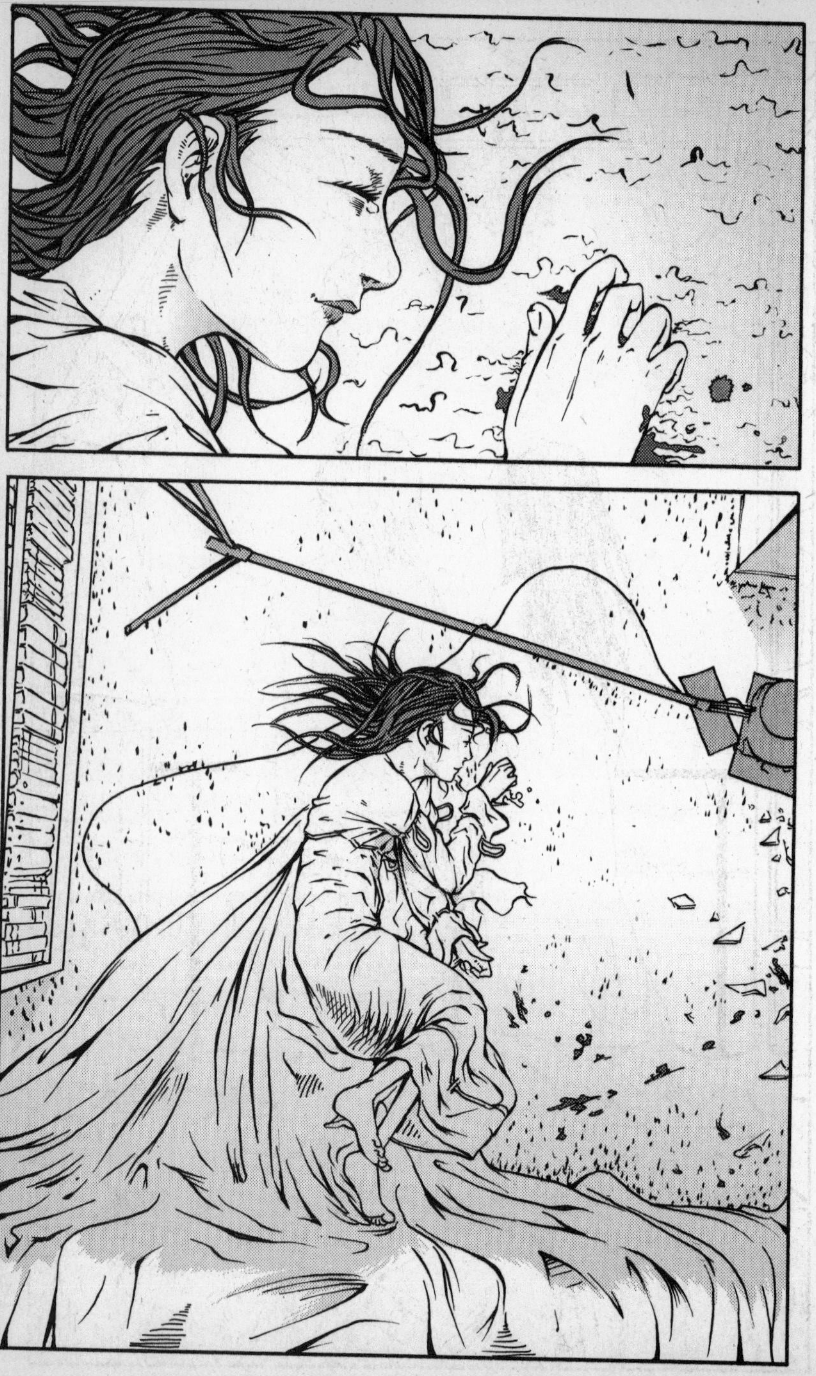

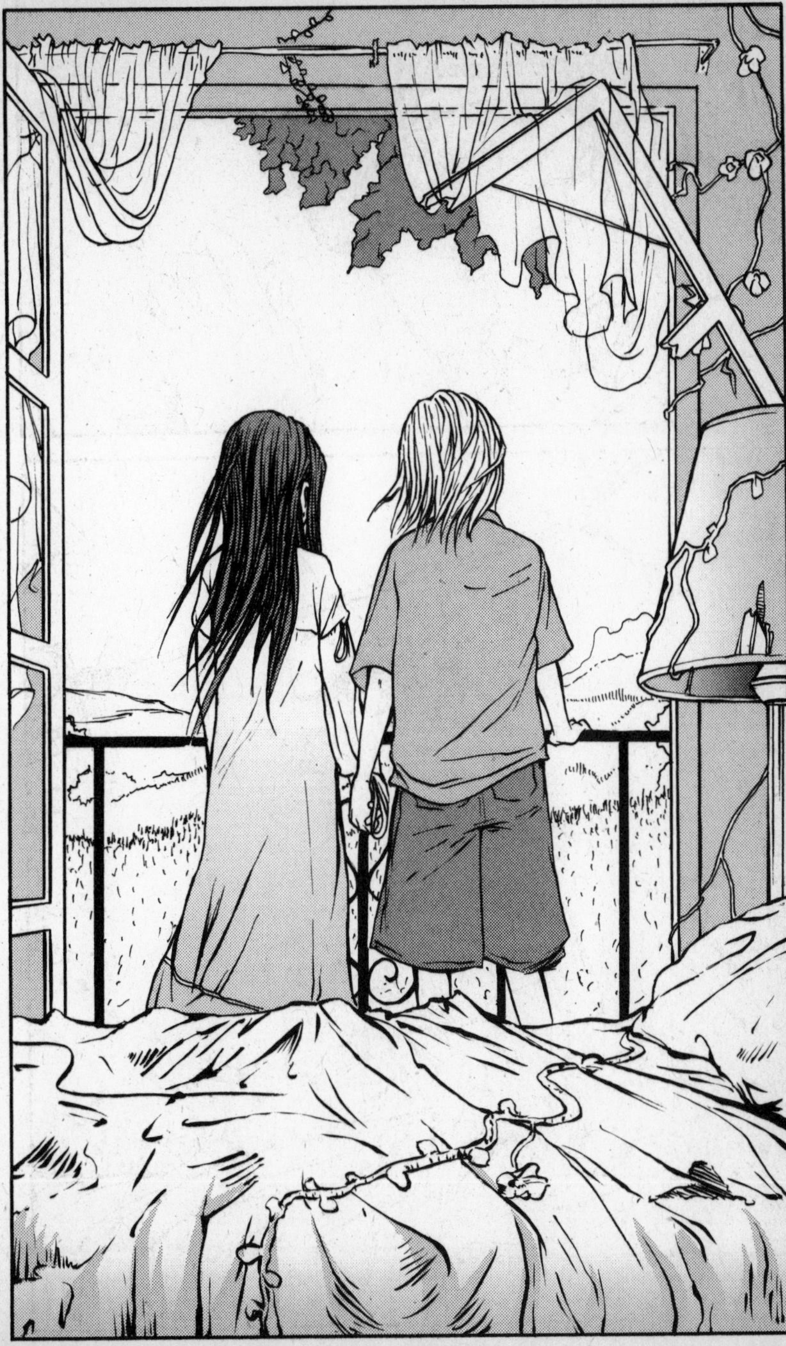

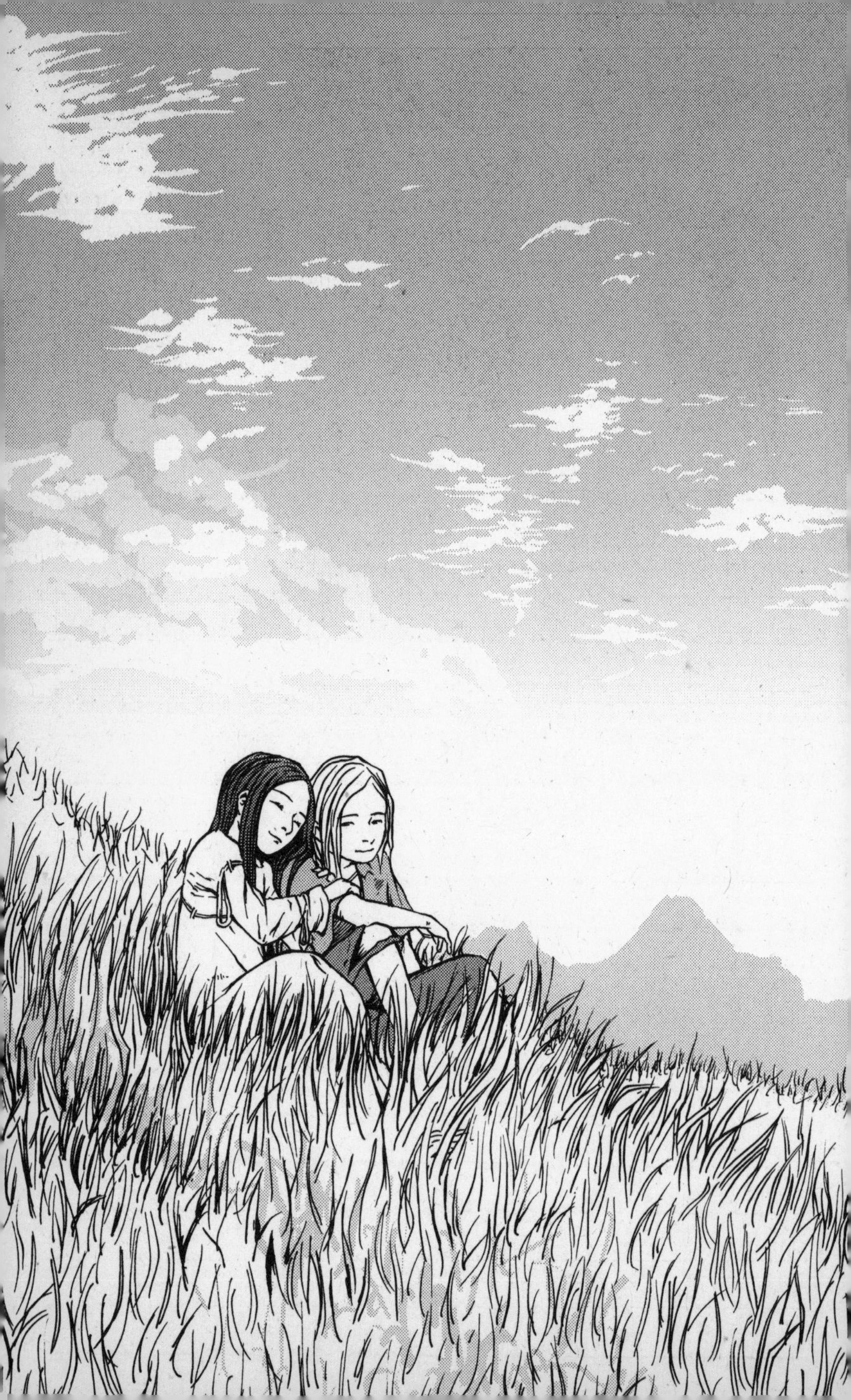

It doesn't hurt anymore.

While I don't have a gift for words or legible handwriting, I want to take the chance at the end of my first real book to express my deepest appreciation to the following people:

- Mom, for teaching me how to color in the lines.
- Mr. Spilewski, Ms. Daglean, Mr. Whitehead, and Ms. Bacon.
- My various teachers through the public school system who didn't fail me for drawing all day instead of doing classwork (or homework for that matter)...
- Becky, whose zeal infected me before I even met her.
- Lisa, for listening to my endless rambling and always managing to keep me optimistic.
- Phil and Mike, for saying they actually <u>wanted</u> to see this story get drawn.
- Dan, for all the hours in Edgewater discussing and filling plot holes with me.
- Carol, who has been the lone catalyst of every good memory I've had in the past year. Thank you for lending me your sharp eyes, your encouragement, and your creativity. I'm in your debt forever.

And finally, to everyone who's read this far in the book and to everyone who's ever said a kind word about my odd little drawings.
I hope to continue working for your enjoyment for years to come.

Yours,
George Alexopoulos

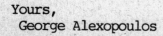

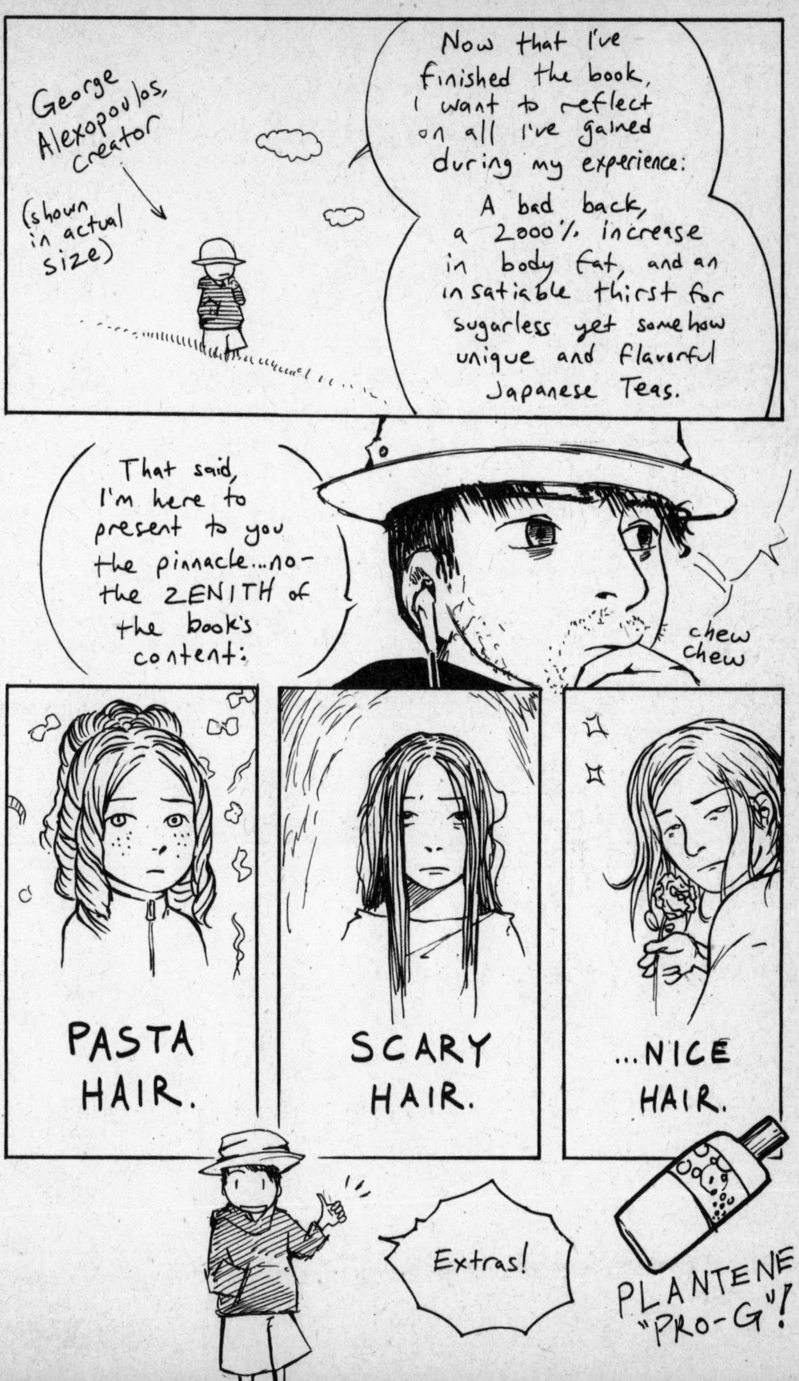
George Alexopoulos, creator
(shown in actual size)
Now that I've finished the book, I want to reflect on all I've gained during my experience: A bad back, a 2000% increase in body fat, and an insatiable thirst for sugarless yet somehow unique and flavorful Japanese Teas.
That said, I'm here to present to you the pinnacle...no- the ZENITH of the book's content:
chew chew
PASTA HAIR.
SCARY HAIR.
...NICE HAIR.
Extras!
PLANTENE "PRO-G"!

Yet to be Determined...

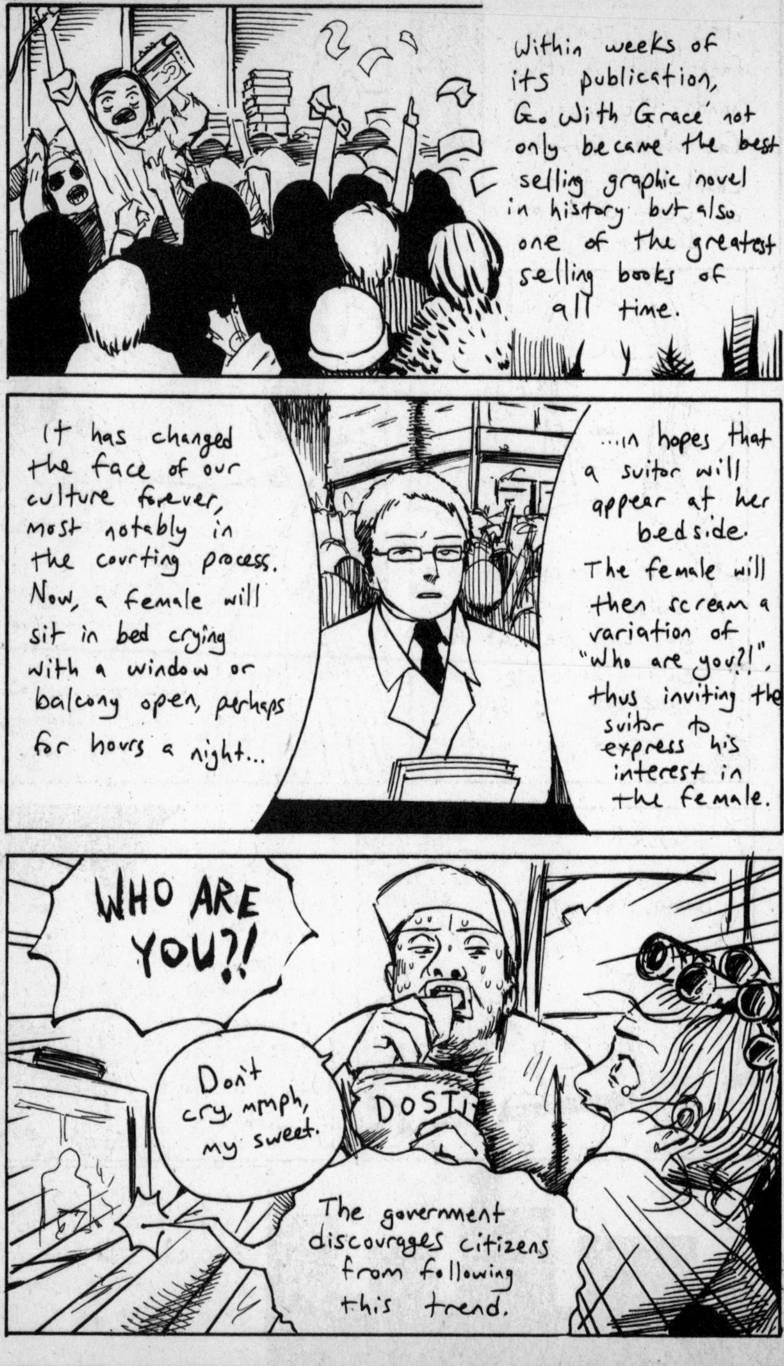
Within weeks of its publication, Go With Grace' not only became the best selling graphic novel in history but also one of the greatest selling books of all time.
It has changed the face of our culture forever, most notably in the courting process. Now, a female will sit in bed crying with a window or balcony open, perhaps for hours a night...
...in hopes that a suitor will appear at her bedside. The female will then scream a variation of "Who are you?!", thus inviting the suitor to express his interest in the female.
WHO ARE YOU?!
Don't cry, mmph, my sweet.
DOST
The government discourages citizens from following this trend.

It's a scary fact, but in other hands the story of Go With Grace could have gone in a very different direction.

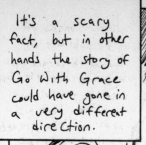

Here, take this sword! With it, you can defeat the evil sorcerer and release my spirit from his clutches!

Okay!!

Quest into the hills! There you will find a crabby but kind-hearted witch who will show you the way!

I won't let you down, Andy!

Huzzah!

kekeke... now all I have to do is lead her around for 20 volumes and surely she'll fall in love with me!

And sensing an opportunity had been missed, someone in a dark office slams their fist on a table.

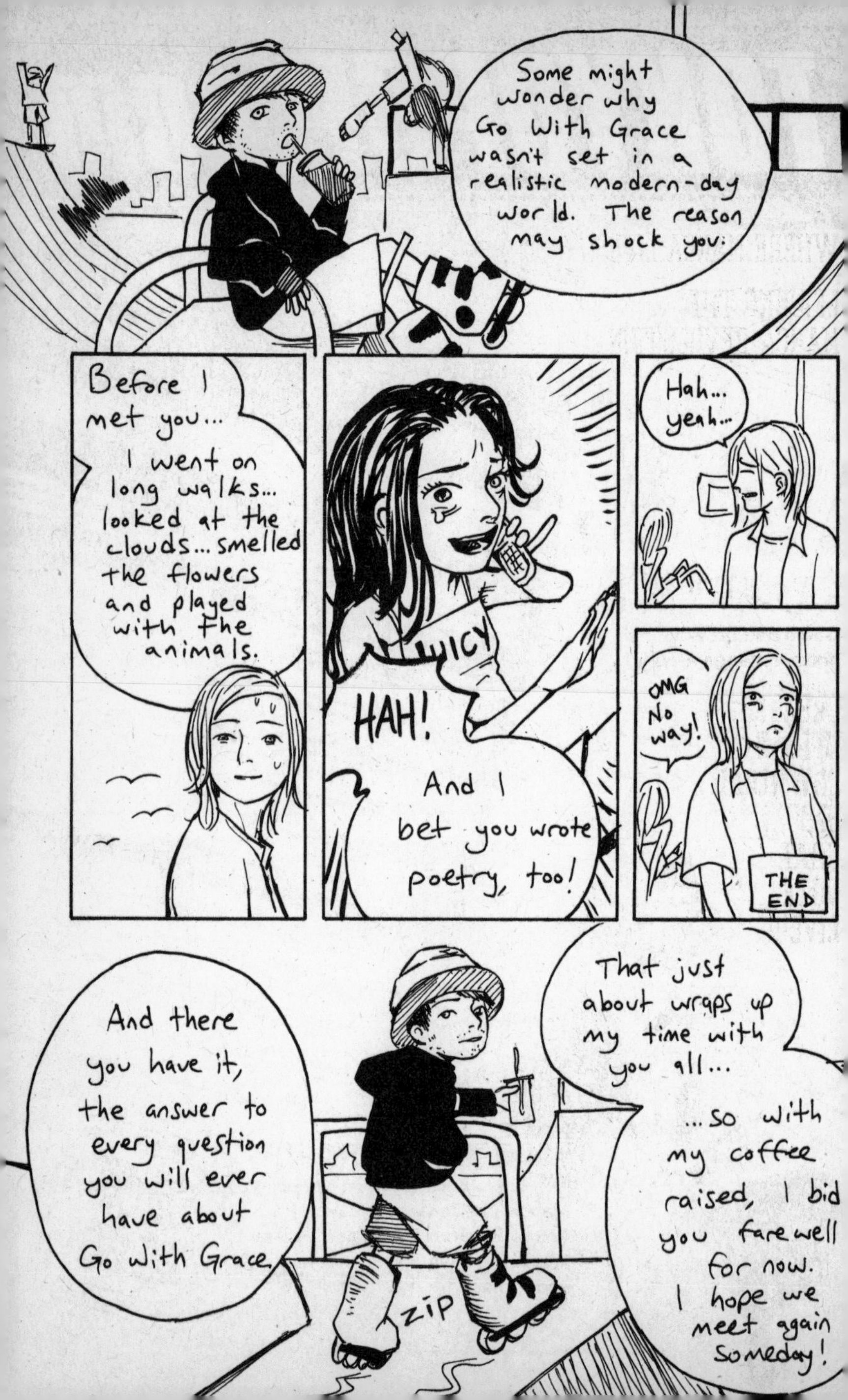
Some might wonder why Go With Grace wasn't set in a realistic modern-day world. The reason may shock you:
Before I met you... I went on long walks... looked at the clouds... smelled the flowers and played with the animals.
HAH!
And I bet you wrote poetry, too!
Hah... yeah...
OMG No way!
THE END
And there you have it, the answer to every question you will ever have about Go With Grace.
That just about wraps up my time with you all...
...so with my coffee raised, I bid you farewell for now. I hope we meet again someday!
ZIP

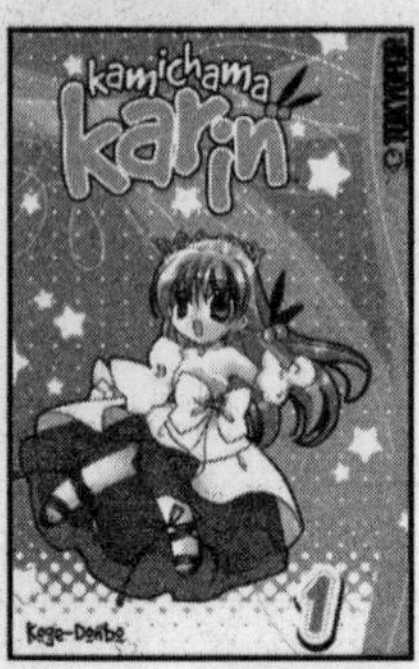
kamichama karin
1
Koge-Donbo

ROMANCE

Y YOUTH AGE 10+

KAMICHAMA KARIN

BY KOGE-DONBO

This one was a surprise. I mean, I knew Koge-Donbo drew insanely cute characters, but I had no idea a magical girl story could be so darn clever. *Kamichama Karin* manages to lampoon everything about the genre, from plushie-like mascots to character archetypes to weapons that appear from the blue! And you gotta love Karin, the airheaded heroine who takes guff from no one and screams "I AM GOD!" as her battle cry. In short, if you are looking for a shiny new manga with a knack for hilarity and a penchant for accessories, I say look no further.

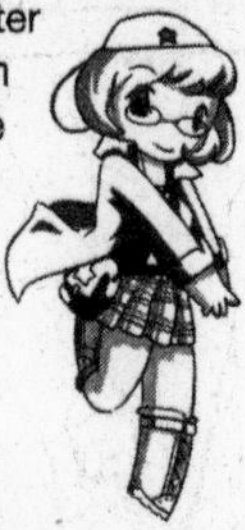

~Carol Fox, Editor

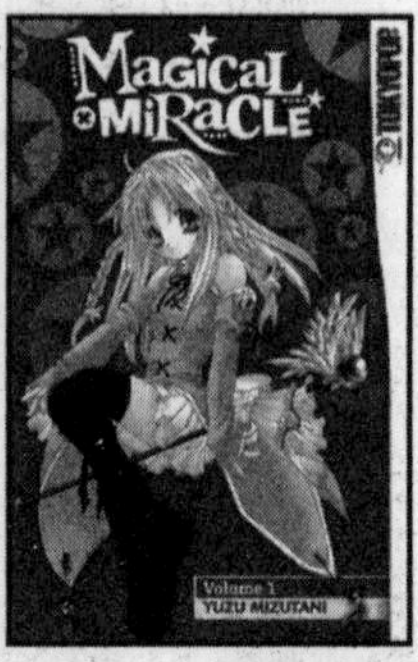
Magical X Miracle
Volume 1
YUZU MIZUTANI

FANTASY

T TEEN AGE 13+

MAGICAL X MIRACLE

BY YUZU MIZUTANI

Magical X Miracle is a quirky—yet uplifting—tale of gender-bending mistaken identity! When a young girl must masquerade as a great wizard, she not only finds the strength to save an entire kingdom...but, ironically, she just might just find herself, too. Yuzu Mizutani's art is remarkably adorable, but it also has a dark, sophisticated edge.

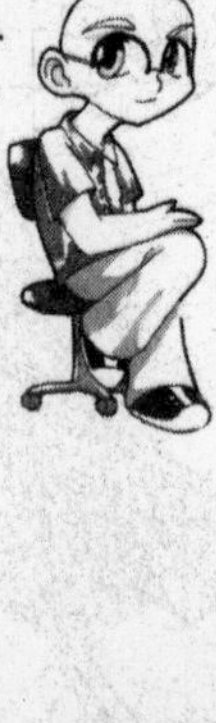

~Paul Morrissey, Editor